Communication Theory
EASTERN AND WESTERN PERSPECTIVES

HUMAN COMMUNICATION RESEARCH SERIES

PETER R. MONGE, Editor

Monge and Cappella:
MULTIVARIATE TECHNIQUES IN
HUMAN COMMUNICATION RESEARCH 1980

Cushman and McPhee:
MESSAGE-ATTITUDE-BEHAVIOR
RELATIONSHIP 1980

Woelfel and Fink:
MEASUREMENT OF COMMUNICATION
PROCESSES 1980

Kerr and Hiltz:
COMPUTER-MEDIATED COMMUNICATION SYSTEMS:
STATUS AND EVALUATION 1982

Hart:
VERBAL STYLE AND THE PRESIDENCY:
A COMPUTER-BASED ANALYSIS 1984

Hunter, Danes, and Cohen:
MATHEMATICAL MODELS OF ATTITUDE CHANGE,
VOLUME 1: CHANGE IN SINGLE ATTITUDES AND
COGNITIVE STRUCTURE 1984

Kincaid:
COMMUNICATION THEORY:
EASTERN AND WESTERN PERSPECTIVES 1987

Communication Theory
EASTERN AND WESTERN PERSPECTIVES

Edited by

D. Lawrence Kincaid
Department of Communication
State University of New York at Albany
Albany, New York

ACADEMIC PRESS, INC.
Harcourt Brace Jovanovich, Publishers
San Diego   New York   Berkeley   Boston
London   Sydney   Tokyo   Toronto

ACADEMIC PRESS, INC.
1250 Sixth Avenue, San Diego, California 92101

United Kingdom Edition published by
ACADEMIC PRESS INC. (LONDON) LTD.
24–28 Oval Road, London NW1 7DX

Library of Congress Cataloging in Publication Data

Communication theory.

Bibliography: p.
Includes index.
1. Communication. 2. Intercultural communication.
I. Kincaid, D. Lawrence, Date
P90.C6335 1987   001.51   87–1257
ISBN 0–12–407470–7 (alk. paper)

PRINTED IN THE UNITED STATES OF AMERICA

87 88 89 90   9 8 7 6 5 4 3 2 1

Contents

Contributors

Numbers in parentheses indicate the pages on which the authors' contributions begin.

Chung-Ying Cheng (23), Department of Philosophy, University of Hawaii, Honolulu, Hawaii 96822

Donald P. Cushman (1, 57, 223), Department of Communication, State University of New York at Albany, Albany, New York 12222

Jesse G. Delia (255), Department of Speech Communication, University of Illinois, Urbana, Illinois 61801

Wimal Dissanayake (151), Institute of Culture and Communication, East-West Center, Honolulu, Hawaii 96848

James S. Fu (45), Department of Foreign Languages, San Jose State University, San Jose, California 95192

Randy Y. Hirokawa (137), Department of Communication, University of Iowa, Iowa City, Iowa 52242

Kyung-wha Kang (235), Department of Mass Communication, Yonsei University, Seoul, Korea

D. Lawrence Kincaid (1, 209, 275, 331), Department of Communication, State University of New York at Albany, Albany, New York 12222

Klaus Krippendorff (189), Annenberg School of Communication, University of Pennsylvania, Philadelphia, Pennsylvania 19104

Sang-Hee Lee (101), Department of Mass Communication, Seoul National University, Seoul 151, Korea

Keizo Okabe (127), The Institute for Journalism, University of Tokyo, Tokyo 113, Japan

W. Barnett Pearce (235), Department of Communication Studies, University of Massachusetts, Amherst, Massachusetts 01003

Gerry Philipsen (245), Department of Speech Communication, University of Washington, Seattle, Washington 98195

Abdur Rahim (173), Department of Communication and Journalism, Osmania University, Hyderabad, India 500007

Akira Tsujimura (115), Department of Social Psychology, Faculty of Letters, University of Tokyo, Tokyo 113, Japan

Joseph Woelfel (275, 299), Department of Communication, State University of New York at Albany, Albany, New York 12222

J. S. Yadava (161), Indian Institute of Mass Communication, New Delhi 110049, India

Muneo Jay Yoshikawa (319), Department of East Asian Languages and Literature, University of Hawaii, Honolulu, Hawaii 96822

June-Ock Yum (71, 87), Department of Communication, State University of New York at Albany, Albany, New York 12222

Preface

The field of communication has entered one of the most exciting periods in its history. The steady, rapid pace of technological development continues to break down the natural barriers of time and space that once made communication on a global scale so difficult. As the natural barriers diminish, the political and cultural barriers seem more formidable than ever.

The number of people studying communication has reached critical new proportions. New ideas challenging the old come from all parts of the world today. Those who listen to many voices will find the reward in the improved quality and scope of their own work.

This book is a positive response to the demand that has developed during the past few years for theoretical approaches to communication which are compatible with the political and cultural realities of Asia and which clearly differentiate between communication as it is practiced in the East and the West, especially the United States. The main purpose of this book is to broaden our thinking about communication as a fundamental process of society.

A look at communication theory from different cultural perspectives will contribute greatly to the future development of the field. For many readers the ideas presented in this book will be new and quite exciting, challenging and stimulating their own thinking about communication. New students of communication will find a richness heretofore unknown.

We have taken an inclusive approach to "theory." Theory is something to be developed, not a finished product. A formal theory consists of several equally important parts: intuitive notions or presuppositions, more precisely defined constructs, postulates or hypotheses that relate the constructs, deduced laws, and experimental tests of the hypotheses. The authors of some of the chapters in this book limit their discussion to basic presuppositions from a particular cultural perspective or define useful new constructs for theory construction. Others formulate postulates or hypotheses capable of empirical test.

Presupposing and defining phenomena a particular way is a prerequisite for perception and intelligent discussion. Good concepts allow us to see new things or to see old things in a new light. At the same time they divert our attention or blind us from seeing other things. Escaping from this paradoxical situation is no easy task. Progress can sometimes be made by borrowing formal language systems developed in other domains of science, as when biologists apply the language of cybernetics to their own problems or physicists apply the concept of evolution to theirs. One who comes to understand and appreciate concepts developed in different cultures and language systems from their own, the *"Tao"* or "feedback" or "dialectical materialism," has gained a new set of tools to see new phenomena in his or her own culture or see the familiar in a new way. By forcing constructs and relationships into the English language which were originally developed in other language systems, we create a new leverage for theory building. Those who pursue what they are introduced to in this book will find their vision of communication enriched forever.

It would be impossible to cover all of the possible theoretical perspectives of both the East and the West in one volume. The Eastern perspective is represented by discussions from four cultures: China, Korea, Japan, and India. The Western perspective is limited to recent trends in North American thinking. This structure leaves room for the inclusion of several chapters that discuss ideas held in common by the East and the West. Together, the full set of chapters makes an important contribution to the study of intercultural communication, where cultural differences must be clearly understood and, if possible, transcended.

Once the idea for this work was set in motion, it could be realized only with the help of a great many people. The East–West Center's Communication Institute, Honolulu, Hawaii, sponsored the international seminar from which many of the papers originated, and Tokyo University sponsored a second symposium in Yokohama, Japan, which allowed the work to continue.

I would especially like to acknowledge the contributions of Chung-Ying Cheng and Joe Woelfel, who have been with the project since the beginning, and Akira Tsujimura and Keizo Okabe, who gave so much support, and all who participated in the two seminars and who contributed papers.

Communication Theory
EASTERN AND WESTERN PERSPECTIVES

CHAPTER 1

Introduction and Initial Insights

Donald P. Cushman and D. Lawrence Kincaid

Human communication theory can be productively explored from a variety of perspectives. It is the purpose of this essay to explore the insights which are provided by examining communication theory from Eastern and Western perspectives. The knowledge on which our discussion is based comes from the papers presented in this same volume which were written by scholars from both Asia and the United States for the purpose of enhancing our understanding of communication theory.

Before entering into the main portion of our discussion we are in need of some analytic tools for exploring what is meant by the concepts, communication and theory. Both of these concepts are at once ambiguous and conventional in their meaning. They are ambiguous in that each of these terms is employed to designate several rather diverse conceptualizations. They are conventional in that there is considerable agreement among philosophers, theorists, and practitioners as to the elements which make up each of these diverse conceptualizations. Let us therefore begin by defining the terms communication and theory in their most general sense and then provide a conceptualization of the elements involved in each of their different and yet conventional usages.

COMMUNICATION THEORY:
EASTERN AND WESTERN PERSPECTIVES

1

Communication in its most general sense refers to a process in which *information* is shared by two or more persons and which has *consequences* for one or more of the persons involved. Much of the ambiguity and controversy regarding the nature of communication stems from the different ways that "information" is defined, and the different approaches that are taken toward the "consequences" of communication. Kincaid (Chapter 15, this volume), for instance, focuses on the physical nature of information, defining it as "a difference in matter-energy which affects uncertainty . . . " To him, the most important consequences of communication are *between* the persons involved, in terms of their mutual understanding, mutual agreement, and collective action.

This recent approach to communication may be contrasted with that of Cushman and Whiting (1972), who define communication as "the successful transfer of symbolic information." This definition focuses attention on the act of transfer and the nature of success, especially about for whom the transfer is successful: source, receiver, or both? In fact, the introduction of the term, "success," emphasizes an instrumental aspect of communication which is so often associated with Western ways of thinking in general. If success is limited to external criteria, to the effective manipulation of the external world including other people, then the Western bias of this definition is evident and can be traced back to Aristotle's principles of rhetoric. On the other hand, if success is interpreted more broadly we can make room for a greater variety of approaches to communication, perhaps even those which are compatible with Eastern ways of thinking.

First, successful communication can be claimed to have taken place when an individual can subjectively make sense out of his perceptions of experiences and incoming messages. Such a conception of successful communication focuses on the internal information processing capability of an individual. It is communication rooted in *psychological processes* and represents an individual's own subjective estimate that the symbolic patterns confronting that individual have been interpreted correctly. Such personal understanding occurs when one reads a poem or practices meditation, from either external or internal experiences. Understanding gives a personal interpretation to the patterns of information taken from those experiences. From this perspective successful communication is a matter of personal understanding.

Second, successful communication can be said to have occurred when two or more individuals interactively arrive at a common set of interpretations for patterns of information. Such a conception of successful communication focuses on agreements between individuals. It is communication rooted in social consensus and represents two or more individuals' estimates that the information pattern confronting them has been interpreted correctly as a consequence of their interaction. From this perspective successful communication is a matter of mutual understanding and agreement.

Third, successful communication can be said to have occurred when some institution of authority provides a criteria for the correct interpretation of patterns of information. This is communication rooted in institutional authority and represents imposed standards or conventions for interpretation. Examples of institutional conventions for correct interpretations of symbolic patterns are found in various religious ceremonies, cultural conventions for greeting others, and ideological interpetations of government policy. From this perspective, successful communication is a matter of institutional understanding.

Human beings can depend on psychological, social or institutional processes and criteria, or combinations of all three to arrive at coherent, meaningful interpretations of experience based on their shared patterns of information. Defined this broadly, "success" is a question of *how* understanding is reached as a consequence of communication.

The concept *theory* like that of communication has both general and specific conventional uses. In its most general sense, theory is simply a coherent set of hypothetical, conceptual, and pragmatic principles which function as a frame of reference for some field of inquiry. A *principle* is a propositional statement about some aspect of reality which provides a basis for reasoning or a guide for action. A principle serves reasoning to the extent that other statements or propositions can be logically derived from it. In other words, a principle is the ultimate basis from which other statements take their origin.

In the case of scientific theory, we can be much more formal and specific: a theory is a collection of theorems. "A theorem is a proposition which is a strict logical consequence of certain definitions and other propositions" (Rapoport, 1974, p. 260). The logical validity of any given theorem is ultimately derived from assertions which are not proved but simply assumed and terms which are not defined but simply listed. In science as opposed to other fields of study, some of the terms must be related extensionally to referents and at least some of the assertions must be empirically verifiable. The accuracy of these assertions about the empirical world is what makes a scientific theory successful. On the other hand, it is the nature of the theorems that makes a theory part of an exact science. The exact sciences have completely rigid rules for deducing theorems, usually mathematical rules. "It is the rigidity of these rules, not the accuracy of the assertions or precision of measurements which makes an exact science" (Rapoport, 1974, p. 261). Because of its deductive nature, one of the interesting aspects of theory is that none of the statements (theorems, propositions, or equations) remains isolated: every statement is either "an initial premise (hypothesis, axiom, or datum) or a logical consequence of a set of initial assumptions" (Bunge, 1972, p. 227).

There is an unwarranted expectation in some fields of inquiry that to qualify as a theory a set of propositions must not only be internally consistent but also finished or complete. If these two requirements are both met, however, such a theory cannot be extended without becoming inconsistent. Such a theory is dead; nobody works on it anymore. On the other hand, incomplete theory can be extended without necessarily becoming inconsistent. This is especially obvious in the case of factual, scientific theories, where the purpose is to build better and better theories and to apply them a wider range of empirical cases.

> . . . in factual science, theories must be able to grow by the addition of subsidiary hypotheses and data: i.e., they must be incomplete. Otherwise they cannot be general, or they cannot be applied to special cases nor, consequently, subjected to empirical tests (Bunge, 1972, p. 242).

The statements of a scientific theory are thus essentially something to be developed and, in fact, must be developed to properly communicate intelligent thought.

One of the reasons why scientific theories are incomplete and thus constantly developing is because they are part factual and part theoretical, comprised of what one observes and what one supposes or invents (O'Neil, 1969). The inventive or theoretical part fills in the gaps in what can be observed and increases our understanding of it. The theory part gives us more powerful explanations of the world, and it unifies our knowledge by covering a wide range of observed, empirical phenomena and by making connections among empirical concepts and results not linked before (Thomas, 1979). Because it is so well-known, the theory of evolution is a good example. No one ever observed the whole process supposedly covered by the theory of evolution. It is an invention or supposition which incorporates (is consistent with) some of the phenomena which are observed, but as a whole it remains a supposition. It is only natural that a well-accepted theory such as the theory of evolution sometimes comes to be believed as if it too were an observed fact. To shake us out of a false sense of certainty often requires that someone else propose a substantial alteration of the theory or challenge it with a radically new theory accounting for the same facts. The primary purpose of the present book is to make just this kind of challenge, by juxtaposing a very diverse set of theoretical papers about communication from Eastern and Western perspectives. The main focus will be on the fundamental principles that emerge from different cultural orientations.

Three different, but related, types of theoretical principles will be included. The first type refers to the set of background presuppositions or philosophical principles which constitute one's perspective on life. Such *philosophical principles* form the network of attitudes, values and beliefs, or traditions which shape a way of looking at and thinking about experience. When we refer to Eastern and Western perspectives, we are suggesting that there are certain cultures, religions, and political principles which mark these philosophical perspectives as different. Such philosophical principles constitute one's conception of theory—a perspective or philosophical inclination view of theory (Hanson, 1958).

The second type refers to the *processual principles* of communication which govern and guide the process by which information is shared and processed within a particular social and cultural context. These principles govern and guide our interpretations of poetry, news, stories, radio and television programs, as well as our daily interaction patterns. Such principles constitute an interaction or processual view of communication theory.

The third type refers to those *practical principles* which govern and guide how communication is to be employed to obtain goals beyond those of information processing. Such goals as increasing food production, population control, and capital accumulation require the practical adaptation of communication to some task at hand. Such practical principles constitute a goal attainment or practical view of theory (von Wright, 1971).

Human communication theorists can productively inquire into the nature, function, and scope of the philosophical, processual, and practical principles which govern and guide human communication in order to produce a faithful or adequate conceptual reconstruction or symbolic picture of that sector of reality.

Central to an exploration of these general and specific communication principles from within Eastern and Western perspectives is the assumption that such principles differ in regard to those two perspectives and that knowledge of those differences will inform the manner in which we come to construct and understand communication theory. While it is most certainly true that there is considerable diversity within both an Eastern and Western perspective—and the ensuing chapters of this book highlight and explore those differences in some detail—it is equally true that there exists some commonality. We shall therefore begin our inquiry by explicating the core principles which form the basis of this commonality and then contrast the Eastern and Western perspectives with one another. However, before we do so it is important to note that for the purposes of this volume, the Eastern perspective is represented by and limited to the work of indigenous scholars from China, India, Japan, and Korea. Similarly, the Western perspective is represented by and limited to the work of indigenous scholars from within the United States.

From a Western point of view, the most frequently discussed goal of human communication within an Eastern perspective is its *spiritual goal*. While this is no longer either the most important or common goal of communication within an Eastern perspective, an understanding of how communication functions within spiritual processes can provide a profound insight into the contemporary uses of communication in China, India, Japan, and Korea. Historically, the goal of communication within this religious process was to achieve a *spiritual harmony* between man and nature. Central to the process of achieving this spiritual harmony with nature was an individual's ability to transcend personal interests and prejudice in order to become one with the universal essence which constitutes harmony in nature. If communication is to serve the function of disengaging an individual from personal interest and inclination in order to achieve harmony in nature, then the individual must learn how to employ ritual, reflective imagination, metaphors, and myth in order to attain a life of the spirit (Mohanty, 1980).

The function of ritual in this process is to interrupt the historical time of everyday life and synchronize it with sacred time. Reflective imagination can then be employed to elevate human thought and perception onto a metaphorical plane in which the events of everyday life find parallels or are viewed as instances of sacred and universal principles. This use of ritual, reflective imagination, and metaphor leads one into a mythical world of harmony between man and nature. Mythical symbols thus do not appear as symbols, rather they are transferred into sacred objects or beings with a reality of their own (Avens, 1980). In so doing, they promote a spiritual consciousness of a new intermediate realm of reality in between the subjective and objective world, a realm of images and pure imagination, a realm of solitude, unity, and harmony. Such a process of successful symbolic information transfer transforms an individual's subjective interpretations into the sacred institutional interpretations of a disciplined spiritual experience.

Notice several important characteristics of this Eastern spiritual use of the communicatin process. First, it is the subjugation of individual interest and inclination to a strong hierarchial authority. Second, this subjugation is achieved and maintained by a symbolic perception of harmony. Third, this harmony is established and maintained by the belief that everyday events find their only true meaning as manifestations of sacred and universal principles. Finally, all of this is achieved through the ritualistic, imaginative reflection on the metaphorical qualities of life and their embodiment in a sacred myth.

Intermediate between this traditionally Eastern use of communication to achieve a life of the spirit and the contemporary uses of communication in the East, arose a group of political and social leaders who 'sought to transform Eastern spiritual and communication principles into a dynamic set of political principles capable of guiding significant national action. The first generation of such leaders sought to fuse religious and philosophic principles in such a manner as to achieve a national identity. Frequently, later generations of leaders attempted to complement philosophic principles with the authority of military rule or to replace philosophical principles with the principles of a political ideology. These transformations of the primary spiritual goal of communication and the means for achieving that goal have taken on three rather specific patterns in contemporary Eastern societies.

First, some societies such as India and Japan have attempted to integrate democratic and capitalistic principles of political and economic organization with their indigenous religious principles. Second, some societies such as China have attempted to replace traditional religious spirituality with the political and economic ideology of their unique brand of communism and socialism, as in the People's Republic of China, or democracy and capitalism, as in Taiwan, while maintaining the traditional respect for authority, unity, and harmony. Third, some societies such as Korea have developed a military government whose goals and communication principles parallel, but are kept separate from, the philosophical desire for authority, unity, and social harmony.

The unique philosophical perspectives, communication patterns, and practical uses of communication which follow from these specific subdivisions of the Eastern perspective are the subject of the next several sections of this volume. Our purpose here has been to indicate their common beginnings in Eastern spirituality and their transformation into national philosophies and ideologies and to highlight the common characteristics of these transformations: (1) the subordination of individual prejudice and inclination to a strong hierarchical authority, (2) a subjugation achieved and maintained by a symbolic perception of harmony, and (3) a harmony established and maintained by the belief that events find their meanings as manifestations of universal principles. Communication thus becomes the reflective transformation of individual subjective interpretations into sacred institutional interpretations of experience. Such a reflective process is internal to the individual, although it may be assisted by external messages.

From an Eastern point of view, the most frequently discussed aspect of communication within a Western perspective or more specifically the United States perspective is its role in establishing and maintaining political, social, and economic *freedom for the individual.* This function of communication has both a historical and a contemporary significance. Historically, the United States has been the haven for those individuals who wanted to escape political, economic, and social persecution. It was a place where one could seek individual freedom from such constraints. More recently, individual freedom has been carried to its logical extreme, with most American citizens viewing the principle goal of communication to be to provide for *individual self-realization* (Yankelovich, 1981).

Communication is thus employed in order to rationally manipulate others to assist one in the achievement of personal goals. Thus, communication in the West is often dominated by the *instrumental* function of achieving goals in the external world. Central to achieving individual self-realization is the use of self-analysis, rational reflection, audience analysis, and message adaptation. Self-analysis consists of locating one's personal goals and developing one's potential for achieving those goals. Rational reflection involves the step-by-step analysis of how one's potentials might be developed and goals attained and what resources must be brought under human control in order to achieve those personal goals (McKeon, 1957). Currently, *science* and its companion *technology* are viewed as the rational instruments par excellence for bringing both human and natural resources under the control of individual inclination.

Audience analysis consists of the rational determination of the attitudes, values, and beliefs of those individuals whose cooperation is necessary to achieve one's goals. Message adaptation is the rational determination of what communication strategies must be employed in order to motivate and guide *others* to coordinate their behaviors in such a manner as to assist in one's own goal attainment.* Such a process normally involves a recognition of others' needs for self-realization and an indication of how a given course of action can assist in mutual self-realization. This is achieved through a rational use of interpersonal, organization, and mass communication strategies for goal attainment. The function of communication in such a context is the practical realization of individual or group preferences. Communication as such is tied intimately with personal and group inclinations and prejudice and the practical context in which such inclinations and prejudice seek realization. Such a process of communication transforms an individual's subjective interpretations into the negotiated consensus of social interpretations for self- and other realization (Cushman & Tompkins, 1980).

---

* This contrasts greatly with the Confucian doctrine regarding the good leader as one who begins by cultivating himself to attain the ideal model for others to follow.

Eastern and Western perspectives on communication theory present interesting contrasts in regard to their goals, means for achieving those goals, and the role of the individuals in the communication process. An Eastern perspective emphasizes selflessness and submission to central authority as an institutional means for achieving unity and harmony between man and nature as the principle goal for communication. A Western perspective emphasizes self-realization and the subjugation of human and natural resources to individual control as the central means for achieving individual and group goal attainment. An Eastern perspective emphasizes ritual, reflective imagination, metaphor, and myth as the chief instruments for transforming individual prejudice and inclination through symbolic meditation into an institutional unification of man with nature. A Western perspective emphasizes self-analysis, rational reflection, audience analysis, and message adaptation as the chief instruments for achieving the practical cooperation from others necessary for self-realization. An Eastern perspective asks an individual to imaginatively communicate with himself and nature in order to transform his subjective temporal experiences into universal philosophical and ideological experiences. A Western perspective asks an individual to communicate rationally with others in such a manner as to allow for the development of his own and others' self-realization. Finally, an Eastern perspective focuses on and motivates human action by the individual's participation in a collective institutional structure and controls communication to that end. A Western perspective focuses on and motivates human action by the individual's desire for political, social, and economic self-realization and employs communication to that end.

What makes these traditional contrasts between Eastern and Western perspectives so relevant and worthy of our consideration at this time is the fact that such rapid social and economic changes are occurring throughout the world today, irrespective of any artificial boundaries that might designate one part of the world as East and the other as West. The amount of contact and communication that occurs between people from Eastern and Western traditions increases every year. Western ideas of individual freedom and progress have spread throughout most of Asia and exist side by side in contradiction at times to many of the traditional values and ways of thinking just discussed. At the same time, the whole notion of unrestrained individual freedom at the expense of the natural environment and harmony in human relationships is increasingly being challenged in the West and has become a major political factor in the United States. Eastern ways of thinking about such matters have had impact in Western countries and pose contradictions which can no longer be ignored.

We shall explore the specifics of how these two general perspectives function philosophically, processually, and practically in the next few sections of this volume. In so doing, we shall come to a deeper understanding of the diverse theoretical principles which guide human beings and their communication within both Eastern and Western perspectives.

PART I

ASIAN PERSPECTIVES ON COMMUNICATION THEORY

CHINA

Our study of communication from Eastern perspectives begins with three essays from the Chinese point of view. Chung-Ying Cheng (Chapter 2, this volume) provides us with a concise, but densely packed, summary of the most important philosophical principles from classic Chinese literature which are relevant to human communication. The six principles which he describes go far beyond what most Western scholars of communication are accustomed to. First, they explicitly state the ontology and epistemology from which communication phenomena are to be considered. Second, the principles encompass the processes of perception and cognition so crucial for communication. Finally, the principles explain how language and symbolic reference function and their inherent limitations for describing the "real world" and sharing that world with others by means of communication.

Professor Cheng's essay is the most appropriate point to begin a study of Eastern perspectives. Much of what is revealed in this initial chapter will reappear in other forms throughout the remaining essays from the Eastern perspective. Here we encounter for the first time the concept of the indivisable *oneness* and *unity* of reality, how knowledge arises in an *indefinite* and *ever-changing* process, the *dialectical* nature of change, and the *paradoxical* nature of ordinary language. From this initial essay we discover the source of Eastern patterns of communication, and we begin to understand why they appear so different from Western patterns.

James Fu (Chapter 3, this volume) brings us forward from the classical period of the *Taoists,* such as Chuang Tzu of the fourth century, B.C., to the chaotic period of the Chinese Republican Revolution of 1911. Taking a literary approach, he selects the immortal short story of *The True Story of Ah Q,* written by Lu Hsun at the end of 1921. As an exemplar par excellence of communication from a Chinese perspective, it confirms that many of the philosphical principles of the classical period are still prevalent and influential in the modern literature of China before the revolution of 1949. Hsun uses irony to the point of *paradox* and accomplishes what language alone cannot directly achieve, a communion between the reader, the character of Ah Q, and the author, in which the meaning of reality beyond appearances is shared.

Overstatements are used to actually *lower* the object by apparently raising it. The reader responds by laughing at the ridiculous. Understatements are used to actually praise a person by apparently blaming him. The reader responds with sympathy for the pathetic. In this story we see the first and the last, even life and death, change places. Ah Q's greatest victory is his greatest defeat, but the beginning of his real victory. After he is destroyed, he exists everywhere. The victim becomes the victor. His silenced cry echos forever. The effect of the story is unintentional.

Contradiction, paradox, and the development of each thing as a movement of opposites remain just as prominent in the postrevolutionary period of Mao Tse-tung. Donald Cushman's analysis of Mao's philosphical principles and their application to contemporary problems (Chapter 4, this volume) shows how all of the modern forms of mass communication, organizational communication, and small group communication function in the same kind of dialectical process of change articulated so abstractly by the philosophical principles from the classical period and illustrated so well by the comic–tragic story of Ah Q.

The cyclical extremes through which China seems doomed to oscillate are made comprehensible by these same principles of contradiction and practice. What seems chaotic to the Western observer becomes a natural process of development and change in which the collective ''struggle'' of the classes and material production are necessary to restore a productive balance and to locate those human forces which favor extremism in order to correct their thinking and behavior. Communication is an indispensable and integral part of that dialectical process.

KOREA

The three papers from the Korean perspective introduce us to the influences of Confucianism and Buddhism on both the theory and practice of communication. June-Ock Yum's first paper (Chapter 5, this volume) provides us with a good background in the two elements of Korean philosophy, which has influenced the practice of communication in Korea today; her second paper (Chapter 6, this volume) elaborates in detail how the concept and practice of *Uye-ri,* proper interpersonal relationships, have developed from the Confucian ideals. Then Sang-Hee Lee (Chapter 7, this volume) gives us a lesson on the teachings of Yulgok Yi, the most distinguished neo-Confucianist scholar of the sixteenth century, who was deeply concerned about the need for well-informed public opinion to guide the head of state and the formulation of national policy.

The influence of Confucianism on communication behavior stems from, above all else, its emphasis on propriety in human relationships. This is achieved first by improving oneself, becoming educated in the sound principles of Confucius. Such devotion to Confucian principles sets off a causal chain of benefit to all. Once one is elevated by Confucian morals, the family will be in order. As families become better ordered, the community is cleansed of many vices, and it becomes better ordered itself. Once the community is in order, the nation is in order—to such an extent that the need for a monarch disappears.

Confucian morality itself specifies that right conduct results from the four positive aspects of human nature—humanism, rightousness, propriety, and wisdom—and deteriorates from the influence of the seven human emotions—joy, anger, sorrow, fear, love, hate, and desire. Communication and interpersonal relationships must accentuate the four virtues and suppress the seven emotions. The emphasis on maintaining proper human relationships makes Korean culture oriented toward accommodation rather than confrontation.

As Professor Yum indicates, this philosophy is manifested in the language itself. The relationship with whom one communicates is reflected in both the choice of vocabulary and grammar, and the importance of the relationship is evident in the implicit and indirect way that communication is practiced. Because of the greater possibility of the seven emotions emerging in spoken communication, written communication is held in higher esteem. Taciturnity in interpersonal relations is preferred, and the emotions are suppressed with the exception of the smile, which is considered a general emotional expression not necessarily linked with the seven improper emotions. Because taciturnity reduces the amount of verbal communication, the subtlety of nonverbal expression increases. Hence, effective communication depends greatly on the development of sensitivity to nonverbal cues.

Although different in purpose and scope, Buddhism only serves to reinforce Korean culture's wariness and disregard for excessive verbal communication. The source, however, may be traced back to the Buddhist three-stage theory of perception. The first stage is pure sensation, the equivalent of experiencing the mathematical point instant. The second stage is pure intelligible intuition. The third stage is recognition through a conceptual mode. The well-known tenant of Buddhism that "this world" is an illusion is based on the third stage of perception: conceptual recognition. The first two stages can be trusted, but knowledge based on pure sensation and intuition is inutterable. Verbal communication is, of course, conceptual, so we must be skeptical of what is spoken and recognize the limitation of our own words.

The apparent communication bind that Buddhist teaching creates is mitigated by recourse to instantaneous communication. It represents true communication in which understanding is achieved in a fleeting moment, in which it is impossible to distinguish source and receiver, and in which the message does not have to be stated at all. Naturally, under such conditions, silence becomes a much more important part of communication than it is in the West. Silence is full of meaning; implicitness and ambiguity turn two into one.

Those familiar with communication behavior in China and Japan, as well as Korea, will recognize a high degree of similarity which cannot be accounted for simply in terms of the historical interaction of the people of these three cultures. One of Professor Yum's main theses is that this similarity in communication behavior is due to the philosophical foundations which they share in Confucianism and Buddhism. Her paper provides an excellent background for those interested in understanding communication within these three cultures and especially intercultural communication between members of these cultures and other cultures.

In Professor Yum's second paper (Chapter 6, this volume), the specific relationship characterized as *uye-ri* is described in detail, including its origins in Buddhist philosophy. It is best understood in relation to its antithesis, *ri*, individual interest or personal profit. The proper relationship, *uye-ri*, is not bound by personal gain but, rather, by a sense of justice or faithfulness (*uye*) which maintains human dignity. The relationship is not a means to something else but, rather, is an end in and of itself. Nor, contrary to what many from the West might think, is it based on immediate reciprocity. Obligation and loyalty are what counts; reciprocity does not have to be equal and may not occur for some time. Such values create strong, interdependent relationships. The give-and-take type of relationship common in the United States, for example, must be kept relatively immediate and equal in order to minimize future obligation. Why? To maintain each party's autonomy and independence. Favors are done and obligations are created in order to increase interdependence in Korea. Thus, the self itself is largely determined by one's standing relationships with others in the social structure. The opposite of this pattern would be individualism, equally independent but voluntarily allied for a while for specific purposes.

Uye-ri relationships can be maintained only when it is possible to have a long-term identification with a small number of groups and when the individual is subordinate to the group. Thus, the *uye-ri* relationships that we have been describing are usually found among persons from the same geographical region of the country, from the same high school, or from the same family clan, with the same high school class creating the strongest bonds. *Uye-ri* contributes to very warm, lasting relationships within these groups. Mutual confiding is expected and communication is quite open because acceptance is unconditional. The restraint against fault finding, however, has its detrimental side in that it inhibits constructive criticism. Theoretically, the tight-knit bonds based on *uye-ri* within groups also create serious problems of devisiveness between groups, and it thus contributes to the relatively high level of factionalism that exists in Korea today.

The paper by Professor Sang-Hee Lee (Chapter 7, this volume) presents the communication theory inherent in the writings of the most distinguished neo-Confucianist scholar and statesman of the sixteenth century Yi dynasty, Yulgok Yi. His writings focus on the relationship between the people and their nation's leader, especially the structures and processes by which the condition of the nation and the wants of the people are formulated as public opinion by the *Sarim,* or intelligentia, and then communication to the king to affect government policies and performance.

Yulgok's political philosophy consists of a Confucianist "democracy," in which the operation of the nation is based on popular support and public opinion. Government is for the people but conducted by sage monarchs. Although sovereignty is conceded to monarchs, they exist for the people, and their legitimacy is founded on public opinion. Professor Lee describes the three "journalistic" court structures that served as the main communication channels from the people to the king. A special communication role is fulfilled by the *Sarim,* or court scholars, who are uniquely capable of canalizing public opinion to the king because they are independent of political power and economic influence. They are responsible for pointing out injustices and irrationalities and proposing alternative public policies which reflect public opinion. Yulgok himself was a member of this *Sarim* class. His theories of proper statecraft were heavily dependent on effective communication.

According to his theory, the fundamental difference between ruling by justice and ruling by force is that just rule recognizes the absolute presence of public opinion. The fundamental proposition is quite simple: A nation survives when its communication channels are open; it falls when they are closed. They are kept open by the *Sarim*. Thus, the state cannot function properly without freedom of expression. The problem is stated in an interesting manner by Yulgok to the king: Under blocked or repressed public opinion, what the king "really has in mind cannot be communicated." To save face, bad kings restrict access to important national secrets, and the bad take advantage of this. It no longer is possible to tell right from wrong. Information must be public and subject to public discussion to counteract this inevitability.

Yulgok distinguishes public opinion from mass opinion. Public opinion is regarded as representing the rational section of all opinions of the people of a society at large. It is useful, constructive, rational, and ethical. Mass opinion consists of the irrational opinions of the rank and file masses. It is volatile, irrational, and emotional because of the low literacy and education of the masses. Thus, it is the *Sarim* that create and form public opinion, then communicate it to the king. Only this class is capable of understanding reality objectively. Informed of the conditions of the nation and the wants of the people, they can control and eliminate irrationality and injustice in state affairs. The second basic proposition is: If the *Sarim* are flourishing and at peace, a nation will prosper; if the *Sarim* become radical and disorganized, a nation will fall. History teaches this.

Professor Lee concludes by comparing the function of the *Sarim* of the sixteenth century to that of the modern journalists in Korea today. Similar comparisons could be made to the influence of journalists on public opinion in other cultures today. The profound insights of Yulgok into the role of communication in politics at such an early time remains impressive, and they have a universal relevance which transcends their particular place and time.

JAPAN

Communication with the Japanese has always presented quite an enigma and mystery to Western observers. Akira Tsujimura's initial paper from the Japanese perspective (Chapter 8, this volume) dispels some of the enigma but, to a great extent, leaves the mystery intact. Our growing appreciation of the effects of Taoism, Buddhism, and Confucianism on human communication is further enhanced by his analysis of Japanese communication. Specifically, he describes what he considers to be the four dominant characteristics of Japanese communication: communication without the use of language, taciturnity, indirectness, and emotional atmosphere.

The instantaneous meeting of minds, introduced briefly in Professor Yum's discussion of Buddhist influences in Korea, is elaborated in Professor Tsujimura's paper. Known as *ishin-denshin* in Japanese, its origin is traced to the search for truth between Zen masters and their disciples then later generalized to ordinary communication as any example of an instantaneous meeting of two minds without the use of language. At first glance, this phenomenon might seem equivalent to the Western concept of "mental telepathy," the transmission of thought from one mind to another without the use of sense perception. It is not the same. *Ishin-denshin* does involve sense perception but only of the first and second stages of perception according to Buddhist philosophy: the pure sensation of the point instant and pure intelligible intuition. Language, of course, being conceptual, corresponds only to the third stage of perception. It is this third stage, given such prominence in Western communication, which is unnecessary for *ishin-denshin*. *Ishin-denshin* is the mutual sensation of something at the same point instant of time, which is, in an ideal sense, no time at all.

Professor Tsujimura attributes the Japanese tendency toward taciturnity to Japan's racial, cultural, and linguistic homogeneity to the restraint imposed on the people over hundreds of years of feudal authority and, socially, to the rather low participation of people in positions of responsibility in social settings. Indirectness would also seem to thrive under these same conditions, where loquacity in general and directness in particular are associated with social and political danger. Indirectness, however, has assumed a high positive value in Japanese culture, something performed well by the most skillful and artistic.

Kuuki, or social–emotional atmosphere or mood, remains perhaps the most mysterious phenomenon. Although it is explained quite well and good examples are given, one is left with the feeling that, like *ishen-denshin,* it must be experienced personally to be fully understood. It is much more than what is referred to as "public opinion," "consensus," or "group think." Once again, these terms are associated with conceptual or cognitive perceptual processes, whereas *Kuuki* is more closely associated with feelings and emotions. When it affects the outcome of a meeting, as Professor Tsujimura's examples demonstrate, it does result in a consensus of feeling but not one that was or ever need be directly expressed. It simply pervades the mood of all present.

The question of indirect communication in Japanese culture is taken up by Professor Keizo Okabe (Chaper 9, this volume). He finds that a certain amount of progress in understanding this phenomenon can be made with the speech act theory developed by Austin and Searle. Although recognizing that this approach is the most promising, in its current state of development it is inadequate to the task.

After a presentation of the important elements of speech act theory which are relevant for the understanding of indirect communication in Japan, he points out that many of the required rules of speech acts are often lacking or violated in much Japanese communication, on the surface at least. For example, many such speech acts have no conventionalized form of expression and are thus *idiosyncratic* to the communication situation. They are often purposely vague and ambiguous in violation of the important rule of maximum cooperation, almost as if—to the uninformed observer—the real intent is to mislead rather than share one's meaning. That such is not the case is difficult to understand from the standpoint of current speech act theory. In Japanese indirect communication, there is often such a discrepancy between the meaning of the surface sentence uttered and the ''real'' meaning intended by the speaker that there seem to be two levels of communication occurring simultaneously. This meaning must be inferred with the help of traditional rules of Japanese communication, and to accomplish this requires a high degree of taking the role of the other.

Just how pervasive are the qualities of Japanese communication which we have reviewed thus far? If they are a part of the daily practice of communication, then some of them at least should show up at the workplace. Randy Hirokawa's paper on Japanese organizational communication (Chapter 10, this volume) finds the ambiguity discussed by Professor Okabe to be an important element of business communication, along with what at first glance appears contradictory, a high level of openness. How can communication be free flowing and relatively distortion free with superiors and subordinates as well as colleagues, while at the same time be ambiguous?

Professor Hirokawa identifies three main factors that account for this high level of openness: the employees' concern for the company's success, management's stress on internal group harmony, and job security which stems from a semipermanent employment system. The ambiguity is accompanied by a deliberate use of understatement, lack of certainty, and at times evasiveness. According to Professor Hirokawa, this preference for ambiguity and understatement is a consequence of a high value on personal humbleness and tolerance for the limitations of others, along with a cultural norm of "saving the face" of others. To avoid embarrassing someone, one makes his/her statements purposely ambiguous and evasive yet still communicates. The pride of each party is left intact, but the meaning is there to be inferred by all. Thus, communication remains open at all levels and even distortion free, to the extent that all participants know the rules of interpretation. In the Western organization, the alternative might very well be either confrontation and embarrassment or the closing of particular lines of communication, no matter how important they might be for the company's success.

INDIA

The three papers from the Indian perspective follow the same format as the previous sections: first a paper which provides us with a general philosophical background for that particular perspective, then two papers which illustrate how such philosophical distinctions affect some aspects of the practice of communication within that culture. Wimal Dissanayake's paper (Chapter 11, this volume) presents a very concise, comprehensive summary of the key elements of Indian philosophy. As a summary, of course, it cannot do justice to the richness and diversity of material that has developed over the last four thousand years. As with Confucianism and Buddhism, it is hoped that the reader will be motivated to do more reading on the topic.

Professor Dissanayake derives a model of communication from what he calls the "guiding image" of Indian philosophy, the eight core ideals of the culture handed down by the great philosophical sources of thought, the *Vedas,* the *Upanishads,* and the *Bhagavad-Gītā,* which span a period from 2500–200 B.C. The model of communication culminating from these ideals is radically different from what is known in the West.

First, the communication model is oriented inwardly toward the goal of self-knowledge rather than outwardly toward the goal of informing and influencing others or manipulating the external world. The result is a form of "transpersonal" communication (versus transactional) in which the oneness of the world is unambiguously perceived. Self-knowledge is achieved by means of intuitive interpretation of the essence of reality, as opposed to the emphasis in the West on communication as expression by means of rational conceptualization. Once again we see the skepticism of all knowledge based on the categorization of language.

By intuition one can comprehend directly the totality of reality. Categorization, in fact all forms of measurement, can be false and deceitful.

Thus, meditation and yoga are seen in a new light, as forms of *intra*personal communication. Liberation from the attachments of the world of illusions, even from time itself, allow one to discover the true oneness of things. Such a spiritual orientation contrasts dramatically with the material orientation of the West.

The core set of philosophical ideals which Professor Dissanayake describes could never have been diffused throughout as large and diverse a country as India by means of meditation alone. The "message" had to have been spread outward to the common people before it could ever have been internalized as part of a shared culture. Professor Yadava's paper (Chapter 12, this volume) addresses this issue explicitly with his account of the five tenets of *Sadharanikaran,* known as the fifth Veda, developed by Bharat Muni. *Sadharanikaran* may be interpreted without too much damage as "communication" but in the very special sense of communication by aesthetic or artistic means: music, drama, dance, poetry, and so forth. As a result of such communication we find no "meeting of minds" but, rather, a diminishing in one's heart of the difference between "I" and "others." The emotional takes precedence over the conceptual.

Professor Yadava's paper then presents us with two related theories of communication: first, the ancient theory of communication developed by Bharat Muni for the purpose of diffusing the great Hindu teachings to the uneducated masses across India in the second century B.C., then a general theory of cultural change and social integration based on these same principles as they are practiced today amid the inconsistencies and contradictions of modern influences.

According to this ancient theory, (effective) communication can only take place among those having a common, sympathetic heart, somewhat similar to the kind of empathy that comes from a common cultural orientation. If this condition exists, then communication (especially aesthetic communication) is capable of creating a state of emotional arousal which in turn leads to one or more of seven distinct pleasurable responses, from the erotic to the peaceful. Although such communication is two way, it is also asymmetrical, from higher to lower status, from the dominant to the subordinant, from the wise *guru* to the obediant *chela*. Finally, to work properly, it must make use of simplification and exemplification. Very complex ideas are simplified with illustrations and idioms appropriate to the locale.

Professor Yadava makes two assertions about the results of this theory and its widescale implementation across India. The emphasis on the transmission of culture through asymmetrical relationships was largely responsible for the growth of Indian culture per se and to the division of labor but at the cost of a highly rigid and hierarchical caste society, stable but static and stagnant. Contrary to what Westerners may think, however, the order and stratification of the caste system had been developed in a manner that made it seem not only natural but also satisfying even to those on the bottom.

The *Sadharanikaran* is no longer in current use as a concept to explain communication processes in India today, but Professor Yadava makes a strong case for its continuity in the communication process of present-day village "gossip groups." He witnesses the application of these five tenets within small groups as a mechanism for both continuity and the introduction of change from the outside. Above all else he sees it function to combat the tendency of social systems to become a set of fragmented and closed subsystems by increasing the flow of information across the natural and social boundaries of society.

Professor Abdur Rahim's paper (Chapter 13, this volume) describes how an innovative rural development scheme in India attempts to integrate modern democratic and capitalistic principles of political organization with some of its most deeply imbedded religious and philosophic tenets: the idea of *Karma* and the ideals of renunciation and nonattachment. In each village participating in the *Antyodaya* scheme, the individual's own selfish desire and prejudice is being subordinated to a hierarchical, centralized,and collective action, creating a symbolic harmony by reaching out to help the poorest of the poor in each village, five families at a time from the bottom up.

Professor Rahim begins by noting that the Hindu culture must be regarded as both a religion and a social system from "birth to death." Next, the important unit of action of Indian society for the majority is not the individual but the group—the extended family and caste. For many, the highest value is still based on tradition-determined action. Finally, he stresses that all three main schools of Hindu thought held a *receiver*-oriented perspective toward communication. All of these elements are built into the *Antyodaya* development scheme. This traditional perspective contrasts fundamentally with the individual and source-oriented perspective of the diffsuion model of communication and social change widely adopted in the Indian national development program since the 1960s.

The tradition-oriented development program, *Antyodaya,* was founded on the most important contribution of the Hindu philosopher, Shankaracharya (seventh century A.D.), the law of *Karma,* that human destiny is shaped by one's actions. Happiness in the next life results from doing good in this life, and for this purpose nothing can command higher respect than renunciation, service, sacrifice, and austerity as expressed so eloquently in the *Bhagavad-Gītā*. In a sense, this development scheme is the ultimate test of India's magnificent tradition against the problems of modern society.

CHAPTER 2

Chinese Philosophy and Contemporary Human Communication Theory

Chung-Ying Cheng

INTRODUCTION

Although communication theory is a relatively new field and only recently developed as a subject of study and inquiry, communication as a process and activity is as old as human civilization itself. Communication is an essential and crucial agent for the advancement of human civilization; it provides the basis for combining and organizing human efforts to achieve common goals, and at the same time, it leads to distinctions and identifications that enrich the quality of life.

In what way is philosophy related to communication? There are several aspects of philosophy that bear on communication as a process and an activity. First, philosophy can be the content of communication. When philosophy is the content, the way that it is communicated depends on the philosophy itself. This becomes clear when one asks how philosophy is to be taught or learned. There are many different ways of teaching and learning philosophy, and the methods themselves may produce different results. Philosophical communication—communication about a philosophy—leads to the further development of philosophical thinking.

Second, philosophy serves as a context for communication. Philosophy as a system of basic beliefs and inceptive orientations forms the background of any adequate understanding and effective communication. In this sense, philosophy provides the implicit conditions for communication, and communication depends on the preestablishment of philosophical thinking. We are assuming here, of course, that communication is conducted for the purpose of achieving understanding, establishing beliefs, and inducing action. However, it makes no sense to speak of understanding, belief, and action without an interacting community that understands, believes, and acts. To identify this starting point in achieving understanding, establishing belief, and inducing action is the only way to make communication possible. But to do this is precisely to identify a philosophical context for communication.

Third, philosophy provides a method of communication, just like any other discipline. To understand a specific philosophy, we have to understand its concepts, theories, and methods; they are the means and substance for understanding philosophy, for they constitute that specific philosophy. This also suggests that philosophy constitutes a fundamental method of communication, because it communicates the most fundamental aspirations, values, beliefs, thoughts, and perceptions of a person, a society, or a culture. Philosophy is communication founded on the most general, and yet most basic, understanding of a person and a society. In this sense, philosophy defines what communication is and what the scope and limits of communication are, at least, relative to the philosophy developed or accepted. Because of its generality, philosophy provides both models and structures for the communication process.

CHINESE PHILOSOPHY
AND COMMUNICATION THEORY

By taking account of the three important ways that philosophy is related to communication theory, we hope to enrich communication theory and advance it to a higher level with a more flexible structure and with more powerful methods of inquiry. Specifically, we introduce philosophy as a content, a context, and a method of communication in order to illuminate many of the unresolved problems of human communication.

Chinese philosophy, in particular, with its rich background and insights into human nature and human understanding, can make many contributions to contemporary communication theory. Its substance sheds light on the nature of the individual, society, and government and, simultaneously, provides solutions and norms for dealing with the fundamental problems of humanity and human communication. Its methodology puts human communication problems into a new light. Seeing these problems in relation to basic philosophical principles should lead to an important form of understanding, which should lead to individual enlightenment, social edification, and political harmonization. Together, the substance and methodology of Chinese philsosophy provide a comprehensive framework for planning and reevaluating communication problems and for locating new foci of communication processes.

This leads us to the second important implication of Chinese philosophy for modern communication theory. Chinese philosophy recognizes the crucial necessity of the human context for communication and suggests a philosophical approach to this context that incorporates practical goals. Chinese philosophy is generally most critically oriented to human existence as a whole and refuses to draw an absolute line of demarcation between theory and practice. How the context of communication affects communication and how one can locate and identify that context are to be answered in light of Chinese philosophy.

Finally, Chinese philosophy provides a method of communication. The way in which Chinese philosophy is conducted and the various tactics for developing human understanding and enlightenment demonstrate how communication can be achieved. In both Taoism and Ch'an Buddhism, we can see that the way of communication is to be understood in a much broader sense than in the mechanistic models of communication that are prevalent today.* The Taoist and Ch'an Buddhist theories can be in themselves a basis for enlarging and emancipating the mechanistic models of communication theory from their mechanical restraints and a means of pushing communication theory into new areas with new conceptual tools.

I shall divide the following discussion into two parts. The first part derives and generalizes some of the basic postulates or principles from Chinese philosophy that can provide new concepts and methods for modern communication theory. Fundamentally, these principles serve as the pillars of a new framework for understanding and evaluating communication as a process and activity. Second, the entire set of principles can serve as an alternative means for *discovering* new communication problems and new communication concepts, as a means for *justifying* methods for resolving communication problems, as well as a means for actually *resolving* new problems of communication. Although the details need

* See Kincaid (1979) or Rogers and Kincaid (1981) for a critique of mechanistic models of communication.

further elaboration, we can begin here with the general, yet essential, aspects of Chinese philosophy.

For purposes of presentation, we derive the six basic principles of Chinese philosophy which are the most relevant to the problems of contemporary communication theory. They are:

The Principle of the Embodiment of Reason in Experience
The Principle of Epistemological–Pragmatic Unity
The Principle of Part–Whole Interdetermination
The Principle of the Dialectical Completion of Relative Polarities
The Principle of Infinite Interpretation
The Principle of Symbolic Reference

THE EMBODIMENT OF REASON IN EXPERIENCE

In Western philosophy since Plato, there has been a tendency to separate the material elements of things from the formal pattern of things in the study of the fundamental nature of reality, traditionally referred to an ontology. This ontological characteristic is reflected in Plato's own distinction between ideas and matter (called receptacle) and in Aristotle's distinction between form and prime matter (an indeterminate substance). In order to explain the formation and transformation of individual things in the universe, Plato had to introduce an agent that creates things by informing ideas in matter. Aristotle had to assume a teleological hierarchy derived from the motivating power of the Unmoved Mover. Such ontological thinking results in the tendency to constantly seek external explanation in terms of definitive causes and their effects, at the expense of ignoring the intrinsic, self-regulating power of things, on the one hand, and ignoring the universal relevance of the totality of things for the eventuality of things, on the other. This ontological tendency also predetermines the epistemological bifurcation between reason and experience, which are considered to have respective autonomies that exclude each other in the validation and construction of human knowledge.

The rationalists, from the seventeenth century to the eighteenth century in Europe, represented by Descartes, Leibnitz, and Spinoza, rejected experience and sensation as being vague, blurred, and incorrect representations of reality and, thereby, advocated rational intuition and reasoning as the only avenues to correct and valid knowledge. The empiricists, on the other hand, during the same period in Europe, whose spokesmen were Locke, Berkeley, and Hume, viewed reason as no more than the inherent powers for sensible perception and considered knowledge to be derived not from reason but from sensory experience alone. For Hume, not only are the basic forms of knowledge of the external world based on individual impressions but the concepts of causation and self-identity are to be regarded as subjective constructions with no objective validity. This epistemological separation of reason and experience is no doubt rooted in the ontological separation of form and substance, namely, matter. It also has its own peculiarity; however, for while some creative agent in classical Greek philosophy was introduced to link form and substance, there has been no clear link between substance and reason or between mind and body in major philosophical systems since the seventeenth century. For example, in the Cartesian system, reason and experience have been so conceived and defined that, logically, they would have to exclude each other.

In the view of Chinese ontology, form and substance or matter cannot be separated. Consequently, there cannot be pure forms without informing forms in matter, nor can there be pure matter without being informed by form. Reality is the totality of things, each of which has its own form and own substance, yet this implies neither that form is not a universal nor that matter is uniquely determined. On the contrary, forms are patterns (called *li*) that are embodied in things and unify a variety of things in terms of uniform principles. Forms are the structural patterns of individual things and the *principles informing a variety of things*. In this sense, patterns (or forms) are creative agents for relating various things in a hierarchy of generality and a structure of coordination. On other levels, there are other kinds of interrelating and informing principles. In this sense, forms are not just the forms of things alone but the patterns of relations and relations of relations, and so forth. Chu Hsi says, "There is one source which differentiates into ten thousand varieties." This differentiation of one source into ten thousand varieties is not only true of forms but also of the substance or matter refered to as *ch'i* in Chinese ontology.

Ch'i, as the term is generally used, means the vital energy composing all individual things according to different combinations and organizations. In view of the fundamental source nature of *ch'i, all things are ultimately one,* for all come from the same *ch'i.* Thus, the individuality of things contains two sorts of universality, the universality of *li* and the universality of *ch'i,* which should explain how things are essentially related and essentially transformable. Nothing in the world is a closed window or a closed system, but all things admit change and development. The potential of things cannot be fully exhausted as there is always the possibility for interaction between things, which will generate new forms and new relations of existence.

This unity of form and matter in Chinese ontology has another philosophical consequence, namely, the very unity of the two which mutually determines the other as the basis for creativity in and among things. There is no creative agent apart from unified form and matter in individual things. Each individual thing has its own internal energy for change and interaction, and yet, no individual absolutely determines its own being and relation. Each individual participates in the change and interaction of *all* individuals, not only fulfilling its individual potentiality but also advancing the totality of individual things to a more developed and more structured and newly developed and newly structured network of relations. The advancement of the individual and of the totality is an essential characteristic of reality as conceived by Chinese metaphysical philosophers since the time of the *I Ching* (Legge, 1899/1963). This advancement serves to enable both form and substance to be the creative conditioning for the other in order to fulfill its creative function in the formation and transformation of things. The term *t'ai-chi* ("the Great Ultimate") refers to this open-ended creative function and the relation of individual form and substance in oneness. This concept suggests that even form and substance are a differentiation of one entity.

The unity of form and substance in Chinese ontology has its counterpart in the unity of reason and experience in Chinese epistemology. Chinese philosophical knowledge and its attainment are the results of discovering reason (principles) in experience and inducing experience in reason. It is the perfect fit between the two that is to be established by our natural inclination. In Chinese epistemology, genuine knowledge results from interaction and interrelation between the individual mind and the world. As there is a perfect, shared unity between Heaven (form) and Earth (matter), there is also perfect unity and harmony between heaven (form) and man (form matter), as well as between man and earth (matter).

Human knowledge is a human fulfillment of nature (form-matter) or natural fulfillment of man, that is, the fulfillment of unity and harmony between man and the world. Man is capable of both experiencing and reasoning, and it is man who creates and confronts both. As man is one, so reason and experience are one. Therefore, in Chinese philosophy there is no discrimination against experience and sensation at the expense of reason nor disparagement against reason and logic at the expense of experience. Consequently, no reason or logic is abstracted from the concrete perception and understanding of affairs, and no experience of concrete affairs is void of rational understanding. "Human nature" (*hsing*) is a term used to indicate the basis for such an intimate relation between reason and experience. In this perspective, both reason and experience receive a broader scope of application and a wider connotation.

Experience is not simply sensation as such; it is also the feelings and needs of the total person. Reason is not simply logic as such; it is also the respecting of norms and conventions that have been accepted in the community and that have a practical and aesthetic value. Thus, the fusion of reason and experience entails the harmony not only of man and nature but also of the fit between man and other men in a society. Knowledge, in the end, involves construction of a natural world and a social community in which man can live and enjoy. Knowledge becomes the conspicuous experiences of life endowed consciously and enriched continuously by an individual person's understanding of its importance and meaning. Knowledge, in this sense, is also the construction of values that fulfill the humanity of an individual in the course of fulfilling the humanity of all men in society.

Thus, if we examine how Chinese philosophers speak of knowledge, we find that for most of them true knowledge is not understood as a simple record of factual or theoretical information but, rather, as the understanding (or wisdom) of life that enables one to seek and achieve a better and more harmonious life in nature and in society. Reason and experience are so fused that we cannot distinguish one from the other. They are to be seen as the refined product of culture, art, philosophy, morality, and language. Why science was not developed in China can be answered thus: Science in the Western sense is an abstraction of reason that does not grow out of an organic original unity of reason and experience as embodied in the fulfillment of the nature of man in Chinese philosophy.

EPISTEMOLOGICAL–PRAGMATIC UNITY

Since the origin of Chinese philosophy, action and theory, or practice and theory, have been considered not only as intimately, causally related but as two aspects of the same thing. For knowledge is not to be seen as an isolated phenomenon independent of individual life, society, and political programs and their interactions, nor is it a construction related only to the basic functionings of the mind. No action is regarded as devoid of epistemological significance, as action is always seen as the prior condition or consequent effect of knowledge. The mutual support and mutual determination of knowledge and action perhaps can be understood on the basis of the philosophical works of Confucianism and Taoism. In Confucius' *Analects* (1938), we find that Confucius speaks of "knowing speech" (*chih-yen*), "knowing man" (*chih-jen*), and "knowing destiny" (*chih-ming*). In each case, knowing involves an effort of the knower to put himself in a position and orientation toward the world and other men for the purpose of achieving goodness and harmony, in other words, performing.

Take the example of knowing speech. The point of knowing speech is to be able to communicate with other men so that one can better adjust and relate to them. Thus, to know speech, one has to position or orient oneself in a certain way toward society and other people in order to achieve good human relations. Of course, the effort to relate to others in society is not simply a matter of establishing good human relationships. It is also an essential factor for developing the nature of an individual. One basic perception of Confucianism is that the nature of man needs development and that this development can only occur in the context of the interactions of men. Thus, to react correctly to other men in society induces the healthy development of individuals, as well as inducing stimulus and feedback responses from others that would contribute to the development of the self. In other words, man develops himself only in a society in which he contributes to the development of others.

Society, in terms of human relations and orders that regulate human behavior and channel human energy toward public and nonselfish uses, advances the value of man and provides incentive and the basis for the fulfillment of the nature of man. This is the essence of the Confucian statement, ''If one wants to establish oneself, one has to establish others. If one wants to reach perfection for oneself, one has to reach perfection for others.'' On this basis, knowing is seen as a process toward establishing an ordered society wherein an individual finds his proper place and acquires full satisfaction and realization as a man—that is, an individual develops his nature.

Similarly, actions must also be seen as means for attaining the interhuman goals of the development of the nature of man. Thus, knowledge and action are cofactors for determining a social order and for creating conditions for the development of the nature of man. Of course, it is important to point out that they cannot be codetermining forces for social and individual development unless they are mutually determining and mutually conditioning. For if knowledge is not premised by, or gives rise to, action, knowledge will lose its relevance for life, and it will become an empty concept. If action is not premised by, or gives rise to, knowledge, it will also lose direction, and it will become a blind, unmeaningful movement.

Knowledge becomes meaningful when it conforms with human behavior, individually or socially, according to the perception of one's place or the place of man in the universe, and when it can count on what man could do, should do, or should not do. Knowledge takes in values and value judgments that guide men. Action becomes meaningful when it makes a difference to the human understanding of the self and of the source of life and vitality that is not determined or shaped. It is the antithesis of what knowledge, desire, and action determine or identify. It only emerges when knowledge, desire, and action are void and diminished, for *tao* is void and cannot be experienced if there are determinations created by knowledge, desire, and action and their vicious circle. Thus, for the Taoist, the path to truth and genuine understanding is to "forget language" (*wang-yen*) or to "remain speechless" (*wu-yen*), to "remove knowledge" (*ch'u-chih*), and to "do nothing" (*wu-wei*).*

By getting rid of knowledge, things return to the origin of "no names" (*wu-ming*), and things will be seen in their own right. The simultaneous cessation of knowing and acting is not arbitrary for Taoists. It is an implicit recognition of the intimate relationship of oneness between knowing and doing.

Although Confucianists and Taoists have different evaluations of knowing and acting, they nevertheless agree on the intimate unity of knowing and acting. They also agree that human knowledge inevitably involves a pragmatic dimension because it is part of the process of life activities that condition individual and social existence. This *Principle of Epistemological–Pragmatic Unity* can be said to be dominating principle in Chinese philosophy.

PART–WHOLE INTERDETERMINATION

The part–whole interdetermination principle is an organic–holistic principle that asserts that everything belongs to a whole, and no individual thing can be determined, evaluated, or understood without reference to the whole to which it belongs. It also asserts that everything is organically related to everything else within the system to which it belongs. The identity of an individual is to be ascertained relatively in a network of relations; it is the uniqueness of a network of relations that endows the unique quality or character to any individual. But the unique network of relations that characterizes an individual need not be fully and definitely determined. It could be an open system—a system always open to change, to interaction, and, thus, to modification. In view of this, the individual ascertained by a network of relations cannot be regarded as a closed entity. The individual is open to change and development for it can be viewed as both the recipient and the agent for change and development. One cannot understand an individual unless one understands the

---

* *Wu-wei,* or "do nothing," is sometimes interpreted in English as "do nothing artificial."

network of relations, and one cannot understand the network of relations unless one understands the individual.

This is not, however, a vicious circle that renders understanding impossible. Rather, this mutual dependency or the mutual dependency relationship of the individual and the network is generative of an authentic knowledge in an ever-approaching sequence of gradual approximation and interdetermination. One can start with knowing or understanding the individual and then gain some ground for understanding the network. After one knows or understands a little more about the network, one will move to a more solid stance for understanding the individual, and that understanding will further generate incentive and basis for understanding the network. This process will continue until one reaches a satisfactory understanding of either the individual or the network or both. But of course, because of the open-textured nature of the network and the individual, this understanding of either or both must remain open textured and, thus, capable of being modified, or changed, or improved, but *never fully completed*. Figure 1 indicates the relation between understanding the individual and understanding the network.

It must be recognized that this open series is possible not because of the approximating nature of understanding itself but because ontologically there is a mutual conditioning and mutual constituting relationship of whole and part. Insofar as anything falls into this ontological relationship, to understand it is to have generated or be generating a series of approximations of understanding. This principle is fully explored and utilized by Chinese philosophers, and it is imbedded in the Chinese language. In fact, it is the foundation for understanding what language and knowledge stand for in Chinese philosophy.

To understand Chinese language, one has to understand the meaning of words in relation to one another within the concrete context of sentences and paragraphs. The Chinese word, as is frequently pointed out, bears no grammatical markers for indicating syntactical functions and characteristics. Thus, without a sentential context in a particular use, one cannot determine whether a word by itself is a verb, a noun, or an adjective. But

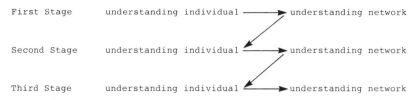

Fig. 1. Understanding as an open sequence of approximation.

once the whole sentence is given the determination of it becomes fairly easy; the word order and meaning of the whole sentence provide a structure in which the individual syntactical functions and characters clearly emerge. This is a good example of how the meaning of the whole determines the meaning of the parts. Although it is also clear that the meaning of the whole determines the meaning of the parts, at the same time, the meaning of the parts determines the meaning of the whole. The meaning of the whole and that of the parts are therefore reciprocally determined. We can also view this reciprocal determination as a sequence of approximations culminating in a relatively definite settlement of the meanings of the whole and of the parts.

To understand reality the same pattern of reciprocal progressive determination between whole and part holds. In Confucianism, the most important thing is to know the primary virtue of how to be a ''man of humanity'' (*jen*). It is to know what is universal among men, together with what one should cultivate in order to bring all men together in a harmonious order. Confucius also speaks of knowing ''heaven'' (*t'ien*) or knowing ''destiny'' (*ming*). All these indicate that one has to know the ultimate and total reality in order to know correctly how one should act on separate occasions. Knowing individual rightness depends on knowing the total standard and norm. Thus, Mencius speaks explicitly of ''establishing the great and then the small cannot deviate.'' For him, one should know the ''four beginnings of virtue'' and the goodness of human nature so that one will attain goodness in individual occasions. In the *Chung Yung,* the stress on understanding the ''mandate of Heaven'' (*t'ien-ming*), the ''nature of man'' (*hsing*), and the ''teaching'' (*chiao*) of the sages is a stress on understanding the totality and ultimate reality as a beginning for understanding the details and minutiae of reality. It is a precondition for gaining understanding of oneself, other people, and society.

Although there is this stress on understanding the totality in order to understand the part, there is also a parallel stress on understanding the part in order to understand the total or for doing things of smaller scope in order to do things of greater scope. Thus, in the *Chung Yung,* there is the statement, ''Nothing is more manifest than the hidden and nothing is more clear than the inconspicuous.'' In the *Ta Hsueh,* the distinction between the root and branch and between ''before'' and ''after'' is made; the root and the ''before'' are things of smaller scope, and the branch and the ''after'' are things of greater scope. Thus, according to the *Ta Hsueh,* if one wants to realize bright virtue in the world, one has to govern well one's state; in order to govern well one's state, one has to regulate well one's family; in order to regulate one's family, one has to cultivate one's person; in order to cultivate one's person, one has to rectify one's mind;

in order to rectify one's mind, one has to make sincere one's intentions; in order to make sincere one's intentions, one has to extend knowledge; in order to extend knowledge, one has to investigate things. This sequence illustrates how one could proceed from doing smaller things to doing greater and greater things. It is clear then that both processes of moving from whole to the part and moving from part to the whole are recognized as equally important and necessary valid conditions for achieving knowledge and insight into reality, as well as essential foundations for developing one's nature and the nature of others.

In Taoism, a similar illustration of the principle can be drawn. But it is sufficient to point out simply that the Taoist philosophers, such as Lao Tzu and Chuang Tzu, always stress the importance of knowing the *tao,* which is the whole, from which all individual things originate. It is only in light of the source reality of *tao* that individual things and their limitations can be understood. On the other hand, Chuang Tzu also points out the importance of seeing the meaning of *tao* in individual, minute things. Thus, a full appreciation of little things, such as sand and dune, is a step to understanding the invisible *tao.* Hence, both the process of knowing the *tao* and the process of knowing small things are recognized. They are essential for grasping the understanding of the relation between *tao* and things and for understanding the full meaning of the *tao.*

THE DIALECTIC COMPLETION
OF RELATIVE POLARITIES

Reality as seen in the eyes of Chinese metaphysicists can be categorized in terms of two opposite and yet complementary principles, referred to as *Yin* and *Yang.* The *Yang* principle stands for the creative, forwarding–pushing, dominating and manifest, systematic force and has the male and heaven as its main images. The *Yin* principle, on the other hand, stands for the receptive, recessive, dominated, hidden, informed, and background force and has the female and earth as its main images. Reality is pervaded by these two forces. Everything in reality is not only regarded as generated from the interactions between these two forces but everything is composed of *Yin* and *Yang* forces. In this sense, everything is a synthetic unity of *Yin* and *Yang* in various stages of their functioning. With this holistic principle in mind, it is clear that everything partakes of many other things in the totality, and its description and understanding is relative to different aspects, standards, and viewpoints. In short, change in reality is to be understood according to the dialectic transformation of *Yin* into *Yang* and *Yang* into *Yin.* But to understand things in their contexts, one has to see and evaluate them in different relative standards of distinctions and classifications. What is most important to observe is that things change dialectically, and this dialectic change forces us to understand them realistically.

Change can be regarded as an occasion for relativism: Change relativizes the standards of evaluation, because it generates new interests, new relationships, and new values. But even independently of change, things can be seen in different perspectives and in different relationships and from different points of view, although the attention of one's understanding may be fixed on one focus. Change over time makes this shift of attention and focus easier and inevitable, but one must bear in mind the distinction between relativization in an absolute sense and relativization in a relative sense. In an absolute sense, relativization is the essential principle for the change and transformation of a thing and a situation. It consists in the creative interchange and reversion of the *Yin* and *Yang* aspects and elements in a thing or situation. The rise and fall, the flourish and decline, the birth and death of things, deeds, and forces in the universe and society or in a man's life are to be accounted for on the basis on this relativization. It has its intrinsic view of opposition, complementation, reversion, and recursion for the *Yin* and *Yang* forces. It is in the innermost nature of change.

On the other hand, relativization in a relative sense consists in seeing and placing things in a different light and at different angles without necessarily requiring a change in time. It means to apply different conceptual schemes to understand a given thing or a given situation in relation to other things or situations contemporaneous with itself. These two processes of relativization are unrelated. It has been pointed out that absolute relativization, which is change, will induce the actualization of relative relativization because it forces a shift in the focus of attention. Relative relativization could, on the other hand, generate creative efforts on the part of the observer or recipient to participate in the change and contribute to bringing about new situations, insofar as no situations or things are closely and absolutely structured and fixed.

Although absolute relativism is primarily an ontological principle and relative relativism an epistemological principle, both can be regarded as principles for understanding reality, as well as for constituting reality. In the case of absolute relativism, we can see things as evolving in terms of the interplay of the *Yin* and *Yang* polarities and, thus, can identify the *Yin* and *Yang* aspects in whatever conceptual system we adopt. The main insight derived from this understanding is that what we see conspicuously need not be the total, nor even the most important, aspect of a thing. What remains unseen must be sought and understood and should be taken into account in understanding the true nature of a thing. Things have to be seen against an amorphous background, their source, and a totality. The totality, the source, and the background equally constitute a part of a thing as its outstanding element. Here the total acquires a special meaning distinct from what is asserted in the *Holistic Principle*. It is the total of *Yin* and *Yang* immediately affecting the nature and change of a thing. The relative relativism is linked to the other sense of the total emphasized in the *Holistic Principle*—the total is the context of total relationships to which a thing belongs. Both senses of the total for a thing are contained in the concept of *t'ai-chi* (the Great Ultimate). The *t'ai-chi*, as mentioned in the *I Ching* and elaborated by the neo-Confucianists, is both the totality to which all things belong and the source from which all things spring forth. It is the totality which defines a thing negatively in terms of *Yin* and defines a thing positively in terms of *Yang*. It is both the actuality and potentiality of a thing. To understand a thing is to understand it in terms of its *t'ai-chi* as the immediate totality and its *t'ai-chi* as involving all possible relations.

INFINITE INTERPRETATION

The dialectic relativism principle has made amply clear that reality has a rich content that unfolds in a polaristic process of change and transformation. But, reality understood in this light need not be regarded as fully determined. Each individual thing involved in the process of becoming can contribute freely to the development of reality. Individual freedom and autonomy have been underlined in our discussion of the part–whole interdetermination principle. What must be explicitly and emphatically brought to light now is the principle that all individuals can creatively contribute to the process of change and can therefore determine an order that is uniquely related to an individual and yet composes the state of affairs of the world. The creative agency presupposes a world which is always open textured and always open to influence from any direction.

This ontological capacity of this creative agency is matched by its parallel epistemological capacity. Reality can be understood in an indefinite number of ways, and there is no absolutely fixed procedure for generating understanding because the object of understanding has no absolutely fixed nature, and there are no two things which are the same. This principle allows us to see things in different perspectives and to make an indefinite number of creative interpretations of them so that we may respond and react to them in creatively different ways. That there are infinite possible ways of understanding a thing or a situation is obvious from the fact that the relative relativization of a thing has no inherent limitation; that is, there are no limitations to the possible relations a thing may have with reference to things in the whole universe. The point of this principle is that to be able to see a thing in its possible relations is a creative contribution toward constituting as well as understanding the thing. It is the source of the creative agency of individual freedom, as it is the basis for developing the individual itself.

In Chinese philosophy, Chuang Tzu has specifically contributed to the formulation and elaboration of this principle. In his essay *Chi Wu Lun* ("Essay on the Equality of Things"), he argues that all things, small and large, are ontologically equal in that they have the same substance, the *tao* ("the ultimate reality and source of reality"), and equally belong to the *tao* of the whole without any real distinction. That means that all things can be regarded as centers of reality and can order and relate to all things from this centralized point of view. It means also that all the distinctions and individuations of things are equally valid outcomes of the creative agency of the *tao,* as well as the outcomes of creative understanding from different perspectives. In this light, Chuang Tzu not only wishes to abolish the egocentric perspective of human beings in comparison with those of the nonhumans, such as insects, fish, and birds, but also he wishes to abolish the biased conventional distinction between reality and nonreality and between life and death. He wonders about the reality of his dreaming of being a butterfly—or a butterfly dreaming of being him—indicating that, ontologically, there is a perfect symmetry and parity between the dream of reality and the reality of dream. In this light, one should not confine oneself to the common belief in reality and should liberate oneself toward the creative possibilities of understanding reality. Consequently, one moves toward the creative grasping of reality, for reality understood in a certain way is reality constituted in a certain way, and understanding or seeing is a way of constituting reality.

On the basis of the parity of the equality principle, Chuang Tzu also draws two conclusions. First, everything is determined relatively to other things, and *there is no absolute truth or falsity* in such determinations. He says, "Nothing is not a *that,* nothing is not a *this.* From *that* one does see *this,* but one will know *this* from *this.* Therefore, it is said that *that* comes from *this*; *this* is determined by *that.* This is the doctrine that *that* and *this* immediately give rise to each other." But *that* and *this* must both be transcended in order to be equally understood and equally accepted. That is to say that one should not attach oneself to *this* or to *that.* This is to recognize the axis of the *tao,* which means that one will not embrace any point of view so that one can see and respond to all points of views equally. Chuang Tzu describes this ontological transcendence and the creative equalizing capacity to respond as "placing the axis at the center of a circle so that one can respond to the infinity." Infinity is the inifinity of *this* as well as the infinity of *that*. It is the infinity of seeing things in the positive way and the infinity of seeing things in the negative way. As things have both positive and negatives sides (*Yang* and *Yin*), the infinity of seeing both ways coincides with the nature of things.

Second, because of the infinite points of views for seeing and understanding things and because the *tao* of the whole reality is an open and ever-changing process, no language or conceptual scheme (which is always limited) is capable of capturing the nature of things, and thus, no language and no system of concepts should be charged with the function of revealing reality. That language and conceptual systems are not complete is obvious from the following two considerations: (1) Language and conceptual systems are logically fixed conventions of distinctions and classification. They may serve a pragmatic purpose for human actions, but they are not uniquely designed for manifesting what reality or the *tao* is. Since there are many possible ways of making classifications and distinctions, language is not able to describe them all. The scope of language is not as comprehensive as the scope of our experience, imagination, or understanding. In other words, the limited resources of language simply do not apply to the infinite reality of the *tao*. (2) Language often generates paradoxical attributions to things, and this shows that ontological reality goes beyond language. The very limited resources of language in facing the ontological complexities of things simply invalidate language by producing paradoxes and contradictions.

Although Chuang Tzu has not yet clearly realized that the paradoxical statements about reality are one way of getting over the limited nature of language as a conceptual network, he has recognized, nevertheless, that language should serve only to *point to* what is to be intended and communicated, namely, to point to the *tao* or to the true nature of things. It is important and imperative that one should not mix the process of pointing with what is pointed out or pointed to. Chuang Tzu notes, "Net is used to catch fish. Once fish is caught, one should forget about the net. Trap is used to catch hare; once hare is caught, one should forget about the trap." In light of this understanding, language would function as a pointer, an indicator, or a lamp that shows but does not describe or classify. One should use language to achieve what it can achieve, and one should confront and understand reality by itself without the medium of language or any conceptual system as an instrument.

These two conclusions from Chuang Tzu's parity or equality principle have specific implications for modern communicatin theory. First, in communication between individual men or between organizations, the participants should explore parallel modes of representation. The more modes of communication that are applied, the more effective the communication will become. A point of view has to be specifically determined, for without a specific point of view there would be no consistent structure, and hence, no meaning. On the other hand, one should not cling to one specific point of view; one should use many points of view to illuminate what is communicated. Second, communication should not be limited to the application of conventional means, such as language. In cases where language and conventional modes are applied, one has to apply them not just in one uniquely predesignated fashion. Specifically, one should be aware of the *showing* or *pointing* function of a specific mode of communication, such as language. To apply one's conventional tools of communication in a sophisticated way, one should design a process of *communication* in its fullest sense and not simply convey one specific set of information.

Furthermore, one should not mix and confuse the mode of communication with the content or outcome of communication. What is communicated should be left free for its own development and should not be tied to a specifically designed mode. There is no contradiction between this and what is said about the first principle, though a medium must be found to suit the meaning of its content. It does not mean that once the goal is achieved, the information should be conceived only in one medium, especially when there is no adequate medium for communicating certain kinds of meaning. One must recognize that what Chuang Tzu teaches is precisely the point that there are many things, including the true nature of things and the nature of the *tao*, which cannot be communicated by any medium, means, or mode of communication. Rather, it must be pointed to indirectly, shown, and reilluminated. In the process, the medium as a pointer must be transcended and abandoned.

In light of the principle of creative interpretation in Chinese philosophy, modern communication theory should recognize that communication involves not only different levels but different relative systems of distinction and classification and that it should always transcend all given levels and distinctions in order to find new ones. This means that communication has to become creative in interpreting as well as in constituting. It should be able to create meaning where there is none and where things originate. Unless communication has constructed meaning and many points of view and can be approached in many ways, it will not become creative. To know and see many points of view and approaches is to transcend them and to find and create new ones.

In this connection, one may learn from the Ch'an master's invention of *koans* as a way of achieving communication. The purpose of this type of communication is to attain enlightenment and the realization of the total nature of reality. There is no conventional method for achieving this. One has to use language to shock one out of what language prescribes. Because language normally carries an ontology of its own and is always conventionally used to prescribe ontology (which obscures the total truth), the language of *koans* is used to rid one of ontologies. This is what I call the *Principle of Ontic Noncommitment*. Once one realizes the emptiness of all linguistically commissioned ontologies, one will open one's eyes to see what reality really is. In doing so, one becomes enlightened, and one will become both free and creative, at the same time, to reconstitute whatever reality suits one's need and purpose without making it a fixed scheme of looking at things. This is what I refer to as the *Principle of Contextual Reconstitution*. My analysis of the use of *koans* has revealed both principles of understanding and communication, which are derivable from, and consistent with, the overall *Principle of Infinite* (or creative) *Interpretation* first suggested by Chuang Tzu.

SYMBOLIC REFERENCE

The *Principle of Symbolic Reference* serves to unique functions in Chinese philosophy. First, it provides an opportunity for the contextualization of the principles which have previously been cited within a communication domain. Second, it allows for one of the most dramatic contrasts between the function of communication within an Eastern and Western perspective.

Previously, we have examined five interrelated philosophical principles which serve to delimit and define the content, context, and method of human communication within Chinese philosophy. The *Principle of the Embodiment of Reason in Experience* emphasized the unity fo form and substance within experience. The *Principle of Epistemical–Pragmatic Unity* emphasized the intimate relationship between knowledge and action within experience. The *Principle of Part–Whole Interdetermination* emphasized the mutual dependency of the individual and the network in generating authentic knowledge and understanding through a process of gradual approximation and incremental determination which is never fully completed. The *Principle of the Dialectical Completion of Relative Polarities* emphasizes the intrinsic view of opposition, complementation, reversion, and recursion through the forces of *Yin* and *Yang* in establishing the innermost nature of change. The *Principle of Infinite Interpretation* emphasizes the open texture of experiences and how all individuals can creatively contribute to the process of change through their differential participation in and interpretation of experience. Throughout the exploration of each of the principles and the analysis which underpines them we begin to recognize the broad outline of the Chinese model of communication. A model in which experience, pragmatic activity, and networks of reality provide the raw materials of understanding while reason, knowledge, and particular interpretations provide a unique, limited, and yet creative understanding of those processes. This reciprocal determination is at once necessary and incomplete. Experience, pragmatic activities, and networks of reality are richer than reason, knowledge, and particular interpretations, and so there is a tension to rise above or go beyond these ways of access to understanding. And yet, reason, knowledge, and particular interpretations are the necessary access points for beginning the interpretative process.

A doctrine of symbolic reference is developed in the philosophy of the *I Ching* (see Legge, 1899/1963), which sets into relief in a most dramatic fashion the difference between the principle of symbolic reference in Eastern and Western communication. Even though the old text of the *I Ching* does not contain a systematic treatment of the relationship between symbol and reference, it seems beyond doubt that the texts were developed for the double purposes of understanding reality and guiding human action. When the "Commentaries" on the *I Ching* were added, the philosphical significance of the *I Ching* as a symbolic system became manifest. But still, we lack a cogent explanation of the meaning and structure of experience embodied in the *I Ching*. Perhaps we should first affirm that the *I Ching* was founded on some primary experience of change and creativity in the cosmos, which both the hexagramic symbolism and the philosophical "Commentaries" are intended to articulate and illuminate (Fig. 2).

Considering the relation between the initial experiences of change and the symbolism, as well as the relation between the symbolism and the "Commentaries," there apparently exist two major systems of symbolic reference in the text of the *I Ching*. First, the system of symbolic reference in the hexagramic symbols presents a clear image of the relationship between language and reality in our perception of change. What these hexagramic symbols represent are multiple entry points one can take which provide diverse interpretations of experience. They are referential symbols for specific realities which when taken collectively form symbolic references for the processes of change inherent in the transformations, influences, confrontations, dominances, harmonizations, reconciliations, oppositions, and so on, of specific experiences.

Because man can penetrate into and participate in the creative activities of the *tao* and *I,* man can articulate the ultimate truth of change and make

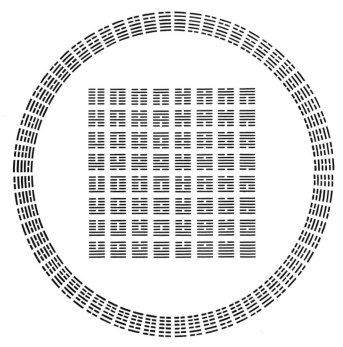

Fig. 2. The Hexagrams, exhibited circularly and in a square, according to the natural process of development from the whole and divided lines, and the order of arrangement ascribed to Fû-Hsí.

correct judgments for action. The very creation of the symbolism of *i* and its practice as presented in the ancient text is the outcome of the wisdom of the sages—the men who have perfected themselves. Thus, the representation of the universal truths of *I* and the *I Ching* already reflect the cosmic participation of heaven and earth. *Hsi Tzu* describes the formation of the *I Ching* in the following way:

> Heaven and Earth determine the scene, and the changes take effect within it. The perfected nature of man, sustaining itself and enduring it, is the category of the *tao* and of justice.
>
> The sages were able to survey all the confused diversities under heaven. They observed forms and phenomena and representations of things and their attributes. These are called images (symbolic images).
>
> The sages instituted the hexagram, so that phenomena might be pereived therein. They apprehended the judgments in order to indicate good fortune and misfortune.

Such a system of symbolic reference with its organic interrelations and hierarchical ordering reveals the structures underlying our experiences and enhances our understanding of the various sources of change.

It also makes clear that each historical instance of human experience illuminates and refines the system of hexagramic symbols present in the *I Ching,* for it brings out a host of possible interpretations of that experience. Thus, while the symbolism illuminates our human interpretation of experience at a given point in time, our sequential experiences of similar events tend to enrich our understanding of the symbolism. The important thing to remember is that what is symbolized can be independently understood and can be used to interpret the symbolism already given. Thus, both experience and symbolism become interdependent. One might say that they represent two processes in the texts of the *I Ching* that are mutually defining, mutually supportive, and mutually illuminating. That this two-fold process of symbolic reference has been most beneficial and practical makes it possible for us to attach great importance to the *I Ching* as a book of philosophical insights.

Finally, while symbols and the things symbolized are mutually and independently understood and yet are interdependent, experience is always somehow richer than that which references it and thus creates the tensions to rise above, to transcend a given symbolic representation to capture the understanding inherent in the broad range of experience. Symbols as such are entry points or perspectives on experience which are at once incomplete and limiting and, in the final analysis, lack the precision, insight, and creativity of experienced life, while they form creative images for gaining access to life and a means for expressing life's experiences in terms of their sequential changing and yet essential configurations.

This forms a Chinese perspective of symbols limited through organically necessary instruments for understanding a reality which is both richer and more diverse than any given symbolic reference. On the other hand, we find some Western philosophers, such as Wittengstein and Hempel, arguing that if a portion of reality cannot be captured by a symbol, there is some question as to its existence. For one, the highest reality exists beyond its symbolic reference; for the other it is its symbolic reference.

CHAPTER 3

Communication in Chinese Narrative

James S. Fu

INTRODUCTION

Chinese fiction represents a union of poetry and history. Therefore, the characteristics of Chinese narrative ought to include those of Chinese fiction, history, and even poetry. In Chinese narrative, especially the short story at its best, whether it originates from literary tales or vernacular stories, the narration tends to become lyrical (Prusek, 1964).

A comparative study of Chinese and Western narrative ought to begin in the two kinds of state of mind or attitude toward reality. In Chinese narrative, events are not often arranged into a linear causal chain as in the Western tradition of realism but form themselves a vast, interweaving process. According to Joseph Needham, the traditional way of thinking in China is "coordinative," whereas that in the West is "subordinative" (Needham, 1956). In coordinative thinking, things react on one another not so much by mechanical causation as by a kind of mysterious resonance. In Chinese narrative, the coherence of the whole is maintained not by subordinating all parts of an external primal cause but by correlating them through an internal harmony. The apparent episodic framework is

COMMUNICATION THEORY:
EASTERN AND WESTERN PERSPECTIVES

precisely the product of this attempt to create such an internally harmonious organism with the linear medium of language.

The best way to examine further the organic view of Chinese narrative and mentality is to study a contemporary Chinese short story. As a literary genre, the short story also forms a small cosmos of its own, self-generating, opening not only on both ends but into many directions. *The True Story of Ah Q* (Yang & Yang, 1972) is a good example of the traditional Chinese narrative. In telling the story of Ah Q, Lu Hsun has woven together at least six kinds of expression: invocation, description, revelation, digression, comment, and narration. The last three are derived from the tradition of Chinese history and are more or less equivalent to the traditional Western narrative method. The first three are derived from the tradition of Chinese poetry and are quite close to the "mythical method" in contemporary Western literature. In *Ulysses, Order, and Myth*, T. S. Eliot said, "In using the myth, in manipulating a continuous parallel between contemporaneity and antiquity, Mr. Joyce is pursuing a method which others must pursue after him . . . . It is simply a way of controlling, or ordering, of giving a shape and a significance to the immense panorama of futility and anarchy which is contemporary history . . . . Instead of narrative method, we may now use the mythical method" (O'Connor, 1964, p. 123).

One of the most difficult tasks for Lu Hsun to achieve here is to bring us into the mind of Ah Q, where we encounter things not only amusingly absurd but amazingly sublime. *The True Story of Ah Q* is considered the greatest of Lu Hsun's stories. For various reasons, many people treat this story as taboo. Though with a universal appeal, the story is unique in many ways.

In our contemporary world, Ah Q is like Franz Kafka's K, who is inexorably an outsider struggling vainly somehow to belong to an order that is impregnably closed by some inscrutable authority. Like many great modern short stories, yet in its own way, the story of Ah Q is also about the cult of frustration, about failure as an invaluable human experience for understanding life. Frustration is essential to the growth of Ah Q's character; later he becomes more and more fearless through the continuous practice of his internal "spiritual victory." At the same time Ah Q demonstrates a readiness to forget and forgive, which is deeply related to the Chinese folk attitude toward the spiritual freedom of Buddhism and Taoism. Though he is treated as a nobody, yet without him, the rest of the characters in the story can hardly have any meaning at all.

Ah Q is more archetypal than most of the prominent figures in Chinese hsitory. His name begins with a common prefix for Chinese pet names, followed by an initial in the Western language, which appears to the

Chinese the picture of a small circle with a rudder or a cipher with a pigtail.

As a mythical hero in the Chinese folk tradition, Ah Q has gone through at least three reincarnations. First, during the Russo-Japanese War of 1904–1905, the Japanese military executed the model of Ah Q by beheading, while the Chinese beside the strapping man had come to enjoy the spectacle. Then at the end of the story proper, Ah Q is shot at the beginning of the Republican Revolution of 1911. Finally, as in a circle, the end is always the beginning; Lu Hsun published *The True Story of Ah Q* at the end of 1921. The spirit of Ah Q has been haunting his mind until it has become so omnipresent that it haunts the imagination of all of us.

COMMUNICATION IN *THE TRUE STORY OF AH Q*

Compared with the Western narrative tradition, the Chinese tradition seems to have far more stories about friendship (between men) and dream. Here again, the story of Ah Q renews the Chinese tradition with innovation. He has no friend as Don Quixote has Sancho Panza. His relation with Young D is only contradictory, but not yet complementary. His daily life including the waking hours is full of dreams, which seem to give form and meaning to his dull life.

The nine chapters in his story can be divided into three sections, each section containing three chapters. In the first section, when he emerges from the pressure of society, his action is internal; in the middle section, his action begins to become external. From Chapter Four to the end, his story proper contains a sustained single action from love to death. The last section combines the internal dream with the external reality. The end of the story is a revelation in reverse, which demands our special attention.

The problem of communication in the story lies in Ah Q's relations with the other characters, with the reader, and even with the narrator. His relation with almost all other characters in the story is marked by his lack of relations with them. Ah Q is able to step out of himself at a crucial moment. Moreover, in his extreme loneliness, his personality often splits into the *alazon* (boaster) and its alter ego, the *eiron* (self-depreciator). The *alazon* often appears in his inner consciousness to follow the lofty tradition, while the *eiron* is often seen in his outer action to react against the heavy society. The *eiron* is often led by the *alazon* but can also balance it. He has a constant revolt against the petty middle class which tends to destroy the individuality of people. As the story goes on, we can see that people like the Chaos and the Ch'iens are losing the colors of their characters, while Ah Q is gaining the intensity of his personality. This phenomenon of course only prepares him for his final sacrifice for their sin of mindless indifference. Under the pressure of the society, he has an inner impulse to surpass his former self by letting the *alazon* and the *eiron* first contradict and then complement each other.

Since irony can help us see reality in its dual perspective, it is an important technique to facilitate the author's expression and the reader's comprehension of the story. Thus, irony here means the discrepancy between appearance and reality. What appears to be true may actually be false. Besides, the story of Ah Q is ironical in its humorous treatments of pathetic themes. Lu Hsun often uses overstatements to actually lower the object by apparently raising it; the result is our laughing at the ridiculous. At the same time he also uses understatements to actually praise a person by apparently blaming him; the result is our sympathy for the pathetic. As a master of irony, Ah Q is full of the *alazon's* overstatements in his inner attitude, while his outer action often embodies the understatements of the *eiron*.

As a good illustration of the universal theme of human loneliness in the short story, Ah Q's seeming relations with most characters are actually no relations at all. Take Amah Wu for example. The widow needs Ah Q or anyone else only to listen to her gossip. On the other hand, Ah Q's expression of love toward her as the representative woman is taken in its worst sense. His death is the result of his inability to hide his love. In the parade before his execution in the town, again he sees Amah Wu, who no longer even recognizes him. With all her pretentiousness, she is but one of the mindless crowd. It is well said in the beginning of Don Quixote's first sally that a knight without a lady is like a body without a soul. Ah Q is a man without a woman. Even in his drunken dream by the candlelight, he imagines himself as a revolutionary hero, yet he cannot find any woman suitable to be his lady. Since people without love cannot understand one another, Ah Q's daily life thus appears to most people as a drunken stupor. Subconsciously, he is searching for love everywhere; eventually, he loses his life because of such a quest. His final death is a breaking away from the pervasive living death in his society.

In his story the only people who have some meaningful relations with him are the two nuns. Contrary to the deception of appearance, Ah Q is actually one of the least harmful creatures in world literature. The only people he can really bully are the two nuns, but only by stealing four turnips from their vegetable garden and by teasing and pinching the little nun on her cheek. The physical touch of that pinch begins a spiritual quest for his own identity and his love with other people. With an awakening effect, that human touch restores his human dignity and rights to a certain degree.

It is more than ironic for such a little virgin, and most probably an orphan, to unconsciously awaken Ah Q from his daily drunken stupor. The nuns have renounced the society to live in the convent called, "Quiet Self-improvement." The society expects the self to play only its role. The little nun is the least pretentious creature in the story. When Ah Q forces her to play her role, her curse in protest soon stops him from playing roles. To deal with the pressure of society, he makes many masks to protect his self. The physical and verbal touch with the little nun not only cuts through all the masks but breaks the tough shell of his ego, making him ready for a communion.

The nuns and Ah Q are the representative victims of the revolution. Their attitudes and actions have discovered new dimensions in life where the ironies become paradoxes. Here, by paradox we mean a reversed development of irony: something false in logic or language yet true to our living experience. Ah Q and the two nuns have once more proved that most of the paradoxes in the new Testament are true to humanity. In the story not only the first and the last but life and death do change places. For instance, Ah Q's teasing the little nun appears to be his greatest victory but proves to be his greatest defeat, which becomes nevertheless the *beginning* of his real victory. To deal with most people, Ah Q is physically defeated yet psychologically victorious. To bully the little nun, however, he is externally victorious yet internally defeated. Unconsciously, she overcomes him from within by revealing to him his false image; such a revelation leads him to his self-realization.

Though living a pious life at the quiet convent, the nuns can hardly keep themselves away from the mindless crowd. On the other hand, Ah Q is like Lu Ta at the beginning of *Water Margin*. At first both characters are forced to live in a quiet temple, and then they involuntarily get involved in the bloody crimes of the society. A more fundamental similarity of the two mythical figures is that both of them appear to the society as simpletons. It has been well said in the East and the West that our deepest insights might appear as follies, and under certain circumstances, as crimes. Like most mythical heroes in world literature, Lu Ta and Ah Q commit only one mistake in their lives. They should not be fully responsible for the mistake, but to make up for it they do much more than enough. Such attitudes and actions to make amends for our sins at whatever cost are redemptive to the society. They can lead to reversing crucial situations.

Soon after Ah Q teases the little nun, deep in his heart he begins to believe her words. While his *alazon* condemns women with inaudible words, his *eiron* worships women with its own kind of ritual song and dance to renew the relation of man and woman in the Chinese tradition. The society allows His Honor Chao to take a concubine, yet forbids Ah Q to have any woman. The "epic fight" between Ah Q and Young D is a dramatic mime, at once humorous and pathetic. The two starving men whose names have been reduced into two initials are the only eyewitnesses of the robbery at the Chaos's house, where the property of the successful provincial candidate has brought violence from town to the "village without a name." Young D sees it briefly with his physical eyes, while Ah Q observes it longer with his mind's eyes.

Both Ah Q and the Imitation Foreign Devil boast about their experience in town. But the Ch'ien lad is a boaster or an *alazon* without the *eiron*. He is a skillful liar and an aggressive robber, while Ah Q proves to be an awkward liar and a timid thief. Ah Q's *eiron* is always there to balance and redeem his *alazon*. Indeed, only the humble people can see sacred things and their significance in the whole vision of life. It seems to me that "Ah Q drawing a circle" has become a parable. Later, we shall discuss in detail how his vision is larger than ours.

As the most crucial event in the story, the revolution also offers various perspectives for our analysis. It is said that real revolution starts with oneself. In Ah Q's mind there are constant syntheses formed by the theses of his *alazon* and the antitheses of his *eiron*. The *alazon* is easily drawn by the revolution to an imaginative flight, while the *eiron* always pulls him back to earth. It is natural for his inner revolution to be intensified with the external revolution of 1911. His internal revolution is of the spirit and prepares him for his final sacrifice, whereas the external revolution is of the letter and proves to be much ado about nothing. The formerly antagonistic Chao and Ch'ien lads join forces to start a "glorious revolution" at the convent at the same time Ah Q finishes his candlelit dream of his internal revolution in the temple. As a mixture of imagination and reality, his dream has become a kind of myth making to fulfill the ritual of his life.

Soon after the revolution at the convent, Ah Q is condemned by the revolutionary court for the robbery at the Chao's house, which of course has nothing to do with him. He lives in the Tutelary God's Temple and never wishes to remove himself even while dreaming of himself as a prosperous hero of the revolution. At first he wishes to have even Young D killed, but soon he orders him to move the Chao's furniture into the temple for his sake. He is arrested from the temple when the revolution needs a bloody sacrifice. As usual, the revolution is a secularization of the sacred. The traditional and the in-between intellectuals rob the convent of its antique censer, and thus, no more incense can be burned to Kuan-yin. In the same way, to kill Ah Q is to sacrifice the local guardian angel.

Now Ah Q has become an archetypal figure who often appears in our dreams to soothe us by taking away our psychological burdens. He is also a prominent figure in comedy, letting us laugh heartily by taking the discomforting incongruities away from our daily lives. To Ah Q himself, the old nun who worships the Compassionate Kuan-yin serves the same function. Being a virgin, she is a mother figure first in the ironic and then in the paradoxical sense. C. G. Jung explains that in dreams and fairytales the grandmother or ancestress often represents the unconscious, which contains the feminine component of the human psyche. Sometimes Ah Q is like an adult who refuses to grow up and, thus, needs more of a mother than a wife. His home, the Tutelary God's Temple, literally means a place to give people shelter and food. When Ah Q is starving because of his tragic love affair, he goes directly to the convent to get some turnips. He is like the fool in the fairytale; he may not be so blessed as the fool, yet to both of them the miraculous is still possible. It is said that his is a comic story with a tragic ending. Still, his story actually ends with a convergence of the comic and the tragic, at a mystic communion beyond our rational grasp or moral judgment.

COMMUNICATION AND COMMUNION

Toward the end of the story of Ah Q, many things come together. First of all, his inner and outer actions become united into one. When he is put in prison, the other prisoners ask him why he is there. He answers directly from his heart, "Because I wanted to revolt." Thus, he pleads guilty for his own attitude rather than his action. It is a mock trial since the captain has beforehand decided to kill him, quoting a folk saying, "Punish one to awe one hundred!" Actually, it is to kill zero to frighten ten thousands. Still, the mock trial is simultaneously a folk ritual and a real sacrifice, since he has now become a nobody forced to take the responsibility of everybody. During the trial, he involuntarily kneels down; in the symbolic action of the ritual, his *eiron* is saluting his *alazon* who consents to die for the crime of the community. Throughout the trial, even more definite than in the whole story, there are two planes of awareness and expression in our misunderstanding one another. The author has thus illustrated the paradoxical aspects of our lvies and language.

Since Ah Q did not know how to sign his name, he was told to draw a circle to accept his death sentence, which was never made clear to him. By making a shape like a melon seed, he has lost the pigtail of the letter Q. To read Lu Hsun's stories as a whole, we can see that the weight of the revolution of 1911 is actually hanging on a pigtail. Since the circle he drew has become a cipher, Ah Q has lost his old identify and has gained a new identity of no identity. Moreover, once this nobody of Ah Q has taken the responsibility of everybody for the universal sin of mindless indifference, the cipher has been transformed into a cosmos.

In his dreaming of himself as the folk hero, and in his daily practicing in irony and the persona, Ah Q creates an image of his own and, henceforth, tries to live up to it. His attitudes toward the society change from dissension to assent and then to acceptance of the role of scapegoat. His character also grows more and more stoic, consistent, and decisive. Through his lifelong frustration, he achieves so much psychological resilience that we never see him completely dejected. He becomes so fearless that the society has to destroy him. After his destruction he at once exists everywhere.

Ah Q once searched for lice in the jacket with Whiskers Wang. His attitude was as serious as in a hunting game of lions. The situation was of course ironic, but now toward the end of the story it reverses and becomes paradoxical. Many soldiers and policemen have come to the temple to arrest him; they even bring a machine gun. Thus, the magnitude of his image has been increasing in his society. He has changed from a louse to a lion, from a timid thief to a fearful bandit, even to a powerful master of martial art in the folk tradition. Ever since Ah Q drew [closed] the circle to consent to die for the community, his action has opened at both ends. They often mean two contrary things at once. Thus, the mock trial is also a mythical ordeal to purify the hero by what is contrary to his former self. No matter how large or small, a circle often gives us the whole vision of two complementary parts, such as the comic and the cosmic. Ah Q is at once a mistaken convict in the revolutionary court and a real sacrifice in a folk ritual from the temple.

At the end of the story we can see the two-in-one unity in his personality. He refuses to play the role, by singing before his execution. During the parade, his eloquent silence is broken only when he sees Amah Wu in the crowd. In his agitation for expression, he utters half a folk saying which he had picked up himself but never used before, "In twenty years I shall be another . . ." Before he could finish it, the crowd roars, "Bravo!" It sounds to him like the growl of a wolf. The eyes of the growling crowd also look like those of a wolf. The eyes look "fierce yet cowardly, dull yet penetrating" and the crowd seems to have merged into one big mouth biting into his soul. Apart from the terror of the image, this is synaesthesis, which shows the intensity of his imagination before his death. Next to the half sentence, his never uttered expression is simply crying for help.

It is said that Ah Q is a victimizer as well as a victim. As we have noted, however, he is one of the least harmful creatures in world literature. At last he grows from a victim into a victor. As we know, a real victor is never a victimizer. Besides, it is not a victimizer but a victim that is necessary to make a victor. At the end of the story, we can no longer say that Ah Q is a victim in appearance but a victor in reality or vice versa. Actually, he becomes a union of a victim and a victor or a *victimor*. The tension between the ironies and the paradoxes has transformed them into oxymora. For instance, here we have the pervasive *living death* in the society, the cruel kindness of the revolutionary court, the eloquent silence of Ah Q since the trial, the fierce cowardice of the crowd, and the passionate patience of the narrator who has learned to tell the story with his heart as well as his head. All these oxymora point to the effort of the author to use his language to discover the whole vision of life anew.

Ah Q has faith in the Chinese folk tradition. Lu Hsun's attitude toward his faith is first objective detachment created by irony and the persona. Then it turns out to be an active involvement, and finally, it is transformed into the integrative principle of a kind of mystic communion. Ah Q is always very lonely. He is still a virgin when he is killed. His desire to have a wife and offspring is never fulfilled. As for the revolution, he is barred from it. Since he is such a loner who belongs to no group, his sacrifice has a universal appeal. Communion between man and nature often comes from our intense awareness of human loneliness. At last, when he tries to cry to heaven for help, he is shot before he can utter the words. His inner voice still creates a resounding echo in the reader's ears as well as in the Chinese folk tradition. Here the comic and the cosmic meet and merge together.

As the central figure of the story, Ah Q transforms from a role-playing stereotype to a living archetype. As a composite picture made up of almost all weak points of the Chinese people, he is sacrificed to awe us for our sin of indifference. When he was shot, "he felt as if his whole body were being scattered like so much light dust." From then on, there has been a little bit of Ah Q in each of us. Is this Eucharist or mock Eucharist? Now many people have realized that perhaps a degree of Ah Q-ism is a necessary element in every man for the preservation of life itself.

In the whole story the author has achieved the union between form and content, style and subject, and art and life (Schorer, 1967). To have an imaginative expression of his experience, he has made his meaning surpass the linear limit of language at the end of the story. When the sound and sense overflow between the lines of his words, the story has been united with music and painting. The unconscious flow of imagery in the author's mind is in harmony with natural phenomena, for example, the Imitation Foreign Devil's staff of the mourner, the white helmets and armour of the revolutionaries in Ah Q's vision, the white vest put on him during the parade, and the bitter lament of the two families after his death.

As natural phenomena beyond the limit of language, they all join together to mourn Ah Q's death.

If we wish to understand Ah Q's world, we must follow his point of view. He is illiterate and does not know the meaning of the black characters written on the white vest. These words are mistaken to Ah Q anyway. If we follow his viewpoint, we can see the vest as a mourning dress for a crucial change in history. The two lamenting families are crueler than the revolutionary court, since they wish to get the robbed goods back from the innocent Ah Q. But if the soul of Ah Q tells us that they are lamenting for his death, we have to believe him. The white helmet and armour are to mourn the lost folk tradition, while the mourner's staff is for the Ch'ien lad to disown his cultural heritage with a foreign stick.

The rambling style and the episodic structure of the story are in harmony with the synchronistic phenomena of nature and the dual nature of oxymora. At the end of the perceptive essay, *To Narrate or Describe?*, Georg Lukacs said, "Man's bodily being as well becomes poetically alive only in the context of human interaction, only in its effect on other human beings" (Steiner and Fagles, 1962, p. 86). To judge the electrifying effect of Ah Q's personality on the other characters, the narrator, and the reader of the story, we must use our hearts as well as our heads. As the author's younger brother and, in a very unique way, his alter ego, Chow Tso-jen said of the story, "The only fault that one can find is that while the author's original intention seems to have been to roundly castigate Ah Q, as the reader approaches the end of the tale he begins to feel that the only really lovable person in all of Wei village is Ah Q. He is certainly the most upstanding person in town, and it is precisely for that reason that he is cut down in the end" (Lyell, 1976, p. 236).

As a great writer of familiar essays himself, Tso-jen cannot be ironic here. By the end of the story, we all feel that the only really lovable person is Ah Q. But still, what Tso-jen called "the only fault" of the story is actually the author's greatest achievement. Tso-jen only mentioned that Tolstoy said something very similar on Chekhov's "The Darling." As Tolstoy said at the end of his comment, what makes the story so excellent is that the effect is unintentional. Chekhov wanted to cast the darling down, but by concentrating on her the close attention of the poet, he raised her up against his own will.

Here we have two good examples of how an author can use his technique as his means to discover the new meaning of life in the process of his creative writing. With the sunshine of a poet's compassionate attention, how much more beauty of humanity can be discovered? Here the poet has returned to the invocation of the epic tradition by humbly asking the muse or the spirit to come to his help. As a result, a communion of man and nature, of the author, the character, and the audience has been achieved beyond the linguistic limits of the story. The author of the story is like the creator of the universe, nowhere and yet everywhere in his created work. He is content to let the characters work out their own actions and, thus, to let the story tell itself.

As the author's attitude toward Ah Q and his language in the story change from conscious irony to unconscious paradox, it is natural for him unintentionally to create the new image of Ah Q with lasting significance. When Ah Q has played out all the roles forced on him by the society, his real self is about to emerge. His final humorous role is only half played when he says, "In twenty years I shall be another . . ." This half of a humorous boast is completed and complemented by his pathetic attempt to cry for help, which, though unuttered in his lifetime, has created a cosmic resonance. Together with his reversed state of mind, the situation of the story and the author's attitude toward him all transform from the absurd to the sublime. All the ironies and satires against Ah Q finally have been turned into blessing paradoxes or redeeming oxymora. Under the sunshine of the author's sympathy and empathy, all the personality defects turn out to be strengths, and the reader is blessed with a higher and more balanced vision of the cosmic order.

Robert Scholes and Robert Kellogg said, "The function of ritual is to interrupt historical time and to synchronize it with sacred time. It is related to empirical actuality and to historical time insofar as it is the vehicle through which human actions are felt to acquire significance, transcending history by identification of the human and the actual with the divine and mythical" (Scholes & Kellog, 1966, pp. 134–135). At the end of the story of Ah Q, we have a mock ritual with a real sacrifice. Still, chronological time has been synchronized with poetic time, while the temporal lines of narrative have become transcended into a cycle of spatial spheres.

How to end the story is really a great problem for all storytellers. Lu Hsun's well-known statement that he took advantage of his editor's absence from town to finish what could have been an interminable series of installments by executing Ah Q points to the fact that like many colloquial tales of the serially chaptered variety, it could have been spun out to almost any length. Ah Q and Lu Hsun join forces in telling the story and in drawing the circle in the trial. The circle is not only a sign of nature but a symbol of the story, for both the circle and the story have no end. If, as Chekhov held, a story should have no beginning and no end, then it can begin and end anywhere. As a work of art, the short story ought to be as natural as "drifting clouds and flowing waters."

Besides, the story needs the imaginative realization of the reader. So long as there are people reading the story, its recreation will never come to a dead end. The imaginative use of the language is to arouse our compassion, to lift us up from our mindless indifference so as to take part in a communion. More than the words on the page, both the song and the story not only mean, but are. The linguistic end of the story is the beginning of our imaginative reenactment.

As Lu Hsun pays more attention to Ah Q, he loves him more and more. The more he loves him, the more he understands him and vice versa. There is also a mutual influence between communication and communion. Without compassionate communion in life, people cannot achieve communication in art or life. On the other hand, as the story tells us, the failure in communication in life and art comes from our universal sin of mindless indifference. Such a sin can be redeemed only by the storyteller's achievement in the communion of the reader and the character, together with the author.

CHAPTER 4

Contemporary Chinese Philosophy and Political Communication

Donald P. Cushman

INTRODUCTION

From its inception in the early 1920s, the Chinese Communist Party was confronted with the traditional problem of what policies to adopt in attempting to unify popular support behind its nationalistic revolution. A general disillusionment with Western ideals had led many Chinese intellectuals to turn their attention toward Marxism. The dialectical perspective of Marxism which viewed reality as a web of contradictions and focused attention on the discovery of the fundamental contradictions which produce change found some interesting parallels in traditional Chinese thought. There are dialectical elements in Buddhism and Taoism, both of which tend to think in terms of opposites and both of which were imbued with the dynamic contradiction of *Yin* and *Yang*. On the other hand, certain basic tensions also existed between traditional Chinese thought and Marxism. The traditional Chinese emphasis on the practical versus the theoretical and the absences of strong class differences between the peasants and an industrial class in the economic realm led many Chinese intellectuals to search for a modified form of European Marxism as a basis for a uniquely Chinese Communist ideology.

By 1926 one of China's more articulate revolutionaries had begun to produce a series of newspaper articles which were to provide in broad outline form the basis for a uniquely Chinese Marxist ideology. In those articles Mao Tse Tung articulated a synthesis of Leninism and the previously mentioned traditional Chinese principles. The main features of the Maoist form of Marxism are outlined by David McLellan (1980, p. 238).

> *Firstly,* China has aimed to develop the agricultural sector in harmony with the industrial sector. The peasantry were thus not the victims of development policy, but mobilized in order to achieve it. China has therefore been able to be a model for most Third World countries, as the Chinese Communist Party was indisputably a peasant party and peasantry formed the vast majority of the population of Third World countries.
>
> *Secondly,* Maoism has emphasized the importance of consciousness. For Marxism is the doctrine of the proletariat and it has therefore been necessary to instil a proletarian or social consciousness into the peasantry. The telescoping of the capitalist phase—both of development and of ideology—into the socialist phase has meant the enhancement of this process. Hence the Cultural Revolution.
>
> *Thirdly,* Mao's doctrines on guerrilla war, evolved in the 1930s, are based on the active cooperation of the peasantry and have had widespread influence in Third World countries.
>
> *Fourthly,* China has evolved forms of anti-bureaucratic struggle that were implicit in *On the Correct Handling of Contradiction Among the People* and put into practice in the Cultural Revolution—though always ultimately under Party control.
>
> *Lastly,* Maoism involves a moral, puritanical emphasis on thrift and devotion to the common good that is reminiscent of Rousseau.

It will be the purpose of this essay to explicate the philosophical principles which underlie contemporary Chinese Marxism and to provide a brief discussion of the political communication system the Chinese Communist Party created to implement their unique ideology.

THE PHILOSOPHICAL PRINCIPLES OF CHINESE COMMUNISM

The basic philosophical principles which underly Mao's form of Marxism were outlined by him for the party in two essays entitled *On Practice* (Mao, 1954a) and *On Contradiction* (Mao, 1954b). The first emphasized man's participation in production and in class ideological struggle as the most fundamental practical activities, activities which alone form the basis for all theoretical knowledge. For Chinese Marxism, the truth of theory is dependent on practice. Participation in production and class ideological struggle are the chief means of overcoming false consciousness and developing theoretical knowledge.

Mao's second essay, *On Contradiction,* attacks static, orderly, and one-sided world views and advocates in their place a search for the causes of fundamental contradictions in a dynamic ever-changing reality as the chief focus of correct action in support of revolutionary change. Mao thus places the dialectical analysis and synthesis of fundamental contradictory forces at the center of practical and theoretical activities. Let us explore each of these philosophical principles in more detail.

The Principle of the Primacy of Practice

According to Mao, human knowledge is the result of direct experience with the means of production or social practice. Since complete knowledge comes from practice, there exists a direct relationship between the questions of knowing and doing. In analyzing the formation of this practical knowledge, we discover a two-stage process of development. Man, at first, comes into contact with the external world and sees only the phenomenal side, the fragmentary, superficial, incomplete aspects of reality. This is the perceptual stage of cognition, the stage of sense perception and impressions. Man sees, hears, and gains something, but he cannot yet form clear concepts which are of a higher order and deeper nature, and therefore, he is unable to understand and reason logically about these perceptions and impressions.

Man's perceptions are impressions which are deepened through the logical stage of analysis. Here, on the basis of the perception of a series of instances, man arrives in a gradual process at a higher stage of cognition. As he comes to understand the internal contradictions in the external world and the laws governing those contradictory forces, he attains a state of more enduring and well-formed logical knowledge. Man deepens cognition through analysis and synthesis by arranging and reconstructing the data of perception. He examines events in their totality in order to extract their essences and to discover the inherent laws which become the theories which govern practice. In short, perception only solves the problem of awareness; theory alone solves the problem of essence. The solving of both these problems is not separable in the slightest from practice.

According to Mao "Seek, the Truth in Facts." This means that a subjective attitude or method running against science is a formidable enemy to research. Research must seek the truth in facts. Facts are the objective events one participates in; truth refers to the discovery of the internal laws which govern those facts.

According to Mao, "Without investigation there is no right to speak." This means that the leadership of the Communist party must know through experience the internal relationships governing experience and how to change experience. Without investigations of this type there is no right to speak.

According to Mao, the formula for success is *Practice-Theory-Practice*. This means that to a Maoist the solution of the important problem of logical knowledge does not stop with understanding a law of the objective world but, rather, requires that one apply that understanding to change the world. The importance of logical knowledge or theory is that it can be used to guide action. To judge our knowledge of objective reality, the Maoist holds that such knowledge is only verified when we achieve the expected results in the process of social practice which may be material production or class struggle. In order to achieve the expected results, we must bring our thinking into correspondence with the laws of objective reality. If they do not correspond, we fail in our practice. Persistence requires us to draw lessons and make corrections to correspond to the law of objective reality and thus turn failure into success.

The Principle of the Primacy of Contradiction

Mao Tse Tung, following in the tradition of Lenin, argued that the law of contradiction in things, that is the law of the unity of opposites, is the basis of all materialistic dialectics. Lenin believed that "the discovery of the contradictory, mutually exclusive, opposite tendencies in all phenomena and processes" is the proper focus for dialectical inquiry. The interdependence of the contradictory aspects existent in all things and the struggle between these aspects determine the life of all things and push their development forward. Contradiction is the basis of simple forms of change and still more so of complex forms of change.

Mao explores the law of contradiction by examining the universal, particular, and fundamental nature of all contradictory processes. The universality or absoluteness of contradiction means that contradiction exists in the process of the development of all things in the world; in the process of development of each thing, a movement of opposites is present from beginning to end. For instance, in life, you have birth and death, love and hatred, new and old, virtue and vice, strength and weakness, development and underdevelopment, poor and rich, oppressor and oppressed, and so forth.

The contradictions peculiar to a certain field of phenomena become the object of study for the scientific branch of knowledge which is built up systematically to become a science. Mao said we should not only understand the universality of contradiction in order to discover the universal cause for the movement or development of things but also should study the particular essence of a thing which is different from one thing to another and the particular cause for the movement or development of that thing.

Mao's thinking is that our knowledge of matter is knowledge of its forms of motion, because certain motion of matter must assume certain forms. When we refer to particularity of contradiction we mean we observe what is particular to this form of motion of matter or the qualitative difference between this form of motion and other forms. Unless we do so, we cannot differentiate things. Every form of motion of matter contains within itself its own particular contradiction. And this particular contradiction consists itself of particular essence which distinguishes one thing from another.

The fundamental contradiction in the process of development of a thing and the essence of the process determined by this fundamental contradiction will not disappear until the process comes to completion, but conditions vary at different stages. Among the countless interwound major and minor contradictions which are determined or influenced by the fundamental contradiction, some become intensified, some are temporarily or partially resolved or mitigated, and some new ones emerge; hence, the process is marked by stages.

According to Mao, *"Different resolutions are required for different contradictions."* In every form of motion of a thing, each real process of development is qualitatively different. Mao held that qualitatively different methods should be used to resolve qualitatively different contradictions. He cited "the contradiction between two opposing forces the proletariat and the bourgeoisie is resolved by the method of socialist revolution; the contradiction between the colonies and imperialism is resolved by the national revolutionary war and the contradiction between the working class and the peasant class in a socialist country is resolved through collectivization and mechanization in agriculture. In reality, new processes and contradictions replace old processes and contradictions, and the methods of resolving contradictions differ accordingly.

According to Mao we require a *"Concrete analysis of concrete conditions."* In order to attain a knowledge of the essence of process, it is always necessary to reveal the particularity of the two opposite aspects of each of the contradictions in that process. Otherwise, the essence of the process cannot be grasped. For instance, the foreign aid programs for each of the less developed countries are extremely different and complex. We must not treat contradictions of many countries in the same way because each country has its own particularity and also because each aspect has its own characteristics.

According to Mao we must apply the *"Principle of the Primacy of*

Practice and the Principle of the Primacy of Contradiction to all problems in order to locate their solutions.'' The following examples serve to illustrate how the Chinese Communist party located a fundamental contradiction and then, through analysis and synthesis of perceptual knowledge, located the logical knowledge or law governing the interrelationship of this conflict and employed that law to change the contradictory forces present in the situation.

The Chinese people know only too well that while the Gang of Four was in power, the Chinese mass media were plagued by what the Chinese called the ultraleft counter revolutionaries. In the Chinese eyes, the media then were notorious for reactionary propaganda, stereotyped writing, frequent fabrication, lack of truthful information, and endless polemics. Then the Gang was arrested and tried, and social life was returned to normalcy and so was the mass media.

In Chinese family-planning communication, the government for a time indicated it was permissible to have two children for each couple in order to keep China's population steady. After finding the life expectancy had become longer, China decided that the policy of one child for each couple should be adopted. When the situation changes, naturally, policy planning and communication should be adjusted to the need of reality.

The relationship between the problem of material incentive and moral encouragement in the past decades in China has changed several times. Before the eventful year 1976, which marked the death of Mao and the downfall of the ultraleft Gang, there had been too much stress on moral encouragement. Finding that it did not work and that something must have gone wrong, the government reacted and reversed the situation, making material incentive predominant. The government sensed through practice that overemphasis on one was just as bad as overemphasis on the other. Thus, a policy of integrating the two was reformulated.

Having examined in some detail Mao Tse Tung's unique brand of Marxism, we are now in a position to explore the system of political communication which the Communist party of China evolved to implement this philosophy into practice.

THE STRUCTURE AND FUNCTION OF CHINA'S POLITICAL COMMUNICATION SYSTEM

Communication in China is not merely an instrument for controlling the population or the means which the rulers use to influence the ruled. Rather, it is the institutionalization of Mao's Marxist ideology. It should be evident by now that what has been called "the Chinese Communication Model'' is actually the crystallization of years of experience in attempting to apply the principles of the primacy of practice and the primacy of contradiction to China's participation in the means of production and social class struggle. Such a communication system is intended to be circular in structure in that information flows from the masses to the masses through an elaborate control system of organizational units and cadre which constitute the super structure of the Communist party of China. The primary functions of this communication system are to mobilize and control the population and to indoctrinate and raise the level of political consciousness in the Chinese people. Let us explore in some detail the specific structure and functions of this system, as well as its effectiveness and problems.

More than half a century of communication practice or the application of the formula practice-theory-practice has led to the evolution of a hierarchical communication structure with its institutionalized means of vertical, horizontal, and cyclical informal flow. This system includes mass, organizational, and small-group structures. A brief overview of these structures and their functions will place us in a position to evaluate their effectiveness and problems.

China's Mass Communication System

The principle function of China's mass communication system is to act as an instrument for the dissemination of information and the mobilization of the population for production and social class struggle. The structures which facilitate these functions consists of a nation-wide television, newspaper, and radio system, as well as an extensive party support display system involving parades, rallies, banners, posters, badges, plays, songs, films, and competitions.

According to Huai Yu (1977), China has 37 television broadcasting stations with 120 relay units. These stations tend to broadcast from four to six hours per day, reaching over 2 million 9½-in. black and white TV sets located primarily in community centers, such as schools, factories, and hospitals, and a small number of homes. In the mornings, China's TV network provides over 400,000 students with access to college courses. In the evening, broadcasts consist of international, national, and local news and programs on science technology, health, literature, art, and sports, which frequently feature the achievements of model production units or model workers. Each day there are children shows featuring songs, dances, and plays designed to instill party spirit. Several times a week stations carry full-length feature films which dramatize important feats of revolutionary heroes. Since television reaches only 2 million of China's

1 billion people, it reaches only a very limited audience located in close proximity to large population centers.

China has an extensive network of national, provincial, district, county, and local newspapers, the two most important of which are the *People's Daily* and *Reference Information*. The *People's Daily* is an eight-page daily paper which produces a four-page daily insert for the provincial and district newspapers. The *People's Daily* and its four-page inserts have a circulation of over 4 million copies which reach all schools, government offices, factories, and rural production teams. The total number of people reached by the *People's Daily* far exceeds its circulation, because many papers are placed on public bulletin boards; still others are read to those who cannot read in reading groups, while still others are rented by the hour at a cost substantially below the cost of the paper at newsstands. Nathan (1979) estimates that each copy of the *People's Daily* reaches about 25 people.

The content of the *People's Daily* is normally divided into four areas: (1) news, (2) party announcements, (3) features on model production units and workers and letters to the editor exposing corruption among party officials and cadre, and (4) advertisements. Chu (1979) reports that in January 1980, a content analysis of the *People's Daily* revealed that of 29 headline front page news stories, 21 dealt with economic issues. Of the 312 front page news stories published during January, 173 dealt with economic issues. Chu also reports that the *People's Daily* received an average of 2000 letters a day from its readers calling public attention to petty corruption and abuse of power by cadre. A special department investigates those complaints, and when found to be true, they are published.

Reference Information is a specialized newspaper for party officials and cadre. Dudman (1977) reported that the circulation of this paper had reached 6 million copies, exceeding the circulation of the *People's Daily*. *Reference Information* reprints, without interpretation, material from foreign newspapers and provides cadre with additional information and features on party programs. However, even with the rapid increase in China's literacy in the past few years and the use of reading groups, Cell (1979) estimates that less than 30% of China's population can be reached on a reliable basis by newspaper.

Radio broadcasting along with its companion direct wire transmission to loud speakers are by far the most accessible means of mass communication in China. In 1975, Ming Ch'en reported that there were 106 million loud speakers installed in China, one for every eight persons (Ming, 1976). Furthermore, these loud speakers are installed in all important public places and are frequently turned on from early morning and play until closing. This combined radio and direct wire system reaches over 92% of the agricultural production teams and 70% of peasant homes. The content of this broadcast system is: (1) news, (2) party announcements, (3) live coverage of criticism meetings, (4) live coverage of study group meetings, and (5) experiences of model production units and model workers.

While television, newspapers, and radio represent the bulk of the Communist party's mass information dissemination system, parades, rallies, banners, posters, badges, plays, songs, films, and competitions represent the party's attempts to get the workers actively involved in the mass communication process. These displays frequently contain the same messages as the media forms but allow the workers a more active means for internalizing those messages and communicating them to others.

China's Organizational Communication System

The Communist party of China operates through a vast network of hierarchically organized work units headed by party member and cadre. These cadre serve as propagandists, organizers, and supervisors. The main organizational units in rural China are: (1) a *study group,* 15–20 members, (2) a *production team,* 100–200 members from 25 to 40 households, (3) a *production brigade,* 1000–2000 members (a village), (4) a *commune,* about 20,000 members (a resource grouping), (5) a *county,* 100,000–1,000,000 members, (6) a *district,* usually 10 counties, (7) *a province,* 20 geographic groups of counties, 5 autonomous regions, and 3 municipalities, and (8) the *nation,* a group of central party functions for 1 billion people.

In the Chinese policy-making process, central committees exist at the top of each organizationl unit of the party. These committees absorb public opinions from each level below it and study and analyze them. After repeated and thorough discussions, decisions are reached and policies formed, promulgated, propagated, and implemented. In the course of propagation and implementation, comments, opinions, and criticisms from cadres and workers are heard, communicated through channels to the top, and then revisions made. Thus, communication from and to the masses passes through the organizational communication system.

China's Small-Group Communication System

All meetings require the participation of the workers involved in an organizational unit, but depending on the type of meeting and audience's goals, the level of participation varies. Four types of meeting are of particular importance to our analysis: (1) mobilization meetings, (2) study groups, (3) criticism groups, and (4) model selection groups.

At the outset of almost every production of class struggle campaign there is a *mobilization meeting*. In this meeting the cadres take political charge of the campaign by making clear to the people the philosophy behind the campaign and their role in implementing it. Frequently, films, pamphlets, slide shows, plays, dances, and songs are employed in conjunction with this meeting. These communication forms are frequently performed by special propaganda teams organized and trained for the occasion by the party. All of these events are aimed at production goals or individual or group targets whose thinking and/or behavior must be changed in the class struggle.

Study groups are by far the most prevalent and frequent type of meetings. In these groups, discussion of current events, local work activities, and/or ideological problems are the focus of inquiry. While study groups meet regularly, their most frequent use is right after mobilization meetings, to educate members of the unit as to how they can help in the campaign and to divide up specific tasks. These study groups tend to meet frequently and serve as feedback groups for adjusting people to goals and goals to people.

Criticism meetings are not as frequent as they once were but do occur during campaigns. They center on the unit's failure to obtain production goals, or they single out target individuals or groups among the masses who are classified as bad elements or enemies. These meetings range in intensity from cadres employing mild self-criticism to public trials of wrong doers. In order to encourage others to participate in the process of criticism and to make the leadership cadre more responsive to the masses, party officials and cadres are encouraged to engage in self-criticism. An editorial in the *People's Daily* told the cadres that:

> When conducting a . . . campaign . . . attention should be given to the gathering of opinion of the masses on the work of the government and on the style of work of the cadres. During conferences, all attempts on the parts of the representatives at criticizing and examining the work of the government and the style of the work of the cadres, it should be accepted with the utmost modesty. It is up to all responsible personnel to carry out criticism and self-criticism in the most responsible, sincere and candid manner so as to increase the masses' confidence in the people's government, improve the relationship between the masses and the cadres, improve our work and conquer the obnoxious inclination for bureaucratism and orderism (*RMRB,* November 14, 1950, in *SCMP,* November 15, 1950, p. 8).

Intermediate in intensity between self-criticism and a public trial is what Mao terms a "struggle." Bennett and Montaperto elaborate:

> In the context of Maoist political behavior . . . "struggle" is a formally defined process in which the target, usually a political offender, is subjected to charge after charge with ever increasing emotional intensity until he admits his guilt. Yet

the purpose of the struggle process is more than just punitive. Rather it is intended to provide the target with a starting point from which to begin actual political and ideological remoulding. Similarly, those who attack are also expected to learn as they do so and thereby to improve their own political and ideological competence. Struggle [is the] . . . acting upon a person or the environment in order to effect a basic change and realize a specific objective (1971, p. 36).

Finally, we have those meetings at which competitions are organized and model units and workers selected. These models are supposed to serve three functions according to Mao:

[Models possess] three good qualities and play three roles. *First,* the role of initiator. That is, you have made surprising efforts and many innovations and your work has become an example for people in general, raised the standard of workmanship and inspired others to learn from you. *Secondly,* the role of the backbone. Most of you are not cadres yet, but you have formed the backbone, the nucleus of the masses; with you it is eaiser to push forward our work . . . *Thirdly,* the role of a link. You are a link between the leadership above and the masses below, and it is through you that the opinions of the masses are transmitted upwards and those of the leadership downwards (*Peking Review,* 1/12/62: 17; see also Chen, 1957, p. 125).

Once individual or collective models are selected, they are reported to higher levels along with propaganda information on their achievement for use in the mass media. Such models are frequently given badges or banners to mark their efforts. Crook and Crook report:

There was . . . a "mobile red flag" awarded every month to one of the companies. As to the model workers, their photos—taken by the commune photographer—were posted at the foot of the Tower of Heroic Ambition, with a brief account of their accomplishments in work, study and physical training; and all were called on to follow their example (1966; p. 84).

Structurally, the Chinese model of political communication was designed to employ mass, organizational, and small-group communication processes in dealing with dialectical inconsistencies in production and class struggle and in adjusting practice-to-theory-to-practice. While there is considerable controversy surrounding the effectiveness of this model in achieving its specific goals, it is possible to draw some general conclusions regarding its effectiveness and problems.

CHINA'S POLITICAL COMMUNICATION SYSTEM: EFFECTIVENESS AND PROBLEMS

Several scholars of China's Political Communication System point with pride to that system's effectiveness in implementing land reform in 1951–1954 and to its Birth Control Program in the mid-1970s (Rogers, 1979).

Clearly, communication from the masses to the masses worked quite effectively in the area of birth control. On the other hand, there are some indications that not every campaign met with this same level of success. Chu (1979) details the numerous campaigns undertaken between 1951 and 1976 aimed at bureaucratic reform—of ridding the party structure and cadre of problems of (1) corruption, (2) nepotism, and (3) commandism. A brief review of these efforts reveals some of the problems involved in the Chinese Model of Communication.

According to the reports of Tze-wen, the minister of personnel, by early 1951 he had uncovered several instances of corruption, nepotism, and commandism by the party cadre. In an effort to restore confidence in the cadre system, the Communist party began the *San Fan Movement* aimed at correcting these bureaucratic abuses at the national, provincial, district, and county levels of the administrative structure. During the first year of this movement, more than 105,000 party cadres or 2.7% of the party cadres were found to have taken bribes in excess of 10 million yuan (*New China News Agency,* February 7, 1953).

In addition to these indiscretions, several cases of nepotism were uncovered. This, according to Tze-wen had led many party cadres to exert little effort in understanding and supervising the work of subordinates. Reports were falsified, field visits were not made, and only good news was reported to higher levels of command (*New China News Agency,* February 9, 1953).

Finally, "Commandism" or the requirement of mass obedience to administrative orders without adequate adaptation of policy to local circumstances led many cadres to file false reports of goal achievements when it was impossible to meet party goals (*New China News Agency,* February 9, 1953).

As part of the San Fan Movement, propaganda teams visited each unit and encouraged the use of mass media criticism techniques to uncover and expose cadre indiscretions. The propaganda unit itself would begin the critical review process by singling out *a known* violator and then encourage others to follow suit. After each meeting those who had accused others were required to remain and examine their own activity to see if they might be subject to the same charges. Thus, by late 1953, the San Fan Movement had begun to restore public confidence in the upper and middle levels of the administrative cadre.

In early 1952, while the San Fan Movement was reaching its peak at the national, provincial, district, and county levels, the party began the *Rural Rectification Program* aimed at correcting cadre problems at the commune, production brigade, production team, and study group levels of the administrative structure. The problems in these rural areas were somewhat different than at other levels of the cadre system. Since these units did not have access to public funds, corruption and bribery were not a problem. Here "commandism" and violations of the land reform laws were more prevalent. These problems were to be corrected by a massive new political education program.

Party cadres at the commune, brigade, and production levels underwent new education programs in order to teach them their roles and responsibilities. Then, by requiring all cadres to visit regularly and communicate continuously with the county cadre above them and peasants below them, the party created a more responsive monitoring system. Supervision from above and criticism from below soon corrected most of the errors in conduct and ideology by cadre. Chu reports:

> No overall statistics were announced, but a few are available. For example, of the 60,360 rural Party members who took part in the initial phase of rural rectification in Shantung Province, 2,363 were found to be counterrevolutionaries (meaning that they were in some related to the former regime), or landlords, or rich peasants, or undefined 'rotten elements.' These were expelled. Another 5,892 were asked to resign from the Party, and 1,856 were given educational reform. The number of disciplinary cases totaled approximately 15 per cent. Thus did the Party purge itself of the undesirable members in its rural organizations (Chu, 1979).

While these two campaigns aimed at restoring public confidence in the cadre system met with some degree of success, it is significant that the party found it necessary to undertake similar efforts in 1957 with the antirightest campaign, in 1964 with the Ssu Ching campaign, and in 1966–1976 with the Cultural Revolution. As late as January of 1982, the Communist party of China announced the beginning of an attempt to purge these party and government officials who support the ousted Maoist radicals and who are now trying to block the implementation of the new leadership policies (*Red Flag,* January, 1982).

SUMMARY

China has made full use of both the crude and sophisticated processes of mass, organizational, and small-group communication processes in an attempt to coordinate its 1 billion inhabitants' efforts at production and class struggle. The Communist party of China has evolved a very large and complex political communication system for operationalizing its guiding philosophical principles. At almost every point in the evolution of this system we have witnessed the appearance of dialectical contradictions between production and consumption, centralism and democracy, discipline and freedom, and revolutionary enthusiasm and logical analysis. The system has on occasions failed to locate the midpoint for productively channeling these forces and has fallen into "extremism." When that happens, "struggle" is required to restore a productive balance and to locate those human forces which favor extremism and to correct their thinking and behavior, thus reasserting the primacy of the principle of contradiction.

Similarly, at almost every point in the evolution of their political communication system, the Chinese people have fought hard to return to practice and, through perception and logical analysis and synthesis, to discover the laws or theories which can again be brought back into practice to guide thinking and behavior. The use of cyclical communication in criticism groups and model groups, as well as mobilization and study groups, is aimed at the realization of Mao's formula, practice-theory-practice, thus reasserting the primacy of the principle of practice.

The lessons drawn for the decade of turmoil (1966–1976, Cultural Revolution) are that the mass, organizational, and small-group communication structures are doomed to failure or to lose their credibility when those in power ignore these philosophical principles and brazenly manipulate the communication processes in complete disregard of the basic interests, wishes, and philosophies of the people. The Gang of Four, having a blind faith in power and institutional authority, ended their abuse of power in utter disgrace. The principles of the primacy of practice and of contradiction were ignored, and democracy or cyclical communication was stifled and "ten thousand houses stood mute." With the silencing of the Gang of Four, the laws of nature returned to their normal dialectical tension, and the Communist party of China's political communication system once again became responsive to problems of the production and class struggle through the use of the principles of the primacy of practice and of dialectical contradictions.

CHAPTER 5

Korean Philosophy and Communication

June-Ock Yum

INTRODUCTION

Communication is the basic social process, and as such it is influenced by the philosophical foundations and value systems of society. Korean philosophical and value systems have been formulated by the combination of several different roots. The three main roots are (1) Korean indigenous belief systems evolved since prehistoric periods and usually categorized as Shamanism, (2) Confucianism originating in China, and (3) Mahayana Buddhism originating in India but imported to Korea through China. If we want to understand Korean thought and communication patterns, it is necessary to have some understanding of these systems and to explore the extent of the impact of each system.

The religious–philosophical systems that have had the greatest impact on the social, behavioral, and thought patterns of Korea, China, and Japan are Confucianism, Buddhism, and Taoism. Lew (1970) suggests that Buddhism rules the mind, Taoism the body, and Confucianism the political society. Buddhism can be said to rule the mind because it strives to control or to eliminate worldly desires so that suffering and pain will disappear from the world. Confucianism is the philosophy of human nature and proper human relationships which are the bases of society. By emphasizing practical human activities and relationships in society, it rules the social order. Taoism is mainly a philosophy of nature and an attempt to transcend the artificial man-made human culture and society. It tries to bring one into closer harmony with nature sometimes by withdrawing one from the world into the isolation of the mountains where one practices a kind of training and asceticism which results in good health and long life. In this sense, Taoism rules the body. These generalizations are somewhat superficial, but they do demonstrate the tendency of each system.

J. T. Kim (1974) suggests that Buddhism approaches the understanding of man through the understanding of the mind, Confucianism through human nature, and Taoism through the understanding of feeling. Buddhism advocates the cultivation of *sim* ("mind"), Taoism *ki* ("energy"), and Confucianism *ri* ("reason"). As a way to transcend the falseness of the world and the suffering due to worldly concerns, Buddhism advocates the cultivation of the mind. Taoism denies rational functions of the psyche for the preservation of energy. Confucianism, on the other hand, advocates that it is reason that rightly absorbs and unifies both *sim* and *ki* (J. T. Kim, 1974).

In Korea, Taoism has not developed into a separate religious or philosophical system but has been absorbed into other belief systems, especially Buddhism. Among the three belief systems, Confucianism has had the most profound impact because it was the official philosophy of Yi dynasty (1932–1910). It was thoroughly institutionalized and systematically diffused to the people. In the following sections, Confucianism and Buddhism will be described, and their impact on communication will be discussed. Shamanism is excluded not because of its lack of impact but because of the emphasis in the present paper on the analysis of the organized religious–philosophical systems.

CONFUCIANISM IN KOREA

In the philosophical and cultural history of the Far East, Confucianism has endured as the basic social and political value system for the past thousand years. Due to their geographical proximity, there have been contacts on both private and official levels between Korea and China since the most ancient times. Therefore, Confusianism arrived in Korea very early, but the exact time is difficult to determine. In 372 A.D., a University (*Taehak*) whose curriculum taught the five Confucian classics was established suggesting that Confucianism was sufficiently developed by this date and that Confucian learning had reached a high enough level to warrant an institution of higher education. At the same time, the equivalent of high schools (*kyung dang*) were established in the outlying districts of the country where all young boys, regardless of class, were taught the Confucian classics, horsemanship, and archery. It is noteworthy that the first significant impact of Confucianism in Korea was the establishment of higher educational systems. The traditional emphasis of Confucianism on education has continued until the present in Korea.

The Unified Silla (688–918) and Koryo (918–1392) periods were best known as the periods when Buddhism reached its peak, but both dynasties adopted Confucianism as the philosophy of politics based on benevolence and righteousness on the part of rulers. In a sense, Buddhism served the people's spiritual needs and left the biggest impact on individual religious life and on art, while Confucianism provided the fundamentals of statesmanship and its educational institutions provided the state with capable officials. In the tenth century, the state examination system for government officers (called *kwaku*) was established. Competent persons were selected and appointed to government posts through examinations in the Five Books of Confucianism and the Three Books of History. By this process of institutionalization, Confucianism played a strong role in supplying an elite which took charge of the functions of government (C. G. Choe, 1972). The same examination system also promoted the diffusion and penetration of Confucianism into the learned section of society. If one aspired to obtain a government post, which was perceived as the most prestigious job at that time, one needed to memorize the Confucian classics by heart.

Confucianism reached its theoretical and philosophical peak as well as becoming a part of daily lives of the general public during the Yi dynasty. Meanwhile, during the closing years of the Koryo period, the political and economic power of the Buddhist monks was such that it was evident that Buddhism had extensively invaded the government apparatus, the traditional domain of the Confucians.

The usurpation of the Koryo dynasty by Yi Sung-Gye, which was supported by Confucian government officials, brought about respect for Confucianism and oppression of the Buddhist policy of the Yi dynasty which had lasted for five hundred years. In the fifteenth and sixteenth centuries, Korea became the center of Confucian learning and produced such scholars as Li Yulgok (1536–1584) and Li T'oege (1501–1570). During the early Yi dynasty, Confucianism reached its highest theoretical and philosophical level by developing the mainstream of neo-Confucianism. By the late sixteenth century, however, the school of rites arose as a reversion against the abstract theorizing of early scholars (Oliver, 1962). The teaching of this school was characterized by the rigid adherence to a highly formalized set of rites or ceremonial patterns of behavior. In reaction to this overemphasis of forms and etiquette, the school of practicalism arose in the seventeenth century. Nevertheless, Confucianism in late Yi dynasty was by and large bogged down with ritualism and petty disagreement in the interpretation of the classics.

Confucianism is a philosophy of humanity. In studying human nature and motivation, Confucianism suggests that there are four human natures from which the right conduct arises: *jen* (humanism), *i* (rightousness), *li* (propriety), and *chih* (wisdom). In contrast, the seven human natures by which people deviate from proper conduct were identified as joy, anger, sorrow, fear, love, hatred, and desire. Therefore, Confucian education strived to elevate and develop the four principles and suppress the seven human passions. Among the four principles, *jen* (humanism) is regarded as the cardinal principle. The concept *jen* defies exact translation into English since it sums up the core of Confucianism. Mencius stated that the concept of *jen* and the concept of man are the same in meaning. Therefore, to ask the meaning of *jen* is to ask the meaning of man—these are one and the same question in the sense that the goal of human nature, the kind of man we are to become, the kind of man we should become, and the kind of man that would exist is summed up in *jen* (H. D. Yi, 1973). In Confucianism the ideal man who is really and fully human is called a man of *jen*.

Lew (1970) stated that there are two functions of *jen*: (1) It is like a seed from which spring all the qualities which would make up the ideal man, and (2) it also refers to the composite possession of these qualities in a high degree. Confucianism contains a view of man as containing something of the devine and of the world which is an expression of Truth which does not change. Confucianism, centered on the concept of *jen*, preaches that humans should be distinguished from beasts. This differs greatly from Buddhism which perceives all living creatures as equally important and preaches not to destroy any living essence.

Hyo (Filial piety) is regarded as the highest embodiment of *jen*. One's relationship with one's parents is regarded as the starting point of all relationships which, in its highest form, should reach beyond and above one's parents and outward beyond one's brothers and sisters.

> Like the rings resulting from a pebble tossed into a lake, the circles radiate outward, upward. Once this process starts, there is a dynamism to it which always seeks to go further, higher . . . . As a man grows, he comes to see more clearly that everything is a gift from above—and above which begins with his parents and gradually stretches, generation by generation, to the very first ances-

tor. In this process, the man recognizes a deep unity with each link in this chain and a sense of gratitude to each link and his chain finally leads him to the cause of it all, heaven.'' (Lew, 1970, pp. 47, 49)

Filial piety encompasses not only one's immediate parents but also previous generations as a benefactor of ego through one's parents and horizontally through other people because they are somebody's parents. In this sense, true filial piety is the vehicle through which *jen* is manifested.

As a philosophy of humanity, Confucianism is most elaborate in explicating proper human relationships and providing proper ways to handle the rituals that function to maintain social order. Confucianism devised five moral codes to regulate the five basic human relationships: *loyalty* between king and subject, *closeness* between father and son, *distinction in duty* between husband and wife, *orders* between elders and youngers, and *faith* between friends. At first glance, these five moral codes seem to be a form of moral coercion imposed from above. But this is not a one-sided relationship with obligations only going upward. Each position has moral obligations. Confucianism takes the attitude that morality basically constitutes reciprocal obligations imposed on all parties concerned and, therefore, that one-sided obligations can never serve morality. Thus, the original meaning of the five moral principles is better described as: father-love, son-filiality; elder brother-brotherly love, younger brother-reverence; king-justice, subject-loyalty; husband-initiative, wife-obedience; and friends-mutual faith. Thus, they stipulate mutual obligations which both sides must fulfill (S. E. Lee, 1967). Therefore, when one side demands that the other fulfill its obligations without first fulfilling its own, the five moral principles are negated.

IMPACT OF CONFUCIANISM ON COMMUNICATION

There are five main areas in which Confucianism has left a significant impact: education, language, public communication, written communication, and nonverbal communication.

Education

The biggest impact of Confucianism on Korean communication is due to its emphasis on learning and gaining knowledge. This aspect has led to the establishment of educational systems, and the high motivation for education that it has instilled in the Korean people has led to a very high literacy rate. Until the early period of the Yi dynasty, Confucianism was studied and practiced by only a few elites, but after the phonetic alphabet was invented for the Korean language in the fifteenth century, Confucian learning spread to the general population. For isntance, after this new alphabet was created, the government engaged in a tremendous amount of publication activity to educate the entire population so that everyone would live according to Confucian teachings. This dedication to education was based on the Confucian philosophy that once one elevates oneself through the learning of Confucian morals, the family will be in order; as families become better ordered, the community is cleansed of many vices and better ordered, and once the community is in order, the nation is in order. The ultimate aim was to create a state in which such a government and such enlightenment arise effortlessly from a people deidcated to their own self-perfection; in a sense to become a state of "needlessness of monarchs" (C. G. Choe, 1972). One of the books published by King Se-Jong in the fifteenth century was called *Sam Kang Do* (*The Picture Book of Three Relationships*). The content of the book was to show the proper relationships between the people and the king, a son and his father, and a wife and her husband. Every other page is a drawing which depicts a scene connected with a story. The story is written above the picture in the Korean phonetic alphabet and on the opposite page in Chinese characters (Lew, 1970). A large number of the books were published and spread across the entire country. It is evident that special effort was exerted to make the book available to be read and understood by the general public.

Language

The Korean language was especially well developed to accommodate the Confucian ethical rules of human relationships. The language is very complex, with special vocabularies for different sexes, for different degrees of social status and degrees of intimacy, and for formal occasions. Correct usage of the proper language for certain occasions and for certain communication partners is regarded as a sure sign of a learned person. By using a certain language, the relationship can be readily defined as intimate or formal, it can establish who is elder and who is younger, and so forth. This type of complex language system is necessary where human relationships are well defined and a certain etiquette is already prescribed in advance. With the influx of Western culture and the lax of Confucian morality, it is inevitable that the young generation today has found that the elaborate language system is unnecessarily complicated and confusing.

The Korean language itself is also abundant with implicitness and indirectness. This aspect is a consequence of the Confucian legacy of putting the highest value on human relationships. Indirect communication helps to avoid the embarrassment of rejection by the other person, leaving the relationship intact. For example, even though both parties know that one's proposition is rejected, it was originally stated in such an indirect manner that both can safely get out of the situation without losing face or damaging the relationship. It makes a negotiation much easier by minimizing the bitter aftermath of a possible failure.

Korean speech is also often interspersed with apologetic and evasive statements like: "It seems to be . . . ;" "It appears like . . . ;" "I dare say that . . . ;" "It may be (quite safely) said that . . . ;" "I am afraid that I may be wrong if I say that . . . "; and "I agree with him but . . ." (C. M. Kim, 1969–1970). If one writes a business letter, four-fifths of it is stringed with greetings and salutations, and the reason that it was written comes at the end usually with profuse apologies. Once again, it is written in such a way as to demonstrate that the human relationship is more important than the business at hand, even though the business is actually what caused the whole interaction. To a pragmatic culture such as the United States this may look like an unnecessary charade, but it is an important procedure to follow in the Confucian tradition of Korea.

Public Communication

Under the Confucian philosophy of politics, government should be *for* the people (even though it was not *by* the people), and Confucian teachings maintain that government should rule with benevolence and righteousness. The power of kings was perceived as absolute, since it was bestowed by Heaven, but only as long as they ruled righteously. If a king violated the Confucian moral code for kings, his subjects were justified or even impelled to arise in revolt and assist in his replacement with a magnanimous monarch (Oliver, 1962). Therefore, Confucianism maintains that the people's mind is heaven's mind. To listen to the public is equivalent to listening to heaven's wish. Therefore, under Confucian political guidelines, the notion that public opinion is the foundation of politics had been in existence since the Three Kingdoms of the third century A.D.. A prominent Confucianist, Lee Yul Gok, suggested that "The rise and fall of a country depends on the opening or closing of communication . . . National policy rests with Public opinion" (Lee Yul Gok, quoted by C. G. Choe, 1972, p. 20).

During the Yi dynasty, there was a special government department which handled public opinion and petitions. The two main unofficial routes for the flow of public opinion were memorials and direct appeal. The *Sagan* officials for expostulation were in charge of receiving memorials and appeals, and they in turn could appeal to the king on a variety of issues and policies. The integrity of these literati-officials, who were devout Confucianists, were held in high regard because sometimes they risked their lives to admonish kings to follow the correct Confucian ways of ruling. C. G. Choe (1972) suggested that the control of power by popular opinion and the existence of literati-officials as intermediaries functioned so well together that it made it possible to maintain the bureaucratic dynasty for five centuries.

These Confucian literati-officials are similar in function to today's journalists and other information gatekeepers. The Confucian tradition of the literati-officials as ombudsman of the government was eventually transferred to the journalists of modern times. In the late nineteenth century and early twentieth century, a large number of modern newspapers were established by the most educated members of the Korean society to inform the public and to keep an eye on the government. Like the literati-officials of the Yi dynasty who were elites that represented the public, the first Korean newspapers were basically elite newspapers. Popular newspapers were slow in appearance, which contrasts with the United States where the early growth of newspapers was based on the broadest possible appeal to the public, sometimes through the yellow journalism of the so-called penny press.

Since being a government ombudsman is regarded as the proper endeavour for the intelligentsia, Korean journalists have come from the most educated groups, such as graduates of Korea's top university, Seoul National University. Becoming a journalist in the past was often a stepping stone to the government itself, since it was not uncommon for renowned journalists to be selected for a high government position such as special assistant to the President, which is strikingly similar in function to the *Sagan* of the Yi dynasty. Furthermore, political journalists have always been regarded as the highest rank among journalists which is again a legacy of the Confucian tradition. Among the Confucianists, Yi Yulgok especially emphasized the importance of public opinion. Lee's paper in this volume discusses his philosophy in detail.

Written Communication Emphasis

Confucianism emphasized written communication and deemphasized oral communication. Under Confucian influences, Korea had no oral traditions such as Western culture's Christian clergymen who preached from pulpits or Greek and Roman debates which led to parliamentary systems. Confucian scholars were supposed to read and record written words. Elites were appointed to government posts by means of written examinations on the Confucian classics and the composition of poems. There was not even one theater in Korea until the middle of the twentieth century, and there was no such course as debate in the school curriculum until today.

Where the written communication was dominant, spoken words were underrated as being apt to run on and on, to be mean and low (C. H. Choe, 1980). To read was the profession of scholars, to speak the act of menials. People were warned that "A crooked gem can be straightened even by rubbing; but a single mistake in your speech cannot be corrected. There is no one who can chain your tongue. As one is liable to make a mistake in speech, fasten your tongue at all times. This is truly a profound and urgent lesson." (Chu Hsi, quoted by C. H. Choe, 1980, p. 47).

In the Yi dynasty, talkativeness was one of the seven reasons that could be used by a man to divorce his wife. This written communication tradition has carried over today in that Korean language programs are basically writing and reading rather than speaking. Taciturnity is still held in higher regard today than volubility. "Man who is only full of words" is a warning against those who talk a lot. This principle is also demonstrated by China's continued preference for Wall Posters in contrast to Western culture's street corner speakers or soapbox preachers.

Nonverbal Communication

Confucianism also left a strong impact on nonverbal communication patterns in Korea. Confucianism maintains that seven human passions are the causes that impede the pursuit of knowledge and truth. It admonishes one to suppress emotion. One is taught to curb one's anger, hide one's sorrow, not to be too obvious in joy, and so forth. One is not supposed to display one's affection to his/her spouse or children in public and much less in the presence of one's elders. Such expressions as the "inscrutable oriental" or "secretive Asian" are due to the lack of understanding that, under Confucian ethics, to reveal one's emotion readily is to indulge in human passion which is a serious deviation from proper conduct.

Korean smiles often baffle those who are not familiar with its culture. Koreans smile when they are happy, amused, or being friendly, but they smile even more vigorously when they are embarrassed or sorry about their own misconduct or shortcomings (C. M. Kim, 1969–1970). They smile when they speak to their elders about something that has gone wrong, and they smile when verbal communication fails, for instance, with foreigners. Unlike laughter, a smile is a neutral expression which does not result from the seven passions one is supposed to suppress. Confucian etiquette prescribes one not to show anger or displeasure on one's face, especially when speaking to or being spoken to by one's elders. Therefore, the smile has become a convenient overall expression. In defending the Korean smile, C. M. Kim (1969–1970) stated that

> It would not be cricket to condemn the smile as self-effacing, self-humiliating, or insincere. It would be wrong to look upon it as a mark of a Korean inferiority complex vis-à-vis Westerners. They are simply being polite in their own way, and in Korean cultural matrices one important way of showing it is to smile (p. 70)

Combining implicitness and indirectness with a lack of expression of one's emotion, one could easily conclude that Koreans do not use much nonverbal communication. On the contrary, Koreans place high value on catching minute nonverbal cues, on reading between the lines, and on hearing between the sounds. Perhaps because information is not forthcoming by verbal means Korean communication must place a great emphasis on nonverbal information. The more subtle the nonverbal communication, the more sensitive or masterful one should become to be a good communicator. For example, to provide someone with something before being asked is regarded as true service since once having asked, the requester has put the other person in a predicament of answering "yes" or "no." *Nun-chi* (roughly translated as perceptiveness or sensitivity with eyes) is regarded as an important communicative quality in Korean culture, since it is through *nun-chi* that one understands what is going on without being told. A person without *nun-chi* is regarded as a crude or unsophisticated person.

To summarize the impact of Confucianism on communication, we can describe a *Gunja* (a man of virtue, a scholar–gentleman that all Confucianists strive to become):

> *Gunja* is a man reasonably well educated, for without education one gets nowhere in Korea. He is a man of principles, has his own opinions—without being overtly opinionated—about the world and, most important of all, lives by them. He is never excited about anything; if he is he never shows it. Ever respectful and courteous, he knows how to deal with people, each according to his background and his worth as a man. He listens to what others have to say more than he himself talks. There is something about him that is sweet, warm and magnanimous. You cannot help admiring him, trusting him, bringing your worries and cares to him for help and guidance. (C. M. Kim, 1969–1970, p. 76)

KOREAN BUDDHISM

Buddhism was first introduced to Korea around fourth century A.D. via China after Confucianism had already been established. When first imported into China, it was inevitable that some of the basic teachings of

Buddhism would conflict with Confucian ethics, especially filial piety which is central to Chinese Confucianism. Buddhism maintained that worldly attachment is a source of suffering and that this world is an illusion. Confucianists found it impossible to tolerate this antifamily, antisociety religion from India. As a result, Chinese Buddhism had to accommodate itself to Chinese cultural imperatives by adopting the basic philosophy that filial piety, i.e., repayment to parental kindness, is the highest morality. The *Ullamban-sutra* (Scripture of Filialial Piety) compiled by Tsung Mi (780–841) expounded the Buddhist version of filial piety and paved the way for the unique development of Chinese Buddhism.

Korea which was also imbued with the Confucian philosophy of filial piety and the importance of human relationships adopted the Chinese version of Buddhism. In spite of this accommodation, Korean Confucianists often criticized Buddhism for its emphasis on life after death, which rendered the present and the cultivation of oneself irrelevant and which isolated the individual from the family and the state (J. W. Kim, 1975). Through its interaction with Confucianism and Korean indigenous Shamanism, Buddhism in Korean was transformed into something less metaphysical but more present oriented, incantatory, and capable of bringing about welfare and happiness to the believer and to his/her family. During the Yi dynasty, Buddhism was oppressed by the Confucianist governments, but because of its egalitarian values it was widely accepted among the lower class and especially by women who were deprived of any social status under Confucian ethics.

According to the monistic view of Buddhism, there is no distinction between mind and body, action and phenomenon, object and subject, or ordinary persons and Buddha. Wholeness and universality lies implicitly within every instance of particularity. The present world is perceived as "ephemeral and illusory" (*maya*). Only by transcending worldly concerns and emptying the mind can one reach Nirvana. Buddhism seeks to return to the original pure mind that rightly sees "phenomena" (*rupa*) as "empty" (*sunyata*) and emptiness as phenomena (Lew, 1975). Buddha is within every ordinary person; the world and Nirvana are the same when one empties one's mind and reaches nothingness. Each particularity is imperfect in that it strives to be one with the original mind. The goal of every individual life is to lose its uniqueness through entrance into Nirvana, the blessed state in which independent existence is no longer a necessity (Oliver, 1962).

Mahayana Buddhism provides several *paramitas* which can be roughly translated as "transcendental virtues," or "higest virtues" for human beings to follow to be true (K. Y. Lee, 1967). The three principle *parami-*

tas are *dana* (giving, generosity, liberality), *sila* (virtuous conduct, morality, righteousness), and *ksanti* (forbearance, patience). They benefit and enlighten all human beings. The three *paramitas* that help individuals to remove worldly concerns are *virya* (energy), *dhyana* (rapt musing), and *prajna* (wisdom). The first three *paramitas* would bring happiness, prosperity, and peace, while the next three let individuals transcend the falsity of worldly concerns and return to the original mind.

Buddhism maintains that poverty, materialistically or spiritually, is due to human greed, and the only way to solve the problem is through *dana,* "generosity," on the one hand, and to transcend the greediness through *virya, dhyana,* and *prajna,* on the other hand. To be generous is the main theme of Buddha's teaching, and it has left a strong impact on many Buddhist societies. In Japan, it was understood as generalized benevolence under such names as kindness, compassion, pity, and empathy and is regarded as a moral virtue (Lebra, 1976). The Buddha is the ultimate embodiment of unlimited generosity. Thus, one is taught to keep benevolent sentiments not only toward fellow human beings but also toward animals, including insects.

In Buddhist logic, two sources of knowledge are recognized: (1) sensation or perception, and (2) inference (H. I. Kim, 1981). The seeming contradiction between the Buddhists' assertion that the world is unreal or illusory and the assertion that we can gain knowledge through perception of this unreal world is solved by qualifying that perception is composed of three moments or stages. The first moment is "pure sensation," and a real datum is given in this first instant (mathematical point instant) of perceptual cognition. The second moment of perception is "pure intelligible intuition," and it is still a form of pure perception. In the third moment, the given datum is synthesized by means of reproductive imagination which is a sort of recognition or rerecognition through a conceptual mode. It is maintained that the illusion of our perception is derived from the third moment of cognition. It is this third moment that constitutes the phenomenal world. Our reproductive imagination is the one that colors the pure sensation or a nonsynthetic unique moment of intelligible intuition.

It is also maintained in Buddhism that "The absolute, i.e., that of the mathematical point instant, the bare particular, nirvana, sunyata, moksa, and so forth which is apprehended directly through 'pure intelligible intuition' is *inutterable*" (H. I. Kim, 1981, p. 81). In comparison to direct and instant perception as a source of absolute knowledge, inference is understood as the source of only indirect conventional knowledge, because inference is bound within the realm of the utterable and functions through the categories of names.

IMPACT OF BUDDHISM ON COMMUNICATION

In Buddhism, there is a general distrust of communication, written or spoken, since it is incomplete, limited, and ill-equiped to bring out true meaning. The words devised to carry out worldly affairs are only approximations and cannot convey what we really mean. *Koo-up,* literally translated as "mouth-khrama," is a burden one has to bear, a source of suffering. Of the 10 proper conducts derived from the aforementioned *paramita,* 4 of them are related directly to communication: Do not lie, do not be engaged in evil-speaking, do not double-talk, and do not use flattery.

Under the premise that absolute knowledge is only given in the first instant, Buddhism teaches that true communication occurs instantaneously, and understanding is achieved in a fleeting moment. Under such conditions, it is impossible to distinguish source and receiver, and the message in the Western sense of the term does not need to be stated at all. True communication is believed to occur only when one speaks without the mouth and when one hears without the ears. The Buddhist holds that the mind is a sixth sense organ and, thus, another means of a specific type of perception (H. I. Kim, 1981).

This principle is often taught by means of an anecdote. For example, a story in a scripture describes a scene in which Buddha was teaching his disciples. At one point he noticed that the sexton who happened to be there broke into a fleeting smile. The meaning of the story is that one instant was enough for the sexton to reach the true understanding, and one fleeting smile was enough for the Buddha to understand that the sexton reached the true mind. Transcending the limitation of words and communicating without resorting to conventional communication means is regarded as true communication. *I-sim jun-sim,* which can be translated as "mind-transference" or "telepathy," is regarded as the highest level of communication that can bring about mutual undersatnding. Professor Tsujimura's paper (Chapter 8, this volume) describes the practice of this type of communication in Japan in detail.

Implicit communication and the ability to discern hidden meaning are highly valued in the Buddhist tradition. Because words are perceived as incomplete, it is sometimes necessary not to take words at face value. The ability to infer the meaning behind them is regarded as a virtuous communication skill. In Korea, one often hears such expressions as "there is a bone within what he/she is saying" or "truth within a joke." A person who "hears one and understands ten" is regarded as an intelligent communicator. To understand without being told is not just a metaphor but a practical communication skill. To catch on quickly and to adjust oneself to another's position before his/her position is clearly revealed is regarded as an important communication skill. Thus, Buddhism elevates silence to an important form of communication. Meditation in silence is a way to reach the true mind, to communicate with the original mind. In contrast, silence is perceived in a Western culture as a state void of communication. In a Buddhist culture it is perceived as pregnant with meaning. Implicitness and ambiguity are used under Confucian ethics as a safeguard to preserve human relationships, while under Buddhism implicitness can turn two communicators into one, complementing one another.

The egalitarian aspect of Buddhism and its teaching to be benevolent to all living creatures contradicts Confucian ethics which emphasizes hierarchy and the distinction between different relationships. However, Buddhism complements Confucianism in that it fulfills other important needs in society. In Buddhism, the temple belongs to nobody and therefore to everybody. Traditionally, Buddhist temples provide shelters and food to whomever asks, and temples are maintained solely by offerings from the people. Buddhism encourages cooperativeness and general benevolence to living things. Not to kill any living thing is the paramount rule of Mahayana Buddhism.

Under the Confucian legacy, there is no provision for communicating with strangers, who are by definition beyond the realm of prescription of the proper human relationships under Confucian ethics. Koreans are very polite and follow an elaborate etiquette but only toward insiders. They can be quite rude toward strangers. Buddhism alleviates this distinction of insiders and outsiders by saying that even a casual brushing together of clothes means a predestined relationship.

Sharing food with a stranger who happens to sit in the next seat in a train is not an uncommon scene in Korea, and Korean hospitality toward foreigners is well-known fact. In other words, Buddhism makes egalitarian communication possible, a communication that cuts across social status or group boundaries, which would otherwise have no place in a purely Confucianist society.

From a very early period, Buddhist scriptures were engraved in wooden block, and block printing was developed to make multiple copies of Buddhist scriptures. From this effort, the first movable types were first invented in Korea some 200 years before the German invention. In that sense, Buddhism also contributed to the development of mass communication in Korea.

CONCLUSION

It is not an easy task to bridge the historical philosophical foundation of a society to current behavioral phenomena such as communication. On the other hand, we cannot adequately describe communication within a social–cultural context without understanding the fundamental patterns. For instance, we can continue to claim that certain communication patterns are idiosyncratic patterns of one society, such as Korea, but when we trace the philosophical origins, we discover the source of the similarity in communication behavior among Korea, Japan, and China as their shared philosophical foundations, namely, Confucianism and Buddhism.

Confucianism exerted a much stronger impact in Korea than Buddhism because: (1) it is a pragmatic, life philosophy, and (2) it was the official ideology of the Yi dynasty for five hundred years, and it was institutionalized and propagated through the educational system and government examinations. Buddhism, on the other hand, was metaphysical and idealistic even after it was transformed to fit Korean soil. Confucianism was said to be the key with which to open the mind and consciousness of the average Korean, so it is where one ought to be looking for the source of Korean national identity (C. M. Kim, 1969–1970). Confucianism is essentially a humanities-oriented philosophy, and many Korean Communication patterns are designed to strengthen the human relationships and place them ahead of actual business transactions and getting things done. This humanities orientation is obvious not only in interpersonal communication but also in organizational communication. In a Korean organization, human relationships take precedence over pure task efficiency. The development of informal relationships among co-workers is encouraged through institutionalized activities. Such activities as company picnics and sports competition among different departments are designed to provide informal communication opportunities among co-workers and between supervisors and subordinates. The seemingly rigid hierarchical status relationships under Confucian ethics are ameliorated by Confucianism's humanistic emphasis which allows or even promotes a certain level of communication among members of different social groups.

Buddhism and Confucianism converge in terms of this humanities orientation, even though the final goal is different. Confucianism enlightens the humanities to establish an orderly, peaceful world where nobody needs to govern or be governed, while Buddhism enlightens each individual to be one with the whole and the whole to be with the one, under the notion that everyone has the potential to be the universe or Buddha. The humanistic orientation in Korea promotes an accommodation-oriented rather than a confrontation-oriented communication style, where advocates manipulate one another and communication is basically a tool to resolve conflicts. The philosophical orientations that underlie a society for thousands of years are the proper starting points to discover the fundamental patterns which influence the communication behavior of the diverse cultures of Asia, and they allow us to make cross-cultural comparisons that go beyond mere description.

CHAPTER 6

The Practice of *Uye-Ri* in Interpersonal Relationships

June-Ock Yum

INTRODUCTION

In Korea, one often hears the expression, "He is a man of *uye-ri*," or one is sometimes admonished not to associate with a certain person because he has no *uye-ri*. A known criminal who was recently arrested in Seoul reportedly commented, "Because of the damned thing called *uye-ri*, I was not able to detach myself from the underworld until it was too late." *Uye-ri* holds the same high value among men that chastity has traditionally held for women. A few years ago, however, in deploring the growing laxity of these principles among both men and women, the two principles were sarcastically reversed to "chastity for men and *uye-ri* for women."

These examples suggest the importance and the prevailing effect of the concept *uye-ri* in the development and maintenance of Korean interpersonal relationships. The term *uye-ri* has three major meanings. The first is justice, righteousness, a just cause, duty, morality, probity, and integrity. The second meaning is obligation, a debt of gratitude, loyalty, and faithfulness. The third meaning concerns the proper relationships between people used in such contexts as *uye-ri* between lord and retainer or *uye-ri* between friends. If the concept is used as a adjective, it means "sworn," such as "they are *uye-ri* brothers." These diverse translations, however, do not capture the complete, or exact, meaning of *uye-ri* as is the case with many culture-bound concepts. English, as a language, developed in a completely different philosophical, cultural, and social context. The concept of *uye-ri* can be fully understood only in the context of the Korean philosophical, cultural, and social context. This is true not only for the meaning of the concept but also for the particular role that the concept plays in communication in the Korean society. In this paper, the origin of the concept of *uye-ri* is explored from the philosophical background of Korea in order to understand the current practice of *uye-ri* and to see the effect of *uye-ri* on interpersonal communication in Korea today.

CONFUCIANISM AND *UYE-RI* IDEOLOGY

Ideologically, Korea has been under the strong influence of Confucianism. The root of the concept, *uye-ri* can be found in Confucianism or, more specifically, neo-Confucianism. In the fifteenth and sixteenth centuries, Korea produced such renowned Confucian scholars as Yulgok (1536–1584) and T'oege (1501–1579).

In neo-Confucianism, the teaching of Confucious became a more ethical and practical approach to life, and it provided the morality for the practice of political principles for self-discipline, for governing the family, for governing a nation, and then for governing the world, that is, secular principles rather than religious or metaphysical principles. The original meaning of *uye-ri* in neo-Confucianism is close to the first definition of the concept, justice or just cause, and it is used as an antithesis to personal or individual interest and profit called *ri*. In the current use of the term, if only *uye* is used, it means just or cause, whereas the meaning of *uye-ri* is closer to faithfulness.

Neo-Confucianism starts with self-examination and introspection. It is the study of oneself rather than study of humanity in general. Therefore, it is a process of self-confirmation and the awakening of self-consciousness. It is based on the Confucius teaching which suggests that if one purifies one's heart, one can lead to better life. As the individual elevates his own standards of conduct, the quality of family life is improved. As families become better ordered, the community is cleansed of many vices. As communities become dependably ethical, the whole nation is more orderly, just, and stable.

Through self examination, however, we transcend self and find the way to understand others since the essence of one's self applies to both ego and alter, and *uye* is the bridge of the ego and alter.

The ideal man in Confucianism is the *gun-ja*, a learned, well-rounded scholar. *Uye* is one of the necessary elements of a *gun-ja*. Therefore, the *gun-ja* seeks *uye* while the *so-in*, or small-minded man who is opposite of the *gun-ja*, seeks *ri*, personal profit or interest. The Confucian scholar *Ju-ja* suggested that *uye* is the product of heaven, and *ri* is the product of human desire. Mencious believed that man has the basic capacity of *uye*. He said that any person who saw a child just about to fall into a well, would feel heartache and pity and therefore rush to save the baby—not because they would expect a reward from the parents or compliments from the neighbors but because of *uye* (Yoo, 1975). In this sense, *uye* is close to the concept of original goodness of human nature (Yoo, 1975).

Uye-ri places value on the internal conscience of human nature as opposed to self-interest or material profit. By behaving according to *uye-ri*, we produce and maintain human dignity. To Mencious, *uye-ri* can be understood and accepted by all human beings, and it is the basis for the social bonds that hold society together.

To Korean neo-Confucianists, the focus of *uye-ri* ideology was to enhance the original human nature and to suppress the secular or physical desires. Not to be tempted by worldly desires but to follow one's true conscience was thought of as the manifestation of *uye-ri*. When Li Sung Gye, the founder of Li Dynasty, usurped the Koryu dynasty, a large number of Confucian scholars refused to be cooped into the new dynasty, and many of them were executed or exiled. These groups of scholars were called *uye-ri* school, and their followers and students maintained the tradition of *uye-ri* by not participating in the politics but by remaining as the main scholarly group that adomonished the king and government of the proper conscience and principles. The *uye-ri* school's resistant tradition was principally derived from the thought that one cannot transfer one's loyalty (*uye-ri*) from one king to another, but it was further expanded to that of accepting a political position to increase one's personal interest and to satisfy human desire, which is the opposite of the true scholar's endeavor to enhance *uye*.

In the early concept of *uye-ri* the notion of reciprocation was weak even though it existed implicitly. In the current form, reciprocation plays an important role in keeping *uye-ri* as a social rule that governs interpersonal interaction.

Another important point is that Confucian ethics is not general or applied universally in every situation. Its ethics are changeable depending on particular interpersonal relationships. In Western thought, an event or matter is objectified by isolating it from personal contexts. In Confucian thought, ethics depends on the nature of specific human relationships.

This changeable form of ethics in Confucian thought is pointed out by Hsu (1963). He hypothesized that the Hindu approach to the world is characterized by supernatural centeredness and unilateral dependence in contrast to the American approach of individual centeredness and independence and the Chinese approach of situation centeredness and mutual dependence.

Confucius says, "In handling all the matters, *gun-ja* will not affirm nor negate but to follow *uye*" (Confucius, cited by D. J. Lee, n.d., p. 138). It means that one should not negate or affirm beforehand but wait until the time and situation are revealed as a concrete reality and then apply *uye* that accommodate the subjective motive and objective situation. One should not be dictated only by objective conditions or by personal whims but should seek propriety.

According to the Western pattern of thought, applying different ethics according to whom you are dealing with is unacceptable, but in Confucian ethics it is natural. Under situational ethics, family, clan, region, and other kinds of interpersonal relationships play an important role. Depending on these relationships, a different source of *uye-ri* applies. Because of this, rational behaviors according to Western criteria were slow to develop in Korea.

PRACTICE OF *UYE-RI* IN KOREA TODAY

The practice of *uye-ri* can be analyzed from two aspects—reciprocity and interdependence. These two aspects are two sides of the same coin, but by looking from both sides we can fully understand the mechanisms by which *uye-ri* regulates interpersonal relationships and communication in Korea today.

Social Reciprocity

Social reciprocity refers to the process of give-and-take in interpersonal communication, both formally and informally. *Uye-ri* involves complementary and obligatory reciprocity, where, in a sense, a person is forever indebted to others (and he, himself, is a recipient of such debts). The alternative variations sometimes found in other societies are: (1) autonomy, where the value is to avoid as many commitments and obligations as possible, all being seen as threats to freedom; (2) symmetrical–obligatory, where a person has obligations primarily to equals or institutions with whom he has established some contractual base.

What appears to be a small request in one society takes on broader implications in another. In the United States, for example, a request to do a favor may imply no necessary reciprocation. It would certainly not imply an obligation that would last forever. In some cultures, however, the expression, "One good turn deserves another," may literally state the rules of social interaction. If you are a close friend or in a position to incur *uye-ri* from another person, you can ask for a very heavy favor from that person because you know that you will be able to reciprocate someday one way or another. The one who is asked also cannot easily refuse the favor because it would mean that he doesn't have *uye-ri,* and eventually this could mean being ostracized from the group to which they both belong. Under *uye-ri,* reciprocity is not necessarily immediate, nor does it have to be promised, for both parties understand that they are bound by *uye-ri.* Sometimes *uye-ri* can be reciprocated by the next generation or by one's spouse in a completely different form than the one originally given/ received. Therefore, for the *uye-ri* to be maintained, the social structure should be compatible. *Uye-ri* can be maintained only when one has a relatively long identification with a small number of groups, and where the individual is subordinate to the group.

The Japanese have the same term with slightly different nuances, pronounced as *giri.* As Kawashima (1951, cited by Lebra, 1976) defined the term, *giri* is generated by and in turn maintains gemeinschaft relationships between particular individuals. The gemeinschaft relationship involving *giri* can be characterized by: (1) duration, not a temporary relationship but permanent ones (for example, the *giri* of regular gift giving), (2) total involvement, the relationship occupying not just a small part of life, such as a pupil learning a skill from a teacher, but the whole sphere of life, including the pupil's marriage and family, (3) an imposition on the individual by virtue of his status, as when *giri* is contrasted with *ninjo,* human feelings, (4) a personal, particularistic relationship involving face-to-face interaction in a physical sense, (5) emotional ties, instead of a contractual relationship maintained from calculations of self-interest (this is when *giri* becomes identical with *ninjo*; even when self-interest is calculated, the relationship must preserve at least a facade of emotional solidarity), and (6) a hierarchical relationship involving an unequal distribution of obligations.

Uye-ri in Korea is an abstract concept that describes the binding rule of social interaction but not a specific action that is to be carried to follow this rule. In Japan, on the other hand, the concept of *giri* can be applied to the general abstract notion of loyalty as well as the concrete act of reciprocation of goods and services received, such as a gift of money, a favor, or work contribution. In Korea, even though there are efforts to reciprocate the favor once one is received and bound by *uye-ri,* since the concept of *uye-ri* is an abstract one, there can never be a straightforward mathematical reciprocation. More often than not a situation occurs in which one is forced to provide assistance to an acquaintance who happens to be from the same village or school and is introduced by one's uncle or a classmate. Even though he may have never received any favor from that person, *uye-ri* to one's village or alma mater comes into play.

The three main *uye-ri* incurring sources in Korea are blood relations, regional relations, and school relations (classmates and teachers). School ties, especially high school ties, are the most important *uye-ri*-incurring groups. It is said that, in the university, people are already concerned about *ri* (personal gain) even in choosing friends, while, in high school, friends are based solely on *uye-ri*. In Korea, school ties are second in importance only to family ties. The concept *uye-ri*, however, is not used to describe one's loyalty to family, which is demonstrated by filial piety. In Japan, besides family, school, and regional relations, one's loyalty (*giri*) is to the company for which one works. Large companies often provide life employment and housing for their employees, which creates opportunities to develop mutually dependent relationships among their co-workers. During the feudal period in Japan, one's loyalty was to one's lord and his clan. When loyalties were in conflict, for example, a samurai was expected to neglect his family in favor of his lord (Vogel, 1963). Korea, on the other hand, never had a feudal system, and the feelings of obligation directly to the king among commoners were weak.

In Korea, classmates look after their fellows when in need. To act otherwise is "treason," "a break in *uye-ri*," against the school and the very order of things. A classmate has the right to demand help from a more fortunate classmate. This goes for the children of classmates as well. This is an obligation that cannot be easily refused or avoided. To fail one's classmate would cause one to lose the respect and goodwill of one's other friends and later opportunity to seek help from them. One might even be exiled from the group as an "unperson." Security in positions in government and in business depends heavily on having fellow alumni in strong positions, where they may assist one another and eventually gain control of an office, a firm, a political party, or the nation itself. For example, the 1961 coup d'état was carried out largely by members of the Eighth Class of the Korean Military Academy, and the recent coup was by the eleventh Class of the same school. Every eleventh Class member, whether or not he actually took part in the coup, gained in power because of the strong *uye-ri* among members of that class. Along with one's specific class, the school one graduates from is important. Two-thirds of the current cabinet members are Seoul National University graduates. To attend any lesser school is to limit one's future chances of a high position in present-day Korea.

The practice of *uye-ri* can create warm, lasting human relationships in Korea because, under *uye-ri,* one does not calculate what one gives and receives. Westerners are sometimes regarded as cold because their relationships seem mostly contractual. The give-and-take of such relationships should always be immediate and kept symmetrical in order to minimize future obligation and maintain autonomy. Very often such impersonal intermediates as lawyers, negotiators, and brokers are involved to handle interpersonal relationships. In the United States, even when friends are going out for lunch or dinner, the check is often accurately calculated and divided evenly among the group. Such a practice is very unusual in Korea and would be considered as quite deviant.

On the other hand, *uye-ri* sometimes creates seemingly irrational or unethical behavior, such as when somebody is hired who is not the best qualified for the job because of *uye-ri.* Although *uye-ri* has a very cohesive power within a group, it can create serious problems of divisiveness between groups. As mentioned before, Confucian ethics are changeable depending on the relationships and the situation. *Uye-ri* toward a certain group is not necessarily the same as or compatible with *uye-ri* toward another group. *Uye-ri,* in its secularized, current form and meaning, has been criticized as the main cause of the serious factionalism in Korea. *Uye-ri* is not based on a universal, rational logic but on a specific group principle or group spirit. Toward the in-group member, one spares nothing. Members are completely involved with each other but very indifferent toward outsiders. Confucian ethics specify the proper interpersonal relationships between king and retainer, father and son, husband and wife, and friend to friend, but one's relationship to the general society as a whole is not developed. One understands one's relationship toward the ruler as an individual but not as a member of the nation.

Interdependence

The concept *uye-ri* can also be understood from the level of dependency or, more accurately, mutual dependency. Interdependence is a pattern where the self is largely determined by a person's current relationships to others in the social structure. The opposite extreme would be individualism, where each self is regarded as equally independent but voluntarily allied with others for specific purposes. The numerous clubs in the United States which one can join or drop out of voluntarily without any group sanctions would be examples. *Uye-ri* can be exercised only in a society where the individual is conditioned to seek mutual dependence, where one is dependent on other human beings as much as others are dependent on him/her and where one is therefore fully aware of his/her obligations to make repayments, however much delayed.

Mutual dependence requires that one be affiliated with relatively small and tightly knit groups of people and have a relatively long identification with those groups. The mechanism that makes *uye-ri* work is that one expects the reciprocation of what one does to the other and that one anticipates that he or she will have to depend on others some other times. The individuals enmeshed in such a human network are likely to react to their world in a complacent and compartmentalized way, complacent because they have a secure and inalienable places in their human group and compartmentalized because they are conditioned to perceive the external world in terms of what is within their group and what is outside it (Hsu, 1963). What is within one's group and what is outside it have drastically different meanings. As one generalizes from this basic assumption, quite different truths emerge for different situations throughout one's life experiences. Principles which are appropriate for one set of situations and people may not be appropriate for another at all, but the principles in each case are equally honorable (Hsu, 1963).

Duty and Obligation

Due to the Confucius tradition of fulfilling one's social obligation depending on the social relationship involved, the concepts of duty and obligation are quite blurred in Korea. While the concept of obligation is well developed and understood by most people, the concept of duty which one has to perform independent of situations or social relations has been slow to emerge. Even though to perform a certain function would be an official duty of a government agent, for instance, people still like to get an introduction from a third person with whom the government official has an *uye-ri* relationship so that his duty becomes an obligation. People send gifts even though they do not have any favor to ask at the moment. It is done as a gesture to maintain a good relationship and also in anticipation of later favors. It is a common custom in Korea for a patient or patient's family to send a rather expensive gift, such as a suit (in the form of a gift certificate so that the receiver may choose his own) or a fine foreign scotch, to the doctor after she/he has performed surgery or delivered a baby. Such medical treatment is a doctor's duty, but Koreans are so accustomed to perceiving human interaction from an obligatory point of view that they feel obligated to show their appreciation by special gifts. A medical bill is simply an impersonal contract with the hospital which is totally inappropriate to accommodate the personal relationship between the patient and the doctor.

Korean students would be very reluctant to ask for a recommendation letter from a professor unless he or she had developed a rather close one-to-one relationship greater than the ordinary student–professor relationship reached through classroom interaction. American students, on the other hand, are quite comfortable asking for such things from their professors because they think that writing a recommendation letter is part of the professor's job. Korean students think that it is a favor the professor would bestow on you if you have been *his* or *her* student and have developed a socially binding relationship. In this type of relationship students show respect and gratitude, and the professor provides knowledge and help.

COMMUNICATION PATTERNS AND *UYE-RI*

As suggested in the previous sections, patterns of interpersonal communication in Korea depend largely on the social relationships or social situations of the people involved in the communication. One of the conditions of *uye-ri* to function as a social rule is that one be able to distinguish between in-group members and out-group members. Therefore, the first impact of the concept *uye-ri* is the development of certain communication patterns that help people initially to differentiate the in-group from the out-group. Once the distinction is made, one's general communication behavior toward the in-group is different from the out-group. As a consequence some communication behaviors are utilized to strengthen the cohesiveness of the in-group and others to further differentiate it from the out-group.

Koreans make clear distinctions among people according to the following three categories: (1) those people who are from the same exclusive group and with whom one has developed close personal relationships over an extended period, (2) those whose background is such that they can draw on *uye-ri* but who are not personally well known, and (3) those who are unknown strangers. The first category includes those who went to the same high school and were in the same class and have become close friends. The second category includes those who went to the same high school and with whom one has become acquainted but who are not necessarily close friends. These three categories are a rough classification. The three main sources that incur *uye-ri* in Korea are blood line (family and clan), regions, and schools. There is a stark difference in communication patterns toward those who are from the same province, are graduated from the same school, and also are personally known and toward those who are strangers from different provinces and schools. Under Confucian logic, there is no universal social rule that can be applied to any individual. Therefore, different social rules and patterns are applied according to the categories to which one belongs.

One of the main differences in communication that actually occurs is the use of language and level of formality. Among the very close friends, the language is almost devoid of honorific terms and is very informal. Even the use of profanity toward each other is often regarded as a sign of closeness between two partners of communication. If there is an age difference between two partners but still a lot of *uye-ri*-invoking sources, the younger one uses polite language but may still behave informally. The older one can even be called *hyung-nim* (elder brother) or *on-ni* (elder sister) even though they are not blood related. Furthermore, it is not uncommon for two persons who started as mere acquaintances and developed a lasting relationship to dismiss the formality and say, "Let's lay away our words," meaning to use nonhonorific language, or if one partner is obviously older than the other, the younger one pleads with the older one to "Please lower your words. I am much junior to you . . . " This process of switching to less formal language and deciding who should use honorific language and who should use common language becomes very easy if the people communicating can find a group(s) to which they mutually belong. Therefore, in Korea if two persons are first introduced, there is a sequence of small talk which establishes the basic socio-demographic information. The first question asked is which school they graduated from. If they both graduated from the same high school or university, the next question is what student number each one holds. This is a subtle way to find out who is senior, because in Korea each student has a student number that shows what year he or she entered the school. Once this information is known, the junior one asks the senior one to lower the level of language toward himself/herself. If they do not share the same school, they try to determine whether they know anyone who graduated from the same school and how many years senior or junior that third person is. Similar information is acquired regarding the regional connection of the person (i.e., province, city, or village), and family and clan connections. This process of obtaining personal information from each other may seem extremely nosey and an intrusion of privacy to many Westerners, but to Koreans it is a necessary initial procedure in order to determine each other's social position and the potential for invoking an *uye-ri* relationship. The social interaction and communication become much smoother once they know whether they share any mutual groups, have mutual acquaintances, who is older, and so forth. It is usually the case that the third party who introduces two people provides the initial cue, such as, "You are both from Seoul National University" or "You are both from Jun-Nam Province."

A stranger in Korea is defined as a person that you would not greet when encountered. Some foreigners visiting Korea are perplexed that Koreans are quite talkative and easily engaged in conversation but, on the other hand, very nontalkative and even rude toward strangers. U. Y. Lee (1966) suggests that Koreans are very polite and follow good etiquette but only toward those who are known and within the same boundaries. Koreans have developed elaborate social interaction patterns for those whose social position and social relationship to oneself is known, but there is no universal pattern that can be applied to anybody who is unknown. This is in stark contrast to the typical American cocktail party in which people get engaged in lengthy and often inconsequential conversation sometimes without even knowing each other's names. After a long time one might say, "Oh, by the way, my name is so and so."

Many American and European novels contain scenes in which strangers who meet for the first time in a bar or on the street open themselves up and confide their life stories to one another, but in Korean novels you seldom find such a scene. One's communication is primarily confined to one's in group and to the sharing of resources within one's own *uye-ri* group.

On the other hand, if you are within the first category, the quality and amount of information shared is very high and one can expect almost unlimited mutual aid. There is very frequently a lending of personal money among close friends without any paper or specific promise regarding when the money would be returned. While in the United States, numerous social brokers such as bank loan officers, lawyers, and social workers, handle and regulate the social action of an individual according to legal contracts. In Korea, many of the functions performed by banks, lawyers, and judges in the United States are fulfilled by one's close friends under a loose, abstract social rule called *uye-ri*.

Some communication patterns function to strengthen the cohesiveness of the group, while others differentiate one's group from others. Confiding in one another functions as the former, while *humdam* (gossip and backbiting) functions as the latter. Once you are in an *uye-ri* relationship with a certain person, you are expected to disclose yourself and withhold no secrets from your close friends. To lay oneself bare to one's very close *uye-ri* group invokes a high level of mutual dependency, and it is done with the expectation that one is not going to be found at fault by the ingroup for whatever one says. On the other hand, when one is dealing with out-group people, Koreans are very careful about what to say and how to talk, which makes such interactions rather formal. If one is found to be confiding with only one person but not with the others within the small *uye-ri* group, then the others will feel hurt and begin to worry whether the *uye-ri* relationship itself is at stake. Especially, if one member is found to be confiding with an out-group person, the in-group members would feel quite betrayed.

Against the other groups, however, it is not uncommon that a large amount of *humdam* is used. *Humdam* literally means conversation about the faults of others. It is not necessarily malignant or intended to be injurious to the target of the *humdam*. It is more often a conversation that reminds them of their being in the same camp and that the other camp has many faults. Of course, this practice of *humdam* is not constructive for intergroup cooperation, and sometimes *humdam* can lead to slander or even trickery. It is sometimes suggested that the fondness for *humdam* is one of the personality defects of the Korean people. It should be pointed out, however, that *humdam* is not a separate, defective communication act by itself but an act embedded in the social interaction patterns of group centeredness, social relatedness, and *uye-ri*. To correct the practice of *humdam* would require more than simply denouncing it as a bad tradition. In Korea one of the expressions of close friendship with somebody is, "We don't have to *hyung-hur-mul* (flaw and blame) each other," meaning that there is no worry about being blamed for certain points with each other. A fault or mistake by a close friend is accepted or even justified, while the same fault or mistake would produce quite a large amount of humdam if found in an out-group person.

CONCLUSION

The concept of *uye-ri* has far-reaching and profound effects on interpersonal relationships in Korea. Through *uye-ri*, people find social, economical, and political support. One can find a close confidant, a money lender, and even a matchmaker in one's closely knit group bound by *uye-ri*. *Uye-ri* as a social rule guarantees reciprocation and mutual dependence. A could lend a large sum of money to B because she/he is sure that B would not fail to pay it back because of *uye-ri* and because she/he knows that she/he can depend on B or other members of the *uye-ri* group in which both A and B belong. To be a man of good *uye-ri* is almost equivalent to having a good credit rating in the United States and being considered a person of "good standing" in the community.

The benefit of such a social relationship has its costs. Confucian tradition provides room for double or multiple standards of morality and conduct and they present the individual with little inner conflict. The main criterion for proper behavior is the social relationship between two people and situations in which the interaction occurs. Since *uye-ri* is called for only among those who belong to the same *uye-ri*-incurring group, factionalism is sometimes inevitable. Because of *uye-ri,* constructive criticism and open discussion often cannot be developed very far. Because of *uye-ri,* if one's professor presented a paper or a theory, one would feel prohibited from making criticisms. Sometimes even making any comments would be regarded as impudent. This condition preempts the need for free discussion which would lead to mutually acceptable ideas.

Whether *uye-ri* will continue to remain as a binding social rule is a matter of speculation. Considering that Korea has gone through tremendous social, economic, and political changes since 1945, tenacity of its social norms can be seen clearly in the modes of interpersonal relations. Social mobility is one of the major factors that determines which is the major *uye-ri*-incurring source and how much *uye-ri* will be abided by the group members. In Japan where the job mobility is low, a life employment system is adopted, and company housing (apartment *dan-chi*) is often provided, the close-knit groups are generally co-workers and one's loyalty resides often with the company (Vogel, 1963). The husband's friends are his co-workers and the wife's friends are her neighbors. In Korea where job mobility is high and a life employment system is not as prevalent, the strongest *uye-ri* incurring group is one's alma mater.

In the United States, where the average person moves every 4 years and travel sometimes requires several hours by air, it is often difficult to develop and maintain relationships that are based on mutual dependence and asymmetrical reciprocity. Therefore, joining voluntary organizations is a prevalent mode of social interaction, and people generally insist on "paying their own way." Since social interaction patterns in Korea and the United States are so different, it is usually quite stressful to move from one country to the other. For example, in a survey of Korean immigrants in Hawaii, 22% of the respondents answered that they do not even have one friend in the United States (Yum, 1984). The mean number of communication contacts in Hawaii was 4.4 compared to 25.4 in Korea, and this difference was the same even among those who have been in the United States for a long time. Most Korean immigrants moved to the United States in their mid-30s, and it was difficult for them to develop new friendship ties according to the pattern of interaction that they were accustomed to, and casual acquaintances could not fulfill their needs for *uye-ri* friends.

Even though one's working place is not one of the major *uye-ri*-incurring sources, moving through several jobs and staying only a short time with each job can be interpreted as a violation of the basic concept of *uye-ri* and, therefore, as something to be avoided. It is quite different in the United States where there is a strong belief that if one wants to climb the ladder, one has to move. The social mobility in Korea will continue to increase due to economic and social development, but since Korea is a relatively small country, Koreans will never have the opportunity for the large scale mobility that citizens of the United States have.

Confucian ethics have dominated the Korean pattern of thought and behavior for over five hundred years, and it is expected that even with substantial social, economic, and political changes, *uye-ri* will continue to exert its influence on the development and maintenance of interpersonal relationships and communication.

CHAPTER 7

The Teachings of Yi Yulgok: Communication from a Neo-Confucian Perspective

Sang-Hee Lee

A proverb says that one who likes to listen to others can become a king, and that one who neglects the ideas of others will fail. If one likes to ask, he will become great, and if not, he will become insignificant.

—Yɪ Yᴜʟɢᴏᴋ (*Yulgokjib,* 1977)

INTRODUCTION

Yi Yulgok (1536–1584) was the most distinguished thinker and statesman throughout the Yi dynasty (1392–1910). He was also a theorist and practitioner; he put theory into practice, while many of his colleagues remained only theoreticians. His ideas on relieving the people of their sufferings came mostly from Confucianism and Mencism and the doctrines of Chutzu. Yulgok's studies embraced the ideas of his leading predecessors such as Cho Chongam, Soh Hwadam, and Yi Toegye. Going a step further, he tried to enhance their ideas in order to make them applicable to contemporary society.

> He advocated the balance between and the unity of *Sugi* (self-improvement) and *Chiin* (rule over the people), and *Chason* (to behave well to oneself) and *Kyomson* (to behave well to others). He thus gave equal value to morality and politics, keeping them parallel. Thus, he taught that there could exist neither *Chiin* nor *Kyomson* without *Sugi* and *Chason*. If one manages to be good to others without improving himself or behaving well to himself, one must be a hypocrite or a dissembler. Also, *Sugi* and *Chason* cannot be achieved without *Chiin* and *Kyomson*. . . . He believed that only those who manage to be good both to themselves and to others, respect morality and politics equally, and learn academic knowledge and administration harmoniously could be recognized as great Confucianists. (P. D. Lee, 1977, p. 4)

Yulgok thought a person should learn Confucianism to educate and enhance himself enough to profess himself to be a *gunja* (true gentleman), to have a good command of the principles of the world, to make friends with good people, and to lead men of ability in the right way. All these things, he firmly believed, would serve public interests.

Yulgok himself served in a variety of key government positions as a statesman, while making remarkable achievements as a scholar. A number of outstanding literary works he left include: in the field of statecraft, *Songhakchibyo, Tonghomundap, Manonbongsa* and many other *So, Yukjogye* and many other *Gye*; and many *Ui* and *Chaek* (*So, Gye, Ui* and *Chaek* are invariably, although slight differences are noted among them, practical recommendations regarding state affairs with philosophical implications to the king). In the area concerning community development there are *Hyangyak, Hakkyomopom,* and *Kyokmongyogyol.*

Songhakchibyo is a textbook arranged for the king, in which Yulgok described in detail the duties of a monarch, using as illustrations historical events during many Chinese dynasties. The work, which covers a wide range of political ideas and topics, was dedicated to the king. *Tonghomundap* is concerned with major issues of the time, which were analyzed for solutions. It is written in the style of a dialogue between a host and guest about important current issues. The book, consisting of 11 parts, reminds one of *Plato's Dialogues.* All Yulgok's recommendations to the king are full of patriotism and love of the people. At the same time, a major characteristic that should not be ignored in the consideration of his recommendations to the king was that they were presented at the risk of his life.

After serving in several initial government positions, he eventually became a cabinet minister and deputy premier. Off and on he left public affairs to think and study. Yulgok taught young students in the countryside whenever time allowed. It is natural that various informal titles were given him such as great philosopher, scholar, political theorist, educationist, writer, and orator. He was a sincere patriot determined to devote himself to the people and state, demonstrating remarkable energetic statesmanship in practical affairs. "He was literally a great Confucianist of talent, personality, knowledge, letters, eloquence, systematic reasoning, judgment and fairness. It is very hard, all told, to find his equal in the history of Korea's Confucianist learning" (P. D. Lee, 1974, p. 13).

POLITICAL PHILOSOPHY

Yulgok's ideas on politics can be termed welfare state politics. This was a political philosophy aiming at realizing the welfare and stability of the nation, based on the Confucian idea that the people are the masters of a nation. The concept that sovereignty rests with the people is to be embodied in reality through *royal politics*. The ultimate goal of politics is to protect the people and to improve their welfare. The sole way to ensure national wealth and power is to ensure the welfare of the people. These political ideas of Yulgok are well reflected in his remarks regarding the relationship between nature and man, the king and the people, and the responsibility of the king:

> Heaven has given birth to all creatures, of which human beings are the most sacred. Of all human beings, in turn, the king is the wisest and thus becomes the father of the people. . . . Heaven is most benevolent to human beings, and particularly so to sages, for sages can be leaders of the people, and they only can take care of the masses like Heaven. As Heaven loves the people like this, the king who is entrusted with Heaven's calling cannot afford to forget that he is the parent of the people. (Yi Yulgok, 1977)

Yulgok thought that human beings were endowed with inalienable rights by Heaven, and the king was the person responsible for the realization of these rights. Still, such realization should be achieved with the affection of parents and never in a high-handed manner. The king's rule, so to speak, should be paternal, not authoritarian.

> Ruling is an art like caring for children. When it is pursued with sincerity, the efforts will succeed, if not fully. Trial and error can be tolerated to some extent. Infants cannot express their desires in communicable language. Their mothers, however, understand what they want. The mothers, of course, may fail to provide fully what the children want. However, such failure will not be serious because the mothers take care of them with extreme caution. What is more important is such heart-to-heart understanding rather than the understanding through knowledge. (Yi Yulgok, 1977)

Yulgok reiterated that the essence of politics is that it be operated with mercy and virtue by the king. A king's concentration on state affairs with humanity and virtue will result in humanitarian politics; if he tries to oppress the people authoritatively and seeks his personal interest, the people will be angered, Yulgok said. They are by no means an insignificant presence; rather, they are an object of fear. The king should treat them with virtue and love. If the king becomes notorious, he will be called a tyrant. No one, however foolish, will follow him. No one can lead a horse with a rotten rope. The people are not an object to be handled recklessly.

A countryman from Maekgu pleaded with Prince Chaehang:

> If a son sins against his father, he may be excused by his father through the mediation of his uncles and aunts. If a subject sins against his king, he may still be exonerated by his king through the apologies of other subjects on his behalf. However, the sins of King Kol and King Chu [ancient Chinese kings] could not be excused, because their commitment of sin was against their subjects and they could find no go-between to make the efforts for the acquittal of the kings. Then, the prince replied, "You are right." (Yi Yulgok, 1977)

The political philosophy of Yulgok can be summarized as Confucianist "democracy" emphasizing "government for the people." It is different, of course, from the Western democracy which emerged in the wake of a bourgeois revolution. If the latter is characterized by "the government of, by, and for the people," the former is the government for the people by sage monarchs. Modern Western democracy upholds the sovereignty of the people, while Confucianist democracy concedes the sovereignty of monarchs but claims that the monarchs should exist only for the people. Consequently, in an ideological sense, the two democracies have a teleological similarity originating from the idea of government for the people. Confucianist democracy, as it were, holds in esteem national administration for the people, which is politics. "To win the world is to realize what the people want through politics. It is the true road to royal politics" (Yi Yulgok, 1977).

For the people when production remained low and the minimum subsistence was the most essential imperative, the most important concern of politics was how to stabilize the economic livelihood of the people. According to Yulgok, the country depends on the people and the people depend on food. Therefore, when the people suffer from food shortages, the country has little to depend on. Yulgok considered the other major source of instability among the people to be excessive concentration on military strength.

Yi Yulgok became seriously concerned about the welfare of the people and state during the latter part of the sixteenth century, about 200 years after the foundation of the Yi dynasty. The country was experiencing setbacks in various parts of society including economic and political frictions and social disorganization and disorder. Politics at that time was also complicated by Yonsangun, one of the most notorious tyrants of the dynasty. There also developed an enmity between old and young court officials and between the ruling camp and the opposition, which led to two purges of scholars—Muo and Kapcha. The land system was revealing unrealistic contradictions, and the system itself was not observed. Some of the landlords and other powerful persons made public property their own private assets. Small farmers who were actually engaged in farming were stripped of most of the crops they produced and were mercilessly exploited. The extortion and oppression of those farmers were extremely great and serious. They had to pay various heavy taxes and were pressed into hard, mean labor. In other words, this Yi era saw political, social, and economic disorder and confusion reach a peak. The period was also threatened by outside enemies who were ready to invade the Korean peninsula at any moment.

To get over this dangerous situation, Yi Yulgok devised two fundamental policy goals. One was socio-economic with emphasis on the stability of people's daily lives, and the other was a reformist initiative calling for a drastic realignment of the law and institutions to adjust them to contemporary social conditions. Whenever occasions arose, he strongly advocated the reformist theory that all ineffective laws and institutions including established ones of long tradition should be reformed. The reformist policy was for the people, particularly for the masses. The objective of his reformism was to protect ordinary people from the arbitrariness and exploitation of the ruling and upper classes.

As stated thus far, his policy goal was to improve the welfare of the general public, especially the lower class, and in no way did he advocate the interests of the upper class. In light of this fact it is understandable that the policies of important value proposed by him largely *failed to be adopted*. The indecisive attitudes of his king, King Sunjo, and the conservative and frivolous attitudes of court officials made it impossible to take his far-reaching proposals seriously.

COMMUNICATION SYSTEMS DURING THE TIME OF YI YULGOK

The function of public opinion in sixteenth century Korean society can be more adequately understood in the context of the systems of communication that existed at that time. The two most important government institutions during the Yi dynasty were *Sahonbu* and *Saganwon*. The two united were also called *Taegan*, which was the most important political institution involved in communication. Officials of *Taegan* were called *Onkwan*, who, unlike other officials, were recognized as elites and granted special favors and privileges.

The main functions of *Saganwon* included *Kanjong* and *Nonbak*. Through *Kanjong*, officials could point out the mistakes of kings and request their correction. Through *Nonbak*, they could review and criticize the personnel management of the government and evaluate the government's effectiveness in handling current affairs. Officials of *Saganwon*, who usually dealt with priority issues and were also called *Kankwan*, were selected from those of noble personality and high intelligence. They were naturally granted a special favor in the court.

> There was no marked distinction of rank among them. They were allowed to drink liquor while attending full-fledged formal meetings. . . . They could enjoy the same legal status as *Taekwan* (officials of *Sahonbu*). Additional privileges were given to them, furthermore. Their workload was smaller and they did not need to observe the court protocol concerning different ranks of court officials. Even while handling public affairs, they could drink. They were, so to speak, the most favored group among all court officials and were consequently highly respected and admired by Confucianist students. The special favors and privileges granted to them apparently aimed at encouraging their pride as they were often practiced at the cost of their lives. (S. H. Choi, 1974, p. 29)

The major affairs for *Sahonbu* comprised the evaluation of state programs and policies, the nation's ethical discipline and customs, and prizes or the punishment of officials. The most important service entrusted to *Sahonbu* officials, or *Taekwan*, was to evaluate current political problems and policy issues. Their role can be compared to that of the mass media today. The *Taekwan*, too, were allowed special privileges and favors, which were not normally given to other officials. They deserved such special incentives since one of their duties was to appraise the achievements of all officials.

While the major concerns of *Kankwan* were directed toward the king, those of *Taekwan* were toward all officials regardless of their ranks. However, they were all responsible for current political and policy issues. The functions of these two government institutions were slightly different from time to time and from king to king. Nevertheless, the officials of the two bodies performed public opinion functions. Consequently, despite the clear separation in legal terms, the two had much in common in their practical functions. It was particularly so in their journalistic activities. That *Taegan* was called *Onkwan* (*On* in Korean means speech in English) underscores the importance of their journalistic roles and activities in public affairs. It is in no way an overestimation to say that their most important role was to promote public opinion based on free speech (Choe, 1974, p. 66). More often than not, the two institutions took joint action in appealing to the king and in impeaching officials.

Another institution, *Hongmunkwan,* a research institute, was occasionally in charge of journalistic duties. Originally, it was responsible for national archives and documents, provided advisory services to the king, and explained the books on Chinese history and classics for the king. During the early days of the Yi dynasty, it was called *Chiphyonjon.* In a strict sense, *Hongmunkwan* was not a journalistic institution. However, it was inevitably involved in current political affairs, as it made frequent contacts with the king to present him with ideas from the Confucian classics. One of the proper duties of the *Hongmunkwan* was to act for the king in an advisory capacity—a duty similar to that of *Onkwan.* After *Hongmunkwan* joined the *Sahonbu* and *Saganwon,* the three were called the *Onronsamsa* (three journalistic organizations). *Hongmunkwan* consisted of senior scholars of nationwide fame, that is, leading scholars of wide learning and experience from *Sarim.* As the major function of *Sarim* was to lead public opinion, the leading scholars from *Sarim* at *Hongmunkwan* played an understandably important communication role, keeping close contact with the king. The three journalistic organizations, in summary, took charge of reflecting public opinion in national policies.

The journalistic activities of *Onkwan* were performed in the form of letters and in the form of direct verbal appeal or recommendations to the king. The most typical in the form of letters were *Sangsomun,* memorials, and recommendations appealing for the king's appropriate actions. They had definite forms and styles designed to honor the king's authority. They had to be transmitted to the king through *Sungjongwon,* the secretariat. It was made a principle for the king to reply to them. Those which had classified contents were put in envelopes. Such letters were called *Pongsa.* Those containing classified contents or containing more than 10,000 words were called *Manonbongsa.* The famous *Manonbongsa* of Yulgok was also a memorial to the king.

A significant portion of the letters to the king were called *Chaja. Chaja* were basically the same as *Sangsomun,* but the form was simpler. *Chaja* were mostly recommendations concerning general administrative problems. Another form of letter memorial was *Kye. Kye* was a "documented" *Chikkyechinpum,* a face-to-face form of recommendation to the king. Because of its face-to-face character, it was felt to be more direct and familiar. Finally, there was *Ui,* whose contents were mostly detailed policy recommendations.

Verbal or face-to-face appeals and recommendations to the king were called *Kyeon* or *Chinon*. Face-to-face communication with the king took place during regular policy discussions in the court, which were called such various names as *Sangcham, Yundae, Chadae,* or *Chinkang*. Such direct communication with the king was also made when the king summoned officials concerned or requested their advice and suggestions.

There were also channels for ordinary officials and *Sarim* in local districts to suggest their ideas or to appeal to the king. However, the procedures involved were too complicated for them to use effectively. Usually such channels were blocked by the established bureaucracy. It was an extremely difficult process requiring hard work and determination for *Sarim* to make recommendations or appeals to the king. The reason is that the motivations for such decisive actions toward the king on the part of *Sarim* were usually rooted in a desire to criticize current situations or to disclose injustices and misdeeds committed by powerful but sly officials. In reality, few opportunities for such bold actions were given to *Sarim* other than *Onkwan*. Therefore, the *Onkwan's* proper duty to promote an atmosphere for liberal discussion was stressed.

Communication channels for the masses were also available. They included *Sinmunko, Pokhap, Kyuhon,* and *Tungjang,* and they represented a system for direct appeal to the king. *Sinmunko* was a huge drum hung in front of the court, which could be beaten by petitioners. *Pokhap* was practiced by kneeling down in front of the court, and *Kyuhon* was a sort of cry to be heard by ranking court officials when they passed by. *Tungjang* was a kind of mass protest and appeal by a group of people to municipal authorities. This was an emergency form of communication by means of demonstration.

In any case, the grass roots, when necessary and according to their own will, could use such extraordinary means of communication with the court. However, the direct appeal system was rarely used except for catastrophes, contingencies, and other extraordinary events. They were ''abnormal'' communication channels. Therefore, *Onkwan* was called on to prevent such undesirable developments by expanding communication channels, through which public opinion could be reflected in the policy-making process.

In Yulgok's days, such communication systems and patterns existed, but they failed to work as intended. Making these communication systems serve the welfare of the state through a royal politics of justice was a major preoccupation of Yi Yulgok, both as a scholar and as a civil servant. For Yulgok their improvement was fundamentally a matter of maintaining open channels of communication and dialogue so that public opinion could be formed properly and brought to bear on the problems of state.

THOUGHTS ON COMMUNICATION

Yulgok's political philosophy was characterized by welfare politics and "government for the people." What, then, was to be the tool to realize it? Yulgok believed in the people's sentiment and "public opinion" to support a government. Application of his political philosophy would be possible only if government policies and programs were carried out on the basis of people's general sentiments and opinions. The Confucian concept of a democratic state is strongly "for the people." It naturally lacks the aspects of "by the people" and "of the people," compared to Western democracy. Yulgok's ideas on welfare politics, however, point to broadly based public opinion among the intelligentsia and the general public.

> A king reigns over tens of millions of people. He cannot listen to all the voices of the people, cannot see all their faces. Songwang [an ancient Chinese king] tried to make the ears and eyes of others his own. Therefore, he was able to fully see and hear the people. Also, others' minds were his mind. Thus, he had a good command of a universe in which the people at large communicated with him. In the past, there were no advisory officials. All court officials, observing their respective duties, directly stated to the king the things that had to be set right. Merchants freely discussed things in the market, and consumers exchanged their opinions with one another as they pleased. The people were virtually functioning as informal advisory officials. . . . The king should hopefully accept frank advice and recommendations and seek diverse opinions of the people to work out effective measures for state management. (Yi Yulgok, 1977)

It was Yulgok's firm conviction that state administration for the people could find its place if the king or government was open to all communication channels. In *Tonghomundap*—his theory in dialogue similar to Plato's dialogues, Yulgok wrote:

> A guest asked, "What will be the first task in politics after decisions are made on right and wrong, and on the desirable and the undesirable?" The host replied, "Improper laws and institutions should be rectified to rescue the people. The reform of laws necessarily requires communication channels in order to collect the best possible ways. All the people ranging from important officials to the rank and file should be permitted to discuss freely all current injustices and improprieties. If a person's ideas are deemed useful, their value should not be judged by the person's social position, but by the inherent value of the ideas themselves. It is not until the eradication of all irregularities is realized by reforming laws that a state works." (Yi Yulgok, 1977)

Yulgok asserted not only that the operation of a nation should be based on popular support and public opinion but also that a national entity's presence itself and legitimacy should have public opinion as their foundation.

> National policies cannot be determined only in verbal terms. What draws popular favor is called public opinion, which determines, in turn, state policies. This

means that national policies are achieved from and through public opinion, as it recognizes their righteousness almost without disagreement. State policies neither court nor dread the people. Even a child, meanwhile, understands they are right. . . . Public opinion wells up in such a natural fashion from the general public that it cannot be prevented. National policies will thus have to be determined according to public opinion. (Yi Yulgok, 1977)

Political power cannot have legitimacy if it is not supported by public opinion. Communication channels, Yulgok believed, have to be expanded to realize welfare politics. True public opinion should live both in the government and in the society. A nation's prosperity depends on whether such communication channels can accommodate public opinion.

A nation survives when its communication channels are open; it falls when they are closed. (Yi Yulgok, 1977)

The most urgent thing right at the moment is to expand public opinion channels. When Your Highness becomes free from personal interest and ambition, your people will be impressed. (Yi Yulgok, 1977)

Only when freedom of expression is ensured can a sound political atmosphere be formed and politics for the people be achieved. Moreover, public opinion is the driving force of the nation; the government should correctly come to grips with national sentiment or public opinion so as to have it reflected in national policies.

Public opinion is the energy to sustain a nation. When it is sufficiently reflected in the input and output processes of a political system, the government is considered to work well; when communication channels are closed and public opinion remains static, only rumors hang in the air and the government falls. If the political atmosphere is restrained and dogmatic and public opinion fades away from the government and the people alike, the nation will collapse. When public opinion is stifled, useful criticism and advice to the government will disappear. Only the voices of those who flatter will be raised.

Although His Highness likes the good, he doubts the honesty of scholars. Although his hatred of the bad is great, he may think dishonest men are not wrong. Hence, the difference between honest scholars and wily flatterers disappears. Honest and wise persons are replaced by crafty and abject creatures. Consequently, foolish persons are more compromised and are allowed to meet frequently with wise and gentle persons. All this confusion will inevitably result in a wide gap between the people and the government. The expulsion of cunning men and the appointment of good persons to important posts will not take place. This development is directly against the real wishes of the people. The government will then fail to listen to the voice of the people and fail to abolish the laws that make the people sick. It will worry only about possible mistakes from reform, and lose the courage to use good and talented persons, even if it likes the good. It will also fail to exclude deceitful persons. Only debate for debate's sake will prevail, fierce wrangles will develop, loyal subjects will lose their places, and sly adherents will try to make their way out. Under these circumstances, what His Highness really has in mind cannot be communicated. (Yi Yulgok, 1977)

The *Songhakchibyo,* quoted above, is a textbook that Yulgok wrote for King Sunjo about the theory and practice of royal rule. Yulgok emphasized the importance of frank remarks in the presence of the King. For the achievement of a royal rule of morality and government for the people, he energetically stressed that general opinion and outspoken advice from loyal government officials are most important. In the same textbook, he particularly pointed out how to select faithful and able personalities and how to purge sly and greedy officials.

Furthermore, he claimed that the king should respect public opinion in state administration, and have opportunities for open discussion with his important subjects in order to lead state affairs in the right direction.

> There has never been a case in which policies succeeded without effective heart-to-heart communication between a king and his subjects. . . . When loyalty and faith are closely linked in the mind, any attempt to split up the two fails. It is as if a king and his subjects are of the same mind and what a fish is to water. . . . Kings of later ages, however, were otherwise. They were in a supreme position, lived in majestic palaces, and alienated good subjects. They knew those who were good, but did not want to have them nearby; they knew those who were bad, but did not want to purge them. Their only command, by which they saved face, was that subjects should not have easy access to important national secrets. As a result, men of virtue were not allowed to do their best for the country, while men of small caliber took advantage of such opportunities. If this happens, one cannot tell vice from virtue and wrong from right. Finally, state affairs will become unmanageable. The king ought to be cautious of this possible event. (Yi Yulgok, 1977)

This points out that an open attitude of the government toward various information required in decision-making and decision-executing processes is a fundamental requirement for the politics of justice. All policy makers including the king should discuss the problems involved candidly. They have to take in reasonable public opinion as it is, and information should be made public and be subject to public discussion. If there is not such an atmosphere for open dialogue, only blind followers and flattering people will appear, and the state will decline.

> Those who remain silent, pretending to know nothing, are regarded as men of broad outlook, those who make recommendations are considered nuisances, and those who abide by routine practices are deemed moderate. Those who are firm in their convictions are dubbed crafty and eccentric. Then, trickery and improprieties prevail in society. A frivolous way of life against this background will inevitably fail to achieve anything progressive. The country will gradually fall into darkness. (Yi Yulgok, 1977)

Yulgok wanted to ensure that the intelligentsia are called on to play a decisive role in canalizing public opinion into the policy-making process. The intelligentsia of that time consisted mostly of scholars, some of whom were recruited as political executives and bureaucrats. The important theoretical concept of this intellectual group, called *Sarim*, is that they be rather independent of political power or economic influence. They stood rather aloof from the world and concentrated on learning and character building for self-fulfillment. Their belief in devotion to the state and people was so strong that they were determined to practice moral politics when opportunities for state administration were offered. Therefore, they tried to point out injustice and irrationality in state affairs, whether they were in or out of office, and then proposed policy alternatives. Occasionally, their proposals were made at the cost of their lives. A typical example of a scholar from this intelligentsia group was Yulgok himself.

Yulgok's ideas on the potential existence of public opinion were based on the presence of the intellectual *Sarim*. This group was strongly motivated to apply their understanding of the nation's situation and what the people wanted to the policy-making process through appropriate communication channels.

> Those who respect established legal norms, practice what Confucianism teaches and speak for rationality are called *Sarim*. If *Sarim* are used for national projects, the nation will thrive. On the other hand, if there is no *Sarim* in the court who can control and eliminate irrationality in state affairs, the nation will become confused. (Yi Yulgok, 1977)

> From ancient times, it has been said that a nation should appreciate highly what *Sarim* recommends. *Sarim* is the principal energy of a nation. Therefore, if *Sarim* is flourishing and at peace, a nation will prosper; if *Sarim* becomes radical and is disorganized, a nation will fall. History teaches this. (Yi Yulgok, 1977)

Sarim's general opinion represents public opinion. State affairs can go well only if the *Sarim* manages to keep up with constructive public opinion that can be sufficiently reflected in state management. It is easy to understand why Yulgok emphasized the role of the intelligentsia's general opinion in politics.

Yulgok believed that *Sarim* had the ability to *form* useful and constructive public opinion, which is different from mass opinion or volatile sentiment. Yulgok distinguished public opinion from mass opinion, which he said may well have an irrational and emotional nature resulting from the illiteracy or low educational level of the masses. He also termed the opinion formed by *Sarim* "mass opinion," when it came from a specific group of *Sarim* inclined to register a partial opinion. The terms used here, public opinion and mass opinion, are different, of course, from the modern concepts, but Yulgok's ideas about them are similar to modern concepts in many respects.

> Once overwhelmed by mass opinion, even *Sarim* fails to develop its opinion fully and public opinion as a frame of reference for policy-making is distorted. Caution is required to protect the public opinion of *Sarim* from the influence of mass opinion. (Yi Yulgok, 1977)

It is clear that Yulgok distinguished public opinion which is based on public interest from mass opinion which has many irrational aspects and is easily affected by temporal emotion. Such public opinion is called *Saron* (the general opinion of true Confucianists) or *Chongron* (authentic and unadulterated opinion). In the modern democracies of the West, public opinion is formed by the "public" or the "masses" in general. According to Yulgok, the *Sarim* should be responsible for public opinion. After the establishment of bourgeois democracy in the West, a general public emerged which had a definite economic status and had been substantially educated. They were deemed capable of reasonably determining social and political issues and of suggesting their own opinions. Accordingly, public opinion can be regarded as representing the rational section of all opinions of the people of a society at large. At the same time, there remained the "irrational" opinions of the "rank and file" masses which were still regarded as those of the "crowd" and which normally counted little in the formation of public opinion. In the Korean society of his time, Yulgok credited the *Sarim* class with performing the important role of *creating and forming* public opinion. To him, only this intellectual class had the capability to understand reality objectively.

Yulgok also touched on the whimsical emotion and rumors among ordinary people. These two elements affecting public opinion are, Yulgok said, *Puui*, which is a mixture of rumors and demagoguery. Yulgok remarked that closed communication channels and the malfunctioning of public opinion would result in the rampant spread of groundless rumors, which would have an adverse impact on state administration.

> The origin of *Puui* cannot be exactly understood. It will grow, however, like a wild fire, rocking the court and causing revolts in key government departments such as *Sahonbu* and *Saganwon*. The whole nation may be engulfed in *Puui*, which may not be brought under control. The potentiality of *Puui* is sharper than a sword, and is heavier than a mountain. Any ranking official, once affected by *Puui* will not be able to survive. Why it is so is hardly explainable. (Yi Yulgok, 1977)

Puui, although their origins is difficult to trace, can spread rapidly, affecting society and the court. They will cause disharmony, enmity, slander, ostracism, and finally disintegration of national unity. *Puui* have irrational elements and can be invented by a person or a clique attempting the expulsion of opponents. Sometimes artificial and negative channels provide traffic for them. Therefore, Yulgok thought that a free and fair political atmosphere which would allow constructive public opinion was necessary and would bring about a national consensus.

> There are two paths leading to the court's peace and national consensus. One is from subjects that are trusted by the king and whose recommendations and advice are accepted by the king. On this path there is no sharp disagreement among subjects. This is unity by means of goodness. The other is "forced silence." Flattering, sly subjects are trusted by the king. There is no disagreement on the surface at least, because their voices are suppressed. This is unity by vice. (Yi Yulgok, 1977)

Yulgok's thoughts on communication developed in the sixteenth century take on a strong character of democracy if they are compared with the circumstances today. His profound insights into the role of communication in politics in such early times are indeed impressive even today, and they seem to have a universal relevance which transcends their particular time and place.

Idealistic royal politics of right, which can exclude the suppression and the dogma of force-oriented politics, can be realized only through public opinion reflecting true national sentiments. The fundamental difference between ruling by justice and ruling by force is that just rule recognizes the absolute presence of public opinion. This is why Yulgok was concerned so much with national sentiments and public opinion and was so emphatic about the role of *Sarim* and their devotion to the sound establishment of public opinion.

CHAPTER 8

Some Characteristics of the Japanese Way of Communication

Akira Tsujimura

INTRODUCTION

In order to describe the characteristics of the Japanese way of communication, it is necessary to return to the past when mass communication had not yet appeared on the scene. Especially in Japan, the ancient philosophies and religions such as Buddhism, Confucianism, and Shintoism have had a strong influence on modern communication.

In the beginning, I would like to underscore the essential elements of the three main religious philosophies and then later show in more detail how they have influenced the Japanese perspective toward communication today.

With regard to Buddhism, which originated in India, Zen has been the most influential on Japanese culture at the highest levels. Zen Buddhism was created in China and imported to Japan in the Kamakura era (1185–1333). One of the final aims of Zen training is to get rid of ego or self and to reach the spiritual freedom of selflessness. Zen training uses a special "question and answer" form of communication (*Zen Mondo*) between

COMMUNICATION THEORY:
EASTERN AND WESTERN PERSPECTIVES

master and disciple. To cite an example, a master once asked a disciple, "What am I presented before you?" When the disciple could not answer, the master hit the disciple with a big stick 20 times. When the disciple replied with some words, the master also hit him 20 times. According to Western logic or ordinary logic, this is not understandable, but Zen Mondo tries to drive the trainees into just such a dilemma to help them to get rid of their ordinary selves. This denial of spoken words at the level of ordinary logic is reflected in the phenomenon of *ishin-denshin,* which is described below.

The main influence on Japanese culture of Confucianism, which also originated in China, is the regulation of human relations, especially with regard to authority in social hierarchies. Man must respect those senior to himself, elders and those above him in positions of power. Taking these delicate human relations into consideration, the Japanese use different expressions and different words in daily communication according to one's position relative to others. They have different expressions between males and females and special expressions and words to show respect (*Keigo*). The heavy emphasis put on in these human relations has a relationship to indirect communication which is described in the fourth section.

Shintoism, which is originally Japanese, places great weight on simplicity. The architecture of typical Japanese Shinto shrines are characterized by simple design and colorlessness, which shows a clear contrast to colorful Chinese and Korean temples and palaces. Refined simplicity which is easily noticed in various facets of Japanese culture, such as architecture, brush painting, the tea ceremony, short poems, and even the design of swords, was partially derived from Shintoism as well as Zen Buddhism.

In the next part of the paper I discuss in more detail four of the main characteristics of the Japanese way of communication: *ishin-denshin,* taciturnity and its social causes, indirect communication and respect for reverberation, and *kuki,* the function of mood or atmospheric constraints.

ISHIN-DENSHIN: COMMUNICATION WITHOUT LANGUAGE

I discussed the characteristics of Japanese communication before the appearance of mass communication in my previous work, *Japanese Culture and Communication* (Tsujimura, 1968). Among the distinctive qualities of the Japanese discussed in the book, the most distinguished one is taciturnity, namely, the reluctance to talk a lot or the use of indirect expression rather than direct expression.

When taciturnity is carried to extremes, communication occurs when nothing is said. Such is the nature of *ishin-denshin,* which is emphasized in traditional Japanese culture. In modern times, *ishin-denshin* has become degraded into everyday terminology without its real meaning being understood. Originally, it was an indispensable factor of the essence of the high level of Japanese culture. What is *ishin-denshin* like, then? The Japanese dictionary defines it as (1) communication made between a Zen priest and a disciple to initiate the truth and (2) communication of thoughts from one mind to another without using language (*Kojien,* 1955). The latter definition is part of the everyday terminology. For example, a man and wife or parent and child can reach a certain understanding with each other without ever saying a word. Of course, this kind of phenomenon can be seen not only in Japan but also all over the world.

Some excellent examples of the everyday use of *ishin-denshin* in Japanese culture can be found in modern fiction. The power of this form of communication is illustrated well by the following dramatic excerpt from Akutagawa's ''In a Grove'' (in *Rashomon,* 1954/1970, p. 28). The thief who has tied her husband to a tree has just knocked her down as she came to his side. ''Just at that moment I saw an indescribable light in my husband's eyes. *Something beyond expression . . .* his eyes make me shudder even now. That *instantaneous look of my husband, who couldn't speak a word, told me all his heart* [italics added].''

In the following passage from Kawabata's *The Sound of the Mountain* (1970), the character Shingo is able to understand exactly what Kikuko means at a particular instant even though her face is hidden behind a mask used in the traditional *No* dramas of Japan. The mask allows no expression except through movement.

> She had a small face, and the tip of her chin was almost hidden behind the mask. Tears were flowing from the scarcely visible chin down over her throat. . . .
> ''Kikuko,'' said Shingo. ''Kikuko. You thought if you were to leave Shuichi you might give tea lessons, and that was why you went to see your friend?''
> The *jido* Hikuko, nodded. (p. 133)

These are examples of *ishin-denshin* which fit the second, everyday use of the term. The *ishin-denshin* which is traditional and essential in Japanese Zen culture belongs to the first definition, which will be given more attention in this paper.

The traditional form of *ishin-denshin* originates from the historical fact that Buddha's disciple, Kasho, was induced and spiritially awakened by Buddha's casual action (*Keitoku-dentoroku,* biography of Buddha's disciples written in the Sung period of China, the tenth century). The disciple succeeded in attaining higher perception of the truth, triggered not by

Buddha's repetitious preaching but by his casual and trivial action. Actions such as twisting flowers or smiling triggered the disciple Kasho's enlightenment. This is precisely what "communication from mind to mind" is. Had the disciple not accumulated rich experience and training, such communication could not have been accomplished even with a million words. In contrast, if a disciple accumulates a tremendous amount of training, he can attain spiritual enlightenment by receiving hints from his master's most trivial behavior. Properly speaking, this is precisely what *ishin-denshin* is all about.

The ethos of *ishin-denshin* usually can be seen in the ascetic practices of Zen, as described in *Zen in the Art of Archery* written by Herrigel (1971). Herrigel, a German Philosopher, stayed in Japan and taught at Tohoku University for 6 years from 1924 to 1930. During his stay, he was fascinated by Zen and strived to practice archery under the guidance of a former Samurai named Kenzo Awa. In the end, he became a master of the art of archery (a fifth grade archer) and succeeded in seeing into the heart of Zen. According to his book, he struggled hard against difficulties. Now, let's take a look into the course he followed to reach such a stage of spiritual development, from which we can realize the discrepancy of logic between the West and the East, especially the different conception of language and communication. Tsujimura stated in *Japanese Culture and Communication*:

> There are some steps in the process of the practice of archery such as the right breathing in the beginning, right distribution of strength in drawing the bow, and right breathing when releasing the arrow. The master gave Herrigel nothing but simple directions, and there were many things incomprehensible in terms of Western ways of thinking. As a result, questions came to him in great numbers. He tried to manage with those questions, using Western logic (or Western rationalism). Nonetheless he could hardly reach the realm of freedom of self or "free handling." In order to achieve this goal, he had to get rid of himself or to abandon himself, which was hard for him to do and understand. Then, he held the following meaningful dialogue with the Master. The dialogue started after the Master emphasized that he must release the arrow in the state of egoless, in which he gets rid of himself.
>
> **Herrigel:** "How can the shot be loosed if 'I' do not do it?"
> **The Master:** "'It' shoots."
> **Herrigel:** "How can I wait self-obliviously for the shot if 'I' am no longer there?"
> **The Master:** "'It' waits at the highest tension."
> **Herrigel:** "And who or what is this 'It'?"
> **The Master:** "Once you have understood that, you will have no further need of me. And if I tried to give you a clue at the cost of your own experience, I should be the worst of teachers and should deserve to be sacked! So let's stop talking about it and go on practicing." (Herrigel, 1971)

What is drawn from this dialogue is that all the advice about enlightenment is worthless after all. Therefore it is essentially necessary to devote oneself not to such language communication but to practice. When Herrigel advanced in his learning, his master's attitude toward him was very modest, as quoted in the following: "Only after a considerable time did more right shots occasionally come off, which the Master signalized by a deep bow." (Herrigel, 1971)

While he has self-consciousness to loose the shot excellently or to hit the bull's-eye, right shots did not come off. When he let go of himself and yielded himself to some unknown transcendental strength, "It", and time was ripe, he could loose the correct shot. It is the last goal of practice to reach the stage of "free handling" where "self" is erased. Therefore, it is not important at all whether he hits the target or not. As the result, even if he missed the target, the Master bowed deeply and humbly, as long as the shot is loosed in the state of egolessness and spiritual freedom.

In short, at the stage of a master-hand at any art, language is inadequate and futile. Similarly in the area of Zen, communication cannot be accomplished by language. What is called communication in Zen, is made through experience. Once one gains experience, he can understand all even if he is told nothing. Here *ishin-denshin* or telepathic communication has been accomplished. (Tsujimura, 1968, pp. 59–61)

SOCIAL CAUSES OF TACITURNITY

Although it may be true that the Japanese tend to be taciturn or untalkative, we would go too far to say that the Japanese owe this characteristic to the tradition of *ishin-denshin* mentioned in the preceding section. We can perhaps boast that the essence of Japanese culture was established by *ishin-denshin* among great masters. Such a high level of communication, however, has little to do with common people and their daily lives. From this standpoint, we need to seek the origin of traditional taciturnity in Japan, not only from the level of the nobility's culture but also from the level of the common people and their everyday experiences.

One of the sources of taciturnity is Japan's racial and linguistic homogeneity. It is a matter of course that people can understand each other easily with few words if they are monolingual and monoracial. In this sense, the United States represents the opposite extreme: a high level of diversity and verbosity. The United States, often called a racial melting pot, has always had a relatively large population of immigrants. Such conditions force people to overcome a variety of difficulties created by language barriers, different life-styles, and different ways of feeling and thinking in order to understand one another. Thus, Americans have no choice but to fully explain and exhaust their words; the social context in which they live often requires it.

An American psychologist, Barker, studied the effects of social psychological environments in great detail. He created the concept of "behavior setting" (Barker, 1960, 1968). According to Barker, the behavior setting is given to individuals from the outside, transcending the individual's own existence. Further, he indicates that the laws which regulate the behavior of human beings in a behavior setting are different from those of the psychology of individuals.

Barker emphasizes that much attention must be paid to behavioral settings rather than individual psychology in order to explain the behavior of human beings. In order to demonstrate his viewpoint, he analyzes the difference between the cultures of the United States and Great Britain based on the differences of the behavioral settings of two small communities in those countries. The results show that the United States is more sparsely populated but supports more behavioral settings with fewer people than Great Britain. Furthermore, the United States overwhelms Great Britain in terms of the number of responsible positions. Responsible positions per person in the States, 7.1, are three times as great as in Great Britain, 2.3. From the result of the analysis, Barker concludes that many responsible jobs must be accomplished with fewer people in the United States than in Great Britain. Americans, therefore, take a larger part in society than the British. Willing or unwilling, Americans have many chances to enlarge themselves and express themselves to the outer world. This is undoubtedly one of the main sources of their characteristic of talkativeness.

Barker (1968) adds, however, that Americans in the past were very interested in social life and were intense in participating in the society, since their culture was historically established in underpopulated behavior settings. The United States is now becoming overpopulated, and this fact will exert an important influence on the American personality and behavior which thus far has been a model for a modern democratic society. A change may take place in the opposite direction.

Applying Barker's theory to the Japanese, we can assume that the ratio of responsible positions per person is small. In a society like Japan, people naturally learn to maintain a passive attitude toward society and leave everything to others. This is a main source of passivity and tactiturnity in Japanese communication behavior.

The most essential origin of Japanese taciturnity in daily life, however, is the historical fact that they subjected themselves to restraint during a long feudal era and to the regulation of speech under totalitarian regimes. From olden times, there are many proverbs which admonish one for being too talkative, such as, "Least said, soonest mended," "Opening the mouth makes it easy to see through the heart," or "Out of the mouth comes evil." These proverbs reveal the fact that in the past loquacity was attended with danger both politically and socially.

Another revealing aspect of Japanese culture is a children's game, a staring contest, in which two people compete with one another to see how long they can glare at each other without bursting into laughter. Why is the one who first bursts into laughter the loser?

French playwright, Pagnol, regards laughter as a kind of expression of a superiority complex (1947). We know from our own experience that we tend to laugh sometimes when we find that we are superior to others in terms of personal worth. Here is a conversation between two deaf people which Pagnol presented as an actual example of his view.

> A deaf person ran into another one who had a rod and line over his shoulder.
> "Are you going fishing?"
> "No, I am going fishing."
> "Oh, that's exactly what I thought." (Pagnol, 1947, p. 83).

Pagnol indicates four spheres of inferiority of the two deaf people that incur laughter.

> The first inferiority is that both of them are deaf. The second is that they are impertinent enough to converse like us, healthy people. The third is that it is proved harshly that they are perfectly deaf. The last one is that their stupid conversation reveals their pitiful attempt to conceal their misfortune from us. (p. 84)

Thus, Pagnol conceives of laughter as the expression of a sense of superiority; therefore, the person who bursts into laughter first must be a winner. In the case of the children's staring contest, however, the person who starts laughing first loses the game. What could this mean? We can infer that a game in which laughter loses is one of the artifacts of the Japanese historical experience of oppression in the feudal era when it was regarded as immodest behavior to grin or to laugh with an open mouth. The social norm which developed places a high value on keeping one's dignity without laughing.

As for the root of the Japanese staring contest, Kodaka (1943) points out that there is a description about the game in the famous classical literature, *Heike-monogatari,* which is assumed to have been written early in the Kamakura Period (1185–1333). This fact shows us that the game existed 800 years ago. His explanation, however, is confined to its origin in terms of literature and period. He does not touch on its social and cultural functions. Today you will see many girls and women laughing who cover their mouths with their hands, although it should not be concluded that this action is correlated with oppression in the feudal era. It seems to me, however, that this action may be a vestige from the old sense of values that it is immodest to grin broadly. Such female behavior does not occur only in Japan. As a matter of fact, this game also exists in China and Korea.

Thus, we may conclude that the tendency toward taciturnity in Japanese communication comes from the spiritual aspect of *ishin-denshin*, from Japan's particular socio-demographic ecology, and from the experience of oppression in the feudal era.

INDIRECT COMMUNICATION AND RESPECT FOR REVERBERATION

Indirect expression is also a distinctive feature of the Japanese way of communication. This aspect of Japanese communication can be illustrated by the *Waka,* a 31-syllable Japanese short poem. The Heian Period (794–1185) is characterized by many novels written by women and by many edited anthologies of short poems. Lovers among the nobility brought about a good understanding of each other by using the indirect method of exchanging *Waka* (poems). They never directly whispered sweet nothings to one another such as, "I love you" or "Je t'aime."

According to *A History of Japanese Manners and Customs* (Fujioka, 1895), in the Heian Period, the nobility decided to marry based on whether the other party was a good poet, rather than on appearance. It is described therein how important the *Waka* (poems) were to communication between people. Regarding the content of the poems, it should be noted that they are full of delicate, indirect, and lyrical expressions, as seen in the famous poems which were composed by Taira and Mibu in a meeting of poetical composition matches. In the meeting held in 960 A.D., being assigned to compose verse with the theme of first love, Taira made the following poem.

> Alas, the blush upon my cheek,
> 　Conceal it as I may,
> Proclaims to all that I'm in love,
> 　Till people smile and say–
> 　"Where are thy thoughts to-day?
> 　　　　　(Porter, 1979)

In response to the verse, Mibu made the verse:

> Our courtship, that we tried to hide,
> 　Misleading is to none;
> And yet how could the neighbors guess,
> 　That I had yet begun
> 　To fancy any one?
> 　　　　　(Porter, 1979)

There was no basis to choose between the two excellent verses. In the end, however, the palm of victory fell to Taira due to the Emperor Murakami's judgment.

These verses allowed them to express their love while containing themselves, as indicated by phrases such as "conceal it" or "tried to hide." No direct and blunt expression can be seen such as "I love thee." The *Waka* (poems) are a very good example of the Japanese way of communication.

The indirect nature of Japanese communication is also demonstrated by the verses on the playing cards of the 100 famous poems (Hyakunin Isshu).* It seems to me that the Japanese have the only culture that would make up an indoor game using art like *Waka*. The popular indoor games of today are *go, shogi* (Japanese chess), mahjong, flower cards (Japanese playing cards), cards, and chess, all of which are unrelated to art. In contrast the playing cards of the 100 famous poems are the only indoor game which uses the *Waka* art.

A careful analysis of the 100 verses on the playing cards reveals much about the essence of the Japanese culture and communication. Verses about love predominate in these 100 poems, which indicate that *Waka* was used to promote better mutual understanding in love affairs. In 19 out of the 100 verses love is conveyed through the description of human relationships, as in the poems above by Taira and Mibu. In 30 of the verses love is conveyed even more indirectly through the description of nature. The following verses are typical of those which express love through nature.

> The rock divides the stream in two,
>   And both with might and main
> Go tumbling down the waterfall;
>   But well I know the twain
>   Will soon unite again.

> The Mina stream comes tumbling down
>   From Mount Tsukuba's height;
> Strong as my love, it leaps into
>   A pool as black as night
>   With overwhelming might.
>   (Porter, 1979)

There are 49 verses about love, almost half of the total number of cards in the game. The second most frequent verses express a view of life. Eighteen verses of this kind convey the theme through the description of nature; nine through a description of human relationships.

---

* The game is played in the following way: 100 cards are scattered on the *tatami* floor. On each card the last two of the five lines of each 100 verses are printed. A designated person reads out loud each verse from the beginning. The participants compete with each other to see who can most quickly match and pick up the card being read, even before the last two lines are read.

Overall, there are 72 verses which contain indirect expressions by means of a description of some aspect of nature, which shows us how closely the Japanese culture is related to nature. It is generally said that the beauties of nature, such as flower·bird·wind·moon or snow·moon·flower, are quite representative of Japanese culture. Among the 76 versus including such words, 45 have either flower, bird, wind, or moon, and 31 have either snow, moon, or flower.

KUUKI: THE CONSTRAINT OF MOOD

The Japanese traditional value of mood or atmosphere is analyzed in an interesting way by Yamamoto (1977). The Japanese word, *kuuki* has peculiar characteristics. Although the word *kuuki* usually means the air we breath as a physical phenomenon, the *kuuki* which Yamamoto studied does not refer to physical air but to the feeling, mood, or atmosphere, in other words, a mental phenomenon which exerts a pervasive pressure on us and on our behavioral patterns. Thus, the word *kuuki* has a double meaning. The English word, "air," does not have this mental or emotional phenomenon in its meaning to the same extent. In English, we would have to use the word, "atmosphere" or "mood," but these are unable to capture the full meaning of *kuuki*, especially its pervasiveness on human conduct.

According to Yamamoto (1977), Hebrew, Greek, and Latin also have words which include the meanings of both physical air and mental air, as seen in the Japanese Language.

Kuuki constitutes a characteristic feature of the Japanese in that it controls their behavior. *Kuuki* in its emotional or mental meaning is as vague as its physical meaning. It broods shapelessly over our world, neither solid nor liquid but penetrating like a gas.

Much of the vagueness can be attributed to the second part of the word, *ki,* which is used in innumerably different ways in the Japanese language. Doi (1973) conducted a thorough analysis of *ki,* which mainly signifies the feelings of human beings. In several phrases in which it appears it indicates the volition of discernment or the exercise of the senses. For example, *ki-ga'kiku* means "having good sense." Being "attentive or scrupulous" is indicated by the phrase *ki-ga'tsuku*. *Ki-o-ushinau* means "to faint," and *ki-ga-susumu* means "to feel inclined to." In *ki-ga-togameru,* *ki* signifies the specific feeling of compunction, guilt. It is a peculiar characteristic of Japanese that one word, *ki,* encompasses the meaning of many different words in English or other European languages. According to Doi (1973), *ki* is similar in meaning to *kokora,* heart, but not the same. It also differs from *atama,* brain, and *hara,* intention.

Doi (1973) regards *ki* as the movement of the mind in an instant; he also interprets it as something floating from moment to moment. The dictionary defines *ki* as the movement, state, and exercise of the mind. In addition, you will find other definitions such as "something filling up the whole universe," which is the definition related to physical air, and "something one feels to be covering and drifting although unseen clearly," which is the definition related to mental or emotional atmosphere (*Kojien,* 1955).

In conclusion, Doi's and Yamamoto's views must be put together in order to define perfectly the concept, *ki. Ki* is mental activity made by human beings from moment to moment in the "air," which should be defined as the unseen atmosphere floating around us, although it is vague like physical air. Japanese action is controlled by a double *ki* in the sense that inside the mind it is controlled by *ki* from moment to moment, and outside, it is restricted by atmosphere. Thus, an ambiguous atmosphere somehow controlling people and events plays an important role in the behavior of the Japanese people.

There is a well-known example of *kuuki* from the second world war. At the end of World War II, Yamato, a Japenese battleship (73,000 tons), which was called the largest in the world in those days, made a reckless sortie for Okinawa and was sunk. Although the sally was evidently an imprudent attempt, it was enforced to do so by the *kuuki* at that time.

Lieutenant General, Jisaburoo Ozawa is reported to have said, "I believe Yamato's sally was a matter of course then, as now, considering the *kuuki* at that time." Yamamoto (1977) commented on this:

> All those who judged that the sally was reckless stood upon detailed data, in other words, reasonable grounds. However, those who insisted on 'a matter of course' were holding no data or reason and the ground of their justification was only by the *kuuki* which made the decision and caused a power against which no one could resist. (p. 58)

Even at the universities in Japan today, the faculty meetings are often dominated by *kuuki*. It is very difficult to resist the dominance of *kuuki* in various communication situations in Japanese society. The existence of a strong *kuuki* of this nature would be difficult for outsiders to recognize, and its consequences on the outcome of communication would undoubtedly be underestimated.

CONCLUSION

The four characteristics of Japanese communication described in this paper have their roots in Buddhism, Confucianism, and Shintoism. *Ishindenshin,* as it has been handed down from the Buddhist monks through the nobility, is a form of instantaneous communication, or "meeting of the minds," that is triggered by seemingly trivial inconsequential behavior. That *ishin-denshin* can function successfully is a reflection of a very high degree of formal training and practice. *Ishin-denshin* may be found today in the everyday communication of the Japanese, in Japanese literature, dramatic film and television productions, and so forth, but it is especially important for many forms of formal, Zen Buddhist training.

The tendency for the Japanese to remain taciturn is related to the spiritual aspect of *ishin-denshin,* but it is attributed to three social causes: the experience of oppression during the feudal era, the high level of racial and linguistic homogeneity, and the small ratio of positions per person in the behavioral settings of Japanese society. Indirect communication, the art of using poetic symbols in an oblique manner to express one's love or human relationships, rather than by means of direct statements, is evident in many of the traditional games and customs of Japan, including the exchange of *Waka* (poems) and the card game of one hundred poems.

The fourth important characteristic of Japanese communication is the extent to which communication is sometimes dominated by *kuuki,* or the constraints of mood and atmosphere. *Kuuki* is a very rich concept which includes both the prevailing movement of minds from moment to moment and the external atmosphere in both a physical and social sense. The Japanese are very sensitive to the influence of mood or atmosphere and adjust their communication accordingly. This implies that anyone not aware of the *kuuki* of a given situation or insensitive to its influence would have much more difficulty communicating successfully than those who are aware.

In order to fully understand and appreciate human communication from the Japanese perspective, it is important to consider the four characteristics described in this paper. The emphasis placed on *ishin-denshin,* taciturnity, indirect communication, and *kuuki* in Japanese culture, as opposed to Western culture, has important implications and consequencies on the communication process as it occurs in Japanese society today.

CHAPTER 9

Indirect Speech Acts of the Japanese

Keizo Okabe

INTRODUCTION

What is communication? How can we represent a model of communication process most properly?

In the popular way of thinking about communication, it is merely transmission of signals or messages. In the field of social psychology, however, it has been often recognized that the process of communication involves more than transmitting signals; to communicate with others is to engage in a social act or social interaction. Mead (1934) was one of the foremost pioneers in studying communication from such a point of view. As is commonly known, he conceived of human communication as a process of sending "significant symbols" and represented the importance of "taking-the-role-of-the-others" in such communication process.

Studies of linguistic communication today tend to stress the social or interpersonal aspect of language behavior. Speech act theory is a typical example of these studies. In this theory a speaker is considered doing something in saying something. In other words, to communicate with others is performing a certain behavior in a social context. So the speech act theory can be a theory of language use in the framework of a general theory of behavior.

In linguistic communication, a speaker usually utters several sentences and means something to a hearer. In doing so, the speaker sometimes intends to mean what the sentences literally mean, and sometimes he intends to mean something more. For example, when a speaker utters, "The door is open," he does not merely describe or report the state of the door that is left open. Instead, he is often asking the hearer to shut the door. It is not unusual at all to find discrepancies between sentence meaning and the meaning the speaker intends to convey. Such communication is an example of an indirect speech act. An indirect speech act is also language behavior that might be explained in the framework of a general theory of behavior.

In this paper I would like to outline the viewpoint of speech act theory very briefly and investigate how the indirect speech acts are to be explained. Then I will inquire into the indirect speech acts of the Japanese and also consider whether they could be fully explained in the framework of "the theory of speech acts."

SPEECH ACT THEORY

It is commonly accepted that the speech act theory stems from an excellent book, *How to Do Things with Words,* written by Austin in 1962. The lecture was delivered first by Austin as the William James Lecture at Harvard University in 1955. Austin rarely used the term "speech act" in this book, but in fact, he has been developing the speech act theory over years. I must note here the term was actually first introduced by Searle (1969) more than 10 years later.

Austin started his argument by classifying utterances into two types: constative and performative utterances. Constative utterances are "statements" to "describe" some state of affairs or to "state some fact," and these utterances could be either true or false. On the contrary, performative utterances do not "describe" or "report" anything at all, and they have no truth value. They are not "true or false." To utter these sentences is to perform an action physically or mentally rather than to say that something is or is not the case. As examples of performative sentences, Austin cited, "I do," as uttered in the course of the marriage ceremony or "I name this ship the Queen Elizabeth," as uttered when smashing the bottle against the stem.

All such sentences must be uttered by appropriate persons in the appropriate circumstances. Otherwise, the utterance become meaningless and sometimes ridiculous. For instance, married people could not swear, "I do," in the course of a marriage ceremony, or a man could not say, "I predict . . . ," after the matter is over. If this is the case, even though utterances are not false, they are indeed inappropriate. Thus, a performative sentence is neither true nor false, but it could be either appropriate or inappropriate. After pointing out this fact, Austin (1975) considered conditions which are necessary to make sentences appropriate utterances and formulated the following "felicity conditions."

A1. There must exist an accepted conventional procedure having a certain conventional effect, that procedure to include the uttering of certain words by certain persons in certain circumstances and further;

A2. the particular persons and circumstances in a given case must be appropriate for the invocation of the particular procedure invoked.

B1. The procedure must be executed by all participants both correctly and;

B2. completely.

C1. Where, as often, the procedure is designed for use by persons having certain thoughts or feelings or for the inauguration of certain consequential conduct on the part of any participant, then, a person participating in and so invoking the procedure must, in fact, have those thoughts or feelings and the participants must intend so to conduct themselves and further;

C2. must actually so conduct themselves subsequently.

Austin argued that if any one of these conditions was not fulfilled, the performative utterance would be infelicitous, and when any of the four conditions from A1 to B2 was offended against, the performative utterance might be "misfired." When either condition C1 or C2 was offended, the performative utterance would be "abused."

Thus, the conditions that make performative sentences appropriate mainly depend on persons or circumstances of the process of communication. In other words, Austin's proposal could be interpreted as an interesting suggestion that linguistic communication is a kind of social behavior, and its success cannot be appreciated without referring to its social context.

But later, Austin came to recognize that the classification of constative and performative was not tenable enough, because the distinction between them was sometimes blurred. He thought of his failure to find a grammatical criterion for performatives and developed the former classification to a three-fold distinction between locutionary, illocutionary, and perlocutionary acts. These were as follows:

1. Locutionary act—an act of saying, or to produce a meaningful utterance;
2. Illocutionary act—an act performed in saying something, e.g., making a promise, asking a question, swearing an oath, naming a ship. These kinds of act must fulfill various felicity conditions mentioned above in order to be successful;
3. Perlocutionary act—an act of effect-making process by means of saying something, e.g., an act of persuading someone to change his mind.

It is important to know that these three categories mean elements or aspects of one and the same utterance. The constative–performative distinction was a kind of exclusive classification; that is to say, an utterance was to be classified as either constative or performative. But in this case, any utterance usually contains these three elements. Thus, we could decide the felicity conditions of any of utterances, so far as its aspect of illocutionary act is concerned. In other words, appropriateness of communication in general could be analyzed in terms of felicity conditions, if only we take into account its aspects of illocutionary acts.

This way of thinking about utterance or linguistic communication was succeeded and further developed by Searle (1969), who conceived of speech acts as basic and minimal units of linguistic communication. Searle hypothesized that linguistic communication is a rule-governed behavior and intended to clarify the nature and form of this rule. So he started his analysis from characterizations of linguistic elements. These elements were:

1. Uttering words, morphemes, or sentences—performing utterance acts;
2. Referring and predicating—performing propositional acts;
3. Stating, questioning, commanding, promising, etc.—performing illocutionary acts.

That is to say, utterance acts consist of uttering strings of words. Illocutionary and propositional acts consist of uttering words in sentences in certain contexts under certain conditions. A word or sentence per se could not be a unit of communication, but the production of such sentences under certain conditions is a speech act, and a speech act is the basic unit of linguistic communication.

Based on these considerations, Searle proceeded with his analysis of rules that govern speech acts or illocutionary acts. Taking "promising" as an example of speech acts, he asked what conditions are necessary and sufficient for the act of promising to have successfully performed in the utterance of a given sentences. Again, we would like to notice that the problem raised here is to consider how to make communication in general appropriate in a given situation.

Thus, Searle (1969) showed the rules of speech acts "promising" as follows:

1. Propositional content rule: Pr is to be uttered only in the context of a sentence (or larger stretch of discourse) T, the utterance of which predicates some future act A of the speaker S;
2. Preparatory rule: Pr is to be uttered only if the hearer H would prefer S's doing A to his not doing A;
   Pr is to be uttered only if it is not obvious to both S and H that S will do A in the normal course of events;
3. Sincerity rule: Pr is to be uttered only if S intends to do A;
4. Essential rule: The utterance of Pr counts as the undertaking of an obligation to do A.

As mentioned above, linguistic communication is rule-governed behavior. The behavior consists in performing speech acts or illocutionary acts, by uttering sentences in accordance with these rules just stated. In communication a speaker performs speech acts and intends for a hearer to understand what his utterance does mean. On the hearer's part, undertanding the utterance consists in knowing the sentence meaning, on the one hand, and recognizing the speaker's intention to make his utterance understood, on the other. When a speaker says, "The door is open," instead of saying, "Please shut the door," a hearer must know the meaning of the sentence, "The-door-is-open," first. At the same time the hearer has to understand the speaker's intention to ask him to shut the door. If the hearer cannot understand the speaker's intention, communication will be cut off.

How can such an understanding of the speaker's intention be achieved? What condition on the hearer's part makes communication successful? These are basic problems in the study of communication, but they are still not satisfactorily answered. Speech act theory contributes much to the study of communication, so far as we examine language behaviors on the part of a speaker, but the model of the process of understanding on the hearer's part still remains to be elaborated.

INDIRECT SPEECH ACTS

In linguistic communication, the speaker says something and he often means something more. For example, when a speaker utters a sentence, "Can you reach the salt?," he means it as a request to pass the salt. In such cases, the speaker's speech act is called an indirect speech act.

In the case of an indirect speech act, a speaker usually performs two types of illocutionary act. For instance, a sentence, "Can you reach the salt?," contains both the act of question and the act of request, and an illocutionary act of request is performed indirectly by way of an illocutionary act of question.

How is it possible for a speaker to perform such two types of illocutionary act at the same time? How is it possible for a hearer to understand the illocutionary act that is performed indirectly? It is certain that some kinds of indirect speech acts are no more than idiomatic language use. So understanding the illocutionary act mainly depends on the knowledge of the iodiom or conventionalized language use. Searle also contended that convention plays an important role in the understanding of indirect speech acts, but in general, Searle (1969) thought three principles are necessary to explain the indirect part of indirect speech acts.

1. The theory of speech acts and general principles of cooperative conversation;
2. Mutually shared factual background information of the speaker and the hearer;
3. An ability on the part of the hearer to make inferences.

Searle was convinced that the theory of speech acts would be able to explain how a speaker performs an indirect speech act. Taking examples of two types of illocutionary acts (request and promise), he conceived of general forms to perform these types of indirect speech act. Then he listed the following generalizations:

1. S can make an indirect request (or other directive) by either asking whether or stating that preparatory condition concerning H's ability to do A obtains;
2. S can make an indirect directive by either asking whether or stating that the propositional content condition obtains;
3. S can make an indirect directive by stating that the sincerity condition obtains, but not by asking whether it obtains;
4. S can make an indirect directive by either stating that or asking whether there are good or overriding reasons for doing A, except where the reason is that H wants or wishes, etc., to do A.

Cooperative principles are argued by Grice (1975) as fundamental conditions or premises necessary for the existence of conversation. The principles mean that both speaker and hearer in conversation must be cooperative so as to continue their communication. In other words, both speaker and hearer have a common purpose to cooperate—even in the situation of disputing, they have the common purpose to dispute. Of course, the degree of cooperation varies in many ways, but without such cooperative efforts to some degree at least, communication could not be maintained. Both the speaker and hearer will be expected to observe such general principles.

More precisely, the principles involve four categories in accordance with quantity, quality, manner, and relation. Grice represented these categories as follows:

Quantity

1. Make your contribution as informative as is required.
2. Do not make your contribution more information than is required.

Quality

1. Do not say what you believe to be false.
2. Do not say that for which you lack adequate evidence.

Manner

1. Avoid obscurity of expression.
2. Avoid ambiguity.
3. Be brief (avoid unnecessary prolixity).
4. Be orderly.

Relation

1. Be relevant.

These principles idealize the conversational process too much. We know that people violate these principles very often, unconsciously or consciously, in the actual process of conversation in everyday life. But violation could not be violation if no ideal principles or standards are presupposed. To put it in another way, a speaker's violation of such principles could not be recognized by a hearer if the hearer does not know about the principles. And in the case of indirect speech acts at least, the fact that the hearer recognizes the speaker's violation is particularly significant, because this recognition could be a clue to inferring the speaker's indirectly performed illocutionary act. For instance, even if a speaker makes an ambiguous utterance, a hearer could still assume that the speaker is cooperating in the conversation and his utterance is intended to be relevant. The hearer enveavers to infer anyway what is the indirectly performed illocutionary act in the ambiguous utterance and what is the speaker's intended meaning of the communication.

Thus, Searle suggested that the principles of cooperative conversation would be one of the apparatuses necessary to explain the indirect speech acts for the hearer. Now we would like to confirm that the principles of cooperative conversation are only a clue to the hearer's inference and that these principles per se could not explain the process or the mechanism of this inference systematically. The problem still remains to be clarified.

As for making such inferences, it is a matter of course that a hearer needs an ability to make inferences. At the same time, background information of the speaker and the hearer is surely necessary to make the inferences successful. To know convention is to have such information. But the nature of an inference ability and the general features of background information are still not explained precisely.

Speech act theory has promising value for the development of the study of communication theory. It does suggest how indirect speech acts are performed and how they are understood, but the problem of the indirect speech acts is so complicated that speech act theory cannot give a full account of the problem as yet.

THE PRACTICE OF INDIRECT COMMUNICATION IN JAPANESE SOCIETY

In the Japanese language there are a great many kinds of expressions which are classified as indirect speech acts. The Japanese have many expressions of the indirect speech acts compared to other cultures. Indirect speech acts are quite common in the Japanese language.

As mentioned above, the utterance, "The door is open," could be an indirect speech act to ask for a hearer to shut the door. The Japanese, instead of saying, "The door is open," often say, "It is somewhat cold today," which is much more indirect, because no words refer to the door. Analogously, if a speaker says, "Let me consider it for a while," when he is asked to do something in a negotiation setting, then the listener usually understand at once that his proposal has been rejected indirectly. Or, in the process of question and answer in the *diet,* ministers often reply to members of the assembly, "We would like to postpone your problem indefinitely." The Japanese understand the utterance, "We will examine your proposal," as an indirect speech act signifying an unfavorable answer.

As stated above, some types of indirect speech act use the standardized form of expression, and the meaning of the expression (or, more accurately, the indirect illocutionary act) is understood by the hearer mostly through his knowledge about the conventional usages of the language. For example, "Do you know Mr. A's phone number?" is not only a question but also a request for the hearer to tell Mr. A's phone number to the speaker. The listener will understand the speaker's intention at once, only if he recognizes the conventional usage of the utterance as a request. Other kinds of speech act have no such conventionalized form of expression and are idiosyncratic to the communication situation. So the hearer cannot depend on the knowledge about the convention in order to understand the meaning of these indirect speech acts. Furthermore, these expressions are often vague and ambiguous. In other words, they are in violation of the maxim of cooperation—not to speak ambiguously or obscurely. Nevertheless, the hearer can understand the meaning of them easily without being aware of their violation of the maxim.

There are several ways of considering this process of understanding. The principles of cooperation and speech act theory suggest a way to answer the question to some extent, but they are not enough for this purpose. To explain the process of indirect speech acts in Japanese, the traditional mode of communication should not be ignored, or rather, its important role must be stressed more than in other societies. For example, to express the speaker's demand, rejection, assertion, or criticism to the hearer directly or straightforwardly is often regarded as impoliteness or as bad manners in human relations in Japanese society. In general, the traditional rule of communication that prescribes "not to demand, reject, assert yourself, or criticize the listener straightforwardly" is a much more dominant principle in Japanese communication than the maxim of "not to speak ambiguously or obscurely." It is true that the industrialization and the modernization of the Japanese society has exerted a strong influence on its patterns of culture. Nevertheless, there still exists a cultural lag in many aspects of social life. The mode of communication is still subject to traditional rules, though this mode has gradually changed since World War II toward a more direct mode of speaking.

In the case of indirect speech acts, there exists more or less a discrepancy between the meaning of the surface sentence uttered and the real meaning which the speaker intends. In the extreme case, the discrepancy between these two meanings becomes so great that the speaker looks as if he were speaking on two levels of communication simultaneously. For successful communication, the listener has to understand the meaning of these two levels, not only to understand the sentence correctly but also to infer the speaker's intention accurately. To do so, the hearer must have knowledge about the traditional rules of Japanese communication which govern speakers' communicative behavior. Thus, the knowledge of traditional rules of communication is essential to the listener's ability to infer a speaker's intentions.

In the case of rejection, sometimes the speaker worries about the listener's feelings about being rejected. The Japanese word, *o-mo-i-ya-ri,* means the "speaker's worries," and usually a speaker is afraid to jeopardize the future relationship with the listener. So the speaker often expresses his rejection indirectly by saying, "Let me consider your proposal for a while." At the same time, the listener can undersatnd what kind of feeling the speaker actually has; he infers the speaker's intention of rejection easily. Both the speaker and the listener are able to take-the-role-of-the-other because of their knowledge about the traditional mode of Japanese communication.

In summary, for the explanation of Japanese indirect speech acts, the theory of speech acts is not completely adequate, though it is a promising way to study the communication process. To explain indirect speech acts, the traditional rules of Japanese communication must be used, because the process of communication involves the use of language within a particular social and cultural context.

CHAPTER 10

Communication within the Japanese Business Organization

Randy Y. Hirokawa

INTRODUCTION

With the recent emergence of Japanese industries as dominant forces in the world's economy, it is not surprising that Western organizational scholars have become increasingly interested in the internal dynamics of Japanese business organizations. Much of this interest is undoubtedly motivated by their desire to discover the Japanese "secret" to success. While that secret (if it exists at all) remains an elusive one to us, the efforts of organizational observers have led us to recognize that Japanese business organizations tend to possess characteristics which distinguish them from comparable firms in the United States.

One of the most frequently identified differences between Japanese and American business organizations concerns the nature of communication within those respective organizations. Several authors, for example, have suggested that Japanese business organizations tend to possess more effective and efficient systems of vertical and horizontal communication than their counterparts in the United States (Abegglen, 1958; Johnson & Ouchi, 1974; Yoshino, 1968). Others, while not necessarily acknowledging the inherent superiority of communication within Japanese business organizations, do suggest that the manner in which Japanese employees communicate with one another represents a unique facet of the Japanese organization (Ballon, 1969; Drucker, 1971; Vogel, 1979; Whitehill & Takezawa, 1978). Most observers of Japanese business organizations agree, however, that an understanding of the unique characteristics of communication within the "typical" Japanese business organization represents an important key to understanding the unique properties of Japanese business organizations in general. As Hirokawa (1981) suggests, the nature of communication within the Japanese organization is so intimately woven with other properties of the organization (e.g., style of management) that it is very difficult to understand one without also understanding the other.

The purpose of this paper is thus to illustrate how the unique nature of communication within the typical Japanese business organization is closely linked to specific aspects of the Japanese way of organizing. In particular, the paper focuses on two unique communication characteristics of the typical Japanese business organization: (1) openness of communication between employees of all levels, and (2) deliberate use of ambiguous communication—and attempts to explain how those communication characteristics are influenced by certain properties of the organization.

OPENNESS OF COMMUNICATION AMONG EMPLOYEES

One of the most frequently identified characteristics of communication within the typical Japanese business organization concerns the relative degree of *openness* among organizational employees. Over the years, several observers have noted that, in contrast to many American organizations which are plagued by restricted and filtered lines of communication, Japanese organizations are frequently characterized by free-flowing and relatively distortion-free communication between superiors, colleagues, and subordinates (Abegglen, 1958; Johnson & Ouchi, 1974; Yoshino, 1968).

Within the typical Japanese business organization, it is not uncommon to find employees willingly exchanging accurate and reliable information with other members of the organization. An employee, for example, will readily admit to his/her supervisor when he/she has made a mistake. Likewise, an employee will generally not hesitate to politely inform his/

her superior, colleague, or subordinate when he/she feels that the individual has committed a mistake or an error in judgment. In fact, when it comes to the daily operations of the organization, there is very little that the Japanese employee will *not* communicate openly with other members of the organization.

Openness of communication between organization members is not limited to matters pertaining to the daily operations of the organization. On the contrary, in certain appropriate situations, it is not unusual for employees to discuss all facets of their professional, social, *and* personal lives with other members of their organization. Nakane (1972) points out, for example, that Japanese workers will typically possess a set of close friends who may be their superiors (*sempai*), colleagues (*dōryō*), or subordinates (*kōhai*). Within the confines of this group of close associates, employees from various levels of the organization openly interact on a variety of topics—both work and non-work related. Nakane notes that within these friendship groups, there is really nothing that a Japanese employee cannot (or will not) share with other members of his/her group: Work problems, personal conflicts, family matters, health problems, and love affairs are all legitimate topics of conversation.

FACTORS ACCOUNTING FOR OPENNESS

Why do Japanese employees tend to be so open in their communication with other members of their organization? This question has long puzzled Western observers. I believe that openness of communication between Japanese employees can be traced to three important properties of most Japanese business organizations: (1) employees' concern for company success, (2) management's stress of internal harmony and group unity, and (3) job security stemming from the existence of semipermanent employment systems.

Employees' Concern for Company Success

One of the principal reasons why Japanese employees communicate openly with each other is because they share a strong desire to ensure the success of their company. Japanese employees tend to be very loyal to their company—often viewing it as a direct extension of their immediate family—and thus frequently adopt the goals of the firm. Not surprisingly, it becomes very important to the employee that his/her company excel over its national and international competitors. It is this strong desire for company success which motivates employees to communicate openly and freely with other members of their organization. That is to say, since Japanese employees want their company to be successful, they will typically do anything (and everything) they can to ensure the success of the firm. Very often, this entails accurately communicating important information to other members of the organization. In short, Japanese employees will typically communicate whatever they feel needs to be communicated in order to ensure the success of their company.

Management's Stress on Internal Harmony and Group Unity

Another important reason why Japanese employees tend to communicate openly with each other can be traced to the impact of Japanese management's stress on internal harmony and unity within the organization. Japanese managers typically assume that the survival and continued success of their organization necessitates that the members of the company work together as a single, harmonious unit. As a consequence, Japanese managers continually impress on their workers the need to identify with the goals of the company and to work cooperatively with each other to achieve those goals. Known as the *wa* spirit, this emphasis on maintaining harmony and unity within the organization functions as a fundamental guiding principle of organizational behavior. Within the Japanese organization, members who abide by the *wa* spirit willingly share necessary information with those who need it because they recognize that cooperative and harmonious effort necessitates that such sharing takes place. As Nakane (1972) points out, the influence of the *wa* spirit on organizational behavior is so powerful that the phrase, "That's his/her problem, not mine," is really not a part of the thinking of the typical Japanese worker.

The stress on internal harmony and unity tends to facilitate openness of communication in still another way. That is, in encouraging workers to function as an integrated, harmonious unit, Japanese managers tend to discourage (and often chastise) individual achievement and success *at the expense* of group harmony and unity. Kitano (1969) points out that the Japanese employee is typically socialized to operate under the premise that it is wrong to commit any action which might bring about individual success and recognition at the expense of harmony and unity within the organization, department, or work group. This self-imposed controlling of actions obviously applies to the willingness of employees to communicate openly with one another. That is to say, the Japanese employee operating under the *wa* spirit would never consider withholding important information, or deliberately falsifying or distorting information, in order to gain a competitive edge over other employees, because such actions could disrupt the harmony and unity within the organization.

Job Security Stemming from Permanent Employment

A third important factor which contributes to the willingness of Japanese employees to communicate openly with one another can be traced to the impact of job security on the behaviors of these employees. Although increasing economic pressures are forcing many Japanese companies to reevaluate and adjust their employment policies, most medium- and large-sized Japanese business organizations still retain the spirit of the permanent employment system (Oh, 1976). Within most of these companies, an employee will enter the organization directly after junior high, high school, or college graduation, and remain with that company for the remainder of his/her working career. In essence, once an employee is invited to join an organization and accepts the offer, an unwritten (though mutually understood) "contract" is struck between that individual and his/her organization which binds both parties into a permanent employment relationship. The strength of this employment relationship is such that only the severest of circumstances (e.g., the company goes bankrupt or the employee commits a major crime against the company) will justify a termination of it.

The influence of the permanent employment system on the willingness of employees to communicate openly and freely with other members of their organization is fairly obvious. The permanent employment system gives an employee a sense of job security and, as such, allows that individual the freedom to say whatever he/she so desires without fear of losing his/her job. For example, if the employee is experiencing difficulty completing an important assignment, that individual would not hesitate to discuss the problem openly with his/her supervisor because the employee is secure in the knowledge that exposing personal "weakness" will not cost him/her a job. Similarly, because the employee is secure in his/her position, that individual is also not likely to be afraid to speak out and question the instructions of his/her superior if he/she believes that the superior is mistaken. In short, the security that life-time employment provides Japanese employees allows them the added freedom to communicate openly and freely with other members of the organization.

DELIBERATE AMBIGUITY OF COMMUNICATION AMONG EMPLOYEES

Another interesting characteristic of communication within most Japanese business organizations concerns the ambiguous manner in which Japanese employees appear to communicate with one another. As Pascale

(1978) notes, in contrast to American employees who strive to communicate with each other in a clear, precise, and explicit manner, Japanese employees often deliberately communicate with one another in a seemingly vague and imprecise manner. For example, suppose a salesclerk in a department store went to her supervisor for advice on how to set up a particular counter display. In the typical American company, the supervisor might respond in a fairly explicit manner: "Ms. Smith, I would suggest that you organize the display so that the most expensive items are easily visible by the customers and are easily reached by them." In the typical Japanese company, however, the supervisor is more likely to respond in a less explicit and precise manner. The supervisor may say, *"Tanaka-san, ki o kikasenasai,"* which roughly translated means, "Ms. Tanaka, do what you think would work best . . . let your imagination tell you what should be done." Japanese supervisors and employees, then, tend to be less directive and specific in their instructions or comments to others than their counterparts in the United States.

An interesting facet of this deliberate use of ambiguity when communicating with others involves the use of *understatements*. For the most part, the Japanese have mastered the art of saying something with considerably less emphasis or certainty than appears warranted. Consider the classic example of the president of a large corporation who stands before the company's Board of Directors and, knowing that his company has made a financial "killing" on the international market, calmly says to them, "It seems we have made a little bit of a profit on our recent international venture." Or consider the opposite case of a manager who, knowing that the sales campaign that he has been in charge of has been a dismal failure, tells the company president, "Sir, it seems that the sales campaign has not worked out quite to our expectations." In short, Japanese employees will often say things which are deliberate understatements of what may actually be the case.

Another interesting facet of the ambiguous manner in which Japanese employees communicate with one another concerns their deliberate use of evasive communication tactics. In general, the Japanese employee will rarely (if ever) come right out with an explicit "no" to another's request. On the contrary, the typical employee will try to be very tactful and diplomatic in conveying a negative response. Imai (1975), in fact, identifies 16 evasive "maneuvers" which can be employed by the Japanese to avoid saying "no."

One of the typical ways to avoid saying "no," according to Imai, is to say "yes" and then follow the affirmative response with a detailed explanation which, in effect, means "no." An experience that happened to a friend of mine illustrates this first evasive tactic. On a recent business trip to Japan, my friend (Mr. Tomita) went into a bank in Tokyo and asked the teller to convert $2000 of American Express traveler's checks into Japanese currency. Since the policy of that bank prohibited the teller from cashing more than $1000 worth of foreign traveler's checks, the teller politely informed my friend that the bank's manager would have to authorize the transaction. The bank manager welcomed my friend into his office and had his secretary bring them both some tea. After a brief exchange of greetings, the manager asked what he could do for my friend. My friend explained that he wanted to convert $2000 of traveler's checks into Japanese currency, but the teller informed him that such a large transaction would have to be authorized by him (the manager). The manager smiled, nodded his head in agreement, and replied, "I don't see a problem here, Mr. Tomita . . . let's see what we can work out." The manager then proceeded to carefully explain the rationale for the bank's policy and provided my friend with about five reasons why the bank could not cash such a large amount of traveler's checks even if they wanted to. After about 20 minutes of explanation, it became quite obvious to my friend that the bank manager was *not* going to authorize the transaction, despite the fact that he had initially responded in a positive manner.

Another evasive communication tactic commonly employed by Japanese employees is to simply avoid answering the question and leave the matter unattended. Imai (1981, p. 8) points out that the postponement of a decision on a pending issue or the abrupt changing of the subject is tantamount to saying "no" to the request. He provides a clear example of this evasive tactic:

Salesman: As you can see, our product meets your specifications and requirements 100%. How soon do you think you can place an order?

Manager: Did you see the *sumo* wrestling last night on T.V.?

Salesman: Well . . . yes, I did. But getting back to our discussion of your order, when would you like to place the order?

Manager: What did you think of Jessie Takamiyama? Wasn't he terrific?

A third evasive tactic often employed by the Japanese is to respond to the request in such a vague and ambiguous manner that the other side has no way of knowing whether the answer is "yes" or "no." Imai suggests that by being deliberately vague and noncommital, the Japanese businessman hopes the other person will get the "message" that the answer is "no." A recent conversation that I had with an executive vice president from a large Japanese electronics corporation illustrates this third type of evasive communication tactic. This vice president had come to our campus to deliver a lecture on Japanese management practices. After the lecture, I had an opportunity to talk briefly with him and inquired about the possibility of doing some research within his company. His response to my request went something like this:

> Ah yes . . . we have always believed that research is good—you know, we have learned a lot from your American scholars like Dr. Peter Drucker. In the past, we have allowed people to conduct studies in our company . . . but that was in Japan before I came here seven years ago. Yes, I think research is always interesting . . . perhaps we can talk more about this study of yours later . . . here's my business card . . . do you have one also?

In my conversation with this executive vice president, it became clear to me that he had no intentions of allowing me to conduct my research in his company. Furthermore, it became obvious that to pursue the matter with him, even at a later date, would prove to be useless. Rather than coming right out and denying my request, however, he tried to be generally positive and encouraging, while at the same time, being very careful not to make any commitments. Imai (1981) suggests that in most instances, such a noncommital response reflects an attempt to deny a request without actually saying "no."

A fourth common evasive "maneuver" is to postpone making a decision on the matter until a later date. In most instances, when a Japanese employee indicates that he/she is unable to make a decision at the present time and requires more time to consider the matter, it usually is a good indication that the employee is unwilling to comply with the request. For example, suppose employee "A" is supposed to work on a particular Saturday but asks employee "B" to substitute for him/her on that particular day so that he/she can attend a baseball game. If employee B does not want to take employee A's place on that Saturday, that individual might say to employee A: "I'd like to help you out, but I can't give you a definite answer right now because I have to check with my wife to see if we don't already have something planned for that day." Imai (1981) suggests that in postponing the decision until he has had an opportunity to check for a previous engagement, employee B is essentially indicating to employee A that he has no interest in switching schedules for that particular day.

A fifth evasive tactic commonly employed by Japanese employees is to give off nonverbal signals which indicate that the request is a difficult one to comply with. Imai (1981) points out, for example, that when a boss calls in an employee and asks him/her to conduct a survey by such and such a date, the employee may signal his/her unwillingness to comply with the request by folding his/her arms, gazing at a spot on the ceiling with a grimace, and mumbling something like, "Saaah . . . that . . . may . . . not . . . be . . . so . . . easy . . . to . . . do." Or the employee may frown, shake his/her head, and say unenthusiatically, "I will see what I can do."

Another commonly employed evasive tactic which also involves the use of nonverbal signals is to provide nonverbal cues which indicate that one is no longer interested in discussing the matter any further. Imai provides an anecdote which clearly illustrates the use of this particular evasive maneuver:

> I once escorted an American company president on a visit to a large Japanese company which he wanted to persuade to adopt a very ambitious scheme. Among the executives from the Japanese company present at the meeting, we noticed that the executive in charge of liaison on the project kept his eyes closed throughout the discussion, and it was not certain whether he was asleep, meditating, or what. But it was clear that he was not listening. As expected, the project never materialized. (1981, p. 8)

Imai (1975, 1981) suggests, of course, that there are many additional ways in which a Japanese employee can avoid saying "no" directly to another person. For example, the employee can suddenly assume a highly apologetic tone as if to signal his/her regret at not being able to provide an affirmative response to the request. Or, the employee can laugh at the request and pass it off as a joke. Still further, the employee can suddenly begin criticizing the other person in an angry tone. Whatever the tactic employed, Imai (1981, p. 10) points out that in the typical Japanese communication, one has to be able to "hear between the lines." He suggests that just as in a *haiku* poem, what is left unsaid may be just as important as what is said.

FACTORS ACCOUNTING FOR DELIBERATE AMBIGUITY

Why do Japanese employees often communicate with each other in a deliberately ambiguous manner? There are, of course, no simple answers to this question. However, at least two plausible reasons can be advanced to partially explain the prevalence of ambiguous communication between members of the typical Japanese business organization: (1) the belief among employees that one should always try to downplay both one's successes, as well as others' failures and (2) the desire among employees to avoid embarrassing both themselves and others.

The Influence of Humbleness and Tolerance

Earlier, it was pointed out that the typical Japanese business organization is characterized by the emphasis that its management places on the development and maintenance of harmony and unity within the organization. In general, the Japanese believe that the development and maitnenance of such harmony and unity can be greatly facilitated if all employees display "humbleness" (the deliberate downplay of one's virtues and success) and "tolerance" (the deliberate downplay of another's failures and shortcomings) when dealing with each other. From the perspective of the Japanese, such actions facilitate harmony and unity within the organization because they tend to minimize the rise of conflicts between employees.

It is this desire to display the appropriate degree of humbleness or tolerance which tends to influence the rise of ambiguous communication between employees. That is to say, the use of ambiguous statements provide the Japanese employee with a convenient way to display the humbleness or tolerance expected of him or her. Consider, for example, the case of the head of an advertising department who is called in by the Board of Directors to present a summary of the results of the company's recent advertising campaign. The department head *knows* that the campaign has been very successful and obviously wants to communicate that information to the members of the Board. However, in communicating that information, the department head also realizes that he/she must display the humbleness expected of all "good" executives. Thus, in order to accomplish both "objectives," the department head would probably resort to the use of some appropriate understatement like, "I'm happy to report that we have experienced a little more luck with the campaign than was expected." Similarly, consider the case of a manager who comes to work in the morning to find that his office has not been cleaned by the janitor. The manager wants to communicate this problem to the head of the janitorial service but realizes that in doing so, he/she must display the appropriate degree of restraint and tolerance because there may be many "legitimate" reasons why his office was not cleaned the night before. Thus, in order to register his/her complaint while, at the same time, displaying the appropriate degree of tolerance, the manager would probably resort again to the use of an appropriate understatement like, "Mr. Fujita . . . I hate to bother you with such a trivial matter, but I was wondering if you could inform whoever was responsible for cleaning my office last night that the office does not appear to be as clean as it once was."

The Influence of the Desire to "Save Face"

While deliberate ambiguity of communication between Japanese employees can often be attributed to their desire to display humbleness and tolerance when dealing with other members of their organization, such ambiguity can also be attributed to their desire to avoid embarrassing both themselves and others. The Japanese appear to be particularly sensitive to the concept of "face" (i.e., one's dignity and self-respect) and thus make every effort to avoid or prevent the "loss of one's face" (i.e., the loss of self-respect and dignity resulting from public humiliation and embarrassment). So powerful is this desire to "save one's face" that it is not uncommon for an individual to voluntarily resign from a company (or in extreme instances, take his/her own life) rather than live with the shame of "losing one's face."

Typically, the Japanese employee will use ambiguous communication to avoid the loss of one's face, or the face of another. Imai (1981, p. 10) suggests, in fact, that the desire to save face is a principal reason why Japanese employees have developed elaborate evasive communication tactics. As Imai puts it, when the Japanese employ evasive tactics, they are essentially saying, "I am sending you all the necessary messages and signals because it would be an embarrassment for me to have to say no and for you to be rejected . . . I hope you will please understand what I mean." In short, the use of ambiguous communication provides the Japanese employee with a convenient opportunity to say what needs to be said without risking the possibility of embarrassing either himself/herself or the other party he/she is communicating with.

In using ambiguous messages to avoid the loss of face, the Japanese employee is very careful to say things in such a manner that both parties are allowed to leave the interaction with their pride intact. That is to say, the employee will attempt to phrase the message in such a way so as to preserve the opporutnity to save face by saying, "Oh, I'm sorry if I offended you . . . it was not meant to sound that way." For example, in criticizing the work of one of his/her subordinates, a Japanese manager may say, "Perhaps you could reflect a bit further on your proposal." What the manager *really* means, of course, is, "You're way off base here . . . this proposal will never work . . . you'd better come up with a more acceptable idea." In phrasing the message in an ambiguous manner, however, the manager is able to register his/her concern with the proposal, while also allowing the subordinate to leave the meeting with his/her pride intact. Similarly, when questioning a decision made by one's superior, a subordinate will carefully select his/her words so that he/she can come close enough to the point to ensure that the superior understands the concern but *not* so close as to embarrass the manager or cause him/her to become defensive. For example, instead of saying, "I think the new schedule of yours will really cause dissention among the workers," the subordinate may say, "I'm wondering if all the workers would feel comfortable with this new schedule?" The latter question still raises the question of whether the new schedule is desirable but does not "crowd" the superior and force him/her to become defensive as does the first statement.

CONCLUSION

The preceding discussion has hopefully convinced the reader that the unique characteristics of communication within the typical Japanese business organization are directly attributable to specific aspects of the Japanese way of organizing. The suggested relationships between specific aspects of the typical Japanese business organization and the nature of communication occurring within it may be summarized by way of the following propositions:

Proposition 1: Communication between members of an organization tend to be more open when those members share a common concern for the success of the organization. The Japanese experience suggests that when employees want their company to succeed and perceive that the accurate communication of information to other members of the organization is essential for bringing about that success, they can be expected to communicate openly and freely with other members of the organization.

Proposition 2: Communication between members of an organization tend to be more open when those members work cooperatively together as a single, harmonious unit. The Japanese experience suggests that when employees identify with the goals of the organization and work cooperatively together to achieve those goals, they can be expected to willingly share information with each other because they recognize that cooperative and harmonious effort necessitates that such sharing takes place. Furthermore, when employees are committed to working cooperatively together as a single, harmonious unit, openness of communication is further facilitated because employees will refrain from deliberately distorting or falsifying information for fear of disrupting the desired harmony and unity among members of the organization.

Proposition 3: Communication between members of an organization tend to be more open when those members are provided job security. The Japanese experience suggests that when employees realize that their jobs are not dependent on what they say (or fail to say) to other members of the organization, they can be expected to communicate more openly and freely with each other.

Proposition 4: The desire to display the appropriate degree of humbleness and tolerance tends to influence the rise of ambiguous communication between employees. The use of ambiguous messages provides an employee with a convenient means of communicating what needs to be communicated while, at the same time, downplaying one's virtues and success *or* another's failures and shortcomings.

Proposition 5: Ambiguous communication between employees is often the result of their desire to avoid the loss of face. The use of ambiguous messages provides an employee with a convenient means of communicating what needs to be communicated without risking the possibility of losing his/her self-respect and dignity *or* the self-respect and dignity of the other party.

Although this paper is somewhat guilty of oversimplifying the nature and dynamics of communication within the typical Japanese business organization, it is hoped that the preceding discussion has provided the reader with a better understanding of both the nature of communication within the typical Japanese business organization, as well as the nature of the typical Japanese business organization in general. More important, however, it is hoped that this paper has provided the reader with a better basis for understanding how the characteristics of an organization (be it American or Japanese or whatever) can influence the nature of communication between members of that organization.

CHAPTER 11

The Guiding Image in Indian Culture and Its Implications for Communication

Wimal Dissanayake

INTRODUCTION

The relationship between philosophy and communication is indeed a fascinating one. Each culture has a set of presuppositions and postulates that guide, and even control, human communication. Therefore, in order to comprehend fully the communicative behavior that is associated with a given culture, it is imperative that we delve into the philosophical underpinnings of that culture. The objective of the present essay is to uncover one very significant philosophical strand in the fabric of Indian culture and to point out its centrality in the understanding of communication in the context of India.

Weaver (1964) provides us with an excellent conceptual focus for this exercise. While underscoring the fact that man is by nature a social animal, he examines the relationship that exists between man and nature at three levels of conscious reflection. These three levels are man's (1) specific conception of and ideas about things, (2) general beliefs and convictions, and (3) metaphysical vision of the world. The first level includes the

COMMUNICATION THEORY:
EASTERN AND WESTERN PERSPECTIVES

thoughts and ideas that men employ in the business of day-to-day living. This level naturally deals with man's mundane existence. The second level is concerned with belief systems and conglomerations of values that men acquire through cultural memory as well as through new human encounters. The third level, which according to Weaver is the highest, represents an intuitive feeling about the imminent nature of reality and a reference point for ideas, beliefs, and actions.

Based on this categorization, Weaver proceeds to make the point that a society is essentially an organized entity which has both structure and hierarchy, and this organization obtains its cohesive force from the centripetal predilections discernible in all cultures. Culture, Weaver emphatically asserts, by its very nature, tends to be centripetal and to aspire toward some unity. As Cushman and Hauser (1973) point out, the world of facts does not possess any organization nor does it display any cohesion. It is only by means of an inward search, a culturally sanctioned reference point, that an ordering principle could be obtained.

In this regard, Weaver's concept of the tyrannical image is pregnant with heuristic significance. By the tyrannical image, he means the ideal, the norm, toward which a cultural collectivity seeks to move. As Weaver remarks:

> There is at the heart of every culture a center of authority from which there proceed subtle and pervasive pressures upon us to conform and to repel the unlike as disruptive. . . . At this center there lies a "tyrannizing image" which draws everything toward itself. The image is the ideal of its excellence. The forms that it can take and the particular manifestations that it can find are various. . . . But examine them as we will, we find this inward facing toward some high representation. This is the sacred will of the culture from which inspiring waters like magnetic lines of force flow out and hold the various activities in a subservience of acknowledgment. Not to fill this magnetic pull toward identification and assimilation is to be outside the culture (1964, p. 11)

As the word "tyrannizing" has certain unhappy associations, I prefer to use the term guiding image. A study of this "sacred well of the culture" can prove to be extremely useful in understanding the contours of any given culture.

In India, as in most other Asian countries, this guiding image is inextricably linked with philosophy and religion. This is especially true in India, where as Radhakrishnan says the pursuit of philosophy is deemed a religious vocation. Therefore, in order to come to terms with the cultural ideal that animates Indian society, we need to examine, brief though they may be, the outlines of Indian philosophy.

Indian philosophical thought has evolved over a period of 4 thousand years. The Vedas, composed somewhere between 2500–2000 B.C. constitute the fountain of Indian philosophy. The hymns contained in the Vedas deal with the relationship of man to nature. Nature is represented in the form of Gods, and man has to live righteously in order not to incur their wrath. The Vedas, and the Brahmanas in which Vedic thought culminates, are closely associated with ritualism.

The Upanishads represent the next stage in the evolution of Indian philosophical thought. The Upanishads exercised a profound influence on the growth and development of Indian philosophy. These works call attention to the value of the knowledge of ultimate truth as a means of liberation. Hence, with the Upanishads, Indian philosophy rises to a higher plane of discourse. Concomitantly, there was a greater emphasis on the need to look inward for a clearer understanding of reality. The basic tenets of the Upanishads—the need to acquire self-knowledge and thereby liberate oneself from wordly bondages—resound through all subsequent confrontations of the Indian mind with the circumambient world.

With the passage of time, a number of non-Vedic philosophical traditions sprang up. The Charvakas placed heavy emphasis on the material world and discarded all notions of transcendentality. Jainism was another tradition of philosophy which was non-Vedic in character. It maintains that both the animate world and the inanimate world are eternal and independent. In accordance with this world view, the Jains developed a logic which upheld the multifaceted nature of reality and the diversity of viewpoints.

Buddhism, another non-Vedic philosophy, constitutes a powerful reaction against the ritualism that characterized the Vedas and the transcendentalism that was associated with the Upanishads. The individual, according to Buddhism, should diligently work out his salvation, that is liberation from pain and suffering, through right knowledge and right living.

Later, Indian philosophy began to move further and further away from the original ways of thinking and, indeed, split into different and competing systems. Although these systems do not by any means constitute mutually exclusive categories, they display sufficient variation to warrant autonomous conceptual status. Of these, there are six that repay close attention. They are the Nyaya, Vaisheshika, Sankhya, Yoga, Mimamsa, and Vendata and Advaita. These schools, too, contributed mightily to the formation of the Indian mind.

This rapid survey of Indian philosophy should underline one important fact; it is by no means monolithic. There were at different periods varying categories of philosophical thinking that were competing for claim on men's imagination and allegiance. Therefore, to talk glibly of the Indian philosophical tradition is obviously inappropriate and inconsistent with the facts as we know them. However, in the consciousness of the people, these diverse philosophical schools (many of which, of course, display a remarkable affinity to each other) have intermingled and contributed to the formation of a "tyrannizing image." Research studies of social anthropologists in Indian culture certainly lend support to this contention. This guiding image, given India's ethnic and religious diversity, is not one that is adhered to by the totality of the population, but it is certainly one that is endorsed by a very large and significant segment.

EIGHT GUIDING PRINCIPLES

Now let us examine in little more detail the guiding image of Indian culture that I have been referring to so far. To my mind, it is indeed a composite that consists of eight constituent elements which emphasize respectively the following themes:

1. Idealism
2. Renunciation and nonattachment
3. Oneness of things
4. Illusions
5. Liberation
6. Nonindividuality
7. Transtemporality
8. Intuition

The traditional Indian attitude toward life is largely shaped by an idealistic strain which has its historical roots in the Upanishadic speculations. By idealism is here meant a philosophy which enforces the point that spiritual values have a determining voice in the ordering of the universe. It is indeed true that during certain periods in the evolution of Indian speculative thought, there were some schools like that of the Charvakas for example, which were inclined to hold up materialism. However, they in no way entered the mainstream of Indian philosophy, and they failed to exercise a palpable impact on the consciousness of the people. It is only fair to say that with the belief in an eternal order, a transcendental reality and the illusiveness of the phenomenal world goes hand-in-hand with the idealistic world view that has come to be so closely associated with the Indian mind.

Closely linked to this propensity is the notion of renunciation and non-attachment. This is indeed a highly cherished Indian cultural ideal. It is almost ascetic in its connotations. A measure of man's greatness, to the orthodox Indian mind, is not what he acquires but what he renounces. It is a firmly held conviction, reinforced by centuries of ratiocination, that desire leads to frustration. Hence, the various Indian philosophies sought to eliminate desire, which was deemed the source of frustration, by upholding the virtues of nonattachment. Words such as austerity, self-sacrifice, charity, asceticism, and renunciation figure prominently in the philosophical and religious lexicon of the Indians.

Another vital component of the Indian guiding image is the belief pertaining to oneness of things. The pivotal concern of Hinduism is to establish the oneness of reality and to indicate the mechanisms through which individual human beings could realize it. In Hinduism the supreme ideal toward which one should strive is the identification with the Brahman. Brahman is neither a personal being nor an impersonal concept. It points to a state in which all distinctions are obliterated and oneness is achieved. Traditional Hindus identified two modes of Brahman, Nirguna and Seguna. Nirguna Brahman, or Brahman without qualities, is the transcendent and indeterminate state of being regarding that nothing can be positively affirmed. Saguna Brahman, or Brahman with qualities, is Brahman as interpreted and affirmed by the mind from its necessarily limited standpoint. In the one, all distinctions are obliterated and overcome; in the other, they are integrated (Deutsch, 1968). In either case, it is indeed the oneness that is indisputably established.

A notion that flows from this is that of interconnectedness of things. To the traditional Indian mind, all events and phenomena and beings are interlinked in a way that forms a composite whole. To treat them as discrete entities, as Westerners tend to do, is alien to the Indian spirit. Very often, in our day-to-day lives, we tend to divide the world into separate entities—things, events, phenomena, etc. Although for practical purposes such a division can prove to be useful, Indian philosophers tell us that at a higher ontological level they are all linked to one another and that they can be meaningfully understood only in relation to one another.

To the Indian mind shaped by tradition and cultural memory, the world is indeed an illusion, but here one has to be extremely circumspect in the use of the term "illusion" (*maya*). It does not really mean that the world is an illusion so much that our point of view that supports the contention that the forms and structures is an illusion. Very often we tend to think of the forms and structures in the phenomenal world as realities of nature rather than as products of our mind, which delights in categorization. By *maya* or illusion is meant the mistake of regarding these categorizations and conceptualizations as the reality itself. This, as Bohm shrewdly points out, has interesting implications. As he says:

> . . . in the East the notion of measure has not played nearly so fundamental a role. Rather, in the prevailing philosophy in the Orient, the immeasurable (i.e., that which cannot be named, described or understood through any form of rea-

son) is regarded as the primary reality. Thus, in Sanskrit (which has an origin common to the Indo-European language group) there is a word "matra" meaning "measure," in the murical sense, which is evidently close to the Greek "metron." But then there is another word "maya" obtained from the same root, which means "illusion." This is an extraordinarily significant point. Whereas to Western society, as it derives from the Greeks measure, with all that this word implies, is the essence of reality, or at least the key to this essence, in the East the measure has now come to be regarded commonly as being in some way false and deceitful. (1980, pp. 22–23)

The implications of this attitude of mind are, no doubt, great.

The idea of liberation (*moksha*) is another important facet of the Indian guiding image. As all Indian philosophers unambiguously demonstrate, the ultimate goal of human effort is the liberation from worldly bondage. Almost all Indian philosophers have had a tendency to commence their work by drawing attention to the causal chain of actions which result in liberation. As Potter (1963) points out, every man is faced with challenges arising from his relationship with impersonal objects and people in business, with objects that are highly cherished, and with close friends. Every time we become conscious of these challenges, we are compelled to recognize the inadequacies in our responses to these challenges which constantly trouble us. According to the traditional Indian philosophers, these inadequacies are reflective of our bondage (Hocking, 1968).

The concept of the individual that is mirrored in Indian culture is strikingly different from that found in Western cultures. In the West, the idea of the individual clearly permeates every facet of society. Furthermore, there is the assumption of the potential individuality. As Hocking (1968) remarks, it is the peculiarity of the West that it assumes individuality as potentially present in the human infant and even in the embryo, wholly apart from any manifestation of capacity to contribute to an "individual" point of view to the judgment of experience. On the other hand, the Indian conceptualization of the individual is totally different. Indian metaphysics does not admit a multiplicity of individuals. To think of individuals along those lines is to succumb to an illusion. The ultimate reality, which is Brahman, is undifferentiated and absolute. As was stated earlier, the supreme ideal of the Hindus is to identify and merge with the absolute. This leaves very little room for the concerns of separate individuals.

The concept of personality that finds expression in classical Sanskrit literary works tends to further strengthen this view. In a typical lyric of a Western poet, say that of Wordsworth, it is the personality of the poet that emerges with increasing vigor and overwhelms us. But in the case of a poet like Kalidasa who exemplifies admirably the quintessence of Indian culture, the personality of the poet does not draw attention to itself. Only a sense of transpersonality makes its presence felt (Dissanayake, 1981).

The attitude to time is another important dimension of Indian metaphysics that invites close scrutiny. It is held that representations of time are essential components of social consciousness whose structure reflects the rhythms and cadences which mark the evolution of society and culture. Indeed, the mode of perception of time is indicative of basic trends of society. Time seems to occupy a central place in the "model of the world" characterizing a given culture (Gurevich, 1976). What is the primary attitude to time as sanctioned by traditional Indian culture? One can, on the authority and testimony of classic treatises on philosophy, religion, and literature say that the Indian conceptualization of time is one of cyclicity. By that is meant the belief in perennial and eternal return. It has been remarked that the identification of time with cyclicity and unreality appears to have contributed to such distinguishing aspects of Indian thought as the depreciation of any metaphysical content to history and the eternal repetition of a basic cosmic rhythm (Fraser, 1975). According to the traditional Indian world view, the only way of escape from the human predicament is to escape from temporality. Many of the Indian thinkers were preoccupied with the formulation of strategies that would permit the escape from the inexorable force of time into timelessness. Hence, one is justified in saying that an attitude of transtemporality animates much of Indian speculative thought.

Finally, the question of inwardness and intuition is important. The desire for inwardness is indeed a distinguishing characteristic of the Indian habit of mind. This, of course, stands in sharp contrast to the Western habit of mind. While the Western mind sought to conquer nature and as a consequence succeeded in producing the stupendous technology that continuously overwhelms us, the Indian mind was engaged in the no less exciting task of conquering itself, hence, the emphasis on such self-conquering techniques and strategies as meditation and yoga.

This inwardness and the stress on intuition are intimately linked. It is said that intuition enables men to comprehend reality directly in its totality. While in the West, great store was set by reason and logic, Indians chose to stress the intuitive capacity in man. Human language, they felt, was inadequate to comprehend reality as it was anchored in a phenomenal experience of plurality; similarly, human logic which is based on human experience is inadequate to comprehend a transcendental reality, hence, the emphasis on intuition. In the Mundaka Upanishad it is said, "To know Brahman is to be Brahman." In other words, to know the highest reality one has to *be* that highest reality. In this arduous endeavor logic and reason are of minimal significance because they have the effect of separating knowing from being. It is only the direct experience through intuition that ensures the nonseparation of knowing from being.

These, then, to my mind, are the constitutive elements of the Indian tyrannical image. Clearly, one can add to this list or collapse some of the categories to broaden typologies. However, it seems to me that in any reckoning the characteristic features that I have sought to delineate are indeed fundamental. They go to form the Indian guiding image. As Radhakrishnan remarks:

> . . . since philosophy is a human effort to comprehend the problems of the universe, it is subject to the influence of race and culture. Each notion has its own characteristic mentality, its particular intellectual bent. In all the fleeting centuries of history, in all the incissitudes through which India has passed, a certain marked identity is visible. It has held fact to certain psychological traits which constitute its special heritage and they will be the characteristic marks of the Indian people so long as they are privileged to have a separate existence. (Radhakrishnan, 1927)

The characteristic Indian features that have been discussed are a part and parcel of that distinct Indian mentality that is being referred to by Radhakrishnan.

A study of the Indian guiding image that I have sought to portray is essentially a spiritual one. As Radhakrishnan says, philosophy in India is essentially spiritual, and the spiritual motive dominates life in India. This spiritual image has exercised a profound influence on the thought, imagination, and behavior of the Indian people. Radhakrishnan makes the observation that

> Throughout the history of Indian thought the ideal of a world behind the ordinary world of human strivings, more real and more intangible, which is the true home of the spirit has been haunting the Indian race. (Radhakrishnan, 1927)

IMPLICATIONS FOR AN INDIAN THEORY OF COMMUNICATION

What implications does this guiding image of Indian culture have for communication theory? To my mind, on the basis of this image, we can construct a model of communication which is essentially Indian, and which differs substantially from the manipulative and transactional models found in Western culture.

In this Indian model, the primary focus of interest is how does the receiver make sense of the stimuli that he receives so as to deepen his self-awareness. In the two generic Western models, the basic questions that present themselves are how does the communicator affect/influence/ manipulate the receiver and how does the communicator and receiver share information and enter into a two-way relatinoship. According to the traditional Indian views, meaning should of necessity lead to self-awareness. Hence, the Indian definition of communication would be that it is an inward search for meaning.

The concept of meaning endorsed by the classic Indian thinkers is radically different from the concept of meaning favored by Western thinkers. In the West meaning is seen as the thing that is conveyed or signified largely through language. This notion is, obviously, tied to a certain model of communication which is Western in form. Here communication is seen as the transference of meaning with the intention of influencing the receiver, but, according to the Indian concept, meaning is that which transcends language. The Western conception of meaning maintains that meaning is inextricably linked to language. This is, indeed, a crucial difference. One can, with a large measure of justification, say that the manipulative and transactional models of communication are language-centered models, while the Indian model that I am presently delineating is language transcending and centered on meaning.

Speaking of meaning, we need to take note of another dimension which is central to the classic Indian conceptualization. Meaning, according to traditional Indian thought, was seen as a process leading to self-awareness, then to freedom, and finally to truth. Here by freedom was meant the liberation of worldly bondages consequent on the perception of the illusoriness of the world and the comprehension of the artificial categories constructed all around us by language and logic.

Another significant point of divergence between the Indian and the Western models is that the Indian model focuses attention on the intrapersonal dimension as opposed to the interpersonal dimension. In Western models, intrapersonal communication leads to interpersonal communication, but in the Indian model interpersonal communication is secondary to intrapersonal communication. However, the Indian conceptualization does not stop at that. It asserts that if communication is to be truly functional, intrapersonal communication must lead to a transpersonal communication in which oneness of the world is unambiguously perceived. This is a significant difference which marks it off from the Western models.

The Indian model of communication that is linked to the guiding image of Indian culture is different in another aspect too. While the manipulative and transactional models place emphasis on the expressive element, the Indian model stresses the receptive element. To put it differently, the Western model is expression oriented; the Indian model is interpretation or reception oriented. The proponents of the Indian model seem to suggest that what is important in human communication is to find out how a receiver makes sense of the verbal stimuli that is received and engages in a search for meaning. This search is an inward one. The traditional authorities maintain that the reality is indeed within man. According to this model, to know it is to be. In other words, there is no distinction between the knower and the known.

This strand of thinking calls attention to another important element in the model: It is a function of communication to escape the conceptual frameworks erected by logic and language. So long as it is maintained that we operate within the conceptual frameworks erected by language, we will not be able to see the reality. It is only by abdicating the artificial categories set up by language that man is able to achieve freedom and realize truth.

According to the Indian view, the realization of truth is facilitated neither by language nor by logic and rationality. It is only intuition that will ensure the achievement of this objective. To know is to be; to know is to become aware of the artificial categorization imposed on the world by language and logic. It is only through an intuitive process that man will be able to lift himself out of the illusory world, which, according to the Indian viewpoint, is indeed the aim of communication. Therefore, if the Western models of communication are ratiocination-oriented models, the Indian one is intuition oriented.

These, then, are the metaphysical underpinnings of the Indian model. In this paper, I am not concerned with the model's practical implications. However, it needs to be pointed out that one cannot understand present-day Indian communicative behavior solely in the light of this model. It is interesting to ponder what the consequences of this guiding image of the culture are on contemporary communicative behavior, especially in view of the fact that modern Western influences have exerted such a disruptive influence on the fabric of Indian society.

CHAPTER 12

Communication in India: The Tenets of *Sadharanikaran*

J. S. Yadava

INTRODUCTION

The importance of information and education in mobilizing people and seeking their willing cooperation and participation in political and socio-economic development is well recognized. Mass education and people's participation were the pillars on which the "father of the nation," Mahatma Gandhi, successfully built the freedom movement. After Independence the concern about reaching the people and communicating with them was reflected in various plan documents. As a result, over the years, all the available methods of communication have been developed and strengthened. But even after 40 years of planning, mass communication continues to be essentially an urban phenomenon. The mass media are not only urban based but urban biased as well. Owing to low literacy and poor purchasing power, the reach of mass media in India is rather limited.

Despite recent technological advances, the reach of the mass media systems to the people of India is inadequate. Furthermore, when communication is viewed from the perspective of the five tenets of *Sadharani-*

karan, the quality of communication by means of modern mass media becomes questionable. After a discussion of the historical and traditional foundations of communication in India, we will present a perspective toward communication developed by Bharat Muni in the second century B.C. and then describe one of the ways that this form of communication persists throughout Indian today, especially in the rural villages.

TRADITIONAL COMMUNICATION SYSTEMS

Indian society is often characterized as one of "unity in diversity" and its villages as "independent republics." These characterizations have important implications for the patterns of human communication in India.

In ancient India, a large number of cultures blossomed in different parts of the Indian subcontinent, to an extent unique and independent of each other, yet deriving strength and inspirations from what is often referred to as the "great Indian tradition" and, in turn, contributing toward a pan-Indian cultural mosaic. This was achieved, despite poorly developed means of transportation, through the long established oral traditions of "communication specialists" dealing with the problems of both day-to-day life on earth and life after death.

At the regional and national levels the communication tasks were performed by roving saints and *sufies.* They propagated the gospels of eternal truth as provided in *Vedas, Puranas,* epic stories like *Ramayana* and *Mahabharata,* and other scriptures, reinterpreted in the context of contemporary realities. In the process they succeeded in communicating the norms and values for proper social behavior on the part of the common man, the only means by which he/she could make progress toward his/her salvation—the ultimate aim of life.

At the micro or community level there existed, and exists even today, *Brahmins,* a class of knowledgeable people who enjoyed the highest social status in the caste system of hierarchical division of labor. They played an effective role in the communication process at the community level serving as "link persons" between the common man of their own community and knowledgeable persons outside.

Village communities were self-sufficient in most, but not all, of their day-to-day requirements. Each had strong and extensive cultural links with the outside world but relatively weak economic and commercial links, usually not extending much beyond neighboring villages and towns. Administrative contacts were minimal, largely confined to revenue collections. Even this task was performed through intermediaries such as the *Nawabs, Zamindars,* and *Lambardars.*

Thus, in ancient or traditional India, there existed effective systems of communication which were both local and pan-Indian in character. All of these systems of communication linked the worldly human being with "other wordly" concepts and ideas by means of a strong deductive logic but with weak or no empirical evidence. Such communication provided meaning and justification for the social norms and order propagated and maintained here on earth. It inculcated the spirit of devotion, love, and blind faith rather than rationality based on empirical evidence.

Indian society was highly stratified and hierarchical. Communication tended to flow along the prevailing societal grooves from persons with higher status to persons with lower status. In any communication situation, the relationship between the source and the receiver was that of dominance and subordination. In spite of this there was some dialogue between the two. Both shared a common frame of reference which made communication smooth and effective, but the speaker was held in high esteem by the listener, a relationship highly idealized and romanticized in the *guru–chela* relationship. Guru was viewed as an authority figure giving "good," "right," and only "proper" messages. The listener was viewed as a subordinate figure receiving proper information, learning, and adopting prescriptions. The element of coercion was not totally absent in such relations, but one of the major functions of communication in those days was to precondition the listener to accept such a relationship as natural and proper. The speaker was viewed as a repository of wisdom and truth. In other words, the emphasis in communication was on reinforcing stability, order, and social harmony rather than individual well-being, progress, and change in general.

THE CONTEMPORARY PERSPECTIVE

With the advent of the British rule in India, along with the increase in administrative links and physical mobility through rails and roads, a new philosophy and culture through Christian missionaries and Macaulay's education system started making inroads into traditional Indian society and culture. The two were incompatible in many ways. As the communication of foreign concepts, ideas, and philosophies became successful, so the conflicts between the Indian and British systems and interests became evident. As a consequence, there were upheavals, turmoils, and ultimately the birth of independent India, under the leadership of Mahatma Gandhi—a master communicator.

It is well neigh impossible to sum up the Gandhian approach to communication in a few sentences. Essentially, Gandhi identified himself with the masses, turning his personal experience into public programs, adopting a simple style and language, and using parables, proverbs, and quotations from the *Bhagavad Gita,* the *Ramayana,* and other sacred books. His salt *satyagraha* is an excellent example of communicating effectively with masses. He communicated instantaneously to millions of people his opposition to foreign rule (a rule that controlled even the daily consumption of salt) and hence the need for home rule. "Gandhi's communication style succeeded in unlocking the door to the hearts of the people" (Singh, 1980, p. 39).

Free India has adopted democracy based on universal adult franchise. As a welfare state it has opted for planned development. These characteristics and its membership in the world community and participation in the technological revolutions of the twentieth century have significant bearings on the communication patterns of modern India. The technological developments, increase in both personal and impersonal communications, and increases in the scale of economic activities have enlarged the range of choices. The philosophy of equality, irrespective of caste, creed, and religion and the compulsions of democratic elections at all levels— village *panchayats* to the Parliament—help to undermine the traditional dominant/subordinate relations at the same time they contribute meaning to the choices opened up in free India.

Communication is no longer confined to religion and social norms, maintaining only order and stability in society. Communication is helping to bring about change and progress as well. The speaker is often still viewed as an authority figure, particularly in rural areas and the listener as a subordinate, but the basis of such a relationship does not go unchallenged. Reports of social tensions from different parts of the country are symptomatic of this change. At the same time, there are situations (among urban educated elites, for example) where communication patterns are more on a basis of equality. Communication is no longer viewed only as a means to stability and harmony but for change as well. Thus, communication in India has become a varied and complex phenomenon. A careful study of communication processes in India raises many questions, interesting hypotheses, and theoretical formulations, which provide quite a challenge to communication scholars today.

INDIAN COMMUNICATION PHILOSOPHY

The earliest known attempt to document communication philosophy in India was made by the sage, Bharat Muni (1967), in his monumental work

Natyashastra. Its precise date is not known. Some put it in second century B.C., while others attribute it to the first century A.D. Baharat Muni codified the principles of human expression. Besides giving practical descriptions of various aspects of dance and drama to the minutest detail, he expounded theories of human communication. Ever since, *Natyashastra* has continued to serve as a fountainhead for Indian arts. In ancient Indian, *Natya* (drama) and *Nrtya* (dance) were intimately linked and closely developed art forms (Vatsyayan, 1968). According to Bharat Muni the purpose of *Natya* and *Nrtya* is to give instruction for orderly public behavior and to entertain the people. Further, he thought that these art forms dealt with the daily life of common men. Through these art forms and human social behavior, his feelings and his environment are depicted with a view to entertain and instruct the audience about proper behavior for the larger social good (Gargi, 1966, p. 13). In other words, Bharat Muni, besides codifying speech, sentiments, gestures, costumes, and other aspects of *Natya* and *Nrtya* art forms, was essentially concerned with human expression and communication. He was the first sage to expound communication philosophy in India.

There is a legend that *Natyashastra,* also known as fifth *Veda,* was written by Bharat Muni for the common man. He condensed the essence of the four *Vedas* relevant to common man's day-to-day life and put it in a form appropriate for his comprehension. This fifth *Veda* is about art as a means of understanding the Absolute and attaining *Ananda,* or pure bliss. The whole purpose of art—music, dance, drama—in Indian philosophy is to help the audience achieve a state of bliss and joyful harmony (Anand, 1969, p. 34).

The term *Sadharanikaran,* literally meaning simplification, has been used for the communication philosophy expounded in *Natyashastra,* which simplified the complex ideas and philosophy of the four *Vedas* for the common people. It is not certain whether Bharat Muni used the term *Sadharanikaran* as such, but in the tenth century A.D., Bhattanayak is credited for use of the term *Sadharanikaran* in his commentary on *Natyashastra* to explain *sutras* related to *Rasa,* that is, feelings (Bhattanayak, in Verma, 1958, pp. 35–37). According to Bhattanayak, the essence of communication is to achieve commonness or oneness among the people. Some scholars after Bhattanayak, such as Vaman Zalkikar and Govinda Thakur (15 A.D.) also considered *Sadharanikaran* as a word for establishing commonness. Later this word was extensively used for explaining the aesthetic aspects of poetry in literary circles. Today *Sadharanikaran* is often employed to convey the idea of commonness and simplification.

THE FIVE TENETS OF *SADHARANIKARAN*

Being *Sahridayas*

In *Natyashastra,* Baharat Muni enunciated a philosophy for communication or *Sadharanikaran.* The most important postulate in the process of *Sadharanikaran* is that it can take place only among *Sahridayas,* that is, those having a common sympathetic heart. *Sahridayas* is perhaps a poetic expression used for those having a common cultural orientation. *Sahridaya* is not coterminous with predisposition in favor or against. It is much more than a mere personality characteristic (Tewari, 1980).

Rasa Utpathi

Bharat Muni also postulated that for *Sadharanikaran* to take place, *Sthai Bhava,* that is, permanent moods in the audience, have to be aroused which will result in the unleashing of the attendant *Rasa,* feelings or aesthetic pleasure, thereby completing the process of communication. He identified the following nine permanent moods or *Sthai Bhavas* and the resultant quality of response, the attendant *Rasa* or feelings relevant to human communication:

Sthai Bhava (Permanent Mood)	*Rasa* (Aesthetic Pleasure)	
Snigdha	Sringara	(Erotic)
Bhayanaka	Bhayanaka	(Furious)
Hrsha	Hasya	(Laughter)
Dina	Karuna	(Compassion)
Vismita	Adhbhuta	(Wonderous)
Krodhi	Raudra	(Odious)
Drpta	Veera	(Heroic)
Jugipsta	Bibhatsa	(Terrible)
Sant	Sant	(Peaceful)

It is evident that the emphasis in *Sadharanikaran* is on emotional arousal which is understandable in the context of drama and dance, the primary concern of *Natyashastra.* According to Bharat Muni, the emotional arousal and feeling of *Ananda* (harmony and bliss) are the ultimate purposes or aims of all communication. *Rasa utpathi,* the state of arousal of aesthetic pleasure or response among those involved in communication, indicates that *Sadharanikaran* has taken place. In other words, *Sadharanikaran* is more than mere transaction or transfer or exchange of messages. It means total invovlement of those participating in communicative events and the sharing of cultural experiences and achieving of commonness among them.

Rasa Swadan

One can find parallels in Bharat Muni's concept of *Sadharanikara* and Aristotle's concept of *Rhetoric*. Of course, Aristotle's thoughts and writings have been extensively researched and interpreted by philosophers and scientists, but hardly any study of Bharat's contribution to the understanding of communication has been done. Both systematized the art of communication in their respective cultural contexts.

There seem to be some basic differences in their approaches. Aristotle viewed rhetoric as inherently persuasive. Bharat Muni veiwed *Sadharanikaran* as pleasurable responses, *Rasa Swadan,* through arousal of *Sthai Bhava,* permanent mood(s) leading to harmony and bliss (*Ananda*). In rhetoric, the communicator tries to persuade the receiver through dialogue and debate. In *Sadharanikaran* the communicator communicates with the receiver/audience with the help of speech, gestures, and other visuals, which are essential parts of dramatics. The message is conveyed, and there is response on the part of the receiver. The receiver is not passive, but the response is not necessarily in the form of dialogue or argument. The receiver not only accepts the message willingly but in the process derives genuine satisfaction and pleasure or *Ananda*. He communicates this back to the communicator as well.

Bhattanayak stated that when a reader or spectator acts to receive the sum and substance of a poem or a play, the difference between "I" and "Others" diminishes in his heart. This peculiar situation ultimately leads to *Rasa Swadan* (feeling and enjoyment of *Rasa*) among *Sahridayas*. The process in which this peculiar situation takes place is known as *Sadharanikaran* (Bhattanayak). Therefore, for *Rasa Swadan, Sadharanikaran* is a must. Thus, *Sadharanikaran* involves much more than mere persuasion.

Asymmetrical

The *Sadharanikaran* theory of communication seems to suggest that communication is linear but not necessarily unidirectional. It may be two-way. Although the purpose of *Sadharanikaran* is to achieve commonness or oneness, the process itself is *asymmetrical*. There is more flow of communication from source to receiver. Thus, in some way it sounds similar to "mechanistic" models of communication. Schramm's postulation of two-way communication is also essentially linear and unidirectional. The source and the receiver change roles giving only the impression of two-way communication (Schramm and Roberts, 1971).

To overcome this difficulty and to represent communication as a truly two-way process, the idea of "conveyor belt" has been introduced by some scholars of communication (B. A. Fisher, 1978). No doubt, such a formulation is an improvement over earlier mechanistic conceptualizations of the communication process and is representative of communication situations in Western societies where sources and receivers in communication would be served by a channel for message/feedback. This can be visualized as a conveyor belt.

It is assumed that the conveyor belt is equally strong all along the line; otherwise it will break, which is a fallacy. This may be true to an extent in Western societies where sources and receivers, at least in principle, talk or communicate as equals, but in Indian society, they are *not* equals. The source is viewed as higher and the receiver as lower in status. The relationship is a hierarchical one of dominance and subordination. The source is held in high esteem by the receiver of communication, a relationship idealized and romanticized in the *guru-chela* relationship. Even though the source and the receiver are unequal, they are *Sahridayas,* having a common cultural orientation, which makes even their unequal relationship/communication satisfying and pleasurable to both parties.

The asymmetrical aspect of *Sadharanikaran* contributed to the blossoming of Indian civilization through efficient communication and division of labor. This was, however, later taken to the level of absurdity, resulting in a highly rigid and hierarchical society. To some extent, it made Indian society into a more or less closed system and thereby contributed toward its stagnancy and decay. It is true *Natyashastra* was written by Bharat Muni to simplify the complex *Vedas* for the benefit of the common man and thereby bridge the gap between the elites, learned priests, and nobles, who could understand the *Vedas,* and the poor ignorant *Sudras.* However, with the passage of time, *Sadharanikaran* resulted in contradictory consequences, that is, further differentiation of society and the institutionalization of differences.

Sadharanikaran, through asymmetrical communication over a period of time, contributed toward the development of more or less permanent and rigid asymmetrical social relationships, as reflected in the caste system. Not only that, it seems that the values supporting the asymmetrical nature of social arousal of permanent mood(s) (*Sthai Bhava*) and aesthetic pleasure in response (*Rasa Utpathi*) made them natural and acceptable as well as satisfying. This contributed to the continuity of the Indian caste system.

Today, to a great extent, the caste system influences communication patterns, particularly in Indian villages. Within a village community, far more communication takes place among the members of a caste than between castes because of the highly stratified and hierarchical nature of the caste system and attendant traditional norms of social commonality. People of "high" and "low" castes accept their position as natural. The asymmetrical relationship between "high" and "low" caste members is not only hereditary but also accepted even by those who are in a disadvantageous position on rational considerations as something natural and satisfying. This situation was even stronger in the traditional caste system.

It may be pointed out here that in India many other sages and saints in different time periods, like Bharat Muni, launched reform movements against social inequalities. They made attempts to further simplify and reinterpret Indian philosophy for the benefit of common people and thereby bridge the gap between elites and commoners that fight inequalities.

Simplification

There is yet another dimension of the *Sadharanikaran* theory of communication. In the process of *Sadharanikaran,* the complex concepts and ideas are simplified by the speaker (source) with illustrations and idioms appropriate to the understanding of the listeners (receiver of messages). This approach makes communication a dynamic, flexible, practical, and effective instrument of social relationships and control.

The roving saints and *sufies* popularized the complex religious and sociocultural concepts and norms by following the simplification and illustration approach of *Sadharanikaran* throughout the Indian subcontinent, thereby contributing toward emergence of a pan-Indian cultural mosaic. At the community level, Brahmins adopted a similar role of propagating religious ideas and cultural norms through simplification and exemplification. The rich tradition of folk form in India also served a similar purpose of popularizing the culture through the length and breadth of the country (Parmar, 1975).

As a matter of fact, this dimension of *Sadharanikaran* seems to have become a common heritage of the Indian people as is evident from the prolific usage of illustrations and idioms by rural folks to make a point in their day-to-day conversation.

THE INTERFACE TODAY

The nature and function of communication in gossip groups, a common feature of life in village India, illustrate the operation of *Sadharanikaran* in the day-to-day lives of the people. It is worthwhile to describe gossip groups in some detail in order to understand the communication process in India, particularly in the context of rural India.

By gossip groups, I mean groups of persons casually talking or discussing something. One generally finds such groups of people at convenient and strategic places, such as tea shops, street corners, and *baithaks* (men's quarters) of some influential and social persons in the village. They may be playing cards, puffing a *hooka,* taking tea, or just basking in the sun, but even so they are usually engaged in some sort of informal discussion. One person makes a point, someone strongly contradicts him, others support one view or the other expressed during the course of discussion or gossip session; occasionally all burst into laughter and then again proceed with their chitchat. They are *Sadridayas* having *Rasa— Swadan* through *Rasa—Utpathi.*

The composition of such gossip groups is not fixed, as persons join in or withdraw from it quite casually, but the process of gossip-group formation is not as casual as it may appear. The principles of social organization operate even in such informal gatherings, though with a certain degree of flexibility. Caste, kinship, and factional ties are important considerations in such gatherings for chitchat (J. S. Yadava, 1979, pp. 627–636). In the formation of such gossip groups, the asymmetrical dimension of *Sadharanikaran* comes into play.

Discussion in these groups could be on any subject under the sun. Topics may be society, economics, politics, religion, or sex and morality. Local, regional, national, or international affairs may be discussed, but more often, current issues form the substance of such discussions. Any new information, particularly a startling piece of news, is likely to be shared with others and become the topic for discussion.

The participants often cite folklore or other cultural stories to make their points, thereby simplifying difficult and complex ideas and concepts. This greatly facilitates the process of communication. Things expressed in cultural idioms and in terms of local experience are easy to comprehend and remember. Opinion leaders make full use of such gossip sessions (J. S. Yadava, 1971). They give their own interpretation of news and topics under discussion and try to influence other participants. In this manner, communication remains basically asymmetrical.

Thus, gossip groups play a very significant role in information processing and dissemination in the village social system and, hence, in the communication process in general. To an extent, they help to make up for the limited reach of mass media in rural India. They also provide an important interface between continuity and change in the social system. The interplay between cultural values and social structure, on the one hand, and communication linkages with the outside world and mass media, on the other, become most manifested in such "quasi-groups," and their study throws into relief the process of social and cultural change.

Viewed from a communication perspective, Bharat Muni and other saints and *Sufies* in ancient India, during the course of their reform movements, were attempting to energize the Indian social system by increasing the flow of information across the natural and social boundaries within the system. Each one of them, in his own way, was combating the tendency of the social system to become a system of fragmented and closed subsystems. From this perspective, the study of commmunication is the study of the structure, function, and evaluation of the Indian social system.

To conclude, though the term *Sadharanikaran* is no longer in current use as a concept to explain the communication processes in India today, it is still very enlightening. The basic tenets of *Sadharanikaran* are still valid today and are operating in the communication process, particularly in the context of rural India. However, with the spread of western philosophy and modernization, the asymmetrical tenet of *Sadharanikaran* and, hence, of social relationships no longer goes unchallenged.

CHAPTER 13

The Practice of *Antyodaya* in Agricultural Extension Communication in India

Abdur Rahim

To action alone hast thou a right and never at all to its fruits

—The *Bhagavadgita*

INTRODUCTION

Human communication processes in any society are largely governed by the communicative behavior of the people living in that society. This behavior is conditioned and cultivated over time by its cultural norms and traditional values. However, these norms and values themselves derive their strength and sustenance from the all-pervasive pressure of philosophical postulates that guide and inspire society. The validity of this statement is to be tested by examining the pattern of communicative behavior in the light of its cultural and philosophical underpinnings in India—a country which boasts of a philosophical and cultural tradition rooted in 4000 years of history.

HINDUISM AND INDIAN SOCIETY

India has often been described as a "land of myriad diversities," constantly exposed to internal and external cultural pressures which have either been absorbed or have led to the emergence of new structural relationships resulting in new aspirations and patterns of behavior. But throughout its history the distinctive features of the Hindu religion and philosophy with its concomitant culture have filtered the awareness and experiences of the overwhelming majority of the people who constitute this ancient country. As a system of religion and philosophy, Hinduism has shown and continues to show a remarkable ability to absorb and combine the most contradictory creeds which have had their origins at different stages of the system's social development. Due to its ability to accommodate dissimilar elements and to give them a relative measure of unity and integration, Hinduism has achieved a complexity and diversity which is probably unequalled in the history of mankind.

The Hindu religion and philosophy primarily deal with how man relates to his Creator (Brahman) and thereby becomes "one with reality." It is relevant here to identify the two most striking features of Hinduism. The first element is the "extraordinary interpenetration of the religious and the profane. Hinduism as a religion and Hindu social organization are so intimately interconnected that it becomes impossible to distinguish the sphere of the sacred from that of the social" (Kapp & Kapp, 1963a, p. 10). Indeed, the relation between the sexes, birth, death, the role of sons and daughters, occupation, the attitude toward work and its fruits, the meaning of freedom and salvation, man's relation to the physical world, including animals (particularly the cow), are all mediated by and integrated into an essentially religious system of vast cosmological proportions and regularities. As a result, Hindu culture must be regarded at the same time both as a religion and as a social system. This is important because it provides religious sanction to a number of facets in the social system which in modern society have become clearly secular in character.

The second important element in Hinduism is the fact that, with the exception of a small urban middle-class elite, the unit of action and the source of inspiration in Indian social life is not the individual but the group as represented by the extended family and the caste. Group membership shapes the aspirations and desires of the great majority of the people of India, and these group aspirations are in turn molded by the traditional patterns of behavior prescribed for the various status groups of Hindu society. The premium is on tradition-determined action. It is therefore evident that "caste, family and village exhibit strong elements of hierarchy. For this reason it is not surprising to find that the awareness of hierarchy is all-pervasive in Hindu life and thought" (Kapp & Kapp, 1963a, p. 8). Also, caste determines not only social status, it molds the behavior patterns of the group and its members. It regulates communications with not only a group's own members but members of other groups; it mediates the form and content of interpersonal relations and channels human affections. "Each caste is a complete society within a society, a kingdom within a kingdom. A caste has its own gods, its own temples, its council which regulates social behavior, its hereditary occupations and status, its own customs about food, dress and marriage" (Kapp & Kapp, 1963a, p. 8). However, far from seriously undermining the hierarchical structure of the system, castes "reinforce the villager's concept that rank and its prerogatives are important" (Mandelbaum, 1959, p. 147).

In all three of the main schools of Hindu thought, the primary focus of human communication was, unlike the Western concept of source-oriented communication, the *receiver*. The importance of the receiver–listener in the process of communication has always been the hallmark of Hindu philosophy.

One of the early descriptions of human communication in the classic Indian tradition is that of Bhartrhari (1971), the eminent poet–philosopher and grammarian, in his book *Vakyapadiya* written around the fifth century A.D.. His basic premise was that the etymological constructs of *vakya*, "sentence," and *pada*, "word," were imperative to cognition. Two of the major questions that Bhartrhari posed in his monumental work were how does a listener make sense of or construct a thought content out of the stream of sounds uttered by a speaker, and what does it mean for language to be the means of communication? His inquiries led him to conclude that the basic unit of meaning is the sentence.

After Bhartrhari, the best known exponent of Hindu philosophy was Shankaracharya in the seventh century A.D. His teachings embodied the cumulative wisdom of the *Vedas* and the *Upanishads*. The major thrust of his teachings was that the Almighty had given man his five senses and *Manas*, "mind," to perceive His presence inside the human body and outside in nature. Therefore, although there is nature all around and humans can perceive it, it is only illusion or *Maya* created by Brahman, the universal power, to test them. By exercising one's cognitive powers, one can know that power in himself as well as outside.

Perhaps Shankara's finest contribution is his description of the law of *Karma* (human destiny shaped by one's actions). He believed that Divine Power decided an individual's happiness or sorrow on the basis of what he had done in his previous life, whatever happened to the individual in his lifetime as the result of his actions in his previous birth. What he does now will have consequences in his next birth. If he wants to be happy in the next birth, he should do the right things in this life. He could even get out of the cycle of birth and rebirth and unite with the Divine by acquiring the right knowledge and understanding of the Self. No other philosophy or tenet in Hindu thought has so permeated the thought actions of the people of this country than the law of *Karma* which is merely an extended version of the eternal return posited by the cyclical concept of time and causation. In fact, viewed in this fashion, "rebirth and the transmigration of the soul appear not only cosmologically plausible and necessary, but may even be said to be a matter of cosmic justice or equitable retribution in nature. For evidently no one can escape or evade the good or evil consequences of his deeds" (Attreya, 1953, pp. 139–140).

Having examined the philosophical perspectives of Hinduism and the way it has colored the cultural ethos and the communicative behavior patterns of the people, it would be appropriate now to examine how these philosophical, cultural, and communicative underpinnings have affected the practice of communication in India, with particular reference to the role of agricultural extension.

AGRICULTURAL EXTENSION IN INDIA

India is a vast country with a population of over 760 million now. While 242 million of its people live in urban cities and towns, the rest of the 518 million live in the 570,000 villages that dot the rural hinterland. India has a close family structure, which, as stated earlier, plays a dominant role in society. Of the total 150 million families in the country, 48 million are urban, and over 102 million are rural families. Despite the growth of GNP during the past decade, India's population is unequally divided among the few rich and the poor masses. It would be evident that all the plans and growth strategies have failed to ameliorate the lot of these poverty-stricken sections of the population.

According to latest estimates given in the Seventh Five Year Plan (1985–1990) document, 36.9% or 280 million people live below the poverty line (less than $270 per annum income). In terms of families, 68 million families live below the poverty line in the country, of whom 15 million live in the urban areas and 53 million in the rural ares. It would be reasonable to say that the rich have become richer and the poor have become poorer, thereby increasing the gap between these two sections of the people.

Since Independence in 1947, Indian planners have largely believed that the best way to increase the pace of development of the masses is to concentrate on the agricultural front, because more than 70% of the population subsists on agriculture. Toward this end, India has been nursing different strategies for agricultural development, with a definite understanding of the role of communication in this process. Indian communicators, who were primarily concerned with broad overall strategies of development, have focused on political and social functions. Those with technical backgrounds and interests have given priority to ways of transmitting modern scientific and technical information.

> It is important to recognize that communication in agricultural development in India has operated within and to some extent been a prisoner of whatever was the dominant model of agricultural change at any given time. As models of agricultural development have expanded so have the strategies for making more effective use of communications media, methods and messages. (Kearl, 1975, p. 2)

The diffusion model was the first widely accepted view of how agricultural development occurs and how it can be promoted. More refinements were brought into this model by Wilkening (1949), Ryan and Gross (1943), and Beal and others (1957), to which a comprehensive summary was provided by Rogers and Shoemaker (1971). However, this model has run into strong opposition since its inception. First Frey (1952) suggested some important modifications followed later by a host of others, prominent among them being Beltran (1976) and Diaz-Bordenave (1976). Rogers (1983) himself has responded to these criticisms of the original model with modifications that treat communication as a process of convergence among members of interpersonal networks (Rogers & Kincaid, 1981).

Even Indian scholars found fault with the diffusion model. The most urgent and difficult problems to overcome in this diffusion model is its conception of communication as a one-way flow from source to receiver finally; a major source of disillusion with the diffusion model is traceable to its heavy identification with the mass media. "This was primarily an accident of ancestry: this model emerged in a western economy and society where a widespread mass media system existed" (Kearl, 1975, p. 9). It was pointed out by all these scholars that the diffusion model overlooked circumstantial, structural factors such as credit, marketing, and the land tenure system and that it benefited only that class of farmers who could afford the kind of technology and technique being promoted.

The World Bank launched an extension scheme in the developing countries based on the model evolved by Benor. The training and visit system of extension work gained a lot of publicity during the 1970s, particularly the "Model Farmer" approach, which helped the extension worker to succeed by focusing his attention on small groups of "receptive farmers." This naturally led to only a section of farmers getting the benefits of modernization and development, while the large mass of poor and marginal farmers went unnoticed.

The basic fallacy of all these models and approaches was the heavy dependence on the top-down flow of communication from the lab or research station through the extension agent to the receiver, farmers. This is basically a Western concept of communication flow, and it took its roots in the culture and philosophy of the "individual."

Nevertheless, the implementation of these models of extension did have an impact during the Green Revolution, particularly in the decade prior to 1980 when India nearly doubled its food production to about 135 million tons. Mass media have also been used for extension. The Farm and Home Broadcasts, started in 1966, provided educational and informational support to agricultural programs in the IADP districts. Over 75 of the 94 radio stations in the country were broadcasting these extension programs. The extension agent in the village coordinated the information received on the radio either in the Farm Listenership meetings or the now-defunct ubiquitous Radio Rural Forums. The Farm-School-on-the-Air also provided the same service to the extension agent in the village in terms of running educational and informational courses for farmers from 16 radio stations.

The *Charcha Mandals* also lent support to extension activities in the villages. During the Satellite Instructional Television Experiment (SITE) in 1975–1976 about 2330 villages in six states in the country were exposed to informational and educational broadcasts over television. The various studies on the SITE experiment have lauded the role of extension wherever they have been used. India is all set to launch its second multipurpose domestic satellite, INSAT I-C, in 1988 and telecast educational and informational programs over the satellite's vast television network. The extension agent plays an important role in the use of television for educational goals under INSAT.

However, despite all this, the case of agricultural extension is going by default due to its singular misdirections. According to the Asian Agricultural Survey of the Asian Development Bank, whose report was submitted in 1980:

> . . . Not only in India, but in most Asian countries, the role of the extension worker has not been clearly identified. It is frequently found that extension agents are more effectively used in facilitating the distribution of inputs, than in disseminating new concepts to farmers. They are being drawn increasingly into broader developmental programmes particularly those built around supervised credit. (Asian Development Bank Report, 1980, pp. 254–255)

This is to a large extent true of an extension scheme launched by the government of India. This scheme is going to be the focus of our attention when we try to correlate the law of *Karma* with its impact on people and their attitudes to certain cultural and communicative behavior patterns.

THE LAW OF *KARMA*

The law of *Karma* supports a general feeling of relative insignificance of human experiences within a given span as compared with the broader and infinitely more important problem of spiritual perfection and release by submission to one's *Dharma;* Due to this, renunciation, service, sacrifice, and austerity have continued to command the highest respect of the majority of the Hindus. These value orientations have found their purest crystallization in the following verse of the *Bhagavadgita* (Radhakrishnan, 1948, Chapter 3, verses 19–25):

> To action alone hast thou a right and never at all to its fruits; let not the fruits of action be thy motive; neither let there be any attachment to inaction. . . . seek out the poorest among you for the service and this deed will make karma reach a higher plain, for man attains the highest by doing this kind of work.

This law of *Karma* has been at the root of all actions in the lives of a majority of Hindus in India. This is also the philosophical backdrop to the extension scheme launched by the government in 1978–1979 called the *Antyodaya* (unto the last man in the line). The supposition is that by reaching out to the poorest among the poor, we will be able to reach out for the whole and work for the development of the whole. While earlier extension and communication schemes helped the middle and upper classes to seek the benefits of development, with this scheme the government, through the concept of group action on the basis of the family, is making efforts to raise the standard of living of the poorest among the poor in India. Mahatma Gandhi once said, "I wish to be in tune with the life of the poorest of the poor. Self-realization is impossible without identification of and service to the poorest."

Gandhi's reinterpretation of the ideal of disinterested action, as embodied in the advice of Lord Krishna in the *Bhagavadgita,* into any act of service to the poorest among the poor is significant in this respect. A noted Indologist pointed out two decades ago that "despite the teaching of Gandhi no successful effort seems to have been made by India's political and intellectual leadership to reinterpret the doctrine of action without desire for the fruits of one's labor so as to support an ethic of social action and of austerity of the wealthy in the interest of the poor among them" (Kapp & Kapp, 1963b, p. 45). The *Antyodaya* scheme of "reaching out to the weakest link in the chain" belies this assumption. The scheme has shown that the doctrine of action without the desire for reward is not antithetical to "the inner drive which harnesses the energies of man and makes him accept the discipline, orderliness and punctuality required for the highly differentiated tasks in modern industrial society" (Kapp &

Kapp, 1963b, pp. 45–46). To Western man, this seemingly inherent contradiction stems from his misinterpretation of the law of *Karma*. Most Western descriptions of this doctrine stipulate *Karma* in terms of fate or destiny, something which is inevitable. This is highly fatalist in nature. While in fact, *Karma* puts deeds and action before destiny—the actions in one's present life decide one's destiny in one's next birth. This interpretation is not only deterministic but intrinsically positive in its connotation. Reincourt (1960) puts this doctrine in its correct perspective when he says:

> Whereas the Bible seems to take a historical and almost sociological-hereditary viewpoint it announces that "the sins of the fathers shall be visited upon the sons," the Hindu has only himself or his *karma* to blame for his suffering. The individual's condition on this earth is presumed to be not even remotely related to the virtues and sins of parents and ancestors, or to society, past and present. It is exclusively connected with his individual "karma" and past incarnations: "Who did sin, this man or his parents, that he was born blind?" To this ever-renewed question, Indian thought replies unhesitatingly: "This man." (pp. 106–107)

It is therefore deeds which decide destiny. In this light the *Antyodaya* scheme provides the rustic villager the opportunity to do a good deed by service to the poorest among his people and thereby improve his *Karma*. A brief description of this scheme at this point will highlight the religious philosophical underpinnings of a communicative behavior as practiced in agricultural extension in India.

ROOTS AND FLOWERS OF *ANTYODAYA*

Since the middle of the 1970s, Indian socioeconomic thinking and action has taken a new dimension. It was postulated that not only should you have "growth with justice" but "growth through justice." It meant that welfare and the economic means of sustaining it should not only be better directed toward the poorer people but should be especially directed toward the poorest. This new thinking produced a new tool, *Antyodaya*, which literally means, "Unto the last man in the line."

In its essence the idea of *Antyodaya* is a very simple one: If a well has dried up you prime it by pouring a little water into it. Under this scheme, five of the poorest families in a village are selected in a meeting of all the people in the village. They then receive a fixed credit from institutional banks and a subsidy from the government to start them in occupations which would, in the course of time, pay back the bank as well as generate income for their subsistence. The relatively well-off people in the village help these *Antyodaya* families in their occupations, not only individually but as a group.

The extension agent publicizes the scheme in the villages, helps to identify the selected families, coordinates the issue of loans and subsidies to them, identifies and later services their chosen occupations, and channels the individual and group efforts of the rest of the villagers in aiding the *Antyodaya* families. The central theme of the extension agent is to *communicate* with the villagers about the need for ameliorating the lot of these "destitutes of society" through individual and group action. His strategy for this gains strength and sustenance from the doctrine of *Karma* and desireless action in the service of the poorest among them, for it is in consonance with the philosophy, religion, and culture of tradition-bound India.

Launched in 1978–1979, the scheme initially covered 2300 Development Blocks in Rajasthan, Gujarat, U.P. Bihar and Madhya Pradesh. The Antyodaya Scheme was renamed Integrated Rural Development Programme (IRDP) on October 2, 1980, and extended to all the 5011 Development Blocks in the country. During the Sixth Five Year Plan (1980–1985), which ended on March 31, 1985, as against the target of reaching 15 million families living below the poverty line, the IRDP assisted 16.562 million families. The number of scheduled caste and tribe beneficiaries alone was 6.463 million families. The total investment until the end of the Sixth Plan was Rs.4,762.78 crores, or $3670 million. For the first two years of the Seventh Five Year Plan the total IRDP investments (government subsidy and bank credit) amounted to Rs.2232 crores, or $1716 million. By the end of the Plan period in 1990 another 20 million families living below the poverty line are proposed to be assisted. The ultimate goal is to lift every poor family in India above the poverty line by the end of the century.

No doubt there have been innumerable problems and difficulties in the implementation of the scheme, right from the identification of the "poorest among the poor" families and leakages and misuse of loans to reluctance of these families to come out of the darkness of their destitution to receive this "water" for their "dried up wells" so that they can be primed for a better life. But even the usually critical media in India has extolled the scheme in no uncertain terms. The influential *The Economic Times* (1981) in an editorial said, "No other tool of Indian planning has devoted greater attention to distributive justice than the concept of the Integrated Rural Development Programme which provides for income-generating employment to the poorest of the poor in villages."

CONCLUSION

The *Antyodaya* scheme is a classic example of how India is attempting to integrate democratic and capitalistic principles of political organization with its own indigenous religious and philosophic tenets. It indicates how through the subjugation of individual prejudices and inclinations to a hierarchical, centralized, collectivist action, a *symbolic harmony* is being achieved, where the poorest among the poor at the bottom of the ladder are being helped on their feet. The actions of the rest of the villagers to help the poorest among them become part of their *Karma*.

Antyodaya relates the India of timeless tradition to the India that is now emerging, a tradition that is as old as civilization, to a new future in the postindustrial society. India has enormous staying power. Throughout its long history it has been an immensely vigorous place, creative, productive, changing, rising and falling, but always staying in business. It cannot just disappear into oblivion as many cultures have done in the past. Certainly one of the most exciting aspects of the contemporary world is the effort of this ancient culture, now about one-fifth of humanity, to come to its own terms with the twentieth century and to devise its own distinctively Indian solutions. As Nehru (1961) stated, ''We cannot discard the past for it is our strength. Nor can we live in it, steeped and surrounded by rituals. We must combine the best of both orders.''

What, therefore, behooves this ancient country, as it stands on the sword's edge of the present, is to take sustenance from its magnificent past and build its future on the bedrock of the all-pervasive, inevitable, and compulsive tools of modern technology.

PART II

PERSPECTIVES ON COMMUNICATION THEORY FROM THE UNITED STATES

Communication theory in the United States is currently in a very exciting state of development. Many of the conventional assumptions of just a decade ago are being challenged. We are witnessing a growing interest in work being done by scholars in Europe, Asia and the Pacific, South America, and Africa. Some are pursuing the unsettling issues of our field from a philosophical perspective. The recent trend is one of increasing diversity and fragmentation. This trend can be easily accounted for by the wide scope of communication as a phenomenon for study and by the rapidly increasing number of scholars dedicated to this topic compared to just 20 years ago. The papers of this section present some of these diverse points of view and provide the opportunity to examine them at one convenient crossroad.

The introductory paper by Klaus Krippendorff (Chapter 14, this volume) summarizes three of the main American paradigms of communication—the control, the network/convergence, and the information seeking paradigms—in order to establish a contrast to the new paradigm which he introduces, the paradigm of *autopoiesis,* derived from recent developments in theoretical biology. Autopoiesis is an organizing process of self-production, in which a living system's interactions continuously regenerate the network of processes that produced them in the first place. It is this type of autopoietic process which constitutes an organization as a concrete unit in space and time. This may be contrasted with an allopoietic organization process which produces something other than itself.

Autopoietic organizations are autonomous, maintain their own boundaries, are self-referential, and are not hierarchical. Applied to processes of communication and development, the emphasis is *within* organized communities rather than on influences originating outside. Two internal changes of interest are explored: changes in the *ecosphere* (matter–energy) and *noosphere* (patterns, information, knowledge). Professor Krippendorff's paper provides a valuable comparison of the four dominant ways of thinking about communication from the American perspective, and he introduces many new ideas on which to build better communication theories in the years ahead.

Professor Kincaid's paper (Chapter 15, this volume) presents the most recent developments in the network/convergence theory of communication. As originally defined, communication is a cyclical process of convergence in which participants create and share information, resulting in a more mutual understanding and agreement over time. This same sharing of information both generates and maintains communication networks comprised of regions of greater density characterized by less variance or less differences in beliefs, attitudes, and values within their local boundaries than between such regions. The unit of analysis shifts from the individual to the dyad, clique, or intact network and to the macrolevel of analysis of intact cultures or subcultures.

In this extension of the theory, Professor Kincaid conceptualizes communication as the fundamental self-organizing process of social systems. The network/convergence pespective is integrated into a single coherent theory of communication, organization, and culture by means of the direct application of the principles of nonequilibrium thermodynamics. The concept and measure of entropy is applied directly to the statistical distribution of beliefs, values, and behaviors of intact cultures and to the structure of their communication networks. This permits the develpment of a general mathematical model of communication, organization, and culture which is consistent with the network/convergence paradigm.

Donald Cushman's contribution (Chapter 6, this volume) is concerned explicitly with the ancient Aristotelian view that human intentions restrict individual behavior. As a teleological model of purposive human behavior, Professor Cushman's rules approach to human communication shares a key element in common with the autopoietic paradigm described by Professor Krippendorff but differs notably from the Galilean/Newtonian paradigm of human communication revealed in the initial paper by Professors Woelfel and Kincaid. The key difference is the shift from the presupposition that human behavior can be conceived from the position of a third-party observer as *motion* as opposed to viewing it primarily as human *action* based on intent and individual choice. The idea that action is something more than a simple physical process implies an even more basic presupposition, the characteristically Western belief in the separation of mind and body. Such a position is at the heart of the argument for the incommensurability of the theory and methods of the "natural" sciences and those of the "human" or "social" sciences.

The rules that generate both the meaning of symbolic information and patterns of human behavior are not imposed from the outside but, rather, are "conventional," generated by the participants themselves in a communication process of coordination in which the intentions or goals of participants can be achieved. The key component of human behavior in such a paradigm becomes the self-concept because of the cybernetic function that it serves in message comprehension, message adaptation, and communicator effectiveness.

The important role that rules play in the communication process can be revealed no more clearly than when members of one distinct culture interact with those of another. Each participant in this situation brings with them a distinct set of rules from their different experiences and some degree of knowledge of, and competence with, the rules of the other culture required for a successful intercultural interaction. It is this problem of communication competence which Barnett Pearce and Kyung-wha Kang consider in their paper (Chapter 17, this volume).

According to the "coordinated management of meaning" theory, there are two ideal types of competence involved in the acculturation process, satisfactory and optimal. Satisfactory competence occurs when a person functions totally *within* the logic of the other's rules system and is thus unable to see alternatives to the meanings and actions prescribed by that system. Optimal competence occurs when a person can control the extent to which she/he is enmeshed in either the other's or one's own culture. In the latter type, one is free to deviate from the conventions of that culture and act uniquely or appropriately to it. Professors Pearce and Kang illustrate this principle with reference to the difficulty of communication *between* a person who is performing under the assumptions of Western, Aristotelian logic and a person who is functioning under an Eastern, Taoist logic where apparent opposites may not be contradictory. Their comments on this problem have obvious relevance to all of the differences in communication theory between the East and West introduced in the present book.

Gerry Philipsen's approach to communication (Chapter 18, this volume) departs significantly from the standard American classification of communication into interpersonal, group/organizational, and mass communication. Basically, he recognizes a missing piece in this framework and provides that piece with "cultural communication." The emphasis in cultural communication is the balance between the forces of individualism and community. Cultural communication is the process by which a code is realized and negotiated in a communal conversation. It includes two components: *enactment,* the playing out and affirming of cultural forms, and *creation,* the creation, adaptation, and transformation of those forms to meet the contingencies of daily life.

It is a particular type of communication which provides members of a society a sense of shared identity which at the same time preserves individual dignity, freedom, and creativity. Three forms of communication—ritual, myth, and social drama—perform the cultural communication function. Societies can be compared in terms of their degree of emphasis on each of these cultural communication forms, and the personal, positional, and traditional types of cultures are differentiated by Professor Philipsen in terms of the three dimensions of elaboration, rhythm, and distance. Cultural communication represents a new line of inquiry in American communication theory, one which focuses on the *forms* of communication and their social functions as opposed to the usual attention given to sources, channels, messages, and receivers.

The constructivist approach to communication as developed by Jesse Delia and his colleagues (Chapter 19, this volume) is based on the principle that human behavior is organized according to the cognitive or interpretive schemes of its participants. A variety of such schemes have developed because of the different life experiences of the members of society, and several of these different schemes may operate simultaneously in any given interaction. They play an especially important organizing role at the levels of intention and strategy, and message structure. Thus, in the study of the development of communication competence, the constructivist approach places emphasis on the content and quality of the communication-relevant interpretive processes the individual has developed and the levels at which these processes provide control over behavior and understanding.

The concluding chapter by Joseph Woelfel and D. Lawrence Kincaid (Chapter 20, this volume) lays bare some of the central issues involved in the question of whether a *science* of human communication is possible. The issues, both pro and con, are presented in the form of a dialogue among three contemporary scholars, one a physicist and the other two social scientists, with names "conicidentally" identical to the three participants in Galileo's famous dialogue 350 years ago.

The first issue raised is the meaning of causality in Newtonian mechanics as opposed to its Aristotelian use. Common misundertandings are clarified during the course of the dialogue including the concept of mechanical (machine-like) causation as opposed to the concept of force in the science of motion (mechanics), "universal laws" as invariant mathematical relationships, free will, and the relationship between theory and measurement. Four general laws of human communication are posited during the course of the discussion: one on cognitive inertia, one on the acceleration of a cognitive element, one on the outcome of all communication, and finally, one on the relationship between the inertial masses of cognitive elements and their rate of convergence. Although three different sides are stated, the weight of the discussion falls decidedly on the side of a science of human communication modeled on the methods established by modern science. This is the Western tradition at its best, in stark contrast to many of the papers from the Eastern perspective.

CHAPTER 14

Paradigms for Communication and Development with Emphasis on Autopoiesis

Klaus Krippendorff

INTRODUCTION

In the following I describe four paradigms of communication relevant to social, economic, and political development of large social systems: the control paradigm, the network-convergence paradigm, the information seeking paradigm, and the autopoiesis paradigm. The first is largely what is practiced. The second is what is currently in vogue. The third is already implicit in some literature. The fourth needs further development and is depicted here in its infancy.

In giving an account of these paradigms, it is difficult to separate communication from development and to conceptualize some sort of dependence of one on the other. I believe communication and development are inseparable, conceptual twins. Both are imbedded in certain ideological modes of reasoning, and both play different roles relative to each other. The task of describing these paradigms is to link the roles of these concepts to particular systems of ideas relative to which they represent different types.

I feel obligated to add that these paradigms are not entirely free of individual values to which various researchers and/or social institutions interested in development subscribe. I too have preferences for explanatory structures in which I would feel more comfortable than in others. I believe such commitments are implicit in any intellectual pursuit and necessary consequences of how theory, methodology, and data codetermine each other in the stabilizing cycle involving the scientific observer and the observed.

THE CONTROL PARADIGM

The control paradigm goes back to Aristotle who described the process of communication as involving a speaker, the speech act, an audience, and a purpose. It is also traceable to another Greek idea, that of steersmanship. Although feedback was then unknown as a concept, it was clearly implied in the notion of teleology underlying both communication and steering. It sees someone in charge of a mechanism whose effects he desires.

Perhaps the earliest communicators having developmental aims in mind were Christian missionaries. When Livingstone traveled through Africa, bringing Western ideas with him, he knew exactly what development meant: conversion to Christianity, introduction of social forms of organization favorable to trade and to the spread of the British colonial empire. Communication was the means to development: the word of God wrapped into sermon, prayer, ritual, and a little bit of magic. These missionaries also conceived themselves as far superior to the people they chose to work with. The indigenous culture of these people was considered primitive, savage, and worthless in content.

Modern communication researchers no longer follow the steps of Christian missionaries, but they have largely retained their form of interaction and refined and generalized their logic. In the Lerner and Schramm (1976) conceptuion, purposive development reduces to a response to appropriately selected communications. To select appropriate communication implies

1. an external criterion for what development is, including how it could be measured;
2. prior knowledge of the receiver's responses to communications, sometimes improved under feedback conditions; and
3. the ability to produce and the power to impose the communications that will induce the desired change.

There are two important modifications of the paradigm. These are often considered antithetical to the above, but I think they are mere refinements of the underlying pattern of reasoning.

The diffusion of innovation approach to communication and development (Rogers & Shoemaker, 1971) and Rogers, 1983, for example) makes internal social structures responsible for the way development messages take effect. By describing indigenous forces as preventing the dissemination and utilization of information and by conceptualizing development in stages of adoption, the control that flows from the development agent is merely considered more indirect. The receiver of these communications is seen as reacting to and at best filtering, transforming, or even compensating for the messages intended to induce desired changes.

The *cultural imperialist* approach to communication and development (Schiller, 1976 and Nordenstreng & Schiller, 1979, for example) recognizes that news, entertainment, and communications technology is far from value free and that the massive production of communications, particularly in the United States with its pressure on and ability to capture and to dominate international markets, has the effect of setting developmental goals and aspirations surreptitiously, serving primarily Western imperialist intentions. Citing statistics on inequalities in production, on one-way flows of communications, and on the domination of mass media content by technologically advanced countries, the approach calls attention to the latent and exogenous effects of unrestricted information flows and of uses of Western communication technology. But by explaining them in terms of the interests served, the theories of development underlying this critique stay entirely within the control paradigm. According to this paradigm:

There is always a *controller* who knows what he wants and what he is up against, who has the means of affecting change, and whose interests are served by his actions.

Even so there may be feedback, the relationship between controller and controlled is *asymmetrical,* undemocratic, one-sided.

Feedback primarily allows the controller to correct his own actions.

Development is seen in a process of adapting the controller's environment to his goals which are extrinsic to that environment.

Meaning and information becomes equal to the persuasive force of communications, and is measured in terms of desirable (manifest) effects.

Research focusses on the properties of the individual receiver, of the mass audiences, or of the aid-receiving country. Interaction effects involving the outside controller are ignored.

The control paradigm is intermeshed with human rationality and is so persuasive that other modes of analysis are often dismissed as nonpurposive, irrational, or impractical. This paradigm is also supported by the structure of a mass communication technology that is predominantly one way and evaluated by its effects. Also the traditionally linear causal reasoning in the constructions of social theory supports this approach to development.

THE NETWORK–CONVERGENCE PARADIGM

The network–convergence paradigm removes the essential asymmetry from the control paradigm and expands on its limitation to two kinds of communicators by including many individuals, which are now seen as linked by a network of communication channels. These communicators alternate between being sender and receiver of messages and constantly engage in and adjust to the flow of information. Inequalities that may arise become a function of the *topology* of the network and are no longer a question of privilege or individual characteristics. The most important feature of the paradigm is its process orientation, making circular processes of communication and mutual causality primarily responsible for development. The network–convergence paradigm is rooted in (first order) cybernetics (Foerster, 1979) and systems theory and has also been called a systems approach to communication (see specifically Kincaid, 1979; Rogers & Kincaid, 1981).

In addition to seeing communication processees as circular (as opposed to one way) and the communicators as essentially democratic and participatory (not unequal to begin with), the network–convergence approach has focused attention to two important consequences of communication. First, as time progresses, interaction among communicators produces a kind of homeostasis. It converges to (and in some special cases also diverges from) individual states that are within limits mutually acceptable. In the course of this convergence, social relations between the communicators emerge.

Social psychologically it means the emergence of personal interdependencies.

Cognitively it means the reaching of mutual understanding, consensus or agreement.

Behaviorally it means the formation of collective or joint action.

Socially it means the genesis of structure and social organization.

I have shown elsewhere that the genesis (creation or emergence) of structure is inevitable under most conditions of communication (Krippendorff, 1971). Second, whatever happens in the course of such interaction, the joint outcome cannot be predicted from the individual properties of the communicators involved. Whereas in the control paradigm, the outcome can be explained in terms of the interests of the controller (individual, social class, institution, or system), the network–convergence paradigm relates it to the ongoing process of communication during which individuals adjust to each other and social relations emerge.

Dialectical theories of development employ similar mechanisms. We recall Hegel's notion of cognitive development as a continuous overcoming of thesis–antithesis contradictions by a synthesis which may invoke another antithesis at a future time. Marx, turning Hegel upside down, applied the idea to social development whereby contradictions (conflicts and oppositions) in society are overcome by new forms of organization and of systems of production which contain the seed of new contradictions. The process ultimately converges toward a society in which forces are balanced, mutual understanding is achieved, and the social structure becomes stable when it fulfills each and every individual's needs.

One important feature of the network-convergence paradigm is that participants communicate with each other on *the same logical level,* i.e., none has a perspective that is necessarily superordinate to that of another (as a controller has relative to the controlled). Even so positions within networks matter; neither individual nor group can therefore be seen as entirely in charge of the relationships to which the process converges.

In reality, the equality of social relationships can be maintained only in rather restricted subsystems in society, such as a small experimental group of individuals, a social club, or a computer conference. While individuals interact in such situations they may show convergence. After the experiment, meeting, or conference is over "metacontrols" decompose that group into its original parts, and convergence no longer takes place. Convergence presupposes that the pattern of interaction is invariant for a sufficiently long period in time (Krippendorff, 1971). Usually, components on a lower logical level have little place in the process either. For example artefacts, the product of collective activity, which often assume a life of their own and may ultimately condition if not break the relationships toward which the circular process has been converging, are outside the process and cannot be coped with by this paradigm. The network–convergence paradigm is thus *decontextualized* and restricted in scope. It ignores the role of various forms of technology and the human potential for introducing a structural or technological innovations.

Summarizing, according to this paradigm:

There are possibly *many communicators* involved with actions, purposes, and means of communication distributed over these.

All participants *are on the same logical level*. While individual differences are thereby not denied, the relationship is essentially democratic (each puts his own weight into the process) and symmetrical except for topologically different positions individuals may take in a network.

Communication is interactive and may be circular (the difference between a "control action" and the "feedback" that would inform the sender of effects is no longer important).

Development is seen in the process of convergence toward social relations, a form of organization or structure which links the communicators into an integrated whole unity.

Meaning and information become the "force" that directs the process of convergence toward some kind of equilibrium (persuasion and individual effects are no longer one way and become, hence, unimportant as analytical constructs).

Research focuses on the forms of interaction and their systemic consequences within a well-confined context constituted by a network of communication channels.

THE INFORMATION-SEEKING PARADIGM

Whereas much of Western theorizing about communication conforms to the control paradigm, emphasizing the production of effective communications to direct social processes in desired directions, the information-seeking paradigm turns its inherent asymmetry around and assigns the communicational initiative to the receiver rather than to the sender. The receiver is in control of the situation. The sender merely responds to the receiver's request. The information-seeking paradigm recognizes:

Someone in need of or interested in information, advice or aid, or desirous of resources he does not have.

A source which is seen as able to provide the needed information.

The act of requesting desired information.

The act of making information available on request.

The act of receiving and ultimately applying the information obtained as intended.

One crucial feature of this paradigm is that it involves several logical *levels of knowledge* or of information which the other paradigms do not need to consider, for example:

The receiver's knowledge of his own informational needs (i.e., knowledge about the lack of knowledge).

The receiver's knowledge of where and how his informational needs can
   be satisfied.
The receiver's knowledge of the means to obtain the needed information.
And finally, the knowledge or information actually needed to create or
   improve the process in question

What knowledge about the lack of knowledge means is intuitively clear
but poses many formal problems. Metainformation of this kind is easily
talked about but difficult to model and to incorporate into a theoretical
framework.

Equally problematic is the reality for which this paradigm might be
applicable: how realistic or helpful it is for understanding of policy formation concerning communication and development and which biases it entails. For example, those social groups that express the needs of a developing country may not be fully aware of the information requirements of
that country, be it because the ruling elite is not representative of the
population at large, because the existence of a widely shared fascination
with Western styles of life and demands for communications media, con-
sumer products, and agricultural techniques for which infractructures do
not yet exist, or because there is a lack of understanding about the cultural dynamics the introduction of information into the knowledge stream
might set in motion. Even on the psychological level full self-awareness of
individual needs is difficult to achieve (see what psychoanalysis seeks to
accomplish).

In aadition, less developed countries are typically unaware of where
and how they can satisfy their informational needs most efficiently. This
subjects them to the pressures of competition by Western producers of
communications for wider market shares. Various scandals associated
with the sales of military equipment and of baby milk shows that developing countries experience difficulties in choosing among what is available
to them precisely because they are prevented, either by their own internal
structure or by the political interests in or preconception by donors or
resource countries, from developing the level of awareness of the information needed to act in the interest of their own indigenous development.

Although the information-seeking paradigm needs further attention, I
do believe that it is fruitful, if not to explain, to at least redirect some of
the uses of communication in society from production to consumption or
from talking to selective listening (see also Krippendorff & Steier, 1979).
Summarizing, the paradigm distinguishes:

A *communicator* with recognized needs and awareness about the connection between information and practice, capable of expressing such
   needs in the context of an essentially information-rich environment.

Communication is both *circular* and takes place *on several logical levels*. Searching, extracting or retrieving, evaluating, and implementing information involves a form of interaction during which both information and information about information is exchanged.

Development is essentially a process of implementing exogenously located information that realizes indigenous desires of which the communicator is aware, which he wants to take place, and for which he seeks guidance.

Meaning and *information* exist on several levels and depend on how communications are put to use in the process of development. It presupposes again an awareness of needs and of available information resources and an assessment of the consequences of implementing these.

Research focuses on how information in the above sense is processed by the communicator, in which form it is stored in his environment and by which means it can be found, received, and applied to yield results.

THE PARADIGM OF AUTOPOIESIS

Biological Origins and Consequences

The concept of autopoiesis originated in recent developments in theoretical biology, particularly, as presented by Varela, Maturana, and Uribe (1974), Maturana (1975, 1981), and Varela (1979, 1981). In search of a definition of life, biologists of the past have ascertained vitalist perspectives and looked for religious explanations, but more recent efforts have focused on two processes: (1) *reproduction* involving a cyclic process of self-description of and by an organism in a medium, such as DNA, and the planting of this description into a fertile environment, in interaction with which a new and, in essential features, similar organization grows and (2) *adaptation and intelligence,* i.e., the ability of an organism to make appropriate choices concerning its environment so as to keep its essential variables within tolerable limits (Ashby, 1956).

Note that both definitions take the notion of an organism as primitive and, according to Varela (1979), they do not get at what seems to be the critical property of living forms. There is no reason for an organism to develop, adapt, or show intelligence in friendly or supportive environments, particularly when a state of adaptation has been achieved. There is no reason why an organism, once grown, could not live forever, without the need of a reproductive mechanism. Especially in social organizations, there is no natural life span after which the organization must die. People, artefacts, and energy resources are continuously replaced, substituted, and replenished. The life span of the whole has little to do with the life span of its parts. Recognizing these basic facts, Varela and Maturana have identified processes of *self-production* as a useful start for a definition of the living organism. According to these authors, *autopoiesis* or, better, an autopoietic organization is one that is constituted by a network of processes of production of components that: (1) through their interactions continuously regenerate and realize the network of procesess that produced them and (2) constitute the organization as a concrete unit in space and in time.

The complement of an autopoietic organization is an allopoietic organization which produces something materially different from itself. A frequent case of confusion is self-reproduction or the replication of forms of interest in biology. Since offsprings are of a different materiality than their parent organisms, self-reproduction is an allopoietic not an autopoietic process.

Autopoietic organizations continuously generate and specify their own organization through the production of their own components under conditions of continuous pertubations by endogenous information or challenges from their environment and not without consumption of energy. The defining feature of autopoiesis is a *process* or *organization* of components that is *indigenous,* i.e., explainable only in and of itself, and involves the continuous *production* (and decay) *of components* that engage in the process of organization of the same components.

Varela and Maturana's theories emerged in biology and are concerned with autopoietic organizations ranging from the cell to whole organisms. Although many social organizations are allopoietic in the sense that they produce components that engage in processes of production of components other than those that produced them, a pharmaceutical plant or a bakery, for example, I argue that a society at any stage of development includes many autopoietic features. An example is an indigenous culture, i.e., the process by which a system of beliefs, customs, and artefacts (from language to technology) continuously regenerates itself in the face of societal changes, which maintains regularities of its own and ceases to exist after a longer period of disruption of the process of transmission.

A theory of autopoetic organization must explain several empirical consequences of autopoiesis. These consequences include characteristics of autopoietic organizations such as autonomy, self-maintenance of boundaries, individuality, and self-reference. Explanations of these characteristics appear below.

First, autopoietic organizations are autonomous. This does not mean autark in the sense of relying on energy, food, and material resources exclusively from within the system. It does not mean isolated in the sense that information in the form of environmental variation has no effect on its behavior. However, it does mean that autopoietic organizations are explainable entirely, or at least in their essential features, from within and are hence operationally closed or as we say *closed to organization*. We can describe machines and organisms as having potentially three kinds of inputs: energy including matter, information, and organization. A computer is organizationally open in the sense that a written program specifies its network of interaction from the outside. A biological organism is organizationally closed in the sense that the locus of control over the processes of interaction constituting the organism is housed inside the organism and stems from the process of interaction itself. Social forms that are truly indigenous and either resist or are unresponsive to external instructions to organize in a certain way are a manifestation of autonomy.

Second, autopoietic organizations maintain their own boundaries. Whereas the boundary of an allopoietic system is arbitrary and drawn at the convenience of and by an observer, autopoietic organizations define their own boundaries, which the observer may then recognize through the ongoing processes of interaction. For example, the etic conceptualization of a family in terms of the scientist's distinction between generational levels, in terms of inside versus outside contracts or in economic terms may not be of concern to the emic processes that constitute the family in practice. To understand the autopoietic features of the organization of a family, the scientific observer, a family therapist for example, has to recognize how that family constitutes itself, the boundary this family draws around itself, before he may draw his own distinctions which always limit his theoretical or practical concerns for that family.

Third, autopoietic organizations have individuality. By keeping their organization invariant, autopoietic organizations identify themselves or mark themselves in contrast to environmental features or phenomena with respect to which they are open. In allopoietic systems the observer's distinction between an organism and its environment is not only arbitrary but also symmetrical. Both sides of the distinction may have many constitutive parts, involve processes, have structure, etc., and the labeling of one as organism and the other as environment is essentially reversible with little effect on the model accounting for the interaction across this distinction. In autopoietic organizations at least one of the distinctions is marked by processes that *constitute* this boundary including that system's identity in contrast to anything outside it.

Fourth, autopoietic organizations are constitutionally self-referential not hierarchical, which is to say that the forms of these organizations are not subordinate to anything other than themselves and are in this sense radically indigenous. The notion, "the production of components that engage in the production of those components" recognizes the essential circularity of self-production, serving no purpose outside of the auto-poietic process. This is not to say that an autopoietic organization may not be part of a larger sytem, but it means that the coordination which the integration of parts into a whole entails does not affect the autopoietic organization of these parts.

I will now turn to processes of communication and development within autopoietic organizations. The emphasis is on *within,* on the *participation,* or on the *constitution* or the definition of self. The explanation of responses to exogenous communications is left to other paradigms. To cope with problems of communication and development, I distinguish changes in the *ecosphere* from changes in the *noosphere* of a social system. The distinction corresponds roughly to the biological distinction between phenosphere and genosphere; the former consists of the totality of actually observable behaviors (products, material changes, energy sources), and the latter is constituted by the information (pattern, differences, and knowledge) which underlies the observable phenomena. The concept of the noosphere has been elaborated by Boulding (1978), and we will draw many conceptions from his work.

CHANGES IN THE ECOSPHERE

When one removes the evaluative component from the notion of development (i.e., when ignoring questions like "toward which goal," "in whose interest," or "by what criteria"), there remain the physical changes one can observe in the ecosphere of a system. Such changes are characterized by a succession of states, or with an ecological perspective in mind, by the creation and/or movement into unexplored niches, or by the production of new material conditions for existence which differ noticeably from those experienced previously. Changes of this kind are essentially allo-poietic, although I will show later how they take part in autopoiesis.

One such change is the incremental and usually nonstructural change that occurs along a few of a system's variables, such as birthrate, quality of life, rate of production, speed of transportation, and energy consumption. In the short run, changes of this type are essentially subsumed under a given social structure, and they optimize, refine, and in a sense reify that structure. In the long run, these changes may lead to homeostasis or, in the alternative, to a breakdown of the system and to major morphological changes. The recognition and description of these changes is based on the observation of a few quantitative variables. However, such quantitative measurements by themselves cannot shed light on the thresholds for structural or qualitative changes toward which such incremental changes may lead.

Another essentially allopoetic change, design, involves the assemblage of parts to form a system, which may then serve the purposes of the designer (who may be an individual, a collectivity, or a representative of other interests). Although design may result in quantitative changes, a new form of organization of components is largely equivalent to a qualitative shift (for example, the shift in use from mechanical to electronic computers). The ability to assemble a novel system from old or known parts, to place it in a suitable environment, and then to set it in motion, making it interact with other parts of the environment, is limited by the cognitive capacity of the designer or by the structure of the organization producing (assembling), implementing (bringing it into interaction), supporting (by a suitable infrastructure), and controlling the system of components so assembled. In practice, large systems are rarely ever designed *de novo* because the ability to invent new systems at will is indeed extremely limited. However, many communication theories of development, especially under the control paradigm, consider it their aim to provide a logic for changes by design and to relate information to innovation about desirable patterns of interaction.

Ecological growth processes involve incremental changes in typically large numbers of different components which produce, disseminate, and selectively interact with each other, as species do across each other's boundaries of existence. These components may consist of artefacts, biological organisms, human individuals, technical systems, and social organizational entities. To the extent these components are reproduced, they show mutation drifts, and to the extent these components select among each other, they collectively evolve to occupy more favorable niches. Growth is manifest in the numerousness, in the variety of components, and in the dynamics implied by their interaction. These processes may involve mutual cooperation parasitism, predation, competition, etc. We are familiar with these forms of interaction between biological species, and we find that the same phenomena occur between machines and social organizations. Ecological growth does not give preferences to humans.

The emergence of interacting media, another example of allopoetic change, brings otherwise distant or independent phenomena into interaction and thereby fosters the development of dependencies among components and the integration of these components into larger coherent systems of its own definition. Relative to nature, humans were probably the first to bring material and energy resources into contact so as to serve human purposes. Transportation systems, modern mass media, computer networks, and governmental institutions all have the effect of making otherwise isolated and geographically dispersed components depend on each other. The integration these interfaces bring about is qualitatively different from the ecological forms of interaction and the social institutions thriving on them, and this integration provides the main source of organization in technologically advanced societies. Current interfacing technology, from the mass media to computer networking, has largely grown beyond individual comprehension, is ungoverned by social purposes, and tends to follow a dynamic of its own.

Changes in the ecosphere essentially *act out the existing potential* of all human and nonhuman participants, converge toward homeostatic equilibria, optimize processes that are subsumed under basically morphostatic conditions, grow to fill all available ecological niches, and integrate more and more components into a possibly hierarchical system of interdependencies. Although communication takes part in processes leading toward this integration, I will now focus on how information may be conceptualized so as to understand social autopoiesis.

CHANGES IN THE NOOSPHERE

Agreeing with Boulding (1978), I conceive of the noosphere as consisting chiefly of patterns or records of organizational activity that take the role of knowledge or information relative to the ecosphere. I suggest that communication and development in autopoietic organizations are intrinsically linked to the interaction between the two spheres. Let me start with the notion of information in this context.

First, according to Varela (1979), one must distinguish between a *symbolic* and a *systemic interpretation* of information. In a symbolic interpretation we ask what a particular pattern means, refers to, or conveys, and asking this question invariably involves the *intentions of the observer* or those of the participant receiver of this pattern. Inasmuch as autopoietic organizations have their own reason for existence, which may be unrelated to the observer's purposes or outside the participants' awareness, it seems preferable to redirect the attention from an observer's intentions to the interpretation of information in terms of the effects a pattern evokes in the context in which it occurs. So, in a systemic interpretation we ask what role a particular pattern plays within the system of which it is a part. Varela (1979) used the term "in-formation" for the systemic interpretation. While it makes sense to apply symbolic interpretations to the inputs or products of allopoietic processes, for autopoietic processes, systemic interpretations are preferable precisely because such interpretations recognize that such processes are potentially self-referential in nature and that they evolve entirely *within a system.*

Second, and with systemic interpretations in mind, one might wish to distinguish *causal* from *specificational consequences* of information. Hitting a nail causes that nail to be driven into some material. Cause and consequence are related in such a way that the energy that affects the consequence comes with its cause. While the transmission (storage and use) of information almost always requires some energy, this fact is largely inessential to the organizational work it does. I prefer to look at information as containing specifications for certain processes which consume energy from sources other than those carried by the information. Blueprints, commands, instructions, policies, and organizational charts exemplify specifications whose energy content is negligible, but they nevertheless perform organizational work when coupled with preexisting processes under conditions of adequate material and energy resources. The prototypical example of interpreting information in terms of specifications is of course the DNA which, when inserted into a fertile womb, becomes engaged in interactions in the course of which an organism is grown. The DNA explains the form of the organism of which it is a part.

I mentioned blueprints and DNA, but even ordinary mass media entertainment can be taken to specify social roles, define norms and expectations, and provide individuals with ideals or with practical plans for action (whether to commit a crime, to be successful with members of the opposite sex, or to perform a complex task). I maintain that all communications within a reasonably large context, which includes all its antecedent conditions and consequences, can be interpreted as doing organizational work or as containing specifications in the above sense.

Third, there are several processes in the noosphere to which information is or may be subjected. There is *replication and dissemination,* yeilding copies of a pattern which have the same or only slightly different points in space and in time. Writing, telephone, mass communication, and xerox copying exemplify that there are very few limits to the replication of information. Besides material limitations, random errors may retard information in the process of replication, while systematic errors can pollute the noosphere by introducing certain properties of the replication or dissemination processes into the information stream. There is *recombination,* the rearrangement of elements from one pattern into a new pattern, having possibly rather different properties than the original. Mutation is an example of random recombination in the genetic realm. The construction of new sentences from old ones exemplifies creative processes in the linguistic domain. Among the most interesting processes by far is the *reproduction* of information *by mating.* Replication and recombination are essentially unisexual forms of reproduction and induce slow drifts or changes within fixed structures. Most biological reproduction is bisexual, which has a tremendous combinatorial advantage over unisexual reproduction. However, in social systems, information is *reproduced multisexually,* which immeasurably exceeds the combinatorial speed of bisexual reproduction. Information may be assembled out of numerous different patterns that have never been together before. Information may be assembled by taking one part from one pattern and a second part from another pattern, or a pattern in one domain may be used to organize parts from another domain (metaphors), etc., thus creating specifications for new artefacts, new organizational forms, and new processes of production with very few limits.

Fourth, inasmuch as information has the potential for accomplishing organizational work, processes in the noosphere can create or limit the potentiality of behaviors that are realizable in the ecosphere. Individual items of information are typically restrictive (for example, a recipe for onion soup allows the cook to prepare onion soup but little else), and the collectivity of items of information in the noosphere of a culture can delineate what is possible to develop in the ecosphere. Information processes applied to the noosphere tend to expand its potentiality. One of the more important tasks of communication research is to explain processes of combinatorial expansion and contraction of societal information in the noosphere and thus describe changes in that society's potentialities.

AUTONOMY IN ECOSPHERE–NOOSPHERE INTERACTIONS

I am suggesting that the ecosphere and the noosphere of a social organization (system or group) are connected by two processes constituting a cycle. These are: (1) *Realization,* i.e., the process by which information is selectively implemented in the process of production, *organizes* a portion of the ecosphere or *controls* its material construction. Examples range from building a house by a plan or by social conventions to engaging in a crime according to a script surreptitiously provided by television. However, not all patterns in the noosphere are realizable in the ecosphere. (2) *Description,* i.e., the process by which (organizational or procedural) phenomena in the ecosphere are described or enter the noosphere (regardless of the medium or language involved). Examples range from studying a foreign piece of equipment to make plans for its reproduction to codifying an organizational practice so that future members of the organization may be instructed more efficiently.

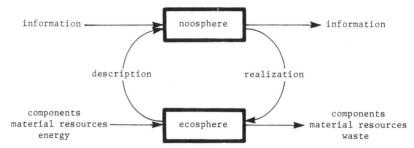

Fig. 1. The circular relationship between the ecosphere and the noosphere through realization and description.

Graphically, we depict the interaction in Fig. 1. The boxes represent processes, respectively operating on information within the noosphere and on the behavior resulting from interaction among components within the ecosphere, and the arrows represent inputs to and outputs from either spheres. The two spheres are thus connected and form a system representing social processes, especially in its informational and morphogenetic aspects.

Most consequences of the realization–description cycle are allopoietic in the sense that the components resulting from the process do not participate in it. For example, the exponential growth of technological development can be seen as a correlate of the production of devices that lead to more efficient production, on the one hand, and to more easily processable descriptions, on the other, which in turn enhances the combinatorial possibilities of realizing more complex arrangements of such devices. The process leads to well-known autocatalytic cycles of development, here, of allopoietic technology. Autocatalysis is most important in social development generally, though rarely recognized in communication research.

I am suggesting that autopoiesis in social systems becomes manifest in the process of self-reference within the realization–description cycle, exhibiting an organization whose form is independent of outside processes, to some extent is resistant to external disturbances, and thus serves as its own explanation. Numerous examples exist, such as the notorious car complex, most of which has no "natural" explanation. It consists of a system of car manufacturers, with their markets of consumers, gasoline and service stations as the outlets of a vast oil industry, road networks maintained by public administrations, driving schools, licensing agencies, individual motivations to own and drive an automobile, etc. The car complex arose in the course of interaction among various social components and has by now become self-defining in the sense that ideas about cars are constantly turned into the practice of production, driving, demonstrative consumption, etc., which in turn explains the ideas people have about cars. Despite the obvious phenotypical changes in the car population, improvements in the network of roads, etc., the self-referential realization–description cycle has produced a rather invariant form of technical and folk literature, social organization, and production which can reasonably be called autopoietic.

Another example is the largely group-specific social definition of "reality," which is constructed in the course of communication among group members. The process alternatingly specifies appropriate individual and collective behaviors and codes that behavior into the stream of communications (instructions, comments, and evaluations) among members, which in turn specifies individual and collective behaviors, etc. It is a self-defining, organization-preserving, indigenous process constituting (at least a part of) the identity of the group in which the process exists. Culture, with its intergenerational transmission and manifestation in individual behavior, social institutions, and production of indigenous artefacts which in turn define what a culture is about, is the more general case in point.

Government, a third example, is embedded in a political system in which members participate by casting votes, protesting, or taking political actions which imply prescriptions for governing elites or which pressure groups to act. Such actions are then again communicated to other members of the government implying further prescriptions for political actions by citizens, etc., which is a process that is ultimately closed. This self-referential process within a realization–description cycle supports a form of government organization and commitment by members, maintains its own boundaries, and thus defines itself by its own processes. Governments collapse when the self-referential process is interupted for sufficiently long periods of time. (When an organization exists only as long as the internal process continues and loses its identity whenever this process is interupted, this usually hints at the autopoietic nature of the organization).

What is rarely realized in mass communication research is that the mass media, by describing social behavior and disseminating information about it to others, may serve as an important link to close a society organizationally and thereby shape and ultimately retain this society's interactionally evolved identity. In technologically less advanced countries, the displacement of indigenous realization–description cycles by modern mass media and the introduction of Western forms of entertainment tend to disturb this identity. While this may not be recognized by short-sighted governing elites or enthusiastic mass audiences, whatever autonomy might have existed within such countries is likely to be diminished in the long run, which will result in a host of social pathologies. Whenever one wants to retain local organizational stabilities, one must inquire into the self-referential processes through which autopoietic organizations persist over time.

I do believe that autopoiesis emerges rather often, and unnoticed, specifically whenever circular processes of realization–description become self-referential. This is all the more likely the more complex and the more information intensive the social processes of production are. However, not all self-referential processes of this kind have the strength to retain their organization over long periods. I hesitate to settle on whether autopoiesis is good or bad, but I am convinced human individuals function better when such circularities exist than when everything is exogenously controlled, historically fixed, or structurally dependent, leading to alienation, loss of identity, and purposelessness.

SUMMARY AND CONCLUSION

Having barely scratched the surface of the emerging paradigm of autopoiesis, I have to remain tentative as to what it entails for communication and development. Nevertheless, let me try to follow the style developed for listing key notions in the other paradigms. Here:

Communication is a process of usually circular coding, dissemination, and processing of information within the noosphere, generating, circulating, and retaining patterns in space and in time.

The communicators are no more essential than the processes in which they are engaged. They are the nodes in a network of ecological processes of production, on the one hand, and the principal locus for collective changes in the noosphere, on the other. The human mind is critical in that it encourages combinatorial processes, such as multisexual mating of information.

Information and meaning are seen in the organizational work a pattern performs within a context or in the specification (of the process of production) that such patterns potentially carry into a particular environment.

Feedback or circular processes are recognized at various points in the process but are of particular importance in realization–description cycles, i.e., in processes by which information performs organizational work, specifying processes of production and of interaction between components, and in processes by which components, and interactions among them, and processes of production become represented in patterns, which are in turn capable of performing organizational work.

Development becomes a process ultimately leading toward organizational closure, enhanced autonomy, increased identity, and higher ability to maintain (organizational) boundaries in the face of continuous influx of information, matter, and energy. The structure toward which this notion of development tends is essentially nonhierarchical. (Although hierarchical forms in the noosphere and in the ecosphere are clearly possible, they are inessential to the paradigm.)

Research into communication and development from this autopoietic perspective must investigate the processes and context of both, the body of knowledge within the noosphere (delineating a system's potentiality) and the material resources and infrastructure constituting the ecosphere of that system in order to map the self-referential cycle of realization (information to organization of production) and description (organization of production to information) through which a system develops it autonomy and identity within the realm of its potentiality. Of particular interest is research into how resistant indigenous communication processes are to new technology, information or administrative aid that might be made available exogenously, and how pregnant such indigenous processes are to bring about structural change once the material conditions are ripe.

In conclusion, I should like to point out that these paradigms are neither classificatory of different portions of reality nor mere alternative constructions of the same phenomena. Each focuses attention on some aspects of communication processes others ignore or are unable to represent in their full complexity. In reality (whatever this is, it certainly must include the observer–actor and is hence self-referential) there are interested parties which pose problems of control, there are processes of convergence that neither participant in the process might seek or be aware of, and there are purposive attempts to gather information residing elsewhere that could aid but also retard development including self-improvement. What the paradigm of autopoiesis does is relate information to processes of organization of production (in the ecosphere), encourage the conception of changes in the domain of information (noosphere) in terms of certain generative processes, and promote the view that communication is also a major stabilizing force, marking a social organization, a culture, or a society as a distinct identity and, being a constitutive part of that organization, producing its organization at the same time. The advocates of the control paradigm have run against this ''stabilizing force'' in the form of obstacles and barriers to social change. The advocates of the network–convergence paradigm have taken this "force" to be fixed or invariant and thereby exclude such organizational processes (not to be confused with the topological properties of networks) from analysis. The advocates of the information-seeking paradigm respect the indigenous nature of the "forces" through which needs are defined and information processing capabilities are realized but tend to be able to cope neither with changes in the noosphere (from inventions to pollution) nor with the organizational work information may accomplish in the domain of production. In contrast to these, the paradigm of autopoieses accounts for processes of communication that make a society see itself as distinct and that make it retain its indigenous form of organization, culture, or mind. In the description–realization cycle, communication becomes the timeless bridge (which thereby transcends the difference) between cause and effect, between creator and the created, and between the observer and the observed. Such organizational processes of communication are explainable only from within a social form and are in the true sense self-referential. Living systems, indigenous culture, self-government, or organizationally autonomous social systems exemplify the empirical domain of this paradigm.

CHAPTER 15

The Convergence Theory
of Communication, Self-Organization,
and Cultural Evolution

D. Lawrence Kincaid

INTRODUCTION

The convergence model of communication (Kincaid, 1979) was created in order to overcome many of the biases that have become evident in the traditional linear, transmission models of communication. The model was derived from the basic concepts of information theory, cybernetics, and general systems theory. Its roots can also be traced to symbolic interactionism in sociology and to small group dynamics in psychology, and, at a more macro level of analysis, to Durkheim's (1966) theory of collective consciousness. Such a formulation is indeed quite general, but then the subject itself—communication—is very pervasive, often referred to as the fundamental social process or as synonymous with culture itself.

There are two key elements in the paradigm: communication as a dynamic process of *convergence* and social systems as *networks* of interconnected individuals who are linked by patterned flows of information (Rog-

COMMUNICATION THEORY:
EASTERN AND WESTERN PERSPECTIVES

ers & Kincaid, 1981). Individuals give different meanings to the information which they share with others. Initial differences in mutual understanding are reduced though a dynamic process of feedback (Ashby, 1956). Although feedback processes reduce differences in meaning among people, the inherent uncertainty involved in information exchange—including the feedback process itself—implies that some differences will always remain. Thus, communication may be described as a series of converging cycles of information exchange among participants who approach, but never exactly reach, the same point of mutual understanding. Mutual understanding provides the basis for mutual agreement and collective action. Communication, then, is defined as a process in which information is created and shared by two or more individuals who converge over time toward a greater degree of mutual understanding, agreement, and collective action. The emphasis is strictly on the mutual relationships between those who share the same information rather than on what one individual does to another individual or mass audience.

This orientation envisions a flow of information through networks of communication. The most important effects of this information flow take place *between* members of such communication networks. That is, the consequences of communication are indicated by changes over time in the relative position between two or more members (in terms of their beliefs, values, and behavior) and in the structure of the networks which they comprise (their patterns of organization). The researcher looks for regions or clusters of individuals within such networks which are characterized by a greater density of information exchange and by less variance or differences within their boundaries than between such local regions. Such regions or local networks are sometimes referred to as subgroups or subcultures within a given culture.

The theory does not rule out divergence within a subculture or local network. In fact, considerable divergence may exist on certain topics. The theory does propose, however, that members of a subculture or local network will tend over time to define and to conceptualize more similarly than nonmembers who have not shared the same information.

The network–convergence paradigm calls for a change in the nature of the research questions which are asked, for new research designs, for new instruments of observation and measurement, and for new methods of data analysis and inference (Barnett & Kincaid, 1983). The "betweenness" aspect of communication is emphasized, shifting the unit of analysis away from the individual to the level of dyads, personal networks, cliques, intact networks, and whole cultures. Information exchange and differences in beliefs, values, and behavior *between* individuals become the central foci of research.

The purpose of this paper is to develop a conceptual framework to integrate the micro- and macrolevels of analysis—the interpersonal level of communication to the level of subcultures or whole cultures. The theoretical framework is derived from the conceptual principles of statistical thermodynamics and the principles of self-organization from nonequilibrium thermodynamics. Specifically, we develop a theory of communication as the fundamental self-organizing process of social systems. The convergence principle and the network perspective are integrated into a single, coherent theory of communication, organization, and culture by means of the application of concepts and principles from nonequilibrium thermodynamics. The concept and measure of *entropy* is applied directly to the statistical distribution of beliefs, values, and behaviors of intact cultures and to the structure of their communication networks. This allows the development of a general mathematical model of communication, organization, and culture which is consistent with the network–convergence paradigm.

ENTROPY

If there are any differences among the members of a social system or subculture in terms of their beliefs, values, or behaviors, those differences are evident in the shape of their statistical distribution. The statistical measure of entropy captures one of the most important characteristics of a distribution, the degree of order that it contains or, conversely, its degree of disorder or randomness. This aspect applies regardless of the phenomena which create the distribution. So, for example, when the mathematical analogy between thermodynamic entropy and information was discovered, it primarily provided evidence that a similar structure existed in two different classes of events: the *distribution* of gas molecules and the *distribution* of a sequence of signals. It is the structure of the distribution of various aspects of culture that provides the missing link between the micro- and macrolevels of communication.

To take this course is not tantamount to wholesale borrowing from the physical sciences; it is simply the description of social phenomena in terms of probability distributions. It is not well known that when Boltzmann did this for the first time in physics, his source of inspiration was social behavior and Darwin's theory of biological evolution. In the middle of the nineteenth century, there was no convincing evidence for the atomic structure of matter. According to Prigogine,

> His starting point was to deal with large systems. Here again, he made analogies
> with social and biological situations. He noticed that we cannot predict the

individual fate of an individual, but that we can describe accurately the average behaviour of groups. Therefore he believed that the first step towards an understanding of the second law should be the replacement of [Newtonian] dynamics by some form of probability calculus. (1973, p. 405)

The concept of entropy is closely identified with that of randomness. The intuitive idea of a random state is that it is characterized by equiprobable and independent events. This describes the maximum entropy state. Lower entropy is characterized by nonrandom, dependent events. Gatlin (1972, p. 29) has developed an extensive list of bipolar opposites to delineate the entropy concept:

Random	Nonrandom
Disorganized	Organized
Disordered	Ordered
Mixed	Separated
Equiprobable	Divergence from equiprobability
Independent	Divergence from independence
Configurational variety	Restricted arrangements
Freedom of choice	Constraint
Uncertainty	Reliability
Higher error probability	Fidelity
Potential information	Stored information

The basic assumption of the convergence theory is that the communication process results in a change in the statistical distribution of the beliefs, values, and behaviors of a culture. For these important theoretical reasons this distribution change should be measured by the mathematical formula for thermodynamic entropy:

$$S = -\Sigma\, p_i \log p_i \qquad (1)$$

where p is the probability of a system being in cell i of its response/ behavior space.

When entropy is interpreted in terms of disorder, an increase in entropy S means that the system of interest has departed further from a defined state of order. In other words, an increase in entropy is an increase in the spread of a statistical distribution. As Denbigh (1975, p. 70) explained, " . . . the whole general idea is perhaps most accurately expressed in terms of the notion of 'spread,' entropy increase is due to a 'spreading' of the system over larger number of available microstates." Hence, the standard statistical measure for the *variance* around the mean of a distribution is also a good measure of this spread, and its inverse may be used to represent the amount of information (R. A. Fisher, 1935). As a consequence of communication among members of a specified culture, we would expect a reduction in the amount of variance in the distribution of the beliefs, values, and/or behaviors associated with that communication.

If measured in discrete categories we would expect a reduction in the measure of the entropy of the distribution.

This change is in the *opposite* direction of that specified by the second law of thermodynamics. In isolated physical systems, the second law states that entropy will increase over time until a state of stable equilibrium is reached. Thus, communication is a process which seems to reverse the production of entropy, one which *seems* to decrease entropy or produce negentropy (order, organization, and so forth). Later we will see how this is possible. By reversing the usual statement of the second law, we have:

$$S_B < S_A \qquad (2.0)$$

$$S_B - S_A < 0 \qquad (2.1)$$

where the entroy S of state B at equilibrium is less than the entropy of state A at an earlier point in time (2.0), or the difference in the entropies of the two states is less than or equal to zero (2.1).

The same relationship may also be stated in the form of a differential equation:

$$dS/dt < 0 \qquad (3.0)$$

where the first derivative of entropy S with respect to time t is less than or equal to zero. That is, it decreases with time toward some maximum limit of negentropy or order.

NONEQUILIBRIUM THERMODYNAMICS AND SELF-ORGANIZATION

That the second law of thermodynamics can be reversed in this manner is implied by the following statement of the law: "This spontaneous tendency of a system to go toward thermodynamic equilibrium cannot be reversed without at the same time changing some organized energy, work, into disorganized energy, heat" (Morse, 1969, p. 43). This statement of the principle is crucial to the argument set forth in this paper. The law implies that the spontaneous tendency can be reversed locally by drawing on the matter–energy resources of the surrounding environment to perform work which is capable of creating or maintaining the order or structure of the localized system. This describes a situation in which the system is not closed but open to the exchange of matter–energy with its environment. This represents a shift to nonequilibrium thermodynamics in which the focus is on dissipative states (self-organizing structures) in which the system no longer moves spontaneously to a state of maximum entropy where it remains, but rather "the system is moving towards a stationary stable state where it remains as long as its interaction with the environment continues to take place" (Prigogine & Stengers, 1977, p. 327).

Prigogine (1978, 1980) developed the following general formula to express the overall change in the entropy of a system as a function of the entropy flow of energy with respect to the system's external surroundings, d_eS, and the irreversible increases of entropy within the system itself, d_iS, (where the dt of each term is omitted for convenience):

$$dS = d_eS + d_iS \qquad (4.0)$$

Only the entropy production within the system, d_iS, has a well-defined sign; in other words, an isolated system can only evolve spontaneously toward greater entropy. This type of entropy production is a function of various thermodynamic forces, such as temperature gradients, and corresponding rates, such as heat flux and chemical reaction rates. "For an open system, however, the competition between d_eS and d_iS permits the system . . . to adopt a new, *structured* form" (Prigogine, 1976, p. 97). Overall entropy, dS, which is the sum of entropy processes within the system, d_iS, and between the system and its environment, d_eS, always increases, thus preserving the fundamental principle of the second law of thermodynamics. In a sense, the self-organization or structure of the system is "bought and paid for" by the system's interaction with its environment, d_eS.

A living organism, for example, obtains food from its environment and destructures it in the process of creating and maintaining its own internal structure. A social system exploits these same energy sources along with others (petroleum, coal, atomic energy, for example) and destructures them in the process of communication which creates and maintains the social system's structure. The negentropy produced by the living organism or the social system is obtained at the expense of the production of greater entropy in the external environment. In a very real sense, the process of communication requires work and produces heat.

COMMUNICATION AND CULTURAL EVOLUTION

The structuring process just described is reminiscent of the role played by Maxwell's demon in the history of thermodynamics. To counteract the effects of the second law, Maxwell speculated on the possibility of an imaginary demon who could sort the fast gas molecules from the slow ones by means of a trap door which separated the two sides of a closed chamber. This possibility seemed to thwart the second law until the paradox was resolved by acknowledging that the energy expended by shining a light on the particles to determine their position/velocity would always exceed the amount of entropy reduced by reordering them (Szilard, 1964).

The cognitive decision processes required for the demon to sort the particles are the same as those required for communication as specified by the convergence model: perception of differences, pattern recognition, understanding, belief, and action. In essence, each of these are decision processes requiring the expenditure of energy (work) which results in greater order, structure, or negentropy. Inanimate particles require the services of a demon or some other third party capable of these cognitive decision processes; living systems can literally sort for themselves. They are linked by the process of sharing the same information. When individuals share information among themselves they simultaneously create and maintain a portion of a communication network in which each one is embedded. Differences in understanding between two or more individuals are reduced by feedback, "a process of approximation which if successful results in a series of diminishing mistakes—a dwindling series of under-and-over corrections converging on a goal" (K. W. Deutsch, 1968, p. 390). This process reduces the independence of each individual and reduces the differences among them. As individuals forfeit part of their uniqueness, they gain a shared culture. The within-group variance or entropy of such a local network in terms of its beliefs, values, behaviors, artifacts, and so forth, decreases as a function of the time devoted to communication about them.

This fundamental principle of communication may be stated in the following manner (Kincaid, Yum, Woelfel, & Barnett, 1983):

1. In a closed social system in which communication is unrestricted among its members, the system as a whole will tend to converge over time toward a collective pattern of thought of greater negentropy (or lower entropy).
2. In a closed social system with no communication among its members, the system as a whole will tend to diverge over time toward a collective pattern of thought of greater entropy.

A closed social system is equivalent to a partially closed, open-ended system: It is closed to inputs of information from the external environment but remains open to the exchange of matter–energy which is required to sustain it as a viable, self-organizing system. This is an idealization which would only be observed in practice for brief periods of time or approximated in the case of extreme forms of social organization found among religious cults, temporary isolation of prisoners or hostages, small groups of people temporarily cutoff from the rest of society, and so forth, or for the case of the world as a whole (global culture).

The principle states that if communication is unrestricted, then a common culture will result, that is, a convergence among the members in terms of their beliefs, values, and behaviors. On the other hand, if all forms of information sharing are cutoff, then over time we would expect the differences among its members gradually to increase, resulting in an overall increase in the system's level of entropy and disorder, or, in more familiar terms, in a breakdown of cultures into ever increasing subcultures of individuals.

Real social systems vacillate somewhere between these two ideal extremes for each content area or tropic that is considered. The use of the ideal states permits the clearest possible expression of the function performed by communication in human societies, in the same way that the law of falling bodies could only be expressed for a perfect vacuum with no friction or external forces.

The next step in the development of the convergence theory is the statement of the factors and conditions which affect the rate of internal entropy/negentropy production in a social system. We would expect the rate of convergence for a particular topic to be a direct function of the rate of information exchange and the size of the initial difference (divergence or entropy). Two other important factors are already specified by the model: boundary conditions created by restrictions in the internal communication networks of a social system and the finite limitations of two key resources for communication: time and energy. Social systems cannot communicate about all topics all of the time. Thus, time and energy place restrictions on communication and the degree of convergence that can be reached at any given time.

Wiley and Brooks (1982), biologists, have developed an evolutionary theory of speciation which is very similar to the model just described. Evolution occurs as a function of genetic variety (entropy of the genetic code) and changes in the level of internal cohesion among members of a species in terms of sexual contact and conception. Panmixia is the term used to describe the ideal state of perfect cohesion: Each member of the species has an equal probability of sexual contact with members of the opposite sex with a perfect probability of conception occurring. Any reduction in this perfect level of cohesion is an increase in disorder in the internal organization of the species or an increase in the entropy of cohesion. For purposes of simplification, Wiley and Brooks consider energy resources to be unlimited in this process, but it seems evident that severe food shortages over an extended period of time would affect the rate of sexual contact and conception among the members of a species, with possible consequences for its evolution.

The mathematical model developed for their theory of the evolution of a species is derived from the basic equation of nonequilibrium thermodynamics proposed by Prigogine (Eq. 4.0). It is readily adaptable to the process of communication and cultural change, and it adds a term which takes into account the organization of a social system in terms of the structure of its communication network:

$$dS = d_iS + d_cS + d_eS \qquad (5)$$

where the overall entropy of the social system dS is composed of the entropy of its stored information d_iS (beliefs, values, and behaviors), the entropy of its internal communication network d_cS (referred to as cohesion), and the entropy production of the system in terms of its energy exchange with the external environment d_eS.

For their description of speciation, Wiley and Brooks (1982) graphically depict the relationship between the change over time in the entropy of information and the entropy of internal cohesion. The entropy of information and cohesion increase together until they reach the point or line of zero cohesion. Zero cohesion is defined as the maximum entropy level for d_cS. Hence, as the cohesion of a species declines, the variety (entropy) of information increases. At the point where cohesion is at its lowest, the species divides into two distinct subspecies followed by a process of differential consolidation within each subgroup. This consolidation is accompanied by a decrease in the entropy of information and an increase in the cohesion within each new subgroup. If the new variety represents an addition to the overall amount of information, then the new species will gradually approach a stationary stable state of entropy which is higher than before. If the new variety represents a substitution of previous information (which disappears), then the new species will gradually approach a stationary stable state of entropy which is about the same level as before.

Causality may work in either direction. For example, if a natural catastrophe (shift in a river bed) or migration over a long distance separates members of a species for a long enough time (reduces cohesion), then genetic variation could occur differentially among two or more separated subgroups. Genetic differences would then further reduce the cohesion among the whole species. Similarly, genetic mutation which is retained among some members would reduce the cohesion among the whole species up to the point where two distinct subspecies would be formed with no interaction between them.

The implications of this model for communication and cultural change are evident. Depending on the level of the social system specified, new information could be produced internally by means of innovation or imported from outside the system by means of external channels of communication. The overall information entropy level of the system would increase accordingly and would affect the overall system to the extent that it became diffused or shared by a greater proportion of its members, eventually leading to a new stationary stable state of higher entropy if it remains a viable addition or approaching the original level of entropy if substitution occurs.

The overall level of information entropy that any given society can support is undoubtedly a function of the amount of resources and time that it has available for processing new information and still maintain a level of cultural convergence necessary for the minimum amount of internal (network) cohesion. Modern communications technology, which increases the amount of energy that can be expended for information sharing, while at the same time reducing the amount of time required, would enable a society to support higher levels of information entropy or cultural diversity (Kincaid, 1983; Woelfel & Fink, 1980).

Support for this theoretical proposition was reported by Rogers and Kincaid (1981) from their study of the family planning communication networks in Korean villages. The degree of connectedness in the communication networks was found to be correlated with the degree of convergence in the villages in terms of the village women's attitudes and knowledge about family planning as measured by the statistical variance around the mean of each village, respectively. Furthermore, it was discovered that communication network connectedness was also correlated in the expected direction with the degree of convergence in terms of the choice of contraceptive method as measured by the relative entropy of the distribution of contraceptive use within each village. Although the study was cross sectional in design, the findings lend support to the mathematical model above which expresses a dynamical relationship between network connectedness for a social system and its degree of cultural convergence.

Kincaid and others (1983) also found support for this proposition in their study of the cultural convergence of Korean immigrants in Hawaii. The shape of the curve which accounted for the most variance in value convergence with the host society was identical to that which describes underdamped harmonic motion (oscillation).

By means of a computer simulation, Krippendorff (1971) has shown that the emergence of structure is logically inevitable under most conditions of communication. The types of structures that emerge are social psychological (personal interdependencies), cognitive (mutual understanding and agreement), behavioral (collective action), and social (organization) (see Chapter 14, this volume).

IMPLICATIONS OF THE THEORY

Reformulated in the language of nonequilibrium thermodynamics, the convergence theory of communication raises several interesting questions about how social systems function. What outcomes would be predicted when conditions depart from the ideal ones in which the theory is stated— when the system is open to information from the outside? What are the sources of diversity and change from within the system itself? What factors affect the rate of convergence within a system? The theory does not take into account conventional theories of power in social systems. Are power and inequity irrelevant to the convergence theory of communication?

Depending on the level of the social system specified, new information can be produced internally by means of innovation or introduced through external channels of communication from the outside (other groups, cultures, nations, and so forth). Initially, the individual or subgroup exposed to this source of new information would have only a minor (though measurable) impact on the overall level of entropy (diversity) of the system. As the number of people exposed to this new information by means of internal or external sources increases, the impact on the system's level of entropy would increase accordingly. Such a cultural change would be subject to the well-known principles of the diffusion of innovations. One of the key questions posed by the convergence theory is whether the new information is added to the current stock or replaces a preexisting item. The overall information entropy level of the system would increase with addition, eventually leading to a new stationary stable state of higher entropy if it remains a viable addition, or it would approach the original level of entropy if substitution occurs.

At the level of nations, governments that want to maintain or increase the existing level of cultural homogeneity should restrict the flow of information entering from the outside to that which is already consistent with the beliefs, values, and attitudes that it wants to maintain. Innovation and creativity from within which deviates from the collective norm should be dampened out as soon as possible. At the same time, policies should be adopted internally which increase the number of channels (network cohesiveness) and flow of information to the system's members for beliefs, values, and attitudes that do conform. Although an increase in one-way, mass media communication would produce the desired outcome (with no competition allowed), a two-way flow of information would represent a much more "unrestricted" flow of information according to the convergence theory. In other words, dialogue is a less restrictive flow of information than monologue. Nations that employ local discussion groups to bring about change consistent with their policies or feature model citizens speaking their mind via the mass media are applying this important principle of the theory.

Although one might assume that the state of communication and cultural convergence just described only applies to totalitarian societies where government control and coercion are quite high, a similar state could occur through the "voluntary" effects of a free market. To the Marxist, for example, the extreme state of cultural homogeneity and conformity in the United States is attributed to the effects of its capitalistic economy. "How else can one explain the similarity one finds on the major television network news broadcasts?" they might ask or the monotony and homogeneity of entertainment programs. The standard response is that only the profitable programs survive, giving the people what they wanted all along. The Marxist attributes this type of cultural homogeneity to a common source, capitalism.

In one society, the level of cultural homogeneity is attributed to the government; in the other society, to the capitalist economic system. In both societies, the convergence theory specifies the conditions which lead to a particular level of homogeneity: boundaries which decrease or prevent the flow of diverse information from entering from the outside, the selection of consistent information for diffusion within the system, and the least restrictions or greatest flow of the selected information within the system.

There is a cost, however, to increasing or maintaining a given level of cultural convergence within a social system. The overall level of information entropy that any given society can support is undoubtedly a function of the amount of resources and time that it has available for processing information. The amount of energy and time which can be applied to the goal of increasing convergence on a given topic is relatively finite. While effort is being exerted on one topic (for example, the women's movement or the nuclear freeze movement) time and effort cannot be expended for other topics (civil rights or protection of the environment). In other words, there are natural limits on the degree of cultural convergence that can be obtained in a given area or topic even if other topics/concerns are not taken into account. If taken into account, the shift of attention from topic to topic over time is a major explanation of cultural oscillation.

As would be expected, the finite limit on the resources and time available for communication can be extended by means of technological development. Modern communication technology, which increases the amount of energy that can be expended for information sharing, while at the same time reducing the amount of time and cost required, would enable a society to support higher levels of information entropy or negentropy (cultural diversity or homogeneity) depending on the nature of the content that is allowed or selected to flow: convergent or divergent, with replacement or addition.

The convergence theory is not a theory of political power; consequently, the term is not employed. As a communication theory, however, it is certainly relevant to discussions of power. An important aspect of power is the capacity to control the selection of information which flows throughout a social system, to control the networks of communication within the system (who talks to whom), and to control the sources and amount of information from outside the system. The "system" of interest in this case could be defined as widely as a division or work group within a large corporation, a religious cult, or national state. Communication power, then, is the capacity to influence or control those aspects of communication specified by the convergence model. Maintaining oneself in power and exercising other types of power are dependent on how much power one has over the communication system. It is no surprise to find, for example, that among the first actions of any revolutionary takeover of a country is the capture of its central mass media systems—radio, television, and the press—followed by the isolation of all major sources of dissenting opinion.

As derived from the basic principles of information theory, cybernetics, and nonequilibrium thermodynamics, the convergence theory of communication is stated at the highest level of generality. Its principles are applicable to all levels of human organization—from dyadic interpersonal communication, through small group and organizational communication, to the processes of mass media communication at the national and international level. It is not designed to replace other theories of communication at each of these levels. What it offers is a way to integrate the wide variety of communication theories that now exist at each contextual level and to unify the field vertically across those levels from interpersonal to mass communication. At the same time, the approach taken to accomplish this integration reduces the distance bewteen the natural sciences, the social sciences, and the humanities.

CHAPTER 16

The Rules Approach to Communication Theory: A Philosophical and Operational Perspective

Donald P. Cushman

INTRODUCTION

It is an ancient view that human intentions restrict individual inclination in selecting what behaviors an individual undertakes. This view has been the basis of numerous accounts of individual conduct and social organization. It is at the heart of the opposition of pragmatism to idealism. It is unequivocally the first principle of rhetorical and communication theory from the time of Aristotle down to the present. The most visible, modern expression of the intentionalist position and related issues is action theory. The action theory tradition centers on a conception of man as a creature of freedom and choice, typically engaged in intentional, goal-directed behavior guided and governed by rules and capable of acting rather than merely being acted on. It will be the purpose of this essay to explore (1) the philosophical assumptions underpinning an action perspective and (2) the self-concept as a cybernetic control mechanism for the rules which govern and guide human communication processes.

COMMUNICATION THEORY:
EASTERN AND WESTERN PERSPECTIVES

PHILOSOPHICAL ASSUMPTIONS

The viability of a rules theory of human communication rooted in action theory depends on a series of assumptions.

The Motion–Action Assumption

First, it is assumed that human behavior can be divided into two classes of activity: those which are stimulus–response activities governed by causal necessity, and those which are intentional and choice-oriented responses governed by practical necessity. The former behaviors are habitual and termed *movements* while the latter are evaluative and termed *actions*. Action theorists restrict their domain of inquiry to those realms of human behavior in which persons have some degree of choice among alternatives, critique their performance, and act in response to practical or normative forces. Fay and Moon (1977) summarize:

> According to this distinction, actions differ from mere movements in that they are intentional and rule governed: they are performed in order to achieve a particular purpose, and in conformity to some rules. These purposes and rules constitute what we shall call the "semantic dimension" of human behavior—its symbolic or expressive aspect. An action, then, is not simply a physical occurrence, but has a certain intentional content which specifies what sort of an action it is, and which can be grasped only in terms of the system of meanings in which the action is performed. A given movement counts as a vote, a signal, a salute or an attempt to reach something, only against the background of a set of applicable rules and conventions and the purposes of the actors involved. (p. 209)

A consensus seems to exist among action theorists that to attribute or ascribe the quality of action to a human behavior is to claim that some agent is the author or cause of what was brought about. Several important implications regarding the nature and the structure of explanation follow from this assumption.

Action theory requires an explanation of human behavior in terms of the intentional link between an agent's perceptions, thoughts, and behavior such that they explain why a given behavior was brought about. Taylor (1970) elaborates:

> Explanation in terms of purpose therefore involved taking into account the conceptual forms through which agents understand and come to grips with their world. That people think of their environment in certain concepts, that is, use certain modes of classification is an element in accounting for what they do. Indeed, it can be said to define what they do. For if we think of actions as defined by the purposes or intentions which inform them, then we cannot understand man's action without knowing the concepts in which they form their intentions. (p. 60)

The structure for explaining human behavior within an action-theory perspective is the practical syllogism in which the conclusions follow with practical rather than causal or logical necessity from the premises (von Wright, 1971).

> A *intends* to bring about B;
> A *considers* that he cannot bring about B unless he does C.
> A *sets himself* to do C.

Intentional reasoning when cast in this structure is termed a first-person practical syllogism. Its distinctive feature is that it is formulated from an actor's point of view, explaining what an actor *considered practically necessary* for the fulfillment of his intention and indicating that an actor *sets* himself to do to fulfill his intention. Note that even if an actor's perceptions of what he must do to fulfill his intentions are in error, the first-person, practical syllogism is still a valid explanation of *why* he set himself to do what he did. von Wright argues that the practical syllogism provides the humanities and social sciences with "something long missing from their methodology: an explanatory model in its own right which is a definite alternative to subsumptive theoretic covering law model" (Cushman & Pearce, 1977, p. 185).

The Information Processing–Coordination Assumption

Second, it is assumed that there exist two classes of human actions, those in which an agent's choice among alternative courses of action and efforts to achieve a goal does not require the cooperation of others and those which do require such cooperation, in which case communication becomes a necessary stage in goal attainment. The former are termed *information-processing situations* and function to regulate human perception and thought in regard to some goal, while the latter are termed *coordination situations* and function to regulate consensus among agents in regard to the cooperative achievement of a goal and restrict their domain of scientific inquiry to coordination situations. Why? Because it is only within the domain of coordination situations that human action requires the transfer of symbolic information or communication to facilitate goal-directed behavior. Cushman and Pearce (1977) summarize:

> . . . (1) there exists a class of human action which involves conjoint, combined, and associated behavior; (2) that the transfer of symbolic information facilitates such behavior; (3) that the transfer of symbolic information requires the interaction of sources, messages, and receivers guided and governed by communication rules; and (4) that the communication rules form general and specific patterns which provide the basis for explanation, prediction, and control of communication behavior. (pp. 173–183)

Several important implications regarding the nature of human communication and its function, structure, and processes within coordination situations follow from this second assumption.

One instance of a coordination task which requires the cooperation of others for goal attainment and is thus governed and guided by communication rules is the traditional marriage ceremony. The goal of such a ceremony is to unite a couple in matrimony. In order to attain such a goal each participant must engage in various sequences of verbal behavior which according to the rules constitutes a verbal commitment. When these verbal episodes are sequenced in a certain way in the appropriate situation they count as a marriage contract. The *function* of human communication in such a context is to regulate the consensus needed to coordinate behavior. The *structure* of human communication is the content and procedural rules involved in regulating consensus. The *process* of human communication involves the adaptation of the rules involved in regulating consensus to the task at hand (Cushman & Craig, 1976).

The Creative–Standardized Usage Assumption

Third, it is assumed that there exists two classes of coordination situations, those in which the interactants attempt through negotiation to generate the rules which will form the basis of episodic sequences in coordinated goal attainment and those in which some generative mechanism already exists which has provided such rules. The former are termed *creative* coordination situations and do not allow for the explanation, prediction, and control of human behaviors in terms of antecedent conditions, while the latter are termed *standardized* coordination situations and do allow for the creation and verification of human communication theories within a traditional measurement model of antecedent conditions. While human communication theories could be developed to explain either creative or standardized interactions, only the latter theories will allow for explanations antecedent to interaction which can predict and verify rules theories. Communication theorists who seek to develop rules theories which employ traditional measurement models thus restrict their domain of inquiry to human actions aimed at coordination within standardized situations. These rules theorists seek to locate as a basis for theory building a coordination task which generates a standardized system of rule-governed, symbol-meaning associations which are relatively persistent because the participants engaged in some task have found the system particularly useful for coordinating their activities in regard to that task (Capella, 1972). Several important implications regarding the empirical verification of rules theories and the use of practical reasoning as an explanatory device for explanation, prediction, and control follow from this third assumption.

The first problem created by the attempt to empirically verify a rules theory is how one can empirically separate rule-governed patterns of behavior from causally determined patterns of behavior. When human communication patterns constitute a rule, they do so because such behaviors are consciously coordinated by being mutually dependent on one another. A rule exists when, and only when, two or more people do the same thing under certain conditions because each expects the other to so behave and each is aware of the others expectation. Thus, a pattern of behavior becomes empirically verifiable as rule governed when a mutual expectation regarding what is appropriate behavior in a given situation can serve as a standard to judge and evaluate (so that one has the *right* to expect certain conduct) and not merely an expectation. While habits are descriptive of human behavior, rules are evaluative of such behaviors and thus monitored by those employing the rule.

In order for empirical research to employ an antecedent model for explanation, prediction, and control within the rules perspective, Cushman and Pearce (1977) argue:

> . . . [First] such research must locate tasks which require coordination because such tasks serve as the generative mechanism for communication rules which take the form of standardized usages and episodic sequences. Next, a researcher must define and measure the generality and necessity of the standardized usage and its various episodic sequences. Finally, we outline three forms which the practical syllogism may take in modeling the generality and necessity of episodic sequences. (pp. 173–183)

Each of these are necessary conditions for rules research to have theoretical import. Collectively, they represent the sufficient condition for such an outcome. Why, because all human actions necessarily involve rules, all actions requiring coordination with others necessarily involve communication, and communication rules and all standardized coordination situations necessarily involve stable communication rules which are carefully monitored in order to avoid deviations and are thus intersubjectively verifiable.

Having examined in some detail the assumptions which underlie the rules-theory approach, we are now in a position to examine the methodological procedures for conceptualizing and operationalizing human action.

SELF-CONCEPT AS A CYBERNETIC CONTROL SYSTEM
FOR HUMAN ACTION

Human actions which take place within a standardized coordination situation require common intentions, an established set of rules for the cooperative achievement of those intentions, and a procedure for manifesting the variable practical force the actors feel for participating in the coordination task. If rules theories of human communication processes seek the explanation, prediction, and control of individual behaviors in such situations, then we are in need of an empirically verifiable construct in terms of which to investigate the link between an individual's perceptions, thoughts, and behaviors. Such a construct will provide a theoretical representation of the conceptual forms through which actors understand and come to grips with the world. We believe that the self-concept provides just such an empirically verifiable construct. Our analysis of why and how the self-concept has the theoretical status of a cybernetic control system for human action in standardized coordination situations will be developed in three stages. First, we will explore the nature, function, and scope of the self-concept and indicate the manner in which it organizes human action. Next we will explore the self-concept as a coordinator of positive and negative feedback, as a cybernetic control system. Finally, we shall review briefly the empirical research which grounds this conceptualization.

The Nature of the Self-Concept

The self-concept traditionally has been viewed as the information an individual has regarding the relationship of objects or groups of objects to oneself (Mead, 1934). An individual moving in his/her environment is confronted by persons, places, things, or concepts. When confronted by such objects, one must, if one is to commit oneself to any action toward those objects, perform two tasks. First, one must determine what the objects in one's environment are by associating them with and differentiating them from other objects of one's experience. Second, one must determine the relationship of the object or group of objects to oneself in terms of what appropriate meanings, evaluations, and behaviors they entail for the actor. One's knowledge of what objects are and how one should act toward them is a product of information based on past experience.

This does not mean the individual only has object relationships in his/her experiential field which include the self as one of the objects. The statement, "Aristotle is dead," for example, provides information about Aristotle without conveying anything about oneself. On the other hand, such statements as, "I am tall," "I am a good democrat," and "I am a good teacher and therefore must have my papers graded on time," do provide information about oneself and, therefore, would be part of the self-concept. Following Thompson (1972), we will divide all such self–object relationships into three classes. First, statements such as "I am tall," designate relationships pertaining to what an individual *is,* that is, they name or label an individual's attributes. These statements form the *identity self.* Second, other self–object statements such as *good,* describe how a person feels about one's relationship to objects or one's self-satisfaction. These statements, then, form the *evaluative self.* Finally, the statement, "I am a good teacher and therefore must have my papers graded on time," in addition to providing information for identifying and evaluating the self, prescribe an appropriate behavior to be performed in regard to the self–object relationship and constitute the *behavioral self.* Consequently, the behavioral self can be represented as a set of imperatives for action, rules governing an individual's behavior with respect to relevant objects in a situation.

The relationships which comprise the self-concept are important in at least three ways. First, the information an individual gleans as a result of an encounter with one object will apply to all other objects one places in the same *class.* An individual can thus make an inference about his/her relationship to an object without encountering that object. One need only have encountered another object which one categorizes with the first. Second, such self-concept structures provide individuals with *expectations* about the nature of those objects they believe to be subsumed under associated rules. The self-concept thus directs perception, causing an individual to notice certain characteristics of an object and to react to an object on the basis of those characteristics. Third, as the self-concept develops, it provides the individual with *preconceived plans* of action. A self–object relationship constitutes a ready made format for processing experience and initiating action. With such a system a person has prepared himself/herself for coping with the future and making sense out of the past. Hence, we regard the self-concept as an organized set of structures which defines the relationship of objects to individuals and which is capable of governing and directing human action. Furthermore, the self-concept, as an organized set of structures, provides the rationale for choice in the form of a balanced repertory of alternative meanings, evaluations, and plans of action.

The Self-Concept as a Cybernetic Control System

We regard the self-concept as the coordinator and initiator of the positive and negative feedback systems in the services of goal-seeking and systematic change. We do not, however, suggest that the process by which an individual forms and executes *all* his/her acts is completely determined prior to performing a particular act. Mead's definition of the act is congruent with our view. The act, Mead asserts, encompasses a complete span of intention with its initial point as an impulse and its terminator in some objective reaction of another which completes the impulse. Between initiation and termination, the individual may be in the process of constructing, organizing, and reorganizing his/her plans for action on the basis of environmental cues (Mead, 1938).

An individual's judgment that a new approach to some situation is useful and worth pursuing requires a previous organizational pattern for comparison purposes. The self-concept provides the previous pattern and the information needed to recognize the implications of the new pattern. Thus, the self-concept is a necessary constituent in the positive feedback system. The new organization and pattern being pursued will also be represented in the self-concept as a new rule or pattern for action in specified situations. Similarly, when the individual has a fixed goal and is in the process of pursuing a standardized pattern of behavior in order to obtain that goal, the self-concept provides the pattern of information needed for a negative feedback system to monitor behavior in accordance with previously established rules for goal attainment. When action is initiated in the external world the actor will engage in a process of feedback evaluation to determine the goodness-of-fit between his/her belief about the appropriate choice and his/her progress toward attainment of his/her purpose.

The self-concept is thus conceptualized as the amount of information an individual has regarding his/her relationship to objects. This information contains identity, evaluative, and behavioral aspects. The internal organization of the self-concept may remain stable or be modified by an individual's interaction with others and the environment. When rules theorists restrict their domain of inquiry to communication behaviors involving human actions in coordination situations governed and guided by standardized rules, they are restricting the portions of the self-concept they seek to measure in three ways. First, they are attempting to measure a stable rather than a dynamic class of self-concept rules. Second, these rules are held in common by all those involved in the coordination task and thus are intersubjectively verifiable through measurement. Third, deviations from this stable set of rules is internally monitored and corrected by those involved in the coordination task. Thus, deviations from the rules are also intersubjectively verifiable.

If the self-concept serves as a cybernetic control system for the rules which govern and guide human understanding and behavior, then we would expect empirical research employing self-concept measures to reveal a necessary and substantial relationship between such measures and message comprehension, message adaptation, and message effectiveness in controlling our own and others' behaviors. Our review of the research literature will attempt to demonstrate that just such relationships have been found to exist. In so doing, we will be demonstrating that the rules which govern and guide human action can be scientifically measured as they are manifest in the self-concept antecedent to and are predictive of an individual's subsequent behavior.

The research literature which pertains to the theoretical relationship between self-concept and essential communication functions involves considerable variation in measurement procedures utilized by investigators, widely differing in theoretical orientations and in the meanings they attach to the specific constructs they are attempting to study (Burns, 1979). However, despite such diversity there is a fundamental commonality. All such studies depend on measures which differentiate, from an actor's point of view, the objects or attributes of objects which constitute that actor's experiential field. Such measures are here termed self-concept measures. These measures normally make three distinctions. First, some measures, principally employ nominal scales to locate the set of objects or attributes of objects in an actor's self-concept. Second, other measures principally employ ordinal scales to locate the hierarchical ordering of objects or attributes of objects in an actor's experiential field. Such measures delineate the *depth* of an actor's self-concept. Finally, still other measures employ interval and ratio scales to locate the distance between self, objects, and attributes or objects in an actor's experiential field. Such measures delineate the *configuration* of an actor's self-concept.

The most frequently used nominal scales are Kuhn and McPartland's (1954) Twenty Question Statement Test and Long, Henderson, and Ziller's (1967) Social Symbolic Task, measures which attempt to delineate the *Scope* of the self-concept or field of perceptual objects. Typical ordinal scales are Kelly's (1955) Rep test and Pitts' (1965) Tennessee Self-Concept scale, which attempt to measure the *depth* of the self-concept or the degree of cognitive differentiation within categories of objects, and typical interval and ratio scales are Osgood, Suci, and Tannenbaum's

(1957) Semantic Differential scale and Woelfel and Fink (1980) Galileo system, which measure the *configuration* of the self-concept or the distances between self and objects.

Message Comprehension Studies

Several researchers have employed self-concept measures to examine the cognitive bases of optimal receptivity to interpersonal interactions. Couch (1955) and Hawes (1964) demonstrated that the *scope* of self-concept differentiation is related to an individual's encoding skill. Triandis (1960), Delia and Clark (1977), and Hull and Levy (1979) demonstrated that the depth of self-concept differentiation is related to social perspective-taking skill. Newcomb (1953), Zajonc (1960), and Carr (1969) demonstrated that the *configuration* of self-concept differentiation is related to encoding skill. Delia and his associates (Delia, Kline, & Burleson, 1979) persistently found that scope and depth of cognitive complexity accounts for between 16 and 54% of the variation in social perspective-taking skills of adults. The information an individual has regarding his/her relationship to objects thus influences that individual's capacity to correctly encode the messages of others.

Message Adaptation Studies

Delia and his associates (Applegate & Delia, 1980) employed cognitive measures to investigate the relationship between social perspective-taking and the creation of listener-adapted messages. Applegate and Delia reported on four studies investigating the degree of association between the scope and depth of interpersonal construct systems of adults and person-centered communication. They found the level of cognitive differentiation to account for 25% of the variation in person-centered communication. Applegate and Delia (1980) and Delia, Kline, and Burleson (1979) demonstrated that construct abstractness accounts for 25% of the variation in person centered communication. Finally, O'Keefe and Delia demonstrated a necessary relationship between cognitive complexity and the number of communication appeals, with the latter accounting for 49% of the variation in the former. Delia and his associates persistently found that social perspective taking accounts for between 16 and 58% of the variation in listener-adapted messages. The degree to which an individual can accurately understand others thus influences his/her capacity to adapt messages to the communication-relevant dimensions of others.

Message Effectiveness

Several researchers have employed self-concept measures and message adaptation measures to explore message effectiveness in influencing attitudes and behaviors. Triandis (1960) demonstrated an independent and substantial relationship between encoding and message-adaptation skills on communication effectiveness. He found that each process accounted for substantial variation in the attitude change of a receiver. Carr (1969, 1970) found that both the configuration of an encoder's cognitive differentiation and his/her message-adaptation skills related to changes in the behavior of psychiatric patients, students, and voters. Finally, Thompson reviewed literature providing support for the relationship between self-concept strength and such message-effectiveness behaviors as (1) overcoming anxiety, (2) attempts to control others, and (3) achievements of communication consensus. Dobson (1970) and G. A. Harris (1968) found strength of self-concept to be negatively related to communication anxiety such that between 25 and 50% of the variation in communication anxiety was accounted for by a weak self-concept. McFarland (1970) conducted two studies aimed at investigating the relationship between strength of self-concept and attempts at control. Strength of self-concept accounted for between 4 and 16% of variation in communication attempts to control others. Cardillo (1971) examined the relationship between self-concept and communication success in achieving consensus. He found that strength of self-concept accounts for 16% of the variation in achieved agreement and 25% of the variation in both achieved understanding and realization. The degree to which an individual can accurately understand others and the individual's message-adaptation skills thus influence message effectiveness in coordinated goal attainment.

CONCLUSION

Our review of the research suggests several important conclusions. First, a relationship exists among scope, depth, and configuration of the self-concept and message comprehension. Second, a substantial and necessary relationship exists between message comprehension and message adaptation. Finally, a necessary relationship exists between both message comprehension and communicator effectiveness and message adaptation and communicator effectiveness, as measured by attitudinal and behavioral change.

Taken collectively, this research suggests that the rules which govern and guide human action are manifest in the self-concept as scientifically measurable relationships between the individual and the objects in his/her experiential field. Further, these scientific measures can be made antecedent to an individual undertaking human action and be employed to explain, predict, and control that individual's subsequent communication behavior, attitudinal change, and behavioral change. We are now in a position to examine the development and validation of such a theory for the formation of interpersonal relationships.

CHAPTER 17

Acculturation and Communication Competence

W. Barnett Pearce and Kyung-wha Kang

INTRODUCTION

Human infants are born "unfinished," with potentials for learning rather than instincts (Geertz, 1973). "Enculturation" or "socialization" names a formative process in which the stories and practices of a particular culture "complete" the gestation of a fully functioning adult. Within one's native culture, communication competence has traditionally meant "fitting in," reproducing—or modifying in contiguous ways—existing patterns of action and meaning. Because there is an assumed congruence between individual action and social forms, communication itself is often taken for granted, a ubiquitous process used to accomplish other purposes, and attention is paid to communication competence only when someone fails to satisfy the exigencies of a particular situation.

This perspective of humans are necessarily enculturated, however, implies a radical reconceptualization of the role of communication and the nature of communication competence. Communication is seen as the process by which social realities—including seemingly permanent social institutions and seemingly intractable personal characteristics—are created and managed. As such, it is far more central to the human condition than has generally been acknowledged. For example, the fifteenth edition of the *Encyclopaedia Britannica* is the first to deal with communication as a topic, and even this treatment focuses on the technologies and theories of "mass communication." If we are right, however, communication as a human process underlies and unifies many of the standard topics by means of which scholars have thought about the human condition (see Pearce, Kang, & Gielis, in press).

Communication competence is systemic, a matter of the relationship between the performance demands of any given culture and the capabilities of particular communicators (Pearce & Cronen, 1980, Chapter 6). Enculturation in a particular society enables communication "like a native" with natives but, simultaneously, makes one unfit for competent communication in other societies. That which "fits in" to a given culture is often strikingly inappropriate for another, and engaging in these behaviors is not simply a performance; it is an expression and reconstruction of individuals' personalities and social institutions—the very moral imperatives by which human life achieves meaning.

This perspective on communication and competence is obscured in monocultural situations, and communication theories which deal only with those situations risk enfranchising the biases of a particular culture into their account of the human condition. What is needed is transcultural concepts in communication theory which illuminate the differences and similarities of various cultures (Kang & Pearce, 1984). Such theories are best based on intercultural comparisons, such as those situations in which individuals from different cultures confront each other or in which a given individual confronts two cultures. The latter is our focus in this paper.

Modern society itself is paradoxical. The performance demands for fitting in require "novelty" or "innovation," which by definition are different from the patterns of thought and action which preceeded them. The effect is ubiquitous change in *mores,* in institutions, in language use, in racial and gender roles, etc. As Marx observed, "All that is solid melts into air" (quoted in Berman, 1982). Those persons enculturated into modern society are perpetual immigrants, continually confronting a changed set of cultural stories and practices (Pearce & Lannamann, 1982). In addition, the latter half of the twentieth century is another time in which there are major movements of individuals across national borders. The entire July 8, 1985, issue of *Time* magazine was devoted to "Immigrants: The Changing Face of America."

The archetypal experience of an immigrant is that of bringing a set of stories and practices from one culture into another in which they do not fit. The task confronting immigrants is that of learning to live and move with acceptable proficiency in the symbolic and behavioral system of the new culture and of dealing with the stories and practices of the culture of origin. This process is usually labeled "acculturation." Significant as a social phenomenon per se, acculturation is a process whose characteristics are likely to expose monocultural biases in theories of communication and competence.

ACCULTURATION

Communication and acculturation are obviously related, but there have been relatively few empirical or conceptual efforts to specify the precise nature of the relationship between these concepts. Y. Y. Kim (1977) summarized the anthropological and sociological literatures as demonstrating the unsurprising phenomenon that persons with different levels of acculturation communicate differently with members of the "new" culture and summarized two unpublished studies in communication discipline as making much the same point: There are individual and intergenerational differences in the communication patterns of ethnic groups in a second culture. (W. H. Chang, 1972; Nagata, 1969).

Two more recent studies used the technique of causal modeling to describe the relation between communication and acculturation more precisely. Y. Y. Kim (1977) found that communication behavior mediated the relationships among variables traditionally thought to affect acculturation and the "perceptual complexity" of Korean immigrants to the United States. Specifically, persons who engaged in interpersonal communication with Americans developed "a greater number of dimensions-worth of information with which to comprehend" the new culture. Use of mass media had a smaller facilitative effect. J. K. Kim (1980) criticized this study for excluding the effect of "ethnically oriented communication variables" and for not demonstrating the conceptual relationship between perceptual complexity and acculturation. J. K. Kim found that intercultural communication facilitated and ethnic communication impeded acculturation of Korean immigrants to the United States. Further, the facilitative effect of intercultural communication increased as a function of the length of time the person had lived in the United States.

The studies by Y. Y. Kim and J. K. Kim clearly show that communicative behavior, particularly interpersonal communication with members of the host culture, improves or at least increases the rate of acculturation. However, three comments are in order.

First, the magnitude of the predicted relationships in these studies is not overwhelming. In both studies, some predicted causal paths were not confirmed, and the strengths of those that were confirmed were relatively modest: The correlation coefficients were .31 between intercultural communication and acculturation, −.21 between ethnic communication and acculturation, .48 between interpersonal communication and perceptual complexity, and .17 between mass media consumption and perceptual complexity.

Second, "communication" in these studies is defined as the number of times a person exchanged messages with other people in the ethnic group or in the new culture or the number of times they watched or listened to mass-mediated messages. This procedure treats communication as something which "increases" as a function of frequency. Qualitative differences between, for example, a fight and a therapy session, are treated as unmeasured error variance.

Third, the conceptualization of acculturation in these studies is problematic. Y. Y. Kim's use of "perceptual complexity" seems contaminated by, among other things, individual differences in the cognitive complexity of her subjects and the variation in types of communication experiences they had with members of the host culture. J. K. Kim defined acculturation as the extent to which Korean immigrants responded as Americans did to questionnaire items which discriminated between monocultural Koreans and Americans.

J. K. Kim's procedure brings the conceptual issue into sharp focus. The person confronting two cultures is in a qualitatively different position than one whose personal history is determinedly monocultural. An immigrant, we suppose, learns how to do things in two (or more) appropriate ways, each of which fits in one culture but not in others. If immigrants' competence is measured only in terms of how well they fit in to one culture, something very important for understanding communication is lost: their position as straddling different cultures. J. K. Kim's concept of acculturation is monocultural; it gives privileged position to learning the ways of thinking and acting in the new culture and ignores (or penalizes) those who maintain some of their native culture and those who find ways to integrate their two cultures into richer social texts than are available for monocultural persons.

An alternative notion of acculturation is to view immigrants as confronting disparate cultures and to ask *how* they handled the differences rather than privileging one potential means of adapting to the new culture. Let "transculturation" denote the experience of polyculturality. There may be many ways of dealing with this experience, of which becoming just like the natives of the new culture is one of the least sophisticated— and perhaps the least satisfying.

Kang's (1984) research on transculturation shows that there is considerable differentiation among immigrants in the way they cope with polyculturality. Some of the more sophisticated procedures include developing a sort of "double vision"; the capacity to envision episodes as appropriate in both cultures. These persons could then choose how they wanted to act—e.g., "like an American" or "like a Korean"—in any given instance.

One of the implications of this sophisticated style of confronting a new culture is that it makes the immigrant inconsistent as viewed by a researcher. Sometimes they are very Korean, sometimes very American. If there is a notion that acculturation is a linear phenomenon of incorporating the stories and practices of the new culture, this type of behavior is very confusing. So much the worse for that notion of acculturation! Many immigrants are able to create stories and practices which are a sophisticated mix of several cultures, and which afford them a great deal of self-control (to the consternation of the social scientist trying to predict how they will act).

This happy news that many immigrants respond creatively to the confrontation of their native culture and a new culture is more than reassuring about the lives of the millions who experience immigration. It also provides a source of enrichment for the cultures to which the immigrants come and for theories of human communication. Specifically, the more sophisticated responses to the experience of polyculturality pose major challenges to concepts of communication competence.

COMMUNICATION COMPETENCE

If communication competence is not just fitting into the local culture, what is it? L. M. Harris (1979) developed a systemic model of communication competence, which defines it as the ability to control the extent to which one is enmeshed in the logic of a particular system. This model has the advantage of describing the relationship between an individual and any number of social systems rather than taking a particular system for granted and supposing that competence means fitting into that system.

Immigrants are initially "outside" the new culture and are thus "minimally" competent. They do not know how to act, cannot judge whether particular acts are right or wrong, and are often surprised by the sequence of events. Learning to be not minimally competent seems an important aspect of acculturation, but there are different ways of doing this.

"Satisfactory" competence describes persons who have gotten "inside" the new system and have accepted its boundaries as their own. This is acculturation as J. K. Kim defined it. Satisfactorily competent immigrants fill out questionnaires in a manner indistinguishable from natives; they define any deviation from the norms as a "mistake" rather than, for example, a choice; they seek to eliminate vestiges of their accent or ethnic identities.

"Optimal" competence describes persons who internalize some combination of more than one culture and thus can control the extent to which they are enmeshed in either the native or the new culture. At times, they move comfortably within the new culture; at other times they preserve their native culture; and at still others they perform uniquely based on their own integrations of several cultural forms.

Consider a conversation among three persons, one a monocultural Korean, one a monocultural American, and the third having had bicultural experience in Korea and America. For the sake of argument, assume that whatever communication difficulties that might occur will *not* be related to difficulties with language. Obviously, cultural differences pose a problem for a three-way "coordinated management of meaning" (Pearce & Cronen, 1980). If the conversation is casual, the American (male) may sit with legs crossed in a "figure 4" with one ankle resting on the opposite knee without realizing the strongly negative significance this has in Korean culture; the Korean may use honorifics and be quietly responsive rather than being "open" and helping initiate the conversation without realizing that this appears "cold" to the American; and the American and Korean may respond quite differently if the conversation reaches a point where the demands of factual honesty conflict with those of role obligations. Both monocultural persons are minimally competent in the culture of the other, and rather predictable communication problems will be encountered as described by Tyler and others (1980).

A different and not so predictable communication problem faces the biculturally experienced person. Ironically, the ability of this person to perceive the meaning of each communicative act from the perspective of both cultures makes him/her more aware of the problems in the situation and less able to act with confidence that he/she will be understood. If this person is acculturated to the extent of "satisfactory competence," he/she will act like the member of the new culture (this is J. K. Kim's definition of acculturation) but with an awareness that this causes problems for the third party. However, if the person is optimally competent, he/she has several choices: he/she may alternate acting like a Korean and like an American, or he/she may do something unique which is simultaneously appropriate for both monocultural conversants.

The qualitative difference between optimal and satisfactory communication competence is important for four reasons. First, the rules for meaning and action in any culture are incomplete and contradictory, and a strategy of learning by imitation and performing by conforming is inherently limited. M. Harris (1974) discussed this problem in his critique of the "new ethnoscience" and summarized his argument in the title of his paper: "Why a Perfect Knowledge of All the Rules One Must Know to Act Like A Native Cannot Lead to a Knowledge of How Natives Act." The problems confronted by ethnographers also confront the acculturating persons and limit the development of their communication competence.

Second, the distinction between satisfactory and optimal competence facilitates the study and perhaps achievement of some of the highest values to be derived from acculturation. Among others, Hall (1977) stressed the personal development which may result from bicultural experience: The person may learn the parameters of his/her own culture as well as the content of a new culture and become more fully human. However, this desirable consequence does not always occur; some immigrants remain perpetual tourists who continually wish that things were like they were "back home," and the human values of bicultural experience are lost by those who acculturate to a satisfactorily competent level because this simply implies the substitution of one culture for another.

There are many training programs designed to facilitate acculturation. However, they may have selected the wrong objective. By identifying the characteristics of optimal competence in acculturation and by determining the conditions under which it is developed, educational programs can be devised which facilitate the achievement of human values in the process of acculturation.

Third, the characteristics of modern society—particularly the prevalence and celebration of change—make satisfactory competence impossible. Lerner (1958) defined "modernity" as "primarily a state of mind—expectation of progress, propensity to growth, readiness to adapt oneself to change." A society this open demands the characteristics of optimal competence as the basic requirement for participation. This is by no means an easy cultural imperative. Using the rubric "Cosmopolitan Communication," we have attempted to articulate some of its implications for ways of thinking and forms of criteria (see Pearce *et al.,* in press).

Fourth, the difference between optimal and satisfactory competence is crucial if communication theory is to avoid simply sanctifying the biases of a particular culture by incorporating it into the timeless terminology of science. Immigrants are important informants (not "subjects"). Their experience teaches us that we are all enculturated and that culture is—in a specific, technical sense—unnatural and unnecessary.

Culture is unnatural because it is the product of human agency and subject to redefinition rather than being an immutable law of nature or an objective phenomenon independent of human knowing. The raw materials of culture are the vicissitudes of time, tide, and circumstance, but the result is the product of the social construction of meaning. Culture is unnecessary because the human mind, particularly in social interaction, can organize meanings in any number of ways rather than following some inherent, necessary principle.

The social realities of cultures pose a problem for theory because they are unnatural and unnecessary. Theorists operate by constructing models and testing the goodness-of-fit to specific phenomena (Harre & Madden, 1975). The scientific revolution in Western culture was the demonstration that a relatively few, comparatively simple "mechanical" models could be used to generate surprisingly useful information about physical events. These models of similar ones cannot be expected to apply to humanly created meanings because these systems have many and changing structures. The terms useful for describing the structure of natural systems are particularly inappropriate in attempting to account for a person's proficiency in moving among two or more symbolic systems. We believe that a science dealing with humanly constructed meanings must be at a level of abstraction different from the physical sciences, employing a metamodel or model of the models which persons themselves use in learning, creating, and managing their symbolic systems.

This theoretical perspective suggests a series of questions, the answers to which should describe the characteristics of optimally competent acculturation. First, how are the two cultures represented in the mind of the acculturating person? We have seen exemplars of four possible ways of representing the cultures. The "perpetual tourist" perceives the new culture as duplicating his/her native culture and, consistent with the concept of minimal competence, defines as mistakes those behaviors by natives which do not fit into his/her expectations. The "cultural convert" perceives the new culture as the only legitimate one and defines as mistakes or shameful foolishnesses those behaviors performed by him/her or members of the ethnic group which fit the old but not the new culture. The "perpetual alien" uses some sort of cognitive balancing procedure and "averages" the differences between the two cultures, in the process rendering himself/herself minimally competent in both. To be optimally competent, the acculturating person must develop a differentiated rule structure including a representation of both cultures.

Second, how does the person "move" within and/or between the logical forces of the two cultures? Differentiating cultures within the cognitive frame of a person poses a problem for coherent interpretation of logical events and for deciding how to act. In fact, some schools of psychology define "integration" as an index of health and/or maturity. An optimally competent person should be able to convert this problem to an opportunity by having at least some volitional control over which set of rules to use when enacting or interpreting an episode. Rather than being confused by the differences or unwillingly "trapped" into either set of rules, optimally competent persons should be able to choose whether to act like an American or like a Korean in particular episodes.

Third, what is the relation between the acculturating person's concept of himself/herself and the logics of the cultures? A minimally or satisfactorily competent person identifies himself/herself with the content and structure of the symbolic system in which he/she is enmeshed. However, optimally competent persons may be "alienated" or "transcendent" (Pearce & Cronen, 1980, Chapter 6). An alienated optimally competent person is estranged from the content and structure of the symbolic system(s) of which he/she is a part, whatever definition of self is implied by these systems, the person must be something other than that. In contrast, a transcendent optimally competent person identifies himself/herself with the fact that he/she is variably enmeshed in multiple systems and is not fully identified by the meanings in any of them; the self is located *simultaneously* and *unproblematically* both inside and outside each of the cultural system of which he/she is a part.

The Western notion of logic—and thus of what relationships are possible—is based on Aristotle's principle of identity, which specifies that a thing cannot be both "A" and "not A" (see Cronen, Johnson, & Lannamann, 1982). This principle must be violated by the reasoning of an optimally competent person. Varela (1975) introduced into formal logic the "autonomous operator" which describes an entity which is indicated by itself and which parallels the characterization of the relationship between the self and the several logical forces in the cognitive system of a transcendent optimally competent person. The autonomous operator is represented by a stylized snake biting its tail (□). This symbol indicated that Varela has formalized a concept long in use in the wisdom literatures of various peoples, particularly in Asia. The descriptions of Hindu or Buddhistic "enlightenment" as well as the "mystic" tradition in the West stress the simultaneous unity with and nonattachment to both poles of what appear to be dichotomies in experiences.

CONCLUSION

The experience of polyculturality sometimes produces optimal competence and, with it, a special, uniquely rich manner of being human. Meanings are hierarchically organized, and maturation (in a qualitative rather than temporal sense) lies in becoming aware of and able to choose at successively higher levels of hierarchical contextualization.

The development of personality is perhaps inevitably a conflict between social imitation (e.g., doing what has always been done without knowledge of alternatives) and individual choice (e.g., doing what one chooses even if what is chosen is to perform in traditional ways). In this process, confrontation with several cultures, however this confrontation is managed, is a powerful process of making persons aware of the alternatives. It solves lower level problems and precipitates high level problems. In this instance, lower level problems refer to the awareness that cultures differ and to the development of sufficient differentiation within the system of rules so that the person can act appropriately in each. Higher level problems refer to the development of an integrative logic such that the self may be perceived simultaneously and unproblematically as enmeshed in incompatible cultures. The practices and stories which express such a logic are not likely to be totally useless in a world which includes economic and political integration of cultures which differ in moralities and aspirations.

CHAPTER 18

The Prospect for Cultural Communication

Gerry Philipsen

INTRODUCTION

Every people manages somehow to deal with the inevitable tension between the impulse of individuals to be free and the constraints of communal life. Such resolutions, of course, are never fixed in some absolute cultural stasis. The reality of a culture as experienced by those who live it moves along an axis with two poles at the opposing extremes, one exerting a pull toward the communal, the other toward the individual, as the dominant themes and warrants of human thought, speech, and action. Locating a culture on this axis reveals a partial truth about it, a kind of cultural snapshot, but in order to perceive the culture fully, one must also know the culture's direction of movement along the axis and the relative strengths of the competing forces pushing it one way or another.

Observers of contemporary Western society characterize its last several centuries in terms of gradual, unchecked movement from a communal culture to an individual consciousness. Recently, this process has been noticed, and this noticing has made possible, and in part stimulated,

COMMUNICATION THEORY:
EASTERN AND WESTERN PERSPECTIVES

countervailing forces, such that there has emerged a history and a critique of the movement away from the communal. On one hand is the plethora of lay, literary, and professional rhetoric pressing for the primacy of the individual conscience and the cultivation of the intimate bond as the context for its nurture and celebration. On the other is a nostalgic yearning for community and memorial ways. It is not known how strong these countervailing forces are, but it seems obvious that Western society is moving toward the individual and away from the communal poles of the axis but also that there are emergent forces—or voices—of counterpoise which must be mapped onto the axis of contemporary cultural life.

In Western society in the past four centuries, the interplay between the individual and the communal motives and sensibilities has been sharply correlated with trends in human communication. Three broad shifts in the discursive terrain, their attendant problems, and consequent conserving reactions can be noted. In his book, *The Fall of Public Man,* Sennett (1976) noted one of these changes. He claims that over the past four centuries the center of moral gravity has shifted from the public to the intimate domain of human expression. The public has been replaced by the intimate as the standard and the setting for communication conduct. In the past, according to Sennett, it was society—the public group— which laid down ways of acting in public, and these rules were important forces in human affairs. Today, by contrast, there is a relative emphasis on negotiation between and among intimates about ways of acting in private, and these rules are the relatively important forces in human affairs (Sennett, 1976).

A second thesis was advanced by Berger, Berger, and Kellner (1974) in their book, *The Homeless Mind.* They claim that "honor" has been replaced by "dignity" as an ultimate term in the vocabulary of motives of Western man. There has been, they said, a shift in the appreciation of persons because of their attained or ascribed status to appreciation of persons because of their personhood itself. Such a shift is manifested in the decline in fashion of *honor*ifics and the contempt by many for their use. Berger *et al.* wrote:

> The social location of honor lies in a world of relatively intact, stable institutions, a world in which individuals can with subjective certainty attach their identities to the institutional roles that society assigns to them. The disintegration of this world as a result of the forces of modernity has not only made honor an increasingly meaningless notion, but has served as the occasion for a redefinition of identity and its intrinsic dignity apart from and often *against* the institutional roles through which the individual expresses himself in society. The reciprocity between individual and society, between subjective identity and objective identification through roles, now comes to be experienced as a sort of struggle. Institu-

tions cease to be the "home" of the self; instead they become oppressive realities that distort and estrange the self. Roles no longer actualize the self, but serve as a "veil of *maya*" hiding the self not only from others but from the individual's own consciousness. (Berger *et al.,* 1974, pp. 93–94)

Steiner, a literary historian and critic, noted a third trend. Based on his analyses of selected literary works in several centuries including the twentieth, Steiner found compelling evidence of a weakening of the tendency to withhold thoughts from public presentation, a loosening of the rules for public utterance. Relatively less time is spent in forming, shaping, and editing speech than was done in previous eras, relatively more is spent in talking (Steiner, 1979).

Although these shifts in emphasis from the communal to the individual have been described here in relatively neutral terms and although they have in part been welcomed by those who document them, there is nonetheless an attendant critique. First, coordinating diverse lines of action becomes problematic when rules for selecting and attaining goals are not widely known and shared. This is the problem of *alignment* (there is a related problem of civility), as manifested in such contemporary conditions as the apparent decline in the capacity for institutional coordination. The apparent inability to perform, without disruption, such public ceremonies as high school graduations, has been observed in the author's community, Seattle, Washington. Such failures are symptoms of a deeper, more chilling problem—the replacement of cultural value by undisciplined force as the locus of control in contemporary life. As Sennett (1976) wrote:

. . . the masks of self which manners and the rituals of politeness create . . . have ceased to matter in interpersonal situations or seem to be the property only of snobs; in closer relationships, they appear to get in the way of knowing someone else. And I wonder if this contempt for ritual masks of sociability has not really made us more primitive culturally than the simplest tribe of hunters and gatherers. (p. 15)

Or, as Berry (1978), a critic of contemporary culture, wrote, "To think or act without cultural value, and the restraints invariably implicit in cultural value, is simply to wait upon force" (p. 169).

Second, a sense of who one is becomes problematic when the burden for personal definition is shifted from society to self. This is the problem of *meaning,* as is manifested in a widespread sense of what Berger called "homelessness":

The individual is given enormous latitude in fabricating his own particular private life—a kind of "do-it-yourself" universe. . . . This latitude obviously has its satisfactions, but it also imposes severe burdens. The most obvious is that most individuals *do not kow how* to construct a universe and therefore become furiously frustrated when they are faced with a need to do so. The most fundamental function of institutions is probably to protect the individual from having to make too many choices. The private sphere has arisen as an interstitial area left over by the large institutions of modern institutions of society. As such, it has become underinstitutionalized and therefore become an area of unparalleled liberty and anxiety for the individual. Whatever compensations the private sphere provides are usually experienced as fragile, possibly artificial and essentially unreliable. (Berger *et al.,* 1974, pp. 186–187)

Third, when the standards for permitting or distributing discourse break down, the interest and quality of speech declines. This is the problem of *form,* as is manifested when an egalitarian ethic works against the highest forms and accomplishments in speech. As Steiner (1977) has written:

Today, the stress is on "saying all," on telling "how it is," in explicit rebuttal to what are regarded as archaic, class-determined, uptight atavisms of censorship and decorum. . . . The approved loquacities of psychoanalysis, of mundane confession (as they are practiced in modern therapy), in modern literature, in competitive gragariousness, and on the media go directly counter to the ideals of communicative reticence or autonomy represented by the private letter, diary, or journal. The telephone consumes, with utter prodigality, raw materials of language of which a major portion was allocated to internal use or to the modulated inwardness of the private, silently conceived written correspondence. One is tempted to conclude that where much more is, in fact, being heard, less is being said. (p. 208)

In their studies, of contemporary American sociability, Riesman, Potter, and Watson (1960), and of contemporary public address, Baskerville (1980), provided disciplined, sobered assessment of the decline in standards of form in contemporary communication.

Problems of alignment, meaning, and form have prompted a rhetoric of lament by some observers of contemporary, Western communication. More positively, such concern is an expression of and a warrant for renewed interest in what Berger called the "human significance of tribalism." From the standpoint of communication theory, attention can productively be focused on *cultural communication.* This essay is a programmatic treatment of cultural communication as an emerging problem of contemporary communication theory, research, and practice. Specifically, I shall treat the nature, forms and functions, variations in styles, and prospects of cultural communication in contemporary society. I hope to propose a way to describe cultural communication and to propose a heuristic framework which lays the groundwork for a theory of ethnographic description and comparative analysis of cultural communication.

THE NATURE OF CULTURAL COMMUNICATION

A culture can be viewed from many perspectives, each of which provides one partial but important glance at the nature of things cultural. Three such perspectives can be discerned in the work of various scholars who have used the culture concept. When the focus is on culture as *code,* an observer examines a system of beliefs, values, and images of the ideal. Culture as code emphasizes the fixed and the ordered and focuses on the system of cognitive and moral constraints represented in a world view or value system. Culture as *conversation* emphasizes a patterned representation of a people's lived experience of work, play, and worship. Whereas code is a source of order, the lived conversation of a people is a source of the dynamism and creativity of culture. Codes and conversations are abstrations which, ultimately, can only be made from or applied to particular, nameable contexts, as part of and in part constitutive of a community. A focus on culture as *community* draws attention to a human grouping whose members claim a commonality derived from shared identity, an identity grounded in a communal ordering of memories or the memory traces of a tribe. Communities, thus, are the concrete settings and scenes where codes are learned and where the communal conversation is played out. These three perspectives, when taken together, afford a comprehensive insight into the nature of culture.

The function of communication in cultural communication is to maintain a healthy balance between the forces of individualism and community, to provide a sense of shared identity which nonetheless preserves individual dignity, freedom, and creativity. This function is performed through maintaining a balance or equilibrium between two subprocesses of cultural communication, (1) the creation and (2) the affirmation of shared identity. Thus, cultural communication is the process by which a code is realized and negotiated in a communal conversation. It includes the processes of enactment, a playing out and affirming of cultural forms, and of creation, the creation, adaptation, and transformation of those forms to meet the contingencies of daily life. As such, a community's discursive life both manifests the community's location on the communal–personal (or code-conversation) axis and serves as the means by which a condition of equilibrium is maintained.

A healthy culture maintains a balance among the subprocesses of enactment and creation. It maintains, in the words of Weaver, in *Visions of Order,* "an equipoise of status and function" (Weaver, 1964, p. 25). Depending on where the culture is located on the communal–personal axis, either enactment or creation will be more prominent than the others, and for maintaining a healthy balance of opposing forces in the culture, it is necessary to expend greater conscious effort at the other subprocess in order to perform the function of affirming shared identity while preserving individual dignity. An emerging problem of Western communication can, thus, be stated in terms of a broad shift which has created an imbalance among these processes, such that it is now important to work at moving from a process of creation to identification of those processes of cultural enactment which lead to affirmation of shared identity. Such efforts can be productively made only in terms of those communication forms which are designed to fulfill the cultural function. It is to those forms that I now turn.

FORMS AND FUNCTIONS OF CULTURAL COMMUNICATION

"At the root of culture must be the realization that uncontrolled energy is disorderly—that in nature all energies move in forms; that, therefore, in a human order energies must be *given* forms" (Berry, 1978, p. 122). Although the way the cultural function is performed differs from community to community, there are characteristic forms used to affirm and negotiate a sense of shared identity. Three of these which figure prominently in cultural communication are ritual, myth, and social drama.

Ritual is a communication form in which there is a structured sequence of symbolic acts, the correct performance of which constitutes homage to a sacred object. An example of a contemporary ritual, as described by two students of Black churches in America, is that of "call-response." Daniel and Smitherman (1976) noted that the sequencing of a call by a minister and a response by the congregation constitutes, in the Black churches studied, a sequence of acts which has grammatical force. The sacred object is Black togetherness and unity in a world of hostile, alien forces. Participation in the ritual performs the function of honoring that unity and of affirming commitment to it. Daniel and Smitherman wrote:

> As a communicative strategy, then, call-response is the manifestation of the cultural dynamic which finds audience and listener or leader and background to be a unified whole. Shot through with action and interaction, Black communicative performance is concentric in quality—the "audience" becoming both observers and participants in the speech event. As Black American Culture stresses communality and group experientiality, the audience's linguistic and paralinguistic responses are necessary to co-sign the power of the speaker's rap or call. They let him know if he's on the right case. A particular individual's linguistic

virtuosity is rewarded with a multiplicity of fervent and intense responses. Thus despite the cultural constraints imposed on individuality, skillful sacred and secular rappers can actualize their selfhood within the community setting. (1976, p. 39)

Rituals function so as to maintain the consensus necessary for social equilibrium and order, especially the nonrational consensus. Their form provides for the celebration of what is shared by participating in known sequences of coordinated action, which, by definition, require—and, once enacted, implicate—the exploitation of shared rules. Thus, ritual, the most highly precoded of the cultural communication forms, is a "declaration of form against indeterminacy" (Turner, 1980).

Whereas ritual provides a tightly woven form or pattern for affirming shared identity, myth offers a looser fabric of expression. A myth is a great symbolic narrative which holds together the imagination of a people and provides bases of harmonious thought and action. An example of contemporary mythic expression is found in Hannerz' study of Black men in a Washington, D.C. ghetto community. Each day, the members of the neighborhood streetcorner groups gathered together to talk about the day's activities. One participant described the activity in these gatherings as, "You just sit there and let your mouth run" (Hannerz, 1969, p. 107). But Hannerz found there is more than that. Each man was given an opportunity to tell a tale, a tale in which he, a Black man, must deal with a White man or woman, and in which he, the Black man, against the odds of his alter's superior moral position, used wit and cunning—usually verbal—to bring off at least some subtle, symbolic victory amid the inevitable degradation of the transactions with these important others in his life world. Hannerz wrote of such "streetcorner mythmaking":

The notion we are entertaining is that reminiscences may be like myths, sociability a kind of mythmaking. Myths, we have often been told, are intellectual phenomena by way of which men reflect on their condition: on myths men ground their beliefs about what moves them and their world. Of course, streetcorner narratives are not in all ways like prototypical myths. They are not sacred tales; they do not deal with primeval times, or with men who are like gods. The time is yesterday or yesteryear and the protagonist may be unemployed, separated, or perhaps most noted as someone who occasionally drinks too much. But ghetto men's reminiscences, when added together, may give the understanding of forces transcending the fate of any particular man, because these forces are the same regardless of who happens to be the narrator and temporary incumbent of that enternal protagaonist's position which we have referred to as Ghetto Man. The forces act from the world surrounding him, but they also move him from within. By sharing these experiences, the men establish the fact that a man can hardly help womanizing, drinking, and getting into trouble.

Myths posit a supersensible world of meaning and value from which the least member of a tribe can borrow something to dignify and give coherence to his life. Schneidau, in his book *Sacred Discontent,* claimed that myths do for the group what dreams do for the individual—they transform desires and fears, and especially conflicts and contradictions, into mental patterns that can be dealt with, faced up to (Schneidau, 1976, p. 7). Whereas ritual is the form whereby cultural actors most directly and most wholeheartedly affirm the past, the traditions, myth is the form wherein they creatively apply and discover the fit between past and present, community and individual. They can use myth to give life coherence, by seeing their own acts as conforming to a pattern which is implicit in the patterned stories of the heroic figures of their tribe's past.

A *social drama,* a "drama of living," can occur when specified personae gather together on some nameable or identifiable ground. Therein is created a scene, in which a particular dramatic action can unfold. Social dramas, with the scene thus set, consist of a dramatic sequence in which social actors manifest concern with, and negotiate the legitimacy and scope of, the group's rules of living. More specifically, as Turner (1980) described in his "Social Dramas and Stories about Them," the sequence of dramatic action follows four phases. In the first, there is a *breach*—a violation of the communal code. There follows a second stage, that of *crisis,* in which members of the community notice, attend to, and publicize the problematicity of the violation. Crisis is followed by *redress,* the third stage of the drama, in which the offender—or his spokesman— repairs or corrects the damage wrought by the breach. Finally, the offender is either *reintegrated* into the community or the community recognizes there is a schism or moral dissensus.

Social dramas play an important function in communal life. Whereas rituals have as their dominant function the celebration of a code and myths have as theirs the using of the code to make sense of the communal conversation, social dramas serve as occasions for defining the boundaries of the group and for reintegrating into the group those individuals whose acts have tested the community's moral boundaries. Whereas ritual is a way to affirm it and myth is a way to articulate and apply it, a social drama is a way to remake and negotiate a particular people's sense of communal life.

Surely there are other forms, and their attendant functions, of cultural communication. But in ritual, myth, and social drama, we have available to us three forms—three processual units—of cultural communication and three attendant social functions, ways of relating the individual to the communal. An understanding of these forms and the communal work they perform can lead to enhanced understanding of cultural communication.

VARIATION IN CULTURAL COMMUNICATION STYLE

Hymes (1974), building on the work of Margaret Mead and others, proposed a taxonomy consisting of a set of dimensions for the description of whole communities and their ways of speaking. The taxonomy includes four ideal-typical ways in which a given community resolves the personal–communal tension. In a *personal* society, as exemplified by the Arapesh, "societies depend, for impetus to or inhibition of community action in public situations, upon the continuing response of individuals. The point of communication is to excite interest and bring together persons who will then respond with emotion to whatever event has occurred" (Hymes, 1974, p. 39). In a positional society, as exemplified by the Iatmul, the societies "depend upon formal alignments of individuals who react not in terms of personal opinions but in terms of defined position in a formal sociopolitical structure" (Hymes, 1974, p. 39). In a third type of society, such as that of Bali, communal effort functions "by involving participation in and respect for known impersonal patterns or codes, and in which communicators act as if the audience were already in a state of suspended, emotional attention, and only in need of a small precise triggering of words to set them off into appropriate activity" (Hymes, 1974, p. 39). To this third category, the traditional type, Hymes added a positional, traditional type, as exemplified by the Zuni.

The differences described by Hymes could be called differences in the style of cultural communication. Style refers to patterned variation in the selection and arrangement of choices. Three attributes or dimensions of style will be employed here, following Weaver (1964). He referred to elaboration, the going beyond what is useful to what is engaging to contemplation; rhythm, the marking of beginnings and endings; and distance, the creation of separation between the users of signs and that which they signify (Weaver, 1964, p. 19). With regard to cultural communication, in different societies the rituals have different sacred objects, the myths different characters and story lines, and the social dramas different rules, violation of which is the basis for a breach. Put in stylistic terms, these are differences in what is elaborated, in what sacred objects are singled out for appreciation and decorous treatment. There are also differences in rhythm, in the rules for sequencing participation in community life, particularly in the degree to which the rules are rigid or flexible. Finally, there are differences in distancing, in the nature and strength of such boundary mechanisms as taboos on topic, interlocutors, and manner, of public communication.

Extending Hymes's schema to cultural communication style, one can refer to a personal, positional, traditional, and positional/traditional style.

Three of these will be amplified here. In a personal society, as exemplified by the West, the sacred object, mythic quest, and source of dramatic exigence is the individual self-concept; rules for participation are relatively fluid, providing for easy participation by all; and public life is pressed into the service of breaking down boundaries, of reducing distance between people. In a positional society, it is the group itself which is the sacred object, mythical force, and dramatic forcus; rules for participation, based on position or status, and public life take on their greatest power when the salience and significance of group life is left unsaid but indirectly affirmed through the use of shared communal symbols. In a traditional society, the code, law, or scripture is the object of elaboration; tradition specifies participation patterns; and it is tradition which carries the greatest degree of unspoken force in regulating public conduct and in affirming shared identity.

Certain communication forms should be most naturally associated with certain cultural communication styles. Where individuality is prominent, as in a personalitistic society, social dramas,which provide for reintegrating the individual into a communal life, should be prominent. Myth, as a loose form which permits individual variation in feeling and behavior to be given coherence within an enduring communal experience, is ideally suited to a positional society, which derives its coherence and force from group heroes and places. Ritual, as a precoded form, is the archetypal form of cultural communication in a traditional society.

These dimensions and types are presented here for heuristic purposes. Comparative analyses of existing ethnographic research would permit revision and development of the crude scheme here presented. But the move proposed is (1) to isolate cultural differences in cultural communication style by postulating, as Hymes did, specified stylistic types, such as personal, positional, and traditional and, further, (2) to extend previous work by suggesting three stylistic dimensions along which various types can be compared and contrasted. With regard to (2), it was suggested that a cultural communication style varies as to its object of elaboration, rhythm, and distance. This development of an existing, heuristic typology should make it possible to do further comparative work in and across societies. It should also make it possible to see variations in cultural communication style as diverse expressions of a common humanity and of a common need for cultural communication.

CHAPTER 19

Interpersonal Cognition, Message Goals, and Organization of Communication: Recent Constructivist Research*

Jesse G. Delia

INTRODUCTION

The present discussion reflects a general constructivist viewpoint that has been elaborated in more detail elsewhere (e.g., see Delia, 1976; Delia, O'Keefe, & O'Keefe, 1982; O'Keefe & Delia, 1986; O'Keefe, Delia, & O'Keefe, 1980). The constructivist approach to communication attempts to draw attention to the complexity of the interpretive processes organizing communicative behavior and to the necessity for analyzing those processes as they are related to particular features of behavioral organization. The present discussion summarizes within the context of this orientation recent ideas and research concerning the role of social cogni-

* This paper has been elaborated through collaboration with Barbara J. O'Keefe; portions of the analysis presented here are developed in O'Keefe and Delia (1985).

COMMUNICATION THEORY:
EASTERN AND WESTERN PERSPECTIVES

tion in the generation of the goal structures organizing interaction and communicative conduct. My effort here is not to make a general statement of the constructivist perspective but to summarize the basic orientation and discuss some general points of analysis growing out of one aspect of my collaborators and my recent work. The discussion proceeds by considering in turn a series of interrelated ideas that define important aspects of our orientation.

HUMAN ACTION, INTERACTION, AND COMMUNICATION ARE ORGANIZED BY INTERPETIVE SCHEMES

The constructivist approach takes as a starting point the idea that human behavior is organized by cognitive or interpretive schemes (see the discussion in Delia *et al.*, 1982). Some interpretative schemes are employed consciously, but most reflect tacit, nonconscious construal processes. The organization and quality of interpretative schemes reflect general characteristics of psychological functioning, including general developmental transformations. Moreover, while interpretive schemes in part reflect the idiosyncracies of an individual's life history, very many interpretative schemes for organizing broad ranges of interactional and communicative conduct are acquired in similar form by persons having similar socialization experiences. Thus, the schemes organizing conduct reflect in complex and varying ways psychological, social, and cultural roots and both similarity and divergence in structure and content. This means that there is no single way of representing such schemes that will reflect their nature and role in organizing conduct. A variety of analytic schemes reflecting various similarities and differences of psychological functioning and similarities and differences in the content and organization of schemes is justified and necessary.

Interpretive schemes reflecting these varying and fragmented roots operate simultaneously to organize understanding and behavior. This point frequently seems lost as the proponents of positions with differing foci of convenience begin to argue about what is really important and fundamental in the organization of interaction and communication. Action is always organized simultaneously at multiple levels from the paralinguistic, through the linguistic and interactional, to the tactical and strategic. We may focus on the role of conscious, reflectively formulated intentions in structuring message choices, but even in such cases tacit, nonconscious (and typically culturally shared) schemes organizing nonverbal gestures, phonological and syntactic levels of language usage, role- and situation-appropriate aspects of behavior, and strategic choices will be present and analytically distinguishable. This points to a need for our being careful in defining our level of analysis in discussing the role of particular kinds or characteristics of interpretive schemes in the organization of interaction and communication.

SCHEMES FOR UNDERSTANDING OTHER PERSONS PLAY AN IMPORTANT ROLE IN ORGANIZING INTERACTION AND COMMUNICATION, PARTICULARLY AT THE LEVEL OF GOALS AND STRATEGIES

Some of my colleagues and my recent work points to a central role in the structure of messages of specific representations of and general processes governing the organization of "receiver-focused" messages. This work builds off the idea that interpersonal constructs and more complex social schemas allow for the representation of communication-relevant features of social situations and thus are directly implicated in the organization of communicative actions. From a constructivist point of view, we have been interested in exploring the impact on the character of communicative goals and strategies of particular systematic developmental differences in interpersonal construct systems (e.g., differences in differentiation, abstractness, etc.). Our expectation has been, of course, that important aspects of functional communication will be revealed to be systematically related to differences in the modes of interpersonal interpretation that reflect, in part, developmental changes.

A substantial body of our research has been guided by this general expectation. In particular our research has focused on the ways in which developments in the quality of one's interpersonal cognitive schemes channelize communicative goals and behavior. In this section recent research on functional communication conducted within our framework is summarized in reference to three topics: interpersonal cognition and the development of receiver-focused communicative strategies, the definition of the situation and interactional objectives, and the social context of interpersonal cognitive and communicative development.

The Development of Interpersonal Constructs and Receiver-Focused Communicative Strategies

The relationship of interpersonal cognition to communication most often has been studied through assessing the role of perspective-taking ability in making listener-adapted message choices (e.g., Delia & Clark, 1977; Delia

& O'Keefe, 1979; Flavell, 1968). However, O'Keefe and Delia (1982) argued for considering other roles that developments in interpersonal cognition might play in communicative behavior, including in particular the role of social cognition in generating the goals that organize receiver-focused message production. Specifically, we advance the thesis that variations in social cognitive development (construct differentiation) lead to differences in the perception of obstacles and subsidiary objectives that must be addressed in the pursuit of a dominant situational goal.

The line of research interpreted as supporting this conclusion is based on the hierarchic ordering of message structures in terms of the degree to which multiple dimensions (obstacles and aims) of complex communication situations are recognized and reconciled in messages. Most of this research involves coding schemes derived from the work of Clark and Delia (1976) and Applegate and Delia (1980).

Clark and Delia's (1976) message-classification system defines general types of messages that might be produced when a child is asked to make a request of a listener. Each message type reflects one possible response to an influence situation in which the persuadee is presumed to be reluctant to grant the request. Clark and Delia identified four basic message strategies: simple request, elaborated requests (in which the needs of the persuader are stressed), counterarguing (in which the objections of the persuadee are anticipated and refuted), and advantage to other (in which the advantages of compliance to the persuadee are stressed). In research on the development of persuasive message production, Clark and Delia (1976; Delia, Kline, & Burleson, 1979) showed that these four message types appear to be developmentally ordered: If children of different ages are studied they are observed first to produce simple requests, then elaborated requests, then counterarguments, and finally messages emphasizing advantages to the persuadee. Moreover, in both developmental research (e.g., Delia, Kline, & Burleson, 1979) and research with adults (e.g., Applegate, 1982b, Burke, 1979), the production of strategies higher in this hierarchy has been found to be positively correlated with individual differences in interpersonal construct differentiation. Moreover, this has been shown to hold in both role-play situations where there is no physically present listener and in actual interaction (e.g., Applegate, 1982b).

In interpreting these results the relationship of the message hierarchy to the structural character of the persuasion situation should be considered. Persuasion occurs when one person wants something from another person who is presumably unwilling to satisfy the want. Thus, the essential structure of a persuasion situation implies two people, persuader and persuadee, with competing agendas. Approached in this way, the ordering of Clark and Delia's four message strategies can be explained as a function of increasing success in reconciling the needs of persuader and persuadee in the message—from emphasizing one's own agenda, to denying the validity of the persuadee's agenda, to manufacturing a common agenda. Clark and Delia's message strategies thus represent four alternative actions that comprise a set of generalized options for dealing with the competing wants of persuader and persuadee. The strategies are not simply ways of adapting messages to listeners, nor are the strategies ordered simply by increasing listener adaptedness or receiver focus, although individual differences in social cognitive schemes clearly are implicated as playing a central role in the perception of situational obstacles and issues.

Research on situations requiring regulative and comforting communication even more clearly demonstrate the role of social cognitive developments in the recognition of obstacles and the possession of multiple aims and reconciliation of primary aims with perceived obstacles and with subsidiary aims. For example, the message-analysis system used to categorize regulative messages (in which the communicator must modify another's behavior) involves a set of nine hierarchically ordered categories which can be seen as reflecting variations in attempts to accomplish multiple aims in messages (see Applegate, 1980a, 1980b; Applegate & Delia, 1980; Kline & Ceropski, 1984; also see O'Keefe & Delia's, 1982, discussion of the coding system). The first three categories (physical punishment, commands, and rule giving) all involve messages produced with a single aim, the primary aim of the subject's assigned task: modify the message recipient's behavior. The next three categories involve messages which address the obstacle of gaining the message recipient's compliance (offering reasons for rules, discussing consequences of noncompliance, and discussing general principles behind appropriate behavior). The final three categories involve messages in which the communicator simultaneously corrects the behavior, offers reasons for compliance, and encourages the message recipient to be empathic in his social conduct (describing feelings produced by inappropriate behavior, encouraging the message recipient to see multiple aspects of the situation in terms of feelings, helping the message recipient to make an empathic response through analogy, leading the message recipient to reason through the situation, etc.)

Messages produced in response to comforting situations (in which conflicts in feelings figure prominently) have been classified using a coding system that essentially reflects the degree to which a communicator increasingly deals with multiple dimensions of interpersonal conflicts, including hurt feelings, the reasons for and consequences of hurt feelings, and the message recipient's ability to understand and empathize in conflict situations (see Applegate, 1980a, 1980b; Applegate & Delia, 1980;

Borden, 1981; Burleson, 1982a, 1983, 1984a, 1984b; Samter & Burleson, 1984). Thus, the lowest level strategies deal with the immediate situation without regard to the message recipient's need for support; strategies at the intermediate levels deal with the situation through acknowledging feelings and providing psychological support; and strategies coded at the highest levels deal with the immediate situation, provide psychological support, and help the message recipient to reason through the situation and to learn from it.

Parallel to the finding on research using the Clark and Delia message-analysis hierarchy, both developmental differences as a function of age and individual differences among children and adults varying in interpersonal construct differentiation have been found for performance within these regulative and comforting message orderings in both role-played and realistic interaction situations (e.g., Applegate, 1980b; Burleson, 1983, 1984a; Kline & Ceropski, 1984; Samter & Burleson, 1984). Taken as a whole this research suggests that interpersonal construct system development plays a central role in the perception of communication-relevant tasks and obstacles and in the use of communicative strategies to organize dominant and subsidary goals in situations.

One striking implication of the forgoing results is that the communicative task seems to be construed quite differently by participants in these studies. For example, it appears that some communicators see as genuinely "regulative" those situations in which there is a normative basis for action; that is, a legitimate and sufficient basis for controlling the message recipient's behavior evidently is attributed by some communicators as inherent in such role relationships as a mother addressing a child or a manager addressing an employee. However, other communicators appear implicitly to represnt such role-defined situations as requiring persuasion, not regulation, since the message recipient is treated as a free and autonomous agent of action responsible for his own conduct. Free and responsible agents are not to be controlled. Rather, they act on the basis of their own autonomous beliefs. Hence, control or regulation must be accomplished by "persuasion," i.e., by leading the other to see the implications of his action so that he will be led to "choose" to act responsibly. In terms of Kelman's (1961) classic analysis of social influence, some communicators appear implicitly to represent control situations as involving individuals who can and should be influenced by compliance structures, while others appear to represent situations as involving individuals who can and should only be influenced by internalization structures. Applegate's (1980a, 1980b; Applegate, Burke, Burleson, Delia, & Kline, 1985) research with mothers and teachers, Husband's (1981) with residence hall supervisors, and Kline and Ceropski's (1984) and Kasch's (1984) with medical practitioners all reveal this distinction in control situations as a function of differences in interpersonal construct differentiation. In the following section, we summarize recent research that directly extends our analysis of the goal structure of complex communication situation within a framework emphasizing the concept of the definition of situation.

The Definition of the Situation and Subsidiary Interactional Aims

In the symbolic-interactionist perspective developed from the perspective of Mead (1934) in American sociology by such theorists as Blumer (1969), the definition of the situation is the symbolic representation of the social situation by interactants: their conceptions of the activity in which they are engaged, of the roles of interactants within that activity, and of the spatio-temporal setting in which the activity occurs. The definition of the situation is the source from which interactants derive their sense of relevance and appropriateness; it is the set of beliefs about a situation which shape and channelize conduct of others. As a result, a joint (mutually imputed) definition of the situation is critical to the efforts of interactants to coordinate their behavior. It is for this reason that symbolic interactionists have devoted considerable attention to the processes through which interactants come to a shared definition of the situation and cope with the misunderstandings and conflicts that threaten the "working consensus" they have achieved.

A number of theorists (e.g., Goffman, 1959; Strauss, 1969; Weinstein, 1969) noted that a central element in the definition of any social situation is the identities of the participants, and Goffman (1959), in particular, argued that in all social situations, "face (the positive social value one claims for oneself)" is the centrally relevant feature of one's identity. Moreover, face is one element of the definition of a situation which is necessarily called into question in a wide range of activities and under a wide range of circumstances. As a consequence, social systems develop routine procedures and strategies for managing recurring situations in which the definition of the situation is threatened by the conflict between the need to protect face and the need to pursue some activity (e.g., making a request, regulating another person's conduct) or deal with some untoward occurrence that reflects badly on the identity of one or more interactants (e.g., someone's knocking over a lamp, someone's being caught in a lie).

There is a considerable literature on the conversational strategies people employ in attempting to avoid or repair damage to face. Much of this research describes and classifies interactional tactics commonly used in dealing with particular problems of identity management (e.g., Gross & Stone's [1964] analysis of embarrassment; Scott & Lyman's [1968] analysis of accounts). By contrast, Brown and Levinson's (1978) analysis of universal structures in politeness offers a deeper and more systematic analysis of the forms discourse may take as it is shaped to meet the needs of face protection. They argued that "face" actually consists of two wants: the want that one's wants be valued by others (positive face), and the want not to be impeded by others (negative face wants). There are a large number of actions which are intrinsically threatening to the face wants of either actors or their interactional partners—for example, requests are intrinsically threatening to the negative face wants of the target of the request, since a request necessarily involves some degree of imposition.

Brown and Levinson pointed out that, confronted with the possibility of performing a face-threatening action (FTA), actors may elect one of four generalized options: (1) do the FTA, badly; (2) do the FTA, but with redress; (3) do the FTa off record; and (4) do not do the FTA. Doing the FTA "badly" involves performing the face-threatening action in a recognizably direct and unambiguous fashion ("on record"). Doing the FTA "with redress" is accomplished through adding features designed to satisfy face wants (such as compliments, hedges, apologies) to on-record FTAs. Doing the FTA "off record" involves performing the FTA with some degree of indirectness (by boldly performing some nonthreatening action which logically or conventionally implies the FTA). One thing Brown and Levinson pointed to is the fact that these four options all represent different ways of resolving the conflict between efficient communication (saying clearly what one wants or means) and face wants. They went on to show how, across a variety of cultures, politeness is instantiated in the form of indirectness and types of redress.

What Brown and Levinson's work represents is a move away from the standard symbolic interactionist practice in analyzing discourse strategies, which is to identify some recurring interactional problem and identify the strategies people commonly use in dealing with that problem. Symbolic interactionists would be unlikely to develop the kind of analysis Brown and Levinson offered, because the discourse strategies available for protecting face are seen as involving not the specific conditions of situations but the rational exploitation of a structured system of discourse options in the pursuit of goals.

However, in all the work on strategies for pursuing identity-relevant objectives (including that of Brown & Levinson, 1978) there has been a common focus on describing the shared repertoire of strategies available to members of a social group for handling identity-related problems within face-threatening situations. All this work has involved the assumption that the interactants involved have the goal of protecting face. Virtually no attention has been given to the question of how people use their strategic repertoires. An individual's use of the shared repertoire of face-protection strategies should, of course, depend on his having face protection as a goal and being able to recognize the identity-relevant implications of actions.

Recent lines of research within the constructivist framework have explicitly addressed the question of how individuals use the strategic repertoire available to them for face protection. One of these lines of work, undertaken by Kline (1981a, 1981b, 1983), was concerned with determining how individual differences in social cognition influence the use of strategies for face protection. In this research, subjects were asked to consider that they are in a position of authority and that they face the task of getting a subordinate to mend his or her ways. This is, of course, a situation which intrinsically threatens both the positive and negative face wants of the subordinate, since both an imposition (negative face) and a negative evaluation of the subordinate's current behavior (positive face) are inherent to the action to be taken by the superordinate. Subjects were asked to write what they would say to the erring subordinate, and their responses were coded along two dimensions. The first dimension along which responses were classified concerned the degree to which the response assigned a negative identity versus a positive identity to the subordinate (e.g., in describing the offense, did the subject cast it as a wrongful or defective act characteristic of the subordinate or in some more positive light). The second dimension along which responses were classified concerned the degree to which the strategy for regulating conduct involved imposition of authority versus some attempt to grant autonomy to the subordinate (e.g., simply giving an order as opposed to engaging to persuade the subordinate—persuasion being an act which intrinsically presupposes and therefore implies some degree of autonomy for the persuadee). Kline explicitly grounded her work in Brown and Levinson's analysis of face, so these two dimensions correspond to what they would describe as positive and negative face.

In studies using this paradigm, Kline (1981a; also see Kline, 1981b, 1983) found that there were considerable individual differences in the use of strategies for protecting positive and negative face and that both the sex of the subject and the subject's degree of construct differentiation were significantly related to strategy use. More often than men, women used face protecting strategies and were particularly more likely to use strategies granting greater autonomy to the subordinate. Subjects who were relatively high as opposed to low in construct differentiation produced responses which were more likely both to grant autonomy to the subordinate and to preserve a positive social identity for the subordinate. This construct differentiation/face support relationship has been replicated among children and adolescents (Burleson, 1982b) and adults (Applegate, 1982a).

In a subsequent study, Kline (1982) sought to determine whether these differences among individuals were attributable to differential knowledge of available discourse strategies or differences in goals. The failure to use a face-protective strategy could result from either not having a strategy available or from not having the goal (face protection) which the strategy is designed to achieve. In one investigation, Kline attempted to disambiguate her earlier findings through employing an experimental manipulation designed to induce subjects to have the goal of face protection if they failed to have it spontaneously. Half the subjects were simply given the standard regulative communication task; the other half were given the regulative communication task and explicitly told that they were to seek to protect the face of the partner. Her findings suggest that the inattention to positive face wants displayed by low differentiation subjects is primarily attributable to their failure to spontaneously have the goal of face protection, since when low-differentiation subjects were told to protect face wants, their performance did not differ from that of subjects high in construct differentiation (the results are less clear for negative face). Thus, while the discourse system available to everyone contains a set of options for designing messages to protect positive face, individuals differ in their exploitation of that system, and it appears that this difference is attributable to differences in the goals they set for themselves in interactions. Moreover, these differences in goals appear to be related in a regular fashion to the cognitive structures individuals have for interpreting social situations and behavior (and thus to individual differences in such cognitive structures).

In other research, Kline (1984) used a research framework involving an independent analysis of the goals individuals defined as relevant to such situations as those included in her earlier research. This analysis yielded such indexes, for example, as the proportion of positive interpersonal goals defined as relevant by an individual subject to reprimand situations or behavioral regulation situations. Kline also assessed the number of strategies an individual could generate as possible means of pursuing each goal. These measures provided an assessment of the individual's strategic repertoire independent of its use in a specific communication situation. Kline took the number and proportion of strategies within particular classes (such as positive interpersonal strategies) that were produced in producing actual messages in a specific situation as reflecting the accessibility or propensity to use a particular range of strategies. Her research shows that communicators with highly differentiated interpersonal construct systems have marginally more positive interpersonal goals but no more extensive strategic repertoires. However, it appears that the positive interpersonal strategies at their disposal may be much more accessible. Kline concluded that her evidence suggests that individuals with more highly differentiated conceptions of others are able to draw on a greater number and proportion of their positive interpersonal strategies to accomplish both their task objectives and their interpersonal objectives in reprimand or behavioral control situations.

What Kline's work suggests is a model of social conduct in which individual differences in structures organizing social cognition lead individuals to have fundamentally different ways of defining and acting toward social situations. Some people apparently are simply less likely to represent social situations in such a way that positive face implications and face protection become part of the scheme of relevance defining the concrete situation. This model is given further support in recent work by O'Keefe and Shepherd (in press).

O'Keefe and Shepherd analyzed the strategies people use to protect the face wants of self and partner and maintain interaction in an interpersonal conflict situation. They asked pairs of subjects who were known to disagree strongly about a policy issue to discuss that issue; each interactant was instructed to try to persuade the other to accept his own position on the issue. These dyadic, persuasive interactions were videotaped and the behavior of interactants was classified as to the degree to which behavior was organized in such a way as to deal with the face-threatening features of the situation and to at least maintain the appearance of a coherent dialogue on the assigned topic.

Given that subjects were told explicitly that they disagreed strongly on the assigned topic and that they were assigned the task of persuasion, every behavioral option available to participants involved some potential threat to their own or their partners' face wants or to the maintenance of continued and coherent discussion or both. In displaying this feature of their experimental situation, O'Keefe and Shepherd argued that there are four basic categories or "modes" of action available to interactants in the situation as publicly defined. These four modes are generated by two decisions interactants must repeatedly make as they organize their actions in relation to the situation as defined. First, they must decide whether to convey acceptance (to some degree) or rejection (to some degree) of the position advocated by the partner—and this decision necessarily involves an orientation to their own position as well, since their own and their partners' positions are opposite on the issue. Second, they must decide whether to explicitly and overtly acknowledge the conflict between the two positions. These two choices, taken together, generate four general classes of action that may be performed in this situation: (1) avoidance and simple agreement (implicit acceptance), (2) explanations (implicit disagreement), (3) arguing (explicit disagreement),and (4) compromise (explicit agreement).

The decision simply to agree with the partner (or at least not disagree) and the decision not to explicitly acknowledge the conflict between positions generates a basic posture of avoidance: People try to avoid discussing the topic and in particular try to avoid expressions of opinions on the topic. Subjects acting within this mode denied having the positions attributed to them by the experimenter (they are known to have lied), introduced topics other than the one assigned, simply agreed with what their partners said while at the same time closing off discussion, and said they did not care about the issue (they are known to have lied) and would take any position on it. While actions falling within this mode involve no direct threat to the partners' face wants, they all create identity problems for the actors (by intrinsically involving a very questionable characterization of their own positions or publicly devaluing their own beliefs or simply accepting the imposition of others' beliefs), and they all create problems for interaction maintenance (it is hard to have a discussion if one interactant refuses to discuss; it is hard to be responsive to the partner in this situation if one participant refuses to express opinions about the assigned issue or encourage the partner's expression of opinion).

The decision to express rejection of the partners' views combined with a desire to avoid explicit acknowledgment of the conflict between positions generates a mode of behavior O'Keefe and Shepherd labeled "explanation." Subjects acting within this mode simply explain their own positions on the issue and the reasons why they personally hold their positions, without criticizing the positions of the partners or engaging in any act which is conventionally recognizable as urging their postions on the partners. Thus, while subjects acting within this mode do express a point of view at odds with the view of the partners, they explain their positions in such a way as to avoid explicitly acknowledging or implying that they see a conflict between their own and their partners' positions. As mentioned earlier, actions that refuse to explicitly acknowledge the existence of conflict make interaction maintenance difficult—this is true of action within the mode of implicit rejection as well. Holding to a posture of simply explaiing one's own point of view makes it difficult to sustain interaction past a few turns and to be responsive to the partner's conversational contributions. Moreover, even though adopting a posture of explanation reduces the face threat to the partner that is intrinsic to any rejecting action, nonetheless there is some residual threat to the partner's positive face wants in the failure to accept the partner's viewpoint and the expression of one's own conflicting position.

The decisions to reject the partner's position and to do so in a way that explicitly and overtly acknowledges the existence of conflict result in a posture of arguing. Subjects acting within this mode actively urged their positions on the partners and criticized the partner's viewpoint. Obviously, the primary interactional problems created by this mode of behavior are face related: in explicitly and unambiguously rejecting the position of the partner, one necessarily threatens both the partner's positive and negative face wants and risks creating a negative identity for oneself (by appearing inconsiderate, unfriendly, and impolite).

The decisions to explicitly acknowledge the existence of a conflict and to express some degree of willingness to accept the partner's position generate a posture of compromise. Subjects acting within this mode offered compromise positions to their partners or acknowledged having been persuaded by arguments made by the partners. Action within this mode poses few problems for interaction maintenance but does pose a direct threat to face. Action within this mode intrinsically trades off one's own face wants against the partner's face wants—to the degree that one repudiates one's own position, one threatens one's own positive and negative face wants; to the degree that one qualifies or limits one's acceptance of the partner's position, one refuses the partner's face wants.

Thus, each of the four modes within which subjects could act in this situation potentially involved some threat to the definition of the situation, either through creating difficulties for interaction maintenance or through threatening face or both. The questions that interested O'Keefe and Shepherd were (1) how interactants might organize their behavior to avoid or deal with these potential problems as they acted within these four modes and (2) what ways individuals might differ in dealing with the conflict among the assigned objective they were given in the situation, the potential goal of maintaining interaction, and the potential goal of maintaining face.

Building on the analysis of O'Keefe and Delia (1982), O'Keefe and Shepherd argued that subjects have available three basic ways to deal with the distinctive problems created by action within each of the four modes. Subjects can fail to recognize or ignore the interactional maintenance and face problems of the mode within which they are acting and simply perform some badly produced action. Subjects can recognize and deal with the interactional problems created by their actions through redressive or mitigating embellishments of the basic act they are performing (e.g., through accounts, hedges, compliments to the partner, and so on). Or subjects can avoid the potential problems created by the mode of action by actively redefining some element of the situation so as to create a new situation in which the conflict among objectives does not exist (e.g., by redefining the assigned task as simply having a conversation or getting to know the other person's position so as to become better acquainted, by redefining the participants' roles as detached but not personally involved analysts of social policy or as teacher and student). Subjects pursuing this third strategy must adopt roles or methods of approaching the task which are at variance with the definition of the situation supplied by the experimenter but which legitimate the mode of action being performed and minimize or eliminate the potential interactional problems of a given mode.

O'Keefe and Shepherd used their analysis of modes of action available in conflict situations and strategies for managing interactional problems associated with the modes to develop a coding system for classifying the behavior interactants produced in the discussions they had. Interactions were segmented into their discrete, pragmatically and semantically coherent units (the unit of analysis corresponded roughly to a subtopic of the assigned topic). The behavior of each participant within each unit was classified as to the mode of action is instantiated and the strategy for managing interactional problems it reflected.

O'Keefe and Shepherd found that there was considerable individual variation in the use of strategies for dealing with interaction maintenance and face threats and that individual differences in strategy use were related to the individual's degree of interpersonal construct differentiation. Subjects relatively high in construct differentiation, as opposed to those low in interpersonal construct differentiation, were more likely to engage in redressive action and more likely to undertake redefinition of the situation to resolve the conflict among objectives. The relationship between construct differentiation and the use of situation-redefining strategies was particularly strong ($r = .61$, $p < .001$). In short, consistent with Kline's previous findings, high differentiation communicators appear more likely to design their behavior in such a way as to avoid or redress threats to face and interaction maintenance. Again it appears that, for high-differentiation communicators but to a much lesser extent for low-differentiation communicators these potential features of the situation are incorporated as dimensions of their definition of the situation and are pursued as interactional goals. In the following section, the implications of these differences for socialization and communicative development are briefly considered.

Receiver-Focused Communication and the Social Context of Interpersonal Construct System and Communicative Development

Earlier it was noted that individuals acquire many of their interpretative schemes in common with others in the context of socialization. In interaction itself, socializing agents force particular differentiations on the child's world view by the ways in which they make manifest in their actions and speech particular domains of experience. This idea has served as the basis for socialization studies in which we have investigated the influence of receiver-focused communication of mothers on their children (see Applegate *et al.*, 1985; Applegate & Delia, 1980; Delia, Burleson, & Kline, 1979; Jones, Delia, & Clark, 1981a, 1981b).

In undertaking these studies we reasoned that mothers who control their children's behavior and deal with their interpersonal problems through discussing consequences, giving reasons, and elaborating on perspectives (as opposed to using commands, rules, etc.) present to the child a social world that includes the psychological domain of experience as a manifest feature of reality. Over time, children raised by a mother using highly receiver-focused strategies should come to develop a differentiated and abstract (psychologically centered) set of constructs that are more readily accessed in perceiving and acting toward persons and social situations. In representing communicative situations within such constructs, the wants, needs, and perspectives of others should be a more salient aspect of the relevance structure defining the situation. Moreover, since the psychological domain of experience should be more manifest in the child's world, the child of such a parent gradually should be led to see as immediately relevant to a wide range of situations communicative strategies that incorporate attention to the wants, needs, and interests of the listeners.

Our research has directly supported this expectation. Jones *et al.* (1981a) found greater receiver focus in maternal communication to be a significant predictor both of children's interpersonal construct system development and of their use of more receiver-focused persuasive appeals. Interestingly, this relationship was stronger among seventh-grade than second-grade children. In a longitudinal study, a similar pattern of results has been obtained showing that person-centered maternal communication becomes an increasingly strong force in shaping the child's interpersonal construct system and communicative strategies from early into middle childhood (see Applegate & Delia, 1980, and Delia, Burleson, & Kline, 1979, for initial reports of this work; also see Applegate *et al.*,

1985, for our analysis of "reflection-enhancing" maternal communication).

While important aspects of interaction and message structure reflect modes of construing persons, equally significant aspects of interaction and message structure will reflect the operation of schemes for organizing other domains of world knowledge. I wish to stress in particular, the importance to communciative action of general schemes for organizing action and interaction and discourse schemes for structuring language comprehension and production. Many such schemes, I would expect, operate relatively independently of schemes for representing roles, social relations, and individual characteristics of persons. For example, in the analysis of schemes structuring the organization of interaction, O'Keefe *et al.* (1980) tied their analysis to interaction-organizing schemes rather than to modes of representing persons.

VARIATIONS IN MODES OF CONCEPTUALIZING PERSONS IS IMPORTANT IN THE OPERATION OF MANY DISCOURSE-ORGANIZING SCHEMES

Several theorists have hinted at a likely role for developments in modes of conceptualizing persons or other aspects of the external world in the mastery and use of such linguistic conventions as those governing passive-voice constructions, relative clauses, and wh-complementizers. Similarly, developments in conceptualizing persons and social relations probably reflect one avenue to turning discourse conventions into strategic conversational resources. Of course, there may be many avenues to this end. The person who becomes reflectively aware of discourse conventions will be able to strategically exploit them. However, reflective awareness of discourse rules is probably not the most typical route to control of discourse-organizing schemes as strategic conversational resources. A much more typical route is probably the differentiation of the schemes in combination with increasingly easy access to differentiated representations of social situations, social relationships, and characteristics of persons. These latter construals should allow for the increasing organization of conduct in reference to a greater range of the "nuances" of the context. This implicit recognition of a greater range of contextual features should lead one to be able to more flexibly pursue one's own overt intentions within the conventions and norms organizing talk in the situation.

This line of reasoning suggests the possibility that modes of conceptualizing persons and social relations may, in fact, play an important role in the operation of discourse-organizing schemes. J. Burke, E. Springer, and I are investigating this possibility in some not yet completed research. We place a participant in a small group discussion; the participant's task, unknown to the other group members, is to work a specified off-topic sentence into the group discussion as naturally as possible. Such a research paradigm, offers the possibility of studying the strategic exploitation of discourse schemes governing turn taking, topical coherence, and the like. It is our expectation that variation in the differentiation of subjects' constructs for conceptualizing persons will relate to the flexibility with which discourse organizing schemes are exploited. But whether we are correct in this specific hypothesis, this kind of investigation points to the importance of beginning to think about interrelations in different sets of schemes organizing interaction and communication.

Another important area for investigation of such interpenetration is the socialization context. As was noted above, initial evidence suggests that variations in modes of conceptualizing persons is related to mothers' propensity to use receiver-focused communication strategies, which in turn influences the development of the child's use of interpersonal constructs and communicative strategies. An equally important question, as yet uninvestigated, concerns how conventions governing the organization of communication within a particular medium such as conversation (discourse knowledge) structure the content of talk and access to knowledge about persons and social relations (social knowledge). There is good reason for believing that these two domains of world knowledge interpenetrate at all levels, and for this reason any adequate account of communication within a constructivist framework must acknowledge the role of the linguistic and cultural context in shaping both the behavioral resources of communication and the interpretive schemes organizing them.

SUMMARY

The constructivist approach thus points to a socio-cultural, psychological, and contextual analysis of the interpretive and behavioral resources of communication and of the ways in which these resources are organized. The constructivist analysis of communication places emphasis on the content and quality of the communication-relevant interpretative processes individuals develop and the modes and understanding and behavioral organization these processes channelize. With social experience, each individual develops constructs and schemes that readily differentiate particular communication-relevant features of situations. Control over communicative behavior at progressively more complex levels is developed in integration with this underlying mode of interpretation. Behavior is interpreted and organized at several levels, including the nonverbal behavioral and paralinguistic, the linguistic (lexical and grammatical), contextual, and interactional, and the tactical and strategic. All these levels are interrelated (hence, for example, social rules may be strategically exploited; syntactic structures can subserve clarity of expression or ambiguity; paralinguistic aspects of speech associated with a particular "accent" may be purposefully adopted; etc.).

The important questions to ask within a constructivist theory of communication thus concern the modes of interpretation and behavioral organization persons have developed and whether these processes are adequate to communicative tasks. For example, schizophrenics have been shown to do as well as normals on an easy referential communication task but much poorer when the task is difficult (Cohen, 1978). Likewise, a typical social actor may be perfectly "comeptent" to carry on normal discourse but have inadequate control over the strategic resources of communication at the sociolinguistic level to "pass" as a member of a particular social group (e.g., see the analysis of Goffman, 1968). Moreover, organization of the resources of communication at a particular level may not be maintained within all contexts, though they can be controlled in some. It is a commonplace observation (given theoretical status within the constructivist framework) that emotional arousal, tension, and the like have a debilitating effect on communicative performance. The organization of interpretation and communication thus cannot be separated in the final analysis from a contextual analysis, for behavior is tied in complex, and as yet not-well-understood, ways to modes of construing contexts.

It is also important to recognize the cultural bases of modes of interpretation and the content and organization of the message-production system. The analysis of particular modes of interpretation, goal structures, and message-organization schemes discussed above reflects the implicit structures of relevance made salient by interpersonal construct systems acquired within particular socio-cultural contexts. Importantly, it should be recognized that our evidence suggests that contemporary American culture (the context of our research) appears to present a variety of pathways for development each of which makes different schemes of interpersonal constructs and communicative goal structures readily accessible. In similar fashion, radically different cultures from the American culture should be expected to channelize interpersonal development into quite different pathways. At the same time, the kinds of concepts elaborated within the constructivist framework should continue to be useful for analysis across cultural contexts, since interpretations of intentions, goal structures, and message strategies expressing and integrating goals are essential features of communication systems in general. Thus, for example, the kind fo framework developed here might prove quite useful in understanding some aspects of the well-known preference among Japanese (and some other cultural groups) for communicative indirectness. Indeed, McCann and Higgins (1984) have shown that a wide range of cultural and individual differences in communication behavior can be understood as reflecting differences in the accessibility and organization of various communicative goals. Among other things, the constructivist perspective thus points toward the utility of comparative analysis both within and across cultures of the character of the interpersonal interpretative constructs and schemes communicators use and the organization of communicative goals and strategies mobilized by varying modes of interpersonal interpretation.

CHAPTER 20

Dialogue on the Nature of Causality, Measurement, and Human Communication Theory

Joseph Woelfel and D. Lawrence Kincaid

INTRODUCTION

The question of causality and its role in human understanding has occupied scholars in both East and West since before recorded history. In the twentieth century, communication scholars still find themselves puzzled. Many communication theorists distinguish three classes of theory within the field, often designated as causal or laws theory, rules theory, and systems theory. Often the utility of causal theory is called into question, while new and sophisticated advocates, like adherents of what is called the "causal modeling" approach, have grown rapidly. Frequently, advocates of the different approaches truly disagree, but often the word "cause" is used ambiguously so that arguments are more apparent than real.

This chapter will present several meanings for the term "cause" as it has been used both past and present and examine the extent to which causal theory in any of its meanings may be usefully applied to the study of human communication.

THE DIALOGUE

Continuing Galileo's (1914) dialogues 350 years after they had occurred was an interesting idea to a physicist like Sagredo, but still some things bothered him. First, while he was glad to have been chosen, he wished it had been for some other reason beside the fact that he was the only scientist they could find named Sagredo. And he was, he admitted, a bit disappointed that the other two scientists with appropriate names, Salviati and Simplicio, were both not actually scientists, but social scientists. At least we will not have to wear pantaloons, though, he thought.

The image of himself dressed as a medieval Venetian gentleman was still in his mind the next day when he noticed Salviati was speaking.

Salv: Well, gentlemen, a great deal has happened since our three namesakes met in this place nearly 350 years ago. Have we learned much more than Galileo knew then? Sagredo, since you're from the same field as "the Academician," perhaps you'd be the one to answer first.

Sagr: Well, I suppose the answer is both yes and no. We've certainly resolved the dynamic questions Galileo raised, at least for ordinary notions of ordinary matter. Newton's laws codify virtually everything Galileo originated in terms of dynamics, and the extensions of Einstein cover situations Galileo never anticipated. And our understanding of the strength of materials is far advanced over Galileo's, especially since we understand so much of the atomic structure of matter . . .

Simp: We're certainly much more sophisticated than Galileo was. If he were here now, he'd have a hard time coping.

Sagr: What do you mean, Simplicio?

Simp: Well, of course Galileo was a great man in his time, but he did believe in a simple mechanical model of the world. By modern standards that implies a fairly naive understanding of causality that nobody accepts anymore. And he had no understanding of quantum mechanics, so he wouldn't understand that modern science is based on probabilities instead of certainties. And the social sciences of his time weren't developed at all, so he had no idea that reality is in the eye of the beholder, that "meanings are in people."

Salv: That's a pretty strong indictment of the "father of modern science," Simplicio. But just what do you mean by a "simple mechanical model" of causality?

Simp: A mechanical model is one in which the world is thought of as a machine, of course, whether the behavior of each part is caused by the behavior of some other part. Like a clock.

Sagr: That's a common belief, Simplicio, but if you're accusing Galileo of accepting it . . . or even Newton, for that matter, I'm afraid they're both innocent. Aristotle, perhaps, and certainly Descartes, might accept your "machine model," but not Galileo. At least not in his maturity.

Simp: But everyone knows Galileo and Newton developed mechanical models . . .

Salv: What everyone knows is not necessarily true, Simplicio, and in this case, Sagredo is correct. In his early life, for example, Galileo believed strongly in the need for machinelike causal connections as explanations for motions, but in his later work he had no use for them and argued strongly against them. Causality he correctly attributed to Aristotle. Take, for example, his famous "Law of Falling Bodies." In his youth, Galileo tried to account for the rate at which bodies rose or fell in terms of a hydraulic analogy. He believed, like Aristotle, that bodies had a "proper place" determined by their weight. The "cause" of their motion was the fact that they were "trying" to get back to their proper place. The rate at which they moved was influenced by the physical resistance of the hydraulic medium—sort of like "ether"—through which they moved.

But in his later work, he argues against this same line of "causal" analysis. His law of falling bodies does not explain why bodies fall, or why they fall at a given rate, but simply describes the rate at which any body will fall. This represents a movement away from "qualitative" causal explanations—that is, explanations of processes in terms of their qualities—and toward "quantitative" causal explanations, which consist of statements of invariant quantitative relationships among variables. It really isn't causal explanation that has been discounted by modern scientists, but qualitative causal explanation.

Newton's gravitational law . . . which is the same as Galileo's . . . doesn't give any mechanical explanation either . . . at least not in the sense in which you mean the word mechanical. It doesn't suggest any mechanism at all. It merely says that two bodies will attract each other with a force proportional to the product of their masses and inversely proportional to the square of the distance between them. He never says why this is, just that it is. In this way, he abandons qualitative causes and instead proposes quantitative laws.

Descartes rejected Newton's theory to his grave because of this "flaw."

Simp: But you can't deny that modern scientists reject the simple mechanical models of Galileo and Newton. And the notion of "laws" is suspect as well, is it not?

Sagr: Oh, yes, of course you're right. But it isn't mechanics that is rejected. You yourself use the phrase "quantum mechanics" to describe one of the most modern of physical theories. Mechanics simply refers to the study of the motion of points in space, in its most technical meaning. And modern scientists reject the notion that the universe is like a giant clockwork, with each piece influencing each other part by direct physical contact. But this is sort of a "straw person" argument, since neither Galileo nor Newton really believed that either. The suspicion modern scientists have for "laws" is probably more an indication of modern caution than some epistemological belief. We've seen our laws overturned so many times that many scientists prefer to speak only of hypotheses rather than laws.

Simp: Do you mean to suggest that modern scientists still hope to find universal laws that admit of no exception?

Sagr: Hope, perhaps, is a misleading word. We have a much greater respect for the difficulties, perhaps, than scientists of a century ago (although both Galileo and Newton felt they had seen virtually nothing of what was to be seen, their successors were often less humble!). And few if any of us actually "expect" to make useful statements that admit of no exceptions whatever. But in practice, when a hypothesis is even slightly inaccurate, we say it is wrong and try hard to correct it. If we don't expect to find theories that are perfectly accurate, we are not satisfied with inaccuracy.

Simp: But aren't you ignoring the lesson of quantum theory? Surely you must admit that quantum theory tells us that no event can be established with certainty, but only to a certain level of probability. And, if Heisenberg is to be believed, this probabilistic character is not simply due to our ignorance but is inherently a characteristic of nature itself.

Sagr: Yes, what you say is true, Simplicio. But there are some reservations. Quantum theory does indeed say that there is an inherent probabilistic nature to subatomic processes. The entities which we study in the realm of the subatomic world are small . . . so small they are smaller than any device by which they may be examined. When we attempt to look at these things, we interfere with them, and this is inherent. Moreover, our current understanding leads us to believe many events in this realm are discontinuous, occurring in discrete "packets." Occasionally, nuclei break apart and emit packets of energy. Theory—which is in good agreement with observation—tells us that we cannot, even in principle, tell which of any of trillions of atoms will break apart this way, although we can tell how many of them will have broken in any interval of time. Nor is this a consequence of our ignorance, according to current theory, but an inherent property of the phenomena themselves.

But misinterpretations of this theory are very commonplace. The most common misinterpretation by far is that the uncertainty principle can be applied to larger phenomena. Quantum theory, and the uncertainty principle which is a part of it, applies to the domain of the subatomic and only to this domain. Attempts to apply it by analogy to larger scale events are inappropriate. It would be quite wrong to say, for example, that the force of attraction between two large bodies—say the sun and the earth—is "probably" equal to the product of their masses divided by the square of the distance between them or that, for N such pairs of bodies, the force of attraction between them is distributed about a mean value proportional to the product of their masses and inversely proportional to the square of the distance between them.

Salv: We should also recall, Sagredo, that modern scientists are indeed humble, accepting nothing as absolute truth not subject to disconformation by later observation. And one of the greatest of modern scientists died believing that the uncertainty principle would someday be shown false.

Simp: You mean Einstein, of course. Well, great man though he was, most scientists think he was tragically mistaken in this belief. And the very mention of Einstein brings up perhaps the strongest of reasons for believing the approach of Galileo and Newton is archaic and useless today.

First, Einstein made it clear that the old absolute view of nature held by Galileo and Newton had no counterpart in reality. In fact, all observations depend on the frame of reference of the observer. Observers taking one viewpoint will experience reality differently from those at another vantage point. And, if I may say so, the work of modern social scientists has made this point even more strongly. We know, in fact, that reality is in the eye of the beholder. As communication researchers often say, meanings are in people. The interactionists, and after them the hermeneuticists and the constructivists have all pointed out that reality is socially constructed. All knowledge is human knowledge, and humans are inherently uncertain. Whether your quantum physicsts are right or wrong about the uncertainty prnciple failing to apply to large scale reality, it is quite certain that it applies to human phenomena. No human actions can be predicted with certainty, but only with probabilities. No mechanical or causal model can ever apply with much accuracy to human beings.

Sagr: I have to admit there is a great deal in what you say, Simplicio. But still it's not completely accurate. In one sense, Galileo and Newton did understand the extent to which observations depend on the observer.

Both knew that the description of events depended on the choice of reference frame and that trajectories that looked like a straight line to one observer might resemble a parabola to another observer moving relative to the first. And both understood that the velocity of, say, a projectile would appear greater to a person approaching the projectile than to one who was standing still or moving away from it. In fact, the changes of reference frame which correct for these differences in reference frame are actually called "Galilean transformations" in physics. There might be a sense in which these kinds of transformations account in part for what social scientists may mean by saying reality is in the eye of the beholder. To a small person, another may appear quite imposing, while to a much taller person the same individual may seem ordinary. As long as we're dealing with objects that are neither very large nor very small, and as long as the objects are not moving at an appreciable fraction of the speed of light, Einstein has nothing to add to either Galileo or Newton. And Einstein's theory doesn't do away with causality or laws of nature at all. Both Newtonian and Einsteinian physics search for laws, and both accept only laws which hold in every reference frame. Of course, in Newton's model, Galilean transformations allow the laws to hold across different observers in different reference frames, while for Einstein, it is Lorentz transformations, but both theories are clearly laws theories.

When you talk about human beings, however, I have to admit you may be right. While I hope I won't offend you in saying it, I'm afraid that few of my physical science colleagues hold much faith in the social sciences and have great doubts that you will discover laws of the sort we have found, even granting all their imperfections.

Simp: I'm glad to see that we can agree on some matters at least. I'm willing to accept the idea that causal laws apply to physical processes with the stipulations you suggest: first, that they do not necessarily refer to some oversimplified machinelike cause and effect mechanism but, rather, to invariant relationships like the one between masses, distances, and rates of falling. And I'm even willing to agree that the word "mechanical" in the special sense you choose to impart to it doesn't necessarily imply the naive machinelike model I once thought. And, of course, we have to understand that these lawlike theories don't apply in the same way to quantum phenomena, since the laws only prescribe probability distributions and not specific states for specific individual particles. Furthermore, I also favor your use of the word "hypothesis" as a substitute for "law," since it seems to me to imply the correct amount of humility before nature that a scientist ought to feel.

Even granting all this, it seems we will still agree that such laws will do me no good, since I am a social scientist. The phenomenon I study is humanity or at least the thoughts and actions of humanity, and I think we can all agree that the notion of causality, no matter how carefully qualified, can't be applied to human matters.

Sagr: I quite agree with you there, Simplicio. Our earlier disagreement about the application of laws to physical phenomena was mainly a result of our different vocabularies and differing perspectives. This discussion has been a great help to us both, since a source of apparent disagreement has been eliminated. But we've not heard yet from Salviati about this. How about it, Salviati, do we all agree?

Salv: I think we've come a long way from our initial confusion. Whenever strangers first meet there is bound to be some initial confusion and disagreement, much of which may be real and some of which may just be the result of different points of view and different uses of language. Our discussion has cleared a good deal of this away, but I'm still not sure that such a short discussion is enough to bring about complete harmony.

In fact, just as we may initially think we disagree when the disagreement is only an illusion brought on by different perspectives and usages of language, we may just as often think we agree when we differ and for the same reasons. Before I conclude that we are of one mind on these issues, I'd like to hear more. Particularly, I'd like to hear why each of you believes that laws—like the law of gravity—can never be applied to human thought and behavior.

Simp: There are good reasons for saying laws of human thinking and behavior do not exist. Foremost among these is free will, the capacity of human beings to make choices. "Particles" can't make choices, but human beings can.

Salv: What you say may or may not be true, Simplicio, for each individual person. But even if it were, wouldn't that bring about exactly the situation we have in quantum mechanics? I mean, of course, that even if the behavior of each individual person (or particle) is indeterminate and unpredictable, still the behavior of the aggregate of all of them or even many of them might be described by laws of the type we have already agreed on. And I'd grant your argument in a flash, Simplicio, even for individuals, if you can only tell me on what grounds you are led to believe that human beings have the power of free choice.

Sagr: Very clever, Salviati! I'm afraid you'll have to go further than that, Simplicio, since Salviati has a point. When you say that human beings make choices freely, you are simply using different words to say their behavior is not governed by laws. And that, of course, is what you are trying to prove in the first place.

Nonetheless, since the earliest days of scientific thought, most scholars have been reluctant to believe human thought and behavior could be modeled by the same kinds of laws as physical phenomena. Many generations of the best effort of the best scholars have failed to find even one law of human behavior. Even if Simplicio may not be able to prove that this quest is impossible, you should recall that the burden of proof is on the affirmative. If you, Salviati, believe that there are laws of human behavior, it ought to be on your shoulders to show it is so.

Salv: Of course, you're right, Sagredo. It is my responsibility to show that such laws are possible and yours to rejoin my arguments, should I find any. Before I begin, it's well worth pointing out that your own remarks go a long way toward explaining why most scholars don't think there are any causal laws of human thought and behavior.

Sagr: My own remarks?

Salv: Yes. You see, you said first that very few scholars believed in the possibility that such laws would be found. Since so few believe in the existence of the quarry, is it unlikely the chase will be futile?

Sagr: A good point, Salviati, but a long way from a convincing argument that laws of human thought and behavior will ever be found. Just how do you expect to argue your case?

Salv: With the strongest possible argument, my friends. I hope to show not only that there may be laws of human thought and behavior but that they have already been discovered.

Simp: Already discovered?

Salv: Yes. And furthermore, not only have they been discovered but you yourselves accept them as true.

Simp: If you can convince us not only that there may be laws of human thought but that we already hold to some, that will be quite a trick, Salviati. Especially since we have all agreed among ourselves that no two humans perceive these matters in the same way.

Sagr: The key problem seems to me that laws of nature, especially causal laws, are meant to explain observations. But if everyone observes social and psychological events through a different set of attitudes and values and beliefs, then there is no common set of observations to be explained.

Salv: Do either of you believe that anyone is ever exempt from this filtering of experience by values and beliefs?

Simp: Are you suggesting, Salviati, that you've found a way to free yourself from your own biases and can see things as they really are? I don't mean any disrespect, but ordinarily people who believe they have penetrated to the secrets of the universe can benefit from some counseling. All of us are at all times subject to the distorting effects of our past experiences. There is no privileged view of the world.

Sagr: I can't help but agree with Simplicio there, Salviati. No self-respecting scientist would accept a law, or even a single observation, as true on the word of one person. Science is an objective process, and it requires the agreement of many scientists to accept anything as fact. We believe pretty strongly that the most honest of observers are subject to the distortion of their own backgrounds, beliefs, and attitudes.

Salv: We all agree, then, that all human perception is filtered through the cognitive structures already existing in each individual. And, as you've both agreed, this view is nearly unanimously shared by physical and social scientists alike, is it not?

Simp: I'd say that view is close to the foundations of modern social science, Salviati.

Sagr: It's wisdom to recognize one's limitations, and humans are pretty limited.

Salv: Since we all agree that present perceptions are influenced by past beliefs and attitudes in every person at all times, why don't we just call this a law, then . . . and a causal law at that? In fact, it would seem to be the law on which all rules-type theories are themselves based.

Simp: I have to give you credit for a clever argument, Salviati, but I'm a long way from accepting your conclusion. You can call this ''perceptual filtering'' a law if you like, but it's quite different, it appears to me, from a physical law, like the law of gravity. For one thing, you law doesn't specify any mechanism by which the filtering takes place . . .

Sagr: That's a dangerous approach, Simplicio, and will soon fail. You'll get trapped in the same mechanistic or machine-like theorizing you argued so strongly against a few moments ago. A law doesn't have to posit any mechanism, and modern scientists don't believe in causality in the way that Aristotle did. The law of gravity just says that two bodies attract each other in a specificable way but not why they do so. We're so familiar with the law that we forget this. But when a small child asks us why things fall we say gravity makes it happen. When he or she asks why or how gravity does this, the greatest of physicists has to change the subject.

But that doesn't mean I accept your view, Salviati. There are still many things wrong with your law, I think. First of all, if it is a law, it's different from the kinds of laws we have in physics. For one thing, it's clearly not the same form as a physical law. It doesn't say how perception is affected by past beliefs and attitudes. I don't mean ''by what mechanism,'' but ''in what way.'' Maybe past experiences influence current perceptions randomly, maybe systematically, but we can't say from the current form of you law. Your law, I'm afraid, is vague enough to be true.

Salv: As I've stated it so far, you are both correct. The law is vague and different in form from physical laws. But I think we also agree on ways the law can be made more precise. Would you say, Simplicio, that social scientists are prone to see new data as more or less favorable to their own view due to this filtering?

Simp: More favorable. But it's not that simple, Salviati. The influence isn't always positive. People don't always misperceive to see what they wish to see. Sometimes the opposite is true. Sentries and guards, for example, often see the enemy when it's not there.

Sagr: That's right, Salviati. In general, scientists often misinterpret results to favor their own theories but not always. Michelson, for example, was quite disappointed that his experiment failed to show the "either drift" he expected, and this led him to ignore the much more profound implications of the constancy of the speed of light which his own experiment showed.

Salv: You're both right. But I don't think it would be accurate to say selective perception biases you to see what you want to see but, rather, what you expect to see, good or bad. Selective perception is like an inertial mechanism. And it is a principle, as many other physical laws are principles. This particular law is an inertial law like Newton's first law. It says that the mind tends to remain the same, to resist "acceleration." It tends to maintain itself as it is. The first law, then, may be stated with precision: *in the absence of outside "forces," cognitive structure tends to remain as it is.*

Sagr: I'll grant you that, in the way you now state it, your "first law" has the same form as does Newton's. And, so that the argument may continue, I'm willing to overlook those of a religious persuasion who might believe human cognitive structure can be miraculously changed in a dramatic way by the intervention of supernatural forces. But even so, Salviati, the notion of selective perception implies more than just this. It implies as well that some change is to be expected when the cognitive structure is not isolated from outside forces. To account for this, you'll need at least one or two more laws. If Newton had left us only the first law, none of us would remember his name today.

Salv: Of course, you're correct, Sagredo. A theory made up of only one law is of little use, but a second law won't be difficult to find if we follow again the example of Newton. We already know that the first law—both Newton's and the one I have proposed—is a principle or stipulation rather than an observation. And so is the second. For Newton, the second law states that the acceleration of any body may be accounted for in terms of two new variables, one of which retards the acceleration of the body and another of which increases it. The former we call "inertial mass" and the latter "force." Neither of these variables has a real existence but are really only logical constructions to help us think clearly about what we experience. As you said earlier, they may as well be called rules as laws. And we may agree to the same rules in our cognitive science by simply stipulating that each attitude or belief indeed has some calculable "resistance to acceleration." We need not at first stipulate any mechanism for this resistance but simply observe that some cognitive elements are easier to change than others. Those that resist change most strongly we will consider high in mass, while those that change easily will be assigned a lower mass.

In the same way, if two occurrences should change the same attitude or belief by different amounts, we will say that the one occurrence was proportionately more forceful than the other. Again it is not necessary to postulate a mechanism underlying the forces. Our second law, then, might simply say that *the acceleration (change in the rate of change) of any cognitive element is directly proportional to the force impressed on it and inversely proportional to its own inertial mass.*

Simp: I've listened with some interest to your remarks up until now, Salvaiti, but this strikes me as the emptiest of philosophical speculation. If I was opposed to the idea that there might be laws of human thought, I'm even more strongly opposed to the idea that they might resemble Newton's laws in any except the emptiest logical sense. And in fact your usage of these laws is empty, since they are not inductions based on honest observations but, rather, stipulations and word games. A physical object has mass because there is some observable matter there. You can feel it and weigh it. It's objective! An attitude or belief or any other cognitive element is subjective. You can't see it or touch it or sense it in any direct way. It's existence has to be inferred, not observed.

Sagr: I'm still extremely skeptical about Salviati's argument, Simplicio, but not for the reasons you mention. In some ways, Salviati is right. Mass isn't objective as you say. Newton thought it could be observed directly, but we now know that's not true. Mass is no longer considered the "quantity of matter" in a body but, rather, is simply defined as its resistance to acceleration relative to some arbitrary standard mass. Masses and forces are inferred by physicists, not observed as you think.

And it is true that both of Newton's first two laws might be considered stipulations or definitions. Many physicists and philosophers do so consider them. But even these two laws alone have no meaning and gain us nothing in explaining either physical or cognitive matters. First of all, some sort of measurement system has to be devised if the laws are to be worth anything. As you say, modern laws are quantitative, and, although your laws may take on a quantitative form, there must still be some way in which these quantities are to be anchored in experience. And second, it seems to me that the third law is what makes the first two useful. Newton's third law relates the two unknown terms force and mass to something we can measure directly—distance. Without these, the other concepts, force and mass, and the laws in which they occur, are quite empty.

Simp: Even though I might be willing to grant the philosophical subtleties philosophers attach to Newton's laws, the idea that they might be applied to human cognition is too far out to consider. Virtually every scholar in the social sciences knows that physical and social experiences are different and that these differences lie in the immaterial, subjective, and uncertain character of human variables. It will take a powerful argument to convince me otherwise, I'm afraid.

Salv: I have no hope that any arguments I could propose in a single conversation could be energetic enough to convince you, Simplicio. But I do hope to show that there is enough plausibility to what I say to warrant my own continued investigations into the matter. And it seems to me as well that some of the principles about which we've already agreed here today provide the basis for a third law, one which makes the other two useful.

Simp: I'd be amazed if we already agreed on a third law when we don't seem to have agreed on the first two yet, but nonetheless, please go on.

Salv: When we first began our conversation, we appeared to disagree about the meanings of certain important words and their application to physical theory. The word "cause," for example, was used differently by each of us, as was the word "mechanical." This led us to disagree about whether or not contemporary physical theory could be called causal. And we initially disagreed about the extent to which the work of Einstein and the new quantum theory had overthrown the works of Galileo and Einstein, but after some conversation we were able to come to agreements about how we would use these words among ourselves. And this, in turn, led us to a closer agreement about the nature of causal and mechanical theory and its use in the physical science. Wouldn't you agree?

Simp: If you plan to suggest that the third law will hold that our views grow similar through communication, I'd have to disagree. It's true that sometimes communication brings people's views together but not always true. Our own conversation is a case in point. While we're closer to agreement about the things you mention, we're farther apart than ever in our beliefs about the application of mechanical or causal theory to human cognition. At first I thought we were closer than we are now and would even have been willing to grant you that there was a sense in which causal theory could be applied to human communication. But once I learned that you had in mind an application of the very laws of Newton to these matters, I grew further from your position than ever! You can see, then, that communication sometimes brings convergence of views among the communicating parties, but sometimes the opposite occurs. And a causal law cannot admit of exception, if I am correct.

Sagr: I'm not sure I agree with you completely, Simplicio. By no means do I agree with Salviati yet about the possibility of applying physical laws to human thoughts, but I do think we've grown closer due to the discussion. At first, we didn't have any idea of just how greatly we differed. In some respects we were closer than we thought, and a little discussion made that clear. And in other areas, we were further apart than we thought. But learning how far apart we were certainly seems to me at least to be a step toward agreement, even if not agreement itself. And perhaps you did not grow further from Salviati's position, but simply realized that it was further from your own than you had at first thought.

But that doesn't mean I'm ready to buy Salviati's argument. And, in fact, we may be somewhat premature in considering Salviati's third law, since he hasn't actually proposed it yet!

Salv: You're both right and wrong, at least insofar as you've guessed what I will propose as a third law. I will, in fact, propose that the third law state that *communication brings the thoughts of contending parties closer together and that this is always the case*. But it is not such a simple law as this.

For one thing, both of you have correctly noted that our convergence on a common viewpoint has been more rapid on some issues than for others. Most notably, we agreed fairly quickly about the meanings of the word "mechanics" and on the sense in which Galileo and Newton's theories were mechanical. But our convergence has been much slower when we consider the extent to which these matters may apply as well to human thought. Is this so?

Sagr: That seems right.

Salv: And I hope you will not take offense, Simplicio, if I suggest that it was your opinion about the meaning of the word mechanical which changed the most rapidly and by the greatest amount?

Simp: I'm sure you're right, Salviati, but that should be no surprise. As a social scientist I have little reason to think often of the word mechanical, and I've read little about it. Sagredo, on the other hand, is a physicist, and so he no doubt has read a great deal in this area. It's quite reasonable for me to defer to his greater knowledge on matters about which he has studied a lifetime and I hardly at all. And, for that matter, you too seem to have read a great deal about these historical matters, and so I'm not surprised that you should know the technical definition of mechanics better than I.

On the other hand, I've spent my whole life studying human communication and, particularly, the means by which one person persuades another—or resists persuasion from another, for that matter—and so you are not so likely to change my opinions about that so easily.

Salv: Exactly. And I'm pleased to note that the explanation you offer for the ease with which some of your beliefs may be changed in contrast to the difficulty of changing others is a causal one. But regardless of whether your explanation is causal, or even whether it is correct, none-theless it is quite clear that some of your beliefs are easier to change than others, as are mine. If you were to tell me, for example, that your name was not really Simplicio, I would believe you at once, since the evidence I have for this amounts only to what you've told me once. But if you told me you were not actually here, the evidence you'd need to present would be enormous, since nearly everything I believe about the physical world would need to be changed before I could accept that.

Sagr: Of course, it's obvious where you're going, Salviati. You'll sug-gest that *the rate of convergence of beliefs and attitudes is the inverse of their inertial masses.* And I have to admit that the notion is a powerful one, especially since we've already established that inertial mass need not make any reference to physical matter but only to resistance to accelera-tions. Even though that view is interesting, it still leaves holes in your argument. You correctly noted that mass and force are reciprocals, de-fined in terms of each other. The only thing that saves the whole of Newton's theory from being an empty logical exercise is that he can establish functional relations between these two terms, force and mass, on the one hand, and the observable—or better still, measurable—vari-able, distance. You haven't shown any such possibility yet.

Simp: At least you'll spare us the absurdity of saying the force of attraction between different beliefs is inversely proportional to the dis-tance between them, then!

Salv: I admit I'm not quite ready to apply Newton's third law to human communication . . . at least not so easily as that. But I do note that you say this position has little attraction for you since it is so far from your own. And of course you are right, Sagredo, in arguing that some measur-able notion of distance is required if we are to progress any further. But why do you suspect this will be impossible? Don't you both make use of this concept in your discussion? Didn't you say, Simplicio, that my views are "too far out" to be considered? And didn't we discuss the extent to which our views were far apart or close, or growing closer or growing farther from each other? Don't we use the notion of distance quite explic-itly in discussing human beliefs?

Simp: Of course we do but only in the vaguest analogy to physical distances. Physical distances are objective. You can see them, and you can measure them. This is certainly not so far distances among beliefs or positions one might hold in an argument. This is poetry, not science. And, if you'll permit me to use the analogy one more time, this argument is taking us all further from common sense every moment!

Sagr: I'm afraid I have to agree with Simplicio, Salviati. It's one thing to formulate laws that have the same form as physical laws but quite another to apply them to experience and expect them to hold. There must be a way to measure your concepts, to expose them to experience, otherwise I'm afraid there is no science involved. Science deals with observations, ultimately.

Salv: Well put, Sagredo. Without observations we have no science. But wouldn't you agree with Einstein when he says, "It is quite wrong, on principle, to base our theory on observable magnitudes alone. On the contrary, it is theory which determines what we can observe"?

Sagr: Well, not being Einstein it's hard to know exactly what he meant, but, in a sense, that is true. Quantum theory, for example, leads us to develop devices which enable us to look for things we would not have been able to see otherwise. And it's also true that the subject matter of modern high-energy physics is completely undetectable to the unaided human senses. But I'm not sure that this is the issue we face in our present discussion. The question before us is whether psychological distance can be measured.

Simp: It should be painfully obvious that psychological distance is merely a mental abstraction, not something tangible such as physical distance which can be touched. Physicists can easily lay a ruler or metric stick between the two objects whose distance apart they are measuring and arrive at a ratio in terms of the number of times the ruler physically fits into the space. Whether it's meters or yards, by means of a straightforward transformation, the distance is the same.

Sagr: Oh, but you do us a disservice by suggesting that all physical measures are readily observable and easier to measure than social phenomena. Your criteria certainly do not apply to the measurement of the distance to the nearest galaxy or of subatomic distances which are not directly observable. The measurement of temperature is another important physical property which has not been completely understood after 300 years of work. Temperature scales would not completely pass the criteria for interval scales, since no two methods of measuring temperature agree across the whole range of values. And what about time? Do you believe that time has a "physical" existence?

Simp: Time?

Salv: Of course! Time is the most precisely measured variable in all of science, yet it has no physical existence and no one can lay down a unit of time next to another interval of time.

Sagr: Well, then Salviati, since I can't think of any reason in principle (short of religious matters) why your intangibles should be any less measurable than my intangibles and, since Simplicio can't provide substantial emprical evidence against the measurement of distances among beliefs and attitudes, possibly you might suggest some ways in which such measures might be carried out?

Salv: Since we are all well aware of the extent to which our choice of reference frame determines our experience, I might suggest that our conception of psychological and cultural experiences may seem as different as it does from our experience of the physical precisely because we have adopted different measurement rules for the two domains. My first suggestion, then, would be to adopt the identical rule for measurement that has proven so successful for science in the past. We might take any two objects or beliefs arbitrarily and assign some numerical value to the distance between them. Individuals might then be asked to estimate the distances between any other pair of beliefs or objects as a ratio to this standard distance.

Simp: That's nothing more than an analogy to the measurements of physical scientists. There's no reason to suspect it will work, respondents won't be able to do it, no advantage will be gained from it, and our field will be embarrassed by the pretense that we are scientific. You can't be scientific simply by imitating scientists.

Sagr: I assume you mean that there is some evidence this method fails? Those who have used it are disappointed?

Simp: No, the users are enthusiastic, but then, they are users and naturally favor their own method. But the method does take somewhat longer—possibly 10% longer—than our more common ordinal scaling methods. Some people claim it yields an extra digit or two of precision, but these claims are probably exaggerated. But mostly, there's just no advantage to be gained from it.

Sagr: Assuming the claims are not too seriously exaggerated, very few physical scientists would reject the chance at one or two digits of extra precision for only a 10% increase in cost, particularly since your present five-point scales are not sufficient to establish even one digit with certainty! As a scientist, the observational evidence is paramount with me, and I can't judge the virtues of these claims without reading the data carefully. But for the sake of continuing the argument, Salviati, suppose I grant the scales are at least as precise as the older methods used by social scientists. What does this have to do with causal theory?

Salv: Since the measurement method is part of the frame of reference, any important change in measurement brings about a change in what we observe. And this, of course, changes the form of the laws we find. Had

Galileo chosen to use the time-honored measurement system of the social sciences, he would not have been able to arrive at the law of falling bodies in its quadratic form.

Simp: But he didn't have to use ordinal scales. We do, since the phenomena we study are themselves only ordinal in character.

Sagr: No, that's not correct. Or at least, at best, we really don't know whether it's correct or not. You see, the fact is that very few social scientists have ever applied the same measurement system Galileo himself used. And those who have appear quite enthusiastic about it. But those who use the categorical system guarantee that their observations will always contain large uncertainties. They're built into the scales.

Simp: Then you believe that human thought processes can be modeled by the laws of Newton?

Sagr: I don't believe anything that hasn't been shown by data, and that hasn't been shown to my satisfaction. The point is rather that I am convinced that your efforts with categorical scales do not prove such experiences may not be modeled by physical methods, possibly even by the very equations of Galileo and Newton nor could they. The fact is, no one knows whether attitudes, beliefs, and values can be modeled by the exact methods of physical science, because so few efforts to do so have yet been made. I, like most other scientists, believed that human variables had stubbornly resisted attempt after attempt to encompass them within the methods of physical science, but our conversation leads me to believe this is not true. Rather, it seems, the methods of physical science have only seldom been attempted, because social scientists believe in advance that they will not work. If the notion of selective perception is indeed a law, then this is certainly an instance of it.

Simp: How then do we get to the third law?

Salv: The first step in such a program is the development of a reference frame within which any such law might take on a simple enough form to be recognized by our limited capacities. This step includes the specification of scales of measurement of sufficient precision and richness to describe our experiences in some detail, and it also includes the stipulation of principles such as the first two laws we have proposed today. In this regard we should note that neither Aristotle nor his successors thought even physical motion capable of measurement of the type we have described and so cut themselves off from the possibility of determining laws of the type described by Galileo and Newton, as have many social scientists today. Moreover, neither did Aristotle stipulate laws of the first two kinds we have described, which have the effect of making accelerations the experiences which require explanation. Without stipulations such as these, laws of a Galilean or Newtonian type are impossible, since they depend on the logical form of this system as well as on the experiences themselves. For surely, as we have all agreed, the experiences are viewed only within such stipulations, and changes in the form of these assumptions bring about changes in the nature of our observations. In fact, the contemporary practices and assumptions of many of our colleagues in the social sciences have the character of a self-fulfilling prophecy, since they render the discovery of causal laws impossible.

Simp: Sometimes what you say is sensible and, at other times, seems the emptiest of sophistry, Salviati. But will you just provide us these logical arguments rather than the third law?

Salv: In the proper spirit of scientific humility it is only fair to say that a complete understanding of cognitive processes awaits future generations of scientists. But the notion that the attitudes, beliefs, values, and other cognitive elements of peoples and cultures converge toward the mean of the values of the communicating parties is quite consistent with the principles we have established here and fits experiences so far collected to tolerances at once worse than the best of physical theory and as well or better than the best of theory developed specifically within the human disciplines.

As to whether the final form of this law will be, indeed, an inverse squares law, we have perhaps some choice. While it may at first seem as if the laws must be discovered, a closer look shows that we may, to an extent, choose the mathematical form of the law which is most convenient in a mathematical sense. It is then necessary to discover the set of transformations which must be applied to the data as measured which will make our observations conform to this form. Perhaps one may be found in which the inverse squares law may be made to apply to communication quite exactly.

Simp: Then you will admit, Salviati, that, as yet, your third law does not fit perfectly to observations, and is thus false?

Salv: Insofar as the fit to data is not perfect, then the law is false. But so, then, are all laws, both physical and human, since no experiment can be performed without error, and no theory conforms to experience exactly. Yet we do not reject such a theory unless a superior theory is kown to us, and in no case is it wise to abandon a theory known to be false in favor of an alternative theory that fits to experience even more poorly.

Simp: Your suggestion that the theory you describe fits experience to better tolerances than other specifically social type theories strikes me as the greatest of arrogance, Salviati, not at all in the spirit of humility that we consider indispensible to science. To be sure, such researchers as have been reported usually reveal relatively high degrees of explained variance, but at least some alternative models may do as well.

Salv: To be sure, Simplicio, humility is a great virtue, but the greatest requirement of the scientist is, above all, honesty. To be sure, the simple models and limited experiments that have been presented in behalf of this type of theory leave great room for humility, since they pale by comparison to the great achievements of Sagredo's colleagues. And no one could doubt that the achievements of social scientists, using totally new methods and facing great limitations, warrant the greatest of praise.

But, in fact, the measurements we've discussed today without exception produce more variance than the categorical scales more typically used by our colleagues. Some erroneously consider this a drawback, but greater variance indicates that the experience measured has been divided up into more and smaller pieces. When an experiment is able to account for a given percentage of a large amount of variance, he or she has provided a better and more precise fit to experience than when the same percentage of a small amount of variance has been explained. I believe that a fair reading of the evidence will show that the very simple hypothesis I proposed as the first steps toward a third law—that is, that the beliefs, attitudes, and values of communicating parties converge toward the mean of their beliefs, attitudes, and values—fits experience at least as well as any other model of communication yet proposed.

Simp: I still don't understand why we should adopt your model. Thinking of human beings as law-governed particles in a mechanical system seems demeaning, even if we understand mechanics in the way we have learned to speak of it today.

And the costs of adopting a causal model such as this are enormous! The equations which would be used to model attitudes as points moving through space are difficult, and very few in our field can grasp them. The kinds of words used by such theorists, such as "tensors" and "Riemann spaces" and "harmonic oscillators," do not enlighten us but, rather, cover over what everyone understands in terminology so turgid that no one can understand. How can this be clarifying?

Sagr: While I have grave doubts that Salviati will accomplish his goals in any short time, if at all, Simplicio, there is no doubt but that there would be great advantages if it could be accomplished. May I remind you that, in my own field, the very same terms have been not only clarifying but essential to our understanding. There is no doubt at all but that they are learned and understood at the cost of great pain and effort, but a proper understanding of physical processes has proven impossible without them.

Salv: Not the least of the advantages to be gained is the unification of the sciences. Perhaps the greatest contribution a scientist can hope to make is to show that experiences once thought to be so diverse and separated as to require completely different methods and theories can actually be embraced by a single theory.

Simp: You speak of the gains, but what of the losses? Is the product of a hundred years of social science to be discarded on the basis of these flimsy prospects? Can an entire branch of human knowledge be foreclosed because you hold to a very tentative hope to unit human processes within the confines of theory meant to refer only to particles?

Salv: No one would be so foolish as to suggest such a plan, least of all myself. This model does not deny all other forms of knowledge. Science is a wonderful and powerful system of knowledge but certainly not the only form of knowledge. Those who pursue this quest do not ask all others to abandon their own search but only for the opportunity to continue this work. For indeed, no matter how pleasant and useful this discussion, only experiment will determine the outcome.

PART III

COMMUNICATION THEORY: EAST–WEST SYNTHESIS

The concluding section presents three papers which compare and contrast certain aspects of the Eastern and Western perspectives toward communication and attempt to transcend the differences with some kind of synthesis.

Joseph Woelfel (Chapter 21, this volume) finds a common origin for both Eastern and Western ways of thinking or "models" of the world, which eventually influenced each region's perspective toward communication. Although his focus is on the development of the Western model, his course in a sense takes the form of a circle in which the Western scientific perspective has returned—substantially refined and improved—to a point which shares much in common with pre-Socratic and Eastern-influenced perspectives toward the world.

The crucial distinction is whether the world is mentally constructed in terms of continual processes or discrete catagories. The former choice leads to a position in which the word concepts of ordinary language are grossly inadequate to capture the true nature of the world—a philosophical position found throughout our Eastern perspectives on communication—but to a position in which dynamic change is not only possible but the focus of attention. The latter choice leads to the development of a logical description of the world in ordinary language terms, but to a static world in which the process of change becomes unintelligible and the focus inevitably turns to initial states and "proper" end states.

The categorical "walls" of Aristotelian logic were tumbled by the combined contributions of Decartes's comparative logic and continuous mathematical reference frame and its subsequent application to the problems of motion by Galileo and Newton. The development of general relativity theory in the twentieth century completed the model of science as we now know it by eliminating the notion that any one observer's coordinate system or frame of reference is privileged or absolute. This change led Einstein himself to conceive of science as a process of finding transformations which link the experiences of any observer with the observations of any other.

Although this revised world model is now shared by scientists in both the East and the West, most communication scientists in the West have retained the pre-Cartesian, categorical model of the world on which to build their theories. Professor Woelfel concludes with a discussion of how a communication theory based on the principles of modern science—and more compatible with many of the assumptions of the Eastern model—should be developed.

Muneo Yoshikawa (Chapter 22, this volume) clearly wants a model of communication on which true *intercultural* communication can take place. The "double-swing" model which he develops allows for just such a process to occur, one in which the members of different cultures can respect each other's cultural uniqueness as well as their differences and similarities. To reach his double-swing model of communication, Professor Yoshikawa first identifies the alternative modes of encounter: the *ethnocentric* mode in which the other's culture is ignored, the *control* mode in which one manipulates the other, the *dialectical* mode in which cultural fusion occurs, and the *dialogical* mode which emphasizes wholeness, mutuality, content and processes, differences, and similarities.

The double-swing model is based on the dialogical mode of communication. Professor Yoshikawa elaborates on this model from both Western and Eastern perspectives. The work of Martin Buber expresses this mode from the Western perspective; the Buddhist principles of pardoxical relations express it from the Eastern perspective. Each mode identified by Professor Yoshikawa is presented both verbally and pictorially by means of simple diagrams which make them intuitively obvious to the reader.

D. Lawrence Kincaid's concluding paper (Chapter 23, this volume) reconsiders some of the overly simplified stereotypes that the East and West have of one another (see Chapter 1, this volume) in light of the new material presented in this volume. Some of the differences between the East and West specified at the outset are indeed confirmed and even accentuated by our contributors; others, however, are to be tempered by our newfound knowledge of the similarities and commonalities of each perspective. Professor Kincaid points out the key points of similarity and difference between Eastern and Western perspectives on communication made explicit by the contributers to this volume, and then he suggests new lines of inquiry for theory development.

CHAPTER 21

Development of the Western Model: Toward a Reconciliation of Eastern and Western Perspectives

Joseph Woelfel

INTRODUCTION

Although communication as a formal discipline is one of the youngest of the sciences, it has roots which extend back through the arts and philosophy at least as far back as the Greeks. Even today, Aristotle's rhetoric plays an important part in the training of many communication scholars.

As a young and eclectic discipline, communication has drawn substance from many related fields and has diversified in theory as well as methods of inquiry. In spite of the diversity of its ancestry and the scope of its ecclecticism, recent developments have led to increased interest in the common characteristics which communication theorists share. Particularly, as communication has begun to find world-wide applications, many workers both theoretical and applied have begun to question the applicability of an essentially Western discipline like communication to problems in the East. This essay, while acknowledging the diversity and frequently sharp differences of opinion among communication theorists and researchers, attempts to trace the development of communication theory back to its origins to determine the extent to which common themes, axioms, and methods might justify classifying contemporary communication theory as a single Western model.

At the outset it is important to stress that the Western tradition, like the Eastern, is diverse and includes widely different viewpoints which coexist in time. At the risk of minimizing these differences, however, it is convenient to divide the roughly 30-century period during which the Western model has developed into four segments according to the prevailing model of the time. The earliest period, usually called the pre-Socratic period, is characterized by loosely defined beginnings of Western philosophical thought and shares much with the Eastern philosophical tradition. The second period begins with Socrates and lasts through the work of Aquinas into the beginnings of the Renaissance. It is dominated initially by the work of Socrates, Plato, and Aristotle and, later, by influences of Christianity, particularly through the works of Aquinas. The third period dates from Descartes and Galileo until the late ninteenth century and marks the beginning of scientific measurement, while the fourth period dates from Einstein and his predecessors and continues through today. It is wrong to assume sharp cleavages between these periods, and it is equally wrong to assume each of these periods is homogenous in viewpoint. Nonetheless, each of them is sufficiently domianted by a particular view with sufficiently definable characteristics to warrant separate treatment.

THE COMMON MODEL

It is by now commonplace to note that Western thought has its antecedents among the Greek philosophers, and it is almost universally agreed that Thales (circa seventh century B.C.) was the first of the Greek philosophers. What is less well known is the extent to which Eastern and Western thinking were merged during these early origins. Miletus, the largest city in the Greek world and the home of Thales, Aniximander, and Aniximines, was the largest commercial trading center of the Greek world and, as such, was in continuous contact with the East. Land travel to Mesopotamia was common, as was sea travel to Egypt, and there is good evidence that Thales himself traveled to Egypt at least once. There is also general agreement that Thales predicted an eclipse of the sun around 585 B.C., a feat which almost certainly would have required a good knowledge of Babylonian astronomy.

Moreover, the views of the pre-Socratic Greek philosophers often bear a striking resemblance to the principles of Chinese philosophy. Thales thought that there was a single underlying substratum which was itself the source of its own motion—like the Chinese notion of *Ch'i*—although Aristotle suggests that Thales later identifies the substratum with water. Along with the monistic model of Thales, there are also pluralistic views, like the atomistic view of Democritus and others. The atoms of Democritus, however, are not dead matter but, rather, living force themselves and the source of their own motion. We find also the notion of relative polarities or polar opposites, and these even form a basis of the more well-developed Aristotelian model several centuries later. Within this framework of philosophy, and like the Chinese model, humans are not distinguished as fundamentally different from or opposed to nature but are rather an integral part of being and change. Speculation, as in Chinese philosophy, is not ethical in character, and concepts of moral guilt are not strong in the philosophy of this period.

Perhaps closest of all to the Chinese model is the philosophy of Heraclitus, whose idea of endless change and restlessness is well-summarized by his dictum that one cannot step in the same river twice. Although Aristotle considered Heraclitus' position to be an extreme one even at the time, it was by no means unique, and its conclusions—such as the impossibility of capturing reality in words so common in the Chinese view—were recognized by other pre-Socratic Greeks like Cratylus, " . . . who finally did not think it right to say anything but only moved his finger, and criticised Heraclitus for saying that it is impossible to step in the same river twice, for he thought one could not do it even once" (McKeon, 1941, pp. 745-746).

Consistent with Heraclitus' view of a universe in constant flux was his relativistic epistemology—a theory of knowledge which denied absolute, unchanging knowledge and emphasized instead an individual, internal, enlightening experience which was at once personal and uncommunicable. In fact, Heraclitus' writings are frequently Koan-like, intended to stimulate the reader into internal considerations and personal enlightenment, and more rationally oriented Greeks sometimes complained that he wrote nothing clearly.

Heraclitus' most formidable opponent was Parmenides. Parmenides adhered strongly to the *Principle of Noncontradiction*—a principle which is itself at odds with the Chinese *Principle of Infinite Interpretation*. The *Principle of Noncontradiction,* along with Paramenides' monistic view of nature, led him to deny altogether even the possibility of motion and change. The sequence of an (apparently) ripening tomato, for exámple, required the annihilation of a green tomato and the creation of a red tomato. The tomato could not be both green and red, nor could the green tomato pass into nothing or the red tomato spring into being from nothing. These philosophical difficulties were enough to cause Parmenides to reject sensory evidence of change as erroneous.

Parmenides was not the only Greek to deny motion and change. Zeno, for example, declared motion to be impossible on the grounds that any moving object would need to pass through an infinity of intermediate points which would require an infinite amount of time.

The pre-Socratic period, therefore, was one in which Eastern thought mingled freely with emerging Greek ideas, and it is not to undervalue the originality of the Greeks to say that Western thought can best be understood in the light of these common origins. The next period—the period beginning with Socrates and ending with the birth of classic science—can be seen as emerging out of the ideas of the pre-Socratic period, both Eastern and Western.

THE ARISTOTELIAN MODEL

Although the pre-Scoratic period is marked by a comingling of Eastern and Western thought, the period which begins with Socrates marks a divergence of Greek thinking from the common model. The first step in this divergence is frequently attributed to Socrates, who began to erode the unity of human and nonhuman phenomena by raising the question of ethics in a serious and formal manner. In fact, later commentators such as Cicero suggested that Socrates " . . . brought it (philosophy) into communal life, compelling it to attend to questions of virtue and vice, good and evil" (Guthrie, 1975, p. 8). Aristotle said of this period that " . . . the investigation of nature came to a stop, and philosophers turned their attention to practical morality and political thought" (p. 8). This separation of people from nature continues to this day in Western thought, and even now the activities of society are thought to be "unnatural," for example, by many in the environmental movement. This separation of mankind from nature gave serious impetus as well to the epistemological question—that is, the question of the connection of people and the world of experience.

The question of human knowledge became central for Greek philosophy. In particular, most Greeks (including Plato and Aristotle) conceived of perfect knowledge as absolute and unchanging, while the world of the senses seemed continually in motion and change. Plato clearly accepted a radical disjunction between humans and the world of experience, granting to the world of experience only a shadowy and epiphenomenal existence. Yet Plato would not accept a solution which prohibited absolute knowledge, and so instead adopted a view of knowledge as real but separate from sensory experience. The object of our knowledge, according to Plato, is no in the world of experience but another perfect and abstract world—the world of ideas—which we know only by recollection from a mythical epoch when we lived there. Sensory experience is of no help in gaining this knowledge, although the dialectic method can sometimes help jog our recollections. This is quite different from the Chinese view in which humans hold no special status, since in the Chinese view all beings, human or otherwise, participate equally in the oneness of nature.

It is difficult to overestimate the centrality of the question of motion and change, perception and knowledge, to the development of the Western model. So taken were the Greeks by the materiality of the world of sensory experience and the changing, particular temporality they ascribed to it that they could not reconcile it with the abstract unchanging perfection of immaterial thought. Zeno and Parmenides were prepared to deny altogether the reality of motion and change; Heraclitus allowed himself to deny the abstract and unchanging character of thought. Plato was willing to accept a radical distinction between the object of knowledge and the world of experience.

Aristotle fully accepted the distinction between the concrete changeability of matter and the abstract permanence of thought and attempted to resolve the problem of motion by attributing to every existing entity two principles: a material substrate, whose restlessness accounted for impermanence and change, and an immaterial form, abstract and unchanging, which inhered in the material substrate. This implied for Aristotle a distinction between two senses in which the word "is" was used in Greek. The first meaning of is was "to be" or "to exist" as in the phrase "Scorates is." Such a usage implies that Socrates exists. The second meaning of is was "to have," in the sense of the phrase "Socrates is tall." This second usage, for Aristotle, implied that Socrates "possesses" something; in this case, Socrates possesses the attribute height. This formal quality or attribute, height, is nonmaterial and abstract, which means that it is universal and unchanging and, hence, can serve as a proper object of knowledge as Aristotle thought of it. Yet the notion of change can be reconciled as well, insofar as matter may at one time possess one form and at another time possess another form. Thus, change is the process by which matter possesses at one time and the next a series of abstract, universal, unchanging forms.

Yet Aristotle needed to account for the progression of forms itself. What caused a ripening tomato to have at one time the form green and at another the form red? Where did the redness of the ripe tomato come from? Taken by the systematic character of nature (that is, green tomatoes, if allowed to mature, always become red tomatoes and never ripen into, say, oak trees) and fleeing also from Parmenides dilemma (that is, nothing can come to be from nothing, and nothing can pass into nothing), Aristotle was led to postulate a higher level of form beyond the mere qualitative aspects of an object (such as its color, shape, size, etc.). This higher form scholastic philosophers now refer to as an entity's "substantial form" or "essence." This higher form, or essence, to Aristotle meant whatever it was that made the entity what it was. This form, or the "nature" of the thing, contained within itself as potential all the secondary forms through which the entity could pass during its development. Thus, the form "human" contains within itself as potential the secondary forms size, color, shape, and so forth, which humans can attain. The process of change is the process of moving through these forms already contained as potential in the essence of the entity from its first moment of existence. Thus, all change, and, for that matter, all motion, was for Aristotle a developmental process, whereby an entity becomes in actuality what it has always been potentially.

There are several important consequences of this view. Change and motion as phenomena of our sense experience are saved, since change can be seen as the process whereby abstract, universal forms are taken on and lost by an entity which itself does not cease to exist in the process. The object of knowledge—which for the Greek mind needed to be abstract and unchanging—is placed back in the world of experience rather than in a world of its own. Like Plato's world of ideas, the object of knowledge is the form which the object possesses. Nor is it necessary to assume that qualities come to be from nothing, since the qualities or secondary forms ("attributes") which any object can take on are contained in potency in its substantial form from its first moment of existence. In spite of its power, the Aristotelian model never provided a satisfactory basis for the scientific understanding of motion and change.

In order to construct his resolution to the paradox of permanence and change, Aristotle was forced to ascribe a certain set of characteristics of motion and change which cause serious difficulties in peculiar ways. Specifically, motion is seen as an interim process between two points of rest, a discrete phenomenon intervening between two discrete states. In the case of physical or local motion, for example, a body must always be thought of as moving from one place to another place. Physical bodies are seen as moving or tending to move, barring interference, toward their proper place. The proper place of heavy objects is the center of the universe, and the proper place of light objects (like fire) is at the periphery of the universe. While the entity is moving, it is not, in the true Aristotelian sense, anywhere. A moving body has no place but, rather, is in the process of giving up one place to settle in another. In the same way, any changing entity is not in any state during its change but, rather, is in a semireal state of transience.

To be sure, there is some advantage to this semireal view of motion and change. It provides one resolution of Zeno's paradox, in that it makes it unnecessary to assume that a body passes through an infinite number of points on its journey from one point to another, thus, using up an infinite amount of time. But there are disadvantages as well.

Initially, such a view focuses attention away from the process of motion itself and places it on the terminals of motion. Since all motion is seen as a discrete bridge between one state of being and another, explanations of motion tend to focus on the state of affairs prior to the motion and the state of affairs subsequent to the motion. Additionally, they tend to force consideration of motion as a qualitative category—that by which new places or states or characteristics are attained—and make it difficult to think of motion and change quantitatively. Motion and change tend to be characterized as means to ends, whether those ends are "intended" or not.

Even though the notion that physical bodies were in some sense moving toward ends was not taken in its most naive sense, that is that the objects in some sense intended their motion, nonetheless, the view of motion as discrete jumps from place to place presented an insuperable barrier to the emergence of a well-developed quantitative physical mechanics. Medieval physicists still believed that, when a force was applied to a body, that body took on an "impetus," and the nature of that impetus determined the distance that the object would travel. When the impetus was exhausted, the body would return to its (natural) state of rest. What happened during the motion, for example, whether the body moved most rapidly during the beginning of its travel and then progressively slower until the impetus was used up, whether it moved increasingly quickly, whether it moved more and more rapidly until midpoint then slowed to rest, or whether its motion would be uniform throughout its flight, was not known. This is well worth noting, since today the notion of quantitative analysis of motion is completely commonplace, and even the lay person thinks naturally about velocity and acceleration, particularly in societies where automobiles are in widespread use. Yet, 17 centuries after Aristotle, the greatest minds of Europe were baffled and frustrated in their attempts to quantify motion. By and large, medieval attempts to quantify the Aristotelian laws of motion were unsuccessful in spite of the work of Bradwardine and others, and even Galileo initially believed that every object moved always at its own "natural velocity," a constant velocity proper to itself at which it tended to move.

It was apparently the middle of the fourteenth century before philosophers began to escape the Aristotelian framework sufficiently to generate dynamic quantitative interpretations of physical motion. The fact that motion had been a specific focus of attention for a large span of time no doubt helped weaken the conception of motion as a mere intermediate stage between two terminal states of being. It was Buridan who seems first to have set down the concept of uniform motion, a concept which is at odds with the idea of motion as an interim process between two "real" terminals. Buridan suggested that, once set in motion, the impetus of the body would endure forever unless opposed by some other force, thus effectively anticipating Newton's first law of motion sometime in the middle of the fourteenth century.

These mathematical difficulties were inherent in the character of the concepts that the medieval scientists inherited from the Greeks and are rooted in the distinction between the continuous and the discrete that permeated Western philosophy. Generally, the quest for a reconciliation of mind and matter described above can be characterized as an attempt to reconcile a conception of motion as continuous with a conception of thought as discrete. The mathematical process of counting or quantifying is essentially a process of establishing a correspondence between the elements of two classes. Thus, when we count the number of coins in our hands, we establish a correspondence between the elements of the class "coins in my hand" and certain of the elements of the whole number system, that is, 1, 2, 3,. . . . If there exists an element in the second class for each element of the first class, then the second class can be said to adequately represent or quantify the first class.

If motion is seen as a continuous phenomenon, and thought as a discrete phenomenon, then no such correspondence can be established. No matter how finely the discrete members of the mental class are divided, an element of the continuous class motion can always be found which will be between any two of them, and thus there will always be an infinitely large number of elements of the class of motion for which no analogue can be found in the class of thought.

Zeno's attempt to reduce motion to a discrete phenomenon, that is to see any moving body as passing through an infinite number of discrete places or points, resulted in an absurd conclusion: Such a passage through an infinite series of points implied the passage of an infinite amount of time. Zeno's conclusion, of course, was that motion was impossible, when in fact what he had really established was a problem inherent in the discrete conception of motion.

Heraclitus, on the other hand, clearly characterized motion as a continuous phenomenon and abandoned any hope of establishing a correspondence with the discrete character of thought as he conceived it. Thus, he abandoned hope of knowing the nature of physical reality in any absolute sense. Parmenides too found the way to discrete characterization of the world of sense experience barred, although for different reasons.

The idea of terminals of motion implies that the spatial manifold in which motion occurs is heterogenous, i.e., that there are some points in space where objects are more prone to go than others. There are places in space toward which objects tend to move, and once having arrived, tend to remain.

The heterogeneity of space implies that motion is not linear and, moreover, that the deviations from linearity may not be very clear. The shortest distance between two points may not be a straight line, since some particularly dense or impermeable region of space may be on the line between two points. This means that motion may at times take on very complex curves even in the absence of any imbalance of forces.

The idea of terminals of motion implies that the point at which a moving object will come to rest is given by the force which initiates the motion. Thus, the natural state of being is to be at rest, and the notion of continuous, uniform motion (Newton's first law) is foreign to this system.

No matter how philosophically satisfying such a theory of motion may be, it presents mathematical difficulties especially for an age in which the special non-Euclidian geometries, the calculus, and the probability theory do not yet exist.

The Aristotelian conception of motion is relevant to human behavior not only because of its epistemological consequences but because locomotion, that is, movement in physical space, is a special case of change in general for Aristotle. Human behavior is itself a type of motion, and Aristotle's psychology parallels his ideas of physical motion exactly. Behavior, for Aristotle, was the semireal state between two states of act. In behavior, as in physical motion, the individual moves through a series of discrete states of conditions (forms). Similarly, Aristotle's notion of causality requires that the cause of each state preexist the state itself, or else one would need to say that an event was its own cause. Thus, Aristotle located the cause of the act proximately in the mind of the actor as a goal (final cause, that is, an end). These goals are themselves dependent on the unbroken chain of causality which traces back to the "uncaused cause." Even Protestant conceptions of human behavior conform in essential respects to this model, although in the Calvinist tradition, the choices made by people have been predetermined by an all-knowing God.

The question of human freedom has always proved troublesome to thinkers who embrace the *Principle of Noncontradiction,* and even in pre-Socratic times, philosophers attempted to account for freedom and volition by ascribing the power of arbitrary motion to the substrate or atoms of which the universe was thought to be composed. Within the Catholic theology, the contradiction between an omniscient God who created all being and the free and voluntary action of individual humans is thought to be resolvable only on the basis of faith as revealed by God. Within the Calvinist tradition, the will is thought to be constrained from the first moment of creation. Even though the question of the freedom of the will, which arises as a consequence of the blend of the Aristotelian entelechy or goal orientation on the one hand and the Platonic–Socratic notion of moral responsibility on the other is still seriously debated today in the West, the foundation of the dispute—that humans do indeed act for ends—is seldom called into serious question.

Like the mores of Sumner (1979), the notion of goal orientation holds sway over the Western mind to a large extent because of the lack of serious alternative models within the Western discourse. Imbued as the West is in the *Principle of Noncontradiction,* it makes no sense to the Westerner to suggest—as do many Chinese philosophers—that we forego goals and not seek ends. While this may be a cause of enlightenment to the Eastern mind, to the Western mind it seems like a contradiction to accept the goal of having no goals. Moreover, imbued as it is in 30 centuries of essentialistic thought, it is hard for Westerners to think of this Aristotelian model as anything but by the way humans "really are," wheras for the Chinese who accept the *Principle of Infinite Interpretation,* it is only one possibility (see Chapter 2, this volume).

THE CARTESIAN MODEL

At the root of the Aristotelian model lies the incompatibility of the continuous flux of experience and the categorical and discrete permanence of thought. Aristotle's solution to the dilemma was to posit a two-fold structure for the world, one part of which was continuous and undifferentiated—the material substrate or primary matter—and the other part—substantial form—which was abstract and categorical, like Aristotle's conception of thought. Thus, Aristotle created a categorical component of experience—substantial form—which was compatible with and therefore the object of human knowledge. This solution resolved old difficulties but created new ones, particularly concerning dynamics. It is now common among scientists to note that in spite of the greatness of Greek mathematics and science, the work of the Greeks was completely static, and dynamics—the quantitative analysis of motion and change—is the unique product of the Renaissance.

The development of Renaissance dynamics may be seen to rest directly on a complete reversal of the Aristotelian strategy. Rather than restructuring our conception of the world as discrete and categorical to fit the discrete and categorical Greek conception of thought, Renaissance scientists instead developed a continuous model of reasoning to conform to the continuity and flux of experience. While the logic of Aristotle is categorical, the logic of Renaissance science is comparative and continuous.

The earliest and perhaps still the clearest description of this new epistemology comes from Descartes. Descartes began by rejecting Aristotle's categorical logic completely and substituting for it a comparative logic:

> But because, as we have often announced, the syllogistic forms are of no aid in perceiving the truth about objects, it will be for the reader's profit to reject them altogether and to conceive that all knowledge whatsoever other than that which consists in the simple and naked intuition of single independent objects, is a matter of the comparison of the two things or more, with each other. (Descartes, 1952, p. 28)

Descartes' comparative logic began by defining the term "dimension" which corresponds to Aristotle's notion of "category" or "attribute."

> By dimension, I understand nothing but the mode and aspect according to which a subject is understood to be measurable. Thus, it is not merely the case that length, breadth and depth are dimensions, but weight is also a dimension in terms of which the heaviness of objects is estimated. So, too, speed is a dimension of motion, and there are an infinite number of similar instances. For that very division of the whole into a number of parts of identical nature, whether it exists in the real order of things or be merely the work of the understanding, gives us exactly that dimension in terms of which we apply number to objects. (Descartes, 1952, p. 31)

While for Aristotle, the categories of attributes were discrete classes to which an object belongs or does not, for Descartes, the dimensions were continuously variable magnitudes, and one inquired as to how much of them an object possesses. This assessment is always made as a ratio comparison to some arbitrary segment of the dimension itself:

> For I can recognize the order in which A and B stand, without considering anything except these two—the extreme terms of the relation. But I can recognize the ratio of the magnitude of two to that of three, only by considering some third thing, namely unity, which is the common measure of both. (Descartes, 1952, p. 32)

Both Aristotle's and Descartes' logic proceed by means of a middle term. But in Aristotle's logic, the middle term is categorical; we may say that A is a member of B, B is a member of C, and, through the mediation of the middle term B, we can see that A is a member of C. But for Descartes, the middle term is not categorical but rather comparative. We can say that A is twice as large as B, that B is three times as large as C, and that, therefore, A is six times as large as C. The middle term serves as a comparative standard against which all other objects are gauged as ratios. Thus, the core of Descartes' logic is continuous rather than categorical. To be sure, Descartes did not invent the logic of the continuous middle term, and its use as a vehicle for measuring physical distances and time predates written history. Even Aristotle knew of it, although it seemed a puzzle to him, and he exhibited his discomfort with it in several places. He said of the measurement of distance and motion, for example.

> Now, one must cognize magnitude and motion by means of the same faculty by which one cognizes time (that is, by that which is also the faculty of memory) . . . " (McKeon, 1941, p. 608).

But later, when he spoke of time, he said:

> There is—let it be taken as a fact—something by which one distinguishes a greater and a smaller time; and it is reasonable to think that one does this in a way analogous to that in which one discerns (spatial) magnitudes. (McKeon, 1941, p. 615)

In this same passage, Aristotle went on to make explicit the notion of ratio comparisons, but the phraseology of the passage seems to indicate a hesitation and uncertainty, and he went on to explain the process and its failures in terms of excessive moisture in the head and abnormally large head sizes.

That the notion of continuous logic by means of ratio comparisons to an arbitrary standard lies at the basis of scientific measurement, however, can be shown clearly by the profuse use of the method by Galileo (1914).

The Cartesian resolution of the problem of a continuous manifold of experience mapped onto a discrete structure of thought, therefore, involves the abandonment of the discrete model of thought in favor of a continuous model as exemplified by the method of ratio-pair comparisons to an arbitrary standard unit. But his logic suffices only to establish how science, as opposed to Greek philosophy, describes experience. The notion of explanation still persists from the Greek period, although with important differences. During the early period of pre-Socratic thought, there was a difference of opinion about what needed to be explained, as we have seen. Some philosophers believed that motion needed to be explained, since the proper state of being was rest, while others suggested that motion was the natural state of affairs and that therefore rest required explanation.

Aristotle was clearly among those who believed that motion required explanation. In Aristotle's categorical system, however, motion was discrete, that is, it occurred or did not, and so the causes of motion were discrete. In the continuous model of Descartes, however, motion and change were variables rather than states, and therefore admit of variation themselves. As such, neither motion nor rest required explanation, but rather changes in the rate of motion became the "explainable" phenomena of science. This notion is formalized in Newton's first law (Newton, 1962). This law is not strictly speaking a law but, rather, a definition of what phenomena are to be considered explainable (Mach, 1915). By definition, Newton required that bodies at rest would remain at rest and bodies in motion would remain in motion unless acted on by some force. By so saying, Newton defined any change in rate of motion (that is, any acceleration) as requiring an explanation. Moreover, since these changes in rates of motions themselves admit of continuous variation, their causes are forces with continuously variable magnitudes.

Through the work of scientists like D'Alembert and Hamilton, "variational principles" have developed whereby we assume that science should seek explanations which minimize the magnitude of unbalanced forces that must be postulated to account for the accelerations observed. On these grounds, for example, we reject the geocentric model of the solar system of Ptolemy, since the unbalanced forces that would be needed to account for the acceleration of the stars in their near-circular orbits around the earth would be vastly larger than the forces that need to be postulated to account for the accelerations of the earth and other bodies in the solar system relative to the fixed stars.

Underlying the variational principles are the related concepts of force and inertial mass. In a categorical system, a motion either occurs or it does not, and the cause of the motion is therefore, either present or absent. From the *Principle of Noncontradiction,* it also follows that the cause must be similar to the effect. But in a continuous comparative logic, accelerations occur in greater or lesser magnitudes, and therefore the *Principle of Noncontradiction* demands that the causes of motion must be proportional to the accelerations observed. Force and mass are derived concepts which are constructed so that a proportionality of cause and effect can always be maintained. Thus, for example, if two objects A and B are struck by the same third object, but A accelerates more rapidly than B as a result of the blow, the differences in the accelerations are ascribed to differential inertial masses of the two objects. Similarly, if the same object accelerates more rapidly when struck by one object than when struck by a second, we say that the force imparted by the first is greater than that of the second in proportion to the differences in acceleration.

THE RELATIVISTIC MODEL

As we have seen, the period of Renaissance science was marked by a shift from a categorical logic of classification to a comparative logic of measurement. This led to important rethinking of the character of motion and change. Rather than the categorical distinction "moving or not moving," scientists could now think of relative degrees of motion. The development of the derived concepts of mass and force led as well to the development of the notions of inertia, momentum, and the conservation principles which followed from them. In one regard, however, the period of Renaissance science retained conceptions from the classic Greek period. Most scientists, including Newton, no less, continued to believe in the absolute distinction between motion and rest, stability and change. To demonstrate that there actually existed what might be called an absolute state of motion, Newton proposed a "thought experiment" in which he conceived of a bucket of water tied to a long rope. The rope was wound tightly and released. At the beginning, the bucket would begin to rotate around the axis of the rope, while the water remained at rest. Later, due to friction, the water would begin to rotate at the same speed as the bucket; finally, when the bucket reached the end of its travel and twisted the rope in the other direction, the bucket would stop, but the water's inertia would continue it in motion.

As Newton suggested, at the beginning, when the bucket was moving and the water still, the surface of the water would remain flat, but as the water began to rotate, it would also begin to climb the walls of the bucket due to centrifugal force. Later, when the bucket had stopped but the water continued in motion, the water would continue to climb the walls of the bucket. By this experiment Newton thought he had established that the motion of water and bucket was not merely relative, i.e., the water and bucket were not only moving relative to each other, but thought that he had shown that one could distinguish the water's motion independent of the motion of the bucket.

Mach (1915), however, correctly reasoned later that Newton had performed only half the experiment. Had he held both the water and the bucket completely still and rotated the entire universe around the axis of the rope, the same effects would be observed. Thus, Newton's experiment could not actually distinguish absolute from relative motion.

The implications of this realization have proven very important to modern science, since it demands that there exist no "priviledged" coordinate system. That is to say, observations made by an observer in one coordinate system need not correspond to observations made by another observer in another reference frame in motion relative to the first. More importantly, however, neither observer's observations deserve any more consideration than the other's, since neither coordinate system can be considered priviledged. When observers in different coordinate frames are in nonlinear motion with reference to each other (i.e., are accelerating relative to each other), the situation is even more confounded, since even the laws of inertia in one reference frame will not hold in the other.

This realization led to a reformulation of the goals of science whose full implications have not yet been understood by all working scientists, particularly those in the social sciences. For if indeed states of absolute motion and rest can never be distinguished, science cannot accept as a goal the understanding of motion and rest. Rather, twentieth-century scientists, particularly Einstein, have been led to reconsider science as the process of finding transformations which link the experiences of any observer with the observations of any other. In its most fundamental sense, science becomes the practice of developing communication systems which link human observers.

As Bohr suggested, science is the process whereby scientists make observations and communicate them to others who must check them. Einstein (1956) went further by saying that what we call "real" is that set of experiences which correspond across multiple observers.

In the modern view, we can see a rapid and important reconvergence of the common model of pre-Socratic times. Most important in this convergence is the undertanding that all viewpoints enjoy an equal epistemological footing—a point very similar to the *Principle of Infinite Interpretation.* Moreover, at the very center of the process of comparing observations across observers lies the question of symbol, or more commonly, language. Prior to any social comparison process, observations must be encoded into a symbol system which enables people to compare experiences. To the extent to which the symbol system is inadequate to the representation of the set of experiences, failure of correspondence—or apparently erroneous correspondences—can happen as a consequence of the inadequate encoding itself.

Here again the same question of the categorical structure of thought and the continuous character of experience arise again, but this time it is the vernacular language which is categorical. In general, words represent categories, and experience defined by modern scientific practice appears as a continuum. More and more scientists have had to abandon the categorical language of the vernacular for the continuous language of mathematics. This has led many modern scientists, like Bohr and Heisenberg, to deny entirely the possibility that modern scientific theory can be expressed in words at all. Often theory is completely expressed in an equation that defies translation into vernacular language. Clearly, we see again a convergence of the Eastern and Western model in modern science, since both accept readily the inadequacy of words for the expression of experience.

Although the modern relativistic model bears important similarities to the original common model, it would be a mistake to think of it as simply a return to earlier thinking. The relativism of modern science is an advanced relativisim that has been enriched by the advances made during the interim period. The development of the comparative method of Descartes made possible the measurement of the flux of experience rather than simply the realization that experience seemed in continuous change. Moreover, the development of the variational principles made possible the rational choice of common reference frames without denying the epistemological equivalence of all such frames. The development of modern mathematics, particularly the calculus, which allows for an approximation of the continuous by the method of infinitesimal analysis, makes it possible not only to realize the inadequacy of words to express the complex flow of experience but to go further toward the development of language systems like mathematics which express experience to a closer order of approximation. These same mathematical tools, along with the variational principles, allow science not only to recognize the differences in experience that follow from different viewpoints and reference frames but to construct transformations which allow for the translation of the experiences of any observer in any reference frame into the experiences of another observer in another frame.

IMPLICATIONS FOR COMMUNICATION THEORY

This classification of the development of the Western model into four discrete stages is not to be taken literally, of course, and we should realize that the progress through these stages has been uneven. Different disciplines and individuals have passed through them at different rates. Only a few sciences today can be said to be primarily relativistic, and it is safe to say that no discipline whatever has wholly rid itself of preconceptions left from earlier periods of its history. Communication is no exception, and it would be rash to expect that a science so newly created from its philosophical and rhetorical ancestry should be among the most advanced of sciences.

In fact, many of the criticisms leveled against contemporary theory in communications suggest that these theories are mechanical, that is, that they imply a Newtonian or premodern notion of communication phenomena. It is the case that several communication theories bear a resemblance in form to Newtonian science, but the resemblance, in my opinion, is only superficial. The reason contemporary communication theory should not be thought of as mechanical is that the mechanical models of the eighteenth century presuppose the Cartesian measurement model and the comparative logic that goes with them, but communication measurement has not yet reached this stage. With important exceptions, the measurement model in the communication disciplines remains wholly categorical, and the categorical measurement model is incompatible both with the mechanical model of the eighteenth and nineteenth centuries and with the modern relativistic view, just as it is incompatible with the underlying premises of the Eastern model.

It is impossible on logical grounds to construct a mechanical or a relativistic model of any phenomena, human phenomena included, within the framework of a categorical measurement model, and the measurement model of communication has remained categorical. Moreover, many communication theorists have resisted the movement toward comparative measurement models in communication on the grounds that human phenomena are categorical inherently, that is, that they are qualitatively different from nonhuman phenomena. This view is neither relativistic nor mechanical but, rather, Aristotelian in character. The difficulties that communication researchers face in examining and explaining communication phenomena offer a philosophical parallel to the difficulties faced by medieval physicists in their attempts to describe and explain motion within the categorical framework of Aristotle.

Although there is considerable diversity of opinion among modern communication theorists, it is probably fair to say that most current Western communication theory is underlaid by a common general theory whose roots lie in the model of Aristotle. In general, that model would assume that there exists in any situation a set of potential behaviors from which individual persons may choose. Choices among these behaviors are made on the basis of beliefs and attitudes which an individual holds. Beliefs are usually thought of as definitions of the nature of the individual, the objects he or she faces, and the situation within which they occur, while attitudes usually hold some motivational component—that is a notion of liking or disliking. Each situation is also characterized by certain objective factors which facilitate or impede the performance of each potential behavior, such as the age or sex or physical condition of the person, the difficulty of the task, the weather, and so forth. These beliefs and attitudes are themselves influenced by information, which impacts the individual from the objective situation and from other persons. Recently, technological developments have led to partitioning this latter source of information into that delievered directly by another person or persons and that delivered via some electronic or print medium. Changes in the flows of information from these sources are assumed to bring about changes in the categories to which the objects that make up the situation are assigned (belief changes) and changes in the intensities and valances (positive or negative) of the attitudes held toward objects and behaviors. Furthermore, again in the spirit of Aristotle, most communication theories imply a "threshold" model of effects, such that accumulations of forces in favor of the performance of a behavior yield no result until they outweigh those opposing its performance. Once they exceed this threshold level the behavior is performed as a discrete unit or act.

The late nineteenth and early twentieth centuries saw the beginnings of attempts at the measurement of beliefs and attitudes. These early efforts have been for the most part categorical and essentialistic, as have the theories from which they arose. Early scaling theory, following primarily from the work of Thrustone, usually assumed that a culture made available several "positions" toward any object or topic and that the attitudes and beliefs of the members of that culture were given by which of these positions they took. Within this model, attitude changes are given by changes of position which are discrete—one might change from "favorable" to "strongly favorable," for example, on some issue, or from "birthcontrol is unacceptable" to "birth control is unacceptable for the unmarried." Later attempts moved closer to the continuous manifold of modern science but maintained vestiges of the Aristotelian categoricalism and essentialism. Osgood, for example, assumed explicitly that the domain of beliefs and attitudes was itself a continuous manifold, but nonetheless Osgood's conception remains basically Aristotelian. Osgood assumed, as did Aristotle, that the basis of human meaning lies in a set of "bipolar adjectives" or relative polarities. Osgood further assumed that there are three such polarities: good–bad, active–passive, and strong–weak. He further stipulated that these three bipolars lie at the ends of mutually perpendicular axes of equal length which cross at a common origin. Each other point in the continuum so defined has an absolute meaning given by its relative distance from the bipolar end points of these axes. The origin itself, following from this rule, is a point of complete meaninglessness (Osgood *et al.*, 1957).

This general model in its many manifestations has shown itself to be a cumbersome one when applied to situations of interest to researchers. Overwhelmingly, research has shown most of the variability in human behavior as it is usually defined is left unaccounted for by the model. These failures have led to modifications of the basic model more consistent with a relativistic posture, and today most communication theorists argue that the meanings of objects and the beliefs and attitudes individuals have toward them are relative to the persons who hold them and the situations in which they are found and that the objective meaning of any object or situation is a negotiated product that arises out of the communication among a set of people. Kincaid (1979; Rogers & Kincaid, 1981) presented a convergence model of human communication in which a continuing reciprocal flow of information among individuals results in successive redefinitions of experience which, under suitable circumstances, results in ever increasing agreement among the parties to the communication about the meaning of the situation in question and the objects of which it is comprised. Although the vernacular language makes it necessary to describe this convergence process as a series of discrete stages, in fact Kincaid views the process as a continuous one best modeled by expressions from the calculus. The rate of convergence, for example, represents a velocity in Kincaid's system, (the first derivative of position) and a change in that rate an acceleration (the second derivative). Changes in the rate of acceleration (the third derivative) represent the intervention of control into the system. Furthermore, this model recognizes that the perspective of neither of the parties to a communication is priviledged so that the question of whether one person's view moves toward the other's, the second toward the first, or both mutually closer cannot be absolutely resolved but depends instead on the stipulation of other common reference markers. Thus, the manifold underlying Kincaid's model is clearly relativistic, like Einstein's, rather than absolute, like Aristotle's, Newton's, and Osgood's models.

Inevitably, these more sophisticated theoretical models place heavier burdens on the measurement apparatus than earlier models and require specifically relativistic and precise scaling models. Category scales (like Likert-type and semantic differential type scales) do not provide data of sufficient precision for these theories, and their essentialistic epistemology is inconsistent with the theories. Much more appropriate for these modern theories are the magnitude estimation–type scales of Stevens (1975) and Hamblin (1974), which implement the ratio-type procedure described by Descartes, and the "ratio judgments of separation" scaling model (Woelfel & Danes, 1979; Woelfel & Fink, 1980), which implements the ratio-type procedure along with the method of complete pair comparisons also recommended by Descartes.

Application of these measurement models to modern theoretical perspectives like Kincaid's model is conceptually simple, although the primitive state of the early technology frequently creates practical technical difficulties which at present limit these applications to more advanced centers. Fundamentally, these procedures involve an initial identification of the social objects which comprise a situation for a set of participants and the initial selection of an arbitrary pair of these objects to serve as a measurement standard. All other pairs of objects are then compared to this standard, and the separations of differences among them are expressed as ratios to the initial standard. The result of these measurements is a space or continuum within which the objects are arrayed in a pattern. Although the initial definitions on which this pattern rests are arbitrary, once such initial decisions have been made, the shape of the configuration becomes an empirical matter, with widely different objects far apart in the pattern and similar objects close to each other in the pattern. Since both behaviors and the self may be construed as objects in any situation, measured distances between self and behaviors can be taken as measures of the likelihood of carrying out each such action. Early research shows reliably that behaviors closest to the self are performed most frequently, and increased distances between self and any behavior yield decreases in rate of performance of the behavior. Changes in the structure of the space correspond to changed definitions of the situation, the self, and the objects which comprise them.

The spaces generated by these procedures have no priviledged origin and no fixed boundaries but, rather, are completely relativistic in the same way as the space of modern cosmologists and ancient Chinese philosophers are relativistic. Since the structure of the spaces is dependent on the initial measurement stipulation, the objectivity of the result rests not on any absolute structure of human thought but, rather, on the consensus surrounding the initial stipulations, as is the case in modern physics. Within this model, communication is also a relative concept and refers to the *process* by which the structures of the spaces of the communicating parties are mutually shared among the parties. Within this model, there is no real point to distinguishing "sender" from "receiver" or "source" from "target," since all spaces are on an equivalent epistemological footing, and the appropriate analysis framework is one like Kincaid's convergence model where the modification of the conceptions of the communicating parties is mutual and simultaneous, rather than linear and sequential.

So far the development of these modern models of communication is too recent for them to have found widespread practical application, particularly in developing nations. Those communication models which have found widespread applications are exclusively the premechanical models characteristic of theoretical thinking of the social science of the 1950s. There is no question but that these early models have been inconsistent with basic postulates of Eastern thought. Less well known, however, is the extent to which these models have been incompatible with contemporary Western scientific thought as well. Fortunately the newer models of communication theory and measurement seem consistent both with the underlying assumptions of Eastern philosophical thought and modern Western scientific theory.

CHAPTER 22

The Double-Swing Model of Intercultural Communication between the East and the West

Muneo Jay Yoshikawa

INTRODUCTION

The rapid development of modern transportation and telecommunications technology has helped to break down cultural and national boundaries. This has resulted in an unprecedented quantitative increase in contacts among nations of different cultures. At the same time, the need for creative and constructive dialogue among cultures, nations, and people is more critical now than at any period of human history.

We must seek new ways of interpersonal, intercultural, and international relations within which people of diverse cultures can respect their cultural uniqueness as well as their differences and their similarities.

The primary purposes of this paper are: (1) to identify various modes of intercultural encounter and communication, (2) to explore the development of dialogical thought on which the dialogical mode of intercultural encounter is based, (3) to describe dialogical thought from both Eastern and Western perspectives, and (4) to present the "double-swing" model and discuss its implications within the context of intercultural communication between the East and the West.

MODES OF INTERCULTURAL ENCOUNTER AND COMMUNICATION

The dialogical mode of encounter and communication is best understood in contrast to three other predominant modes of encounter and communication: the ethnocentric, control, and dialectical modes. The differences are readily grasped by means of the diagrams shown in Fig. 1.

The *ethnocentric* mode depicted in Fig. 1a implies that A perceives B only in A's own frame of reference and that B is a mere shadow of A. The cultural integrity of B's culture, its uniqueness, and differences are simply ignored. Communication is one sided, and feedback is rendered ineffective by well-known psychological processes of selective attention, selective perception, and selective retention.

The *control* mode shown in Fig. 1b implies that B is under A's scrutiny. B is perceived and manipulated as a thing or an object for A's purpose. B's cultural uniqueness and differences are recognized, but they are manipulated in order to achieve A's objectives. This is a form of manipulative communication.

The *dialectical* mode of communication shown in Fig. 1c has three potential outcomes. It is possible that as A's thesis meets B's antithesis a new synthesis will be created which is unique and transcends the differences of both A and B which are lost in C. The prime motive of A and/or B is fusion. In the oneness of C the differences between the two disappear, the tension created by those differences is reduced, and a peaceful equilibrium remains. This state is akin to mystical unity, an ideal form of dialectical unity which needs to be differentiated from the two other potential outcomes which are pseudo-dialectical. In the first pseudo-dialectical outcome, A fuses into B and loses its own identity to become part of B. This type of unity may occur as a result of A's blind or selfless devotion or loyalty to B. In the second pseudo-dialectical outcome, A coerces B to become a part of A. All three outcomes are the result of fusion-oriented communication.

The *dialogical* mode of encounter and communication is depicted in Fig. 1d. A does not appear in its wholeness in isolation but rather in relationship to B. While A and B are separate and independent, they are

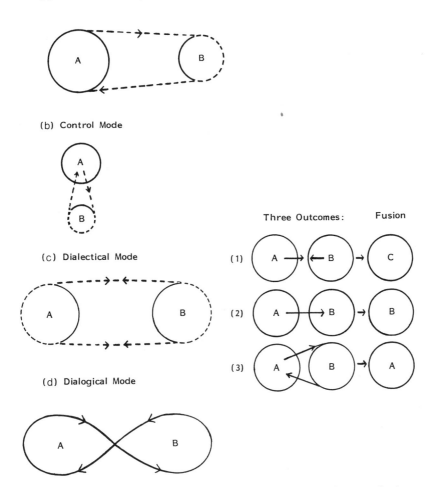

(a) Ethnocentric Mode

(b) Control Mode

Three Outcomes: Fusion

(c) Dialectical Mode

(1)

(2)

(3)

(d) Dialogical Mode

Fig. 1.   Diagrams of the four modes of intercultural encounter and communication.

simultaneously *interdependent*. This type of paradoxical relationship is explained below in terms of Buber's (1958) concept of dialogical relationship and the Buddhistic logic of *Soku* (Nakayama, 1973). The cultural integrity of A and B and the differences and similarities of A and B are recognized and respected. The emphasis is on wholeness, mutuality, and the dynamic meeting of A and B. Even in their union, A and B each maintains a separate identity.

THE DEVELOPMENT OF DIALOGICAL THOUGHT

In order to understand the concept of the dialogical modes of intercultural encounter and communication, we must first begin with the clarification of dialogical thought. I would like to explore this thought particularly with reference to Buber's dialogical thought which was developed in his life-long struggle with the problem of unity and diversity. His struggle may shed new light on the subject of intercultural communication in our emerging pluralistic world in which we ourselves are trying hard to integrate the spirit of universalism (unity) with the spirit of cultural particularism (diversity).

Three different stages in the development of Buber's thoughts have been identified by Friedman (1955), the foremost authority on Buber in America. These are: (1) the mystical stage in which Buber sought for a solution to the problem of unity in mysticism, (2) the existential stage when he was mainly concerned with the concrete and irreplaceable individual beings, and (3) the dialogical stage when he was more concerned with the face-to-face meeting of unique individuals.

Buber's mystical stage occurred at the turn of the nineteenth century when there was a trend toward mysticism in Europe. At that time, interest was shown in Western as well as Eastern mythologies and mysticism and in the religions and philosophies of the Orient (Friedman, 1955). There was a move toward unity and wholeness. This historical period in which Buber's mystical stage falls resembles contemporary life in America and some parts of the world. In particular the reactionary movement against the depersonalization and fragmentation of bourgeois society at the turn of the nineteenth century in Europe has a striking resemblance to the humanistic and counterculture movements of the 1960s and early 1970s in the postindustrial nations of the Free World such as the United States, Japan, Canada, and Western Europe. I believe we can apply Buber's ideas in our search for meaningful interaction in today's pluralistic society.

Transcending and subsuming the mystical experience, Buber moved on to the next existential stage. In the book, *Daniel* (Buber, 1964), we can see the gradual shift in emphasis on unity—from his urge for unity for the sake of unity to his concern for the way the unity is created. He became more concerned with the process and the unique aspect of the individual in and with the world. However, Buber's idea was still basically monological.

In the book, *I and Thou,* Buber (1958) finally reached the dialogical stage. His view of unity was no longer the mystical intrasubjective unity but the intersubjective unity—between the concrete bodily presence of man and man. Buber became more concerned with the dialogical unity which emphasizes the act of meeting between two different beings without eliminating the otherness or uniqueness of each.

Let us now examine more closely Buber's dialogical thought.

Buber's Philosophy of Dialogue

In *I and Thou,* Buber (1958) stated that when a man enters into a relationship with this world, man, and God, he holds two basic attitudes or fundamental stances. They are expressed by the primary terms: I-It and I-Thou. In an I-It relationship, another being is seen as a conceptualized and abstracted object. In the I-Thou relationship, each being treats the other as an immediately whole, living, responding subject or a Thou. The I-It and I-Thou relationships are not entirely separated but are essentially related.

By introducing this polarity of I-It and I-Thou, Buber integrated all the multiple polarities he had been wrestling with: *yin* and *yang,* man and man, man and the world, man and nature, man and God, being and becoming, inner and outer, subject and object, transcendent God and imminent God, idealism and realism, monism and dualism, absolution and relativisim, etc. His view of integration of opposites is not the kind of unity in which only one side of the pole or the world is absolutized by eliminating the other or by merely *absorbing* the two worlds. It is a kind of integration in which two sides of the pole cannot be excluded. For example, Buber's view of union is neither that of the idealist nor that of the realist. Unlike the idealist, Buber does not seek to transcend the multiplicity of the dualistic world into the monistic unity of the absolute world. Unlike the realist, Buber does not reduce the world to the narrow concept of the immediate only. Yet he is an idealist in the sense that he accepts the absolute world of unity. He is also a realist in the sense that he accepts the dualistic world of multiplicity. He is both idealist and realist but neither of these, if taken separately. *So is his view of unity or relation.* It is a paradoxical relation of the two worlds in the monistic world of unity and the dualistic world of separation.

In the last major work, *Knowledge of Man,* Buber's (1965) dialogical thought reached its maturity. Buber clarified the realm of "between" by explaining the concept of "distance and relation." Buber asserted that the principle of human life is two-fold. He viewed this principle as a two-fold movement: the primal setting at a distance and entering into relation. Man gains a separate individuality by setting the other at a distance. Man, now enjoying a separate existence, turns and faces the other who stands over against him, then enters into an I-Thou relationship with it. As a result of this meeting, something of his own uniqueness is sharpened, while the uniqueness of the other is also sharpened. He once more steps back into distance and again reenters into the relation with the other. Through the two-fold movement, self–other awareness is sharpened and deepened. This type of unity may be called an *identity-in-unity* in which the uniqueness of each is intensified over against the other. It is a unity created out of the realization of differences in each object and being. This type of unity does not eliminate the tension created between opposites. It endures the contradictions between basic potential unity and apparent duality.

Buber's dialogical unity can only be created through the meeting of individuals. And in order to meet, we must walk a risky and insecure ridge referred to by Buber as a "narrow ridge" which exists in the "sphere of between." We must take a risk to enter into the insecure "narrow ridge" instead of satisfying ourselves with the security of the "either/or's." Buber's narrow ridge or the sphere of between is no *happy middle* which ignores the reality of paradox and contradiction in order to escape from the suffering they produce. It is rather a paradoxical unity of what are usually understood only as alternatives—love and justice, the love of God and the fear of God, and good and evil.

BUDDHISTIC PERSPECTIVE ON PARADOXICAL RELATIONS

One of the fundamental teachings of Buddhism is that nothing in the world exists independent of a web of conditioning factors. Enlightenment comes when one realizes the arbitrariness and fictional nature of such conditioning factors. Enlightenment is, in one sense, a realization of the nature and process of how reality is categorized. In other words, it is to realize simply how cultural reality is constructed. When one realizes that one does not have to attribute a permanent and unchanging character to things of the world, whether persons or objects, one does not absolutize his cultural reality.

In one sense Enlightenment means the transcendence from the web of conditioning factors. However, mere awareness of the relative nature of reality is not Enlightenment.

According to the essence of Buddhism, acceptance of the view that everything is absolutely relative and conditioned is another type of "clinging"; it is another type of misplaced absoluteness which always functions by way of seizing and clinging, for this means viewing the division between absolute and relative, the conditioned and the unconditioned, the divided and the undivided, and the permanent and the impermanent (Ramanan, 1966). There is an attachment or clinging to either absolute reality or relative reality.

Not clinging to either absolute reality or to relative reality is the "Middle Way." The Middle Way is a nonclinging way, but this should not be construed as a mere compromise position which avoids the two extremes. In the Middle Way, one sees things as they are, recognizes the interdependent and complementary aspects of both unconditioned and undivided absoluteness and conditioned and divided relativeness (Ramanan, 1966). This Middle Way is the dynamic perception of this paradoxical relationship. This idea of paradoxical relationship is well expressed in the logic of *Soku* which is characterized as a logic of "Not One, Not Two."

The idea Not One, Not Two means that the world is neither monistic nor dualistic (Nakayama, 1973). According to Buddhism, the world is viewed as a complementary interplay of the world of category and the world of noncategory.

Enlightenment involves a fundamental change in the way one relates oneself to whatever one encounters—a paradoxical relation which encompasses both separation and unity. It is one's detachment for a more meaningful interconnectedness.

The awakening in Buddhism comes through the dilemma which is experienced as a profound perplexity (Nakayama, 1973). A Zen master, for example, seeks to arouse the dilemma in order to awaken and heighten the perception. One method known as *Kōan* is the composite of two Chinese characters: *Kō* means equality or unity and signifies oneness or wholeness and *an* means the maintenance of separateness or discrimination which signifies many. The term, *Kōan,* then is the unity of the contraries. The purpose of *Kōan* is to have disciples grasp this paradoxical relationship—Not One, Not Two. In Zen philosophy, "Everything in the world is Kōan" (Nakayama, 1973, pp. 39–40). In other words, everything is in paradoxical relationship. With this perspective one perceives the world not "out there" or "in here" but in the dynamic between of "out there" and "in here." Therefore, Zen awakening is awakening to the reality of betweenness which encompasses the mundane (cultural relative reality) and the ultimate (universal absolute reality)—the One and the Many.

The new awareness or perception of Buber's dialogical relation and the Enlightenment of Buddhism call for contact with someone or something that is different from oneself. This contact questions one's attachment to one's only dimensional reality and disconnects one's complete identity in it. This detachment, however, does not mean a negation of one's cultural reality. What is negated is one's view that one's reality is absolute and the other's is relative and that one is a discrete entity, separated from the rest of the world. What is transformed is basically one's perspective and one's relationship to whatever one encounters.

This new perspective and relationship are dialogical perception and relationship which are conceptualized in the form of the double-swing model to which I shall now turn.

THE DOUBLE-SWING MODEL

On the basis of Buber's philosophy of dialogue and the Buddhistic logic of *Soku,* the double-swing model was constructed. The Möbius strip or the infinity symbol, ∞, signifies Buber's idea of two-fold movement and the Buddhistic idea of paradoxical relationship. It signifies the dialogical unity or relationship between, for example, man and his fellow men, man and society, man and God, country and country, religion and religion, subject and object, etc. The double-swing model has several important characteristics.

In terms of structure, the model is neither monistic nor dualistic. While a monistic structure assumes a oneness, which can be represented by a single circle, a dualistic structure assumes separation which can be drawn as two circles without a connection. The mathematician's infinity symbol, ∞, signifies an "identity-in-unity," which embraces the unity of monism and the separateness of dualism, both of which are constantly interactive and complementary. Neither side can be excluded or combined, for both sides represent different realities. To put it differently, this model implies the dynamic double negative—Not Two, Not One. The double negative creates a great affirmation.

The double-swing model pictorially emphasizes the act of meeting between two different beings without eliminating the otherness or uniqueness of each and without reducing the dynamic tension created as a result of meeting.

The double-swing model also shows that one steps out from one's own ground to meet the other. The focus is neither on one side nor on the other, but rather on the dynamic flow of dialogical interaction, a process through which the one and the other are constantly created anew. One is different from the other, yet both are fundamentally interrelated in the same continuum. This model indicates the yielding of one dynamic center to another. It is a "process of centering" (Richards, 1976) by both partners who are opening up their dynamic centers to each other. As this model indicates, it is a dynamic coming together of both, focusing on a point of contact.

This model indicates that one is neither this side nor that side nor beyond both sides, but one is the between. This position of between is, however, not a neutral middle position or a transcendent position "beyond" or a mere dialectical (melting) synthesis which lacks a dynamic process but, rather, is a dynamic, tension-laden "between" in which there is a constant pull from both sides of the pole. One is in constant tension between the various polarities of life, therefore one feels keenly that one is alive.

The double-swing model demonstrates the process of balance between the opposing forces of life. "To be alive as a human being is to maintain a delicate balance between the various polarities of life" (Byrne & Maziarz, 1969, pp. 56–61). For example, one is not always clearly in movement or in rest, spontaneous or planned, purposeful or random, harmonious or dissonant. One is a dynamic mix of those polarities of life. This model shows the bipolar existence of man as well as his different dimensions.

This double-swing model illustrates when the life energy which the Japanese call *ki* flows out of each other. Hoffman, a researcher in practical psychology and parapsychology, identifies this life energy flow with the fundamental pattern of energy flow in the universe called *mana* by the Kahuna, the ancient Hawaiian miracle workers. The energy flows out like "a figure eight or the sign for infinity" (Hoffman, 1976, p. 24). According to quantum theory, the electron waves in the orbits are identified as *ki* energy. They form patterns known as "standing waves" (Capra, 1975) which correspond to the form of the double-swing. One flows in and flows out and flows with it. Both are no longer one or two but one with the other. One is in swinging interaction with the Thou. This double-swing model assumes the continuing existence of both modes of reality independently. It represents a new perspective which is based on a recognition of independence and interdependence.

It should be noted here that the model is not to be construed as a fixed entity or principle but in fact has much to do with the ways we perceive, think, and relate to whatever we encounter. It is essentially related to our basic attitude and life stance. The catalytic thought embodied in this double-swing model can be applied to the whole spectrum of human existence—interaction of man with man, communication between countries, and dialogue among different religions, and so forth. In this paper, however, the focus is on the intercultural encounter of communication between countries and between people.

IMPLICATIONS FOR INTERCULTURAL COMMUNICATION

Difference and otherness which are commonly conceived as problematic in intercultural communication are viewed as positive factors and as essential ingredients for growth. In the double-swing model, the otherness of the other is maximally present, for the focus is the sphere or "between" where each partner allows the other to reach out. In this respect, intercultural communication allows this "existential leap" to happen.

Intercultural communication based on the double-swing model portrays an image of the communicator as an active and creative agent. He is not a passive reactor to outside stimuli but the active creator of his own stimuli. He is not limited by given social and cultural realities—his cultural paradigm. This intercultural communication model then emphasizes the dynamic, creative, changing, spontaneous, and unpredictable aspect of noncultural and nonhistorical aspect of men in a communication process. Unlike the highly controlled approach to intercultural communication, this model brings in an element of surprise and curiosity to the intercultural communication process.

Intercultural communication is viewed as a creative human act. While the existential partners together create a new meaning and form, they are also constantly being created anew.

The model focuses not on the either/or type of polar experience but on the dynamic interplay of polar opposites. It allows one not to possess experience but to experience relationship. It deals with one's capacity to experience and enter into relationship with the other.

The model has a clear and comprehensive philosophical foundation which deals with the whole person. Intercultural communication occurs in the sphere of "between" where the limitation and the possibility of man and culture unfold. In the "between," however, one has a transcending experience.

Intercultural communication is viewed as a process in which one's essential identity takes place. It facilitates both self and other awareness. It is in the sphere of "between" that mutual rediscovery of self takes place. The model places importance on the enlightening aspect of communication.

According to the double-swing model, intercultural communication points a way to a common ground—a sphere of "between"—where East and West meet meaningfully and creatively. Thus, the model is balanced, for it encompasses both Eastern and Western dialogical thought.

SUMMARY

The dialogical double-swing model encompasses both the Western and Eastern ways of thinking. The model points to the common sphere of "between" in which East and West can creatively and dynamically encounter and communicate. The sphere of "between" does not represent exclusively either the Eastern perspective or the Western perspective but rather a third perspective. It is not caught in an either/or type of bipolar structure. This perspective serves as the third alternative which questions the silent cultural assumptions of both Eastern and Western perspectives. The double-swing model is not presented as a fixed model but as a conceptualization of catalytic thinking. Despite its intrinsic fluidity and flexibility, it is destined to be fixed as long as it serves as a framework. It must be tested in the actual stream of life. Thus, the double-swing model requires a constant life and death process.

The sphere of "between" is the sphere of intercultural encounter which is created not by going under the cultures or by going beyond the cultures but by coming through them. Intercultural communication based on the double-swing model does not produce one homogeneous world but rather creates a dynamic, diversified, and pluralistic world.

CHAPTER 23

Communication East and West: Points of Departure

D. Lawrence Kincaid

INTRODUCTION

During recent years, one of the most popular ways to express the nature of communication as a process has been to quote Heraclitus' famous statement that it is impossible to step into the same river twice. Change is constant; no two communication situations are ever exactly the same. To Aristotle this was an extreme point of view; to communication scholars in the 1960s this was an exciting new way to think about their subject. Now in this volume, we are confronted with the even more radical view of Cratylus, who admonished Heraclitus for saying that one could step into the river even once. The assumption that words can have a definite and absolute reference to experience is now seriously challenged.

To challenge and expand the scope of our own thinking about human communication was the original intention of this volume. The skepticism toward language encountered in the Eastern perspective is just one of the many themes that has emerged. The main purpose of this concluding chapter is to compare the main themes that have been found in the Eastern and Western Perspectives and then to suggest some of the fruitful lines for further inquiry. Faced with such a broad range and diversity of papers, the wisest course of action would probably be the one chosen by Cratylus: simply to raise one's little finger and let the readers draw their own conclusions. Such a temptation will be resisted, however, on the grounds that had the ancients of both the East and West emulated this practice, no trace of their thoughts would remain today.

Our concluding discussion draws attention to five basic themes which have emerged from our discussion of communication theory from Eastern and Western perspectives: the unit of analysis, the consequence or purpose of communication, the limits of language and cognition, emotion and rationality, and human relationships. These five themes are not mutually exclusive but, rather, interrelated, and some of the themes encompass subthemes which could just as easily have been treated separately. Although considerable diversity exists within both the Eastern and Western sets of papers, for convenience we will continue to refer to the Eastern perspective and the Western perspective as that represented by the set of papers from each section.

UNIT OF ANALYSIS

One of the dominant themes of the Eastern perspective is the ultimate wholeness or unity of disparate parts. One of the major obstacles of the general systems approach to communication has always been the lack of an appropriate research methodology to study social phenomena holistically. It is conceptually obvious to Western scholars that there is indeed a whole to which the parts studied correspond, but the entire analytical and conceptual apparatus itself has always acted as an obstacle to a clear understanding of this insight.

The oneness of substance and form, of reason and experience, and of knowledge and action are the foundation principles of the Chinese perspective. The philosophy itself goes beyond the usual systems theory presentation. The uniqueness of each part is itself a function of the whole to which it belongs. But more importantly, the part and the whole ultimately *cannot* be separated. One way to say this is that there is no part *and* whole but rather one part/whole. Each "one" defines the other, and indeed *is* the other.

The dialectical completion of relative polarities takes this to the extreme and provides a methodology at the same time. Interpretation is an open-ended, infinite process in which even bipolar opposites, for example, the familiar good and bad of the semantic differential scale, are no longer linear in the Western sense but circular in the Eastern sense. Thus, the good not only complements and defines the bad, it can itself become the bad relative to circumstance and point of view. Good and bad form an inseparable whole.

For communication scholars the most difficult point to which this principle can be applied is to the individual and the society and culture of which he/she is a part and which he/she also creates. Thus, there have always been debates in the social sciences about whether a group is something different from the individuals which comprise it or whether there "exist" characteristics of a whole society apart from the mere aggregation of the characteristics of its individual members.

Communication theories have tended to focus on only one level of analysis, and in the United States, especially, that unit of analysis which has been predominant is the individual. The network–convergence theory attempts to integrate the two levels by means of the network concept (and measurement) and by focusing attention on the statistical dynamics of intact cultures bound together by networks of information flow. A related line of inquiry is the role played by the *hierarchical organization* of individuals in the integration of part and whole, a problem which is explicitly dealt with by the Confucianist scholars and one which becomes important in the new autopoieses paradigm of communication and development. In the Confucianist perspective, we discover a form of mutual causality between part and whole, in which things (society) are not put together by some agent from the outside like machines are but, rather, unfold spontaneously from within like the seed of a flower. Thus, we find a causal loop in which the perfection of the individual leads to the perfection of interpersonal relationships, which in turn leads to the perfection of family relationships, and so forth, ultimately creating a society in which it is possible for individuals to perfect themselves.

THE CONSEQUENCE/PURPOSE OF COMMUNICATION

The term, "purpose," is usually used in a teleological sense as some consciously intended goal or end state which has a causal force on behavior. In practice, the use of this approach must always be accompanied by the notion of "unintended consequences" to complete the picture. Use of the term, "consequences," by itself does not require this because the emphasis is on the unfolding of natural processes irrespective of human intention. In the field of communication, there has always been a certain amount of controversy about which pespective would lead to better theories of human behavior.

In the introductory essay of this volume, we specified three different ways of looking at "successful" communication: personal understanding, mutual understanding, and institutional understanding. But we took no position on these three outcomes with respect to intention or purpose. This aspect does become prominent in the separate papers of this volume, however. Intention or purpose is the basic axiom of the rules theories of communication found in the Western perspective and of action theories in general. In the control paradigm the persuasion of the audience is assumed to be the conscious intention of the source. The network–convergence theory, on the other hand, treats mutual understanding and cultural convergence (negentropy) as consequences of the communication process irrespective of the intentions of the participants. In fact, the theory implies that such outcomes would occur even if they were unintended or undesirable to the participants, in other words, as an outcome of a natural process of information sharing. The self-organization of autopoietic processes is also conceived as a natural outcome irrespective of intention, as are the natural sciences in general. To know *how* a process occurs is to know *why* it occurs.

Outcomes as consequences of naturally unfolding processes is also the predominant position taken in the Eastern perspective. Propriety in the communication patterns of Korea, for example, is not practiced with the purpose "in mind" of producing greater social harmony in a means/ends sense, even though that is one of the consequences. Quite the contrary, propriety is a basic value in and of itself in human behavior. The Korean *uye-ri* interpersonal relationship is another good example of this principle. Westerners find it difficult to understand or believe that the human relationship itself takes precedence over the obligations that are created by it, yet the fact that these obligations are asymmetrical supports this conclusion. The reciprocation may be unequal and delayed indefinitely. The main concern is the maintenance of the *uye-ri* relationship itself. Looked at from a culture which emphasizes *ri,* personal profit, and autonomy, the *uye-ri* relationship makes no sense. "What's the purpose of it?" always comes to mind.

This suggests that it may be misleading to equate the Western goal of individual freedom with the consequence of spiritual and social harmony of the East as was done in the introductory chapter. Independence and individual freedom may be conscious means to one's personal goals in a way that interdependence is *not* a conscious means to harmony. An indication of the difficulty in making such a comparison is the real possibility that in the West most people would predict that disharmony would be the most likely outcome of interdependence, while autonomy would be the best means to harmony. In the Eastern perspective this phenomenon seems to go beyond simple means/ends analysis to a serious underlying question of the *meaning* of the terms that are being used.

Does, for example, freedom mean the same thing in the East as in the West? Some of our papers suggest an important difference. The meaning of liberation in traditional Indian philosophy is intertwined with the related concepts of oneness, nonindividuality, and material nonattachment. Freedom is something attained when one gives up his/her individuality, renounces material things, and spiritually becomes one with something greater than oneself. Freedom, at least in the American sense, is associated with the independence to pursue one's own—often material—interests in fair competition with other individuals. In the West you *do* something to achieve whatever ends make you happy. In the East you *become one* with something greater than yourself for no other conscious purpose. Both speak of freedom.

With the cognitive bias of the West the emphasis is usually on how communication affects one's mind: what the audience thinks and believes. The exception to this, of course, is the third catagory of communication referred to as entertainment and the needs and gratification function of communication. Even the recent interest in this consequence of communication does not compare to the central position it occupies in the approach to communication expressed in Bharat Muni's *Sadharanikaran,* where the form of communication chosen is aesthetic and artistic and the consequence is the diminishing "in one's heart" of the difference (separateness) between oneself and others. The emphasis is on the cultural function of communication in the same sense as it is expressed in the new Western perspective referred to as "cultural communication." The outcome is an emotional and spiritual convergence as opposed to the conceptual convergence emphasized in the network–convergence theory. The aesthetic pleasures which are mutually felt include erotic feelings, feelings of hate, wonder, anger, compassion, and so forth. Sharing these feelings with the performers and others involved creates a spiritual unity and detachment from worldly concerns.

Consequences of this type are *collective* and thus at a higher level of analysis than the individual or even the aggregation of many individuals. The gossip groups of India today which can be traced back to the communication principles of the *Sadharanikaran* are described as functioning to combat the tendency of social systems to become a set of fragmented and closed subsystems by increasing information flow across the society's natural and social boundaries. This is the same function emphasized in the network–convergence theory of communication and which is captured so well by the concept of entropy borrowed from statistical physics.

THE LIMITS OF LANGUAGE AND COGNITION

Since the time of Aristotle's *Rhetoric* communication, theorists in the West have traditionally focused most of their attention on the verbal symbols used in human speech. Although Plato himself considered writing as a form of rhetoric, he claimed that speaking was superior to writing for the purpose of informing as well as persuading. As we have seen, the development of communication theory took quite a different course in the East, where verbal symbols of any kind are treated skeptically, with the least confidence of all placed on the spoken word.

The skeptical attitude toward verbal and rational perception of reality in the East was traced back to the classic Indian theory of perception. More confidence is placed on the direct, immediate perception of reality at the ideal "point instant" of time and on intuition than on perception of the world filtered by conceptual thought. This theory/assumption is the source of the belief that the world itself is an illusion.

Western theories of communication are also based, at least implicitly, on a model of perception. The convergence theory, for example, specifies three levels of information processing—physical, psychological, and social. Information itself is defined as a physical difference or pattern to which one becomes aware through one's senses, interprets or recognizes psychologically, and then understands by means of the application of existing or newly created *concepts*. Concepts themselves have not one but a variety of possible meanings which are pinned down or negotiated during the cyclical process of further information sharing with others at a social level. Such a description of information processing (perception) is consistent with contemporary Western theories of semantics but clearly places the greatest emphasis on the *cognitive or conceptual* interpretation of information (reality). There is not the slightest interest or even mention of intuition or admission that any kind of direct experience is even possible.

The concept of intuition does arise, however, in Western theories of psychotherapy and human relations training, but it has always been treated skeptically in academic circles and considered to be beyond existing methods of empirical research. Empirical research in the social sciences is very dependent on verbal recall and reporting. Intuitive understanding of some aspect of reality very often cannot be put into words. It is often reported as a feeling, for which words do not seem appropriate.

Here then is an important difference between the Eastern and Western perspectives toward communication. The former remains skeptical of conceptual thought and its verbal representation, the latter remains skeptical of intuitive perception because it is so difficult to represent verbally and to measure. Conceptual and intuitive thinking is used in both the East and the West. What we are describing here is the degree of emphasis and confidence placed on these two forms of perception (information processing) in communication theory and practice.

The difference between the East and the West in this respect becomes quite apparent by a comparison of communication from the Chinese perspective in the *Story of Ah-Q* and from the American perspective represented by rules theory. The former places great emphasis on the use of irony carried to the point of paradox, while the latter is exclusively concerned with the straightforward use of logical analysis and means–ends goal attainment. The deeper meaning that emerges from Ah-Q's experience is often the opposite of the surface, literal meaning initially encountered. Irony, paradox, and contradiction are beyond the scope of rules theory and action theory in general. How can a logical syllogism function if the meaning of some of the statements are taken as irony or self-contradiction?

More generally, how can action theory which is based on the conscious (cognitive) intent of the actor be reconciled with the Chinese principle of *wu-wei*? *Wu-wei* is the principle of *nonaction* which is sometimes erroneously interpreted by Westerners as a call for doing nothing. It is more accurately interpreted as "do nothing artificial," where rational, logical thought is construed as artificial. Although such a principle is virtually nonexistent in Western social science literature, the principle is often practiced unknowingly there. When someone advises a young man or woman to act natural and quit trying so hard to win someone's affections, they are advocating *wu-wei,* the principle of nonaction. In a similar manner, it is common practice for doctors to advise couples who have repeatedly failed to get pregnant to quit trying so hard for a while and see what happens. The athlete of any sport is well advised to give up trying to achieve his/her goal as he/she was taught and to simply get into the flow of the game, to visualize himself/herself performing rather than thinking about it conceptually step by step. And finally, direct, overt persuasion is very often the surest way to fail to persuade someone. Modern advertisers and political strategists have certainly learned this lesson. The West has no well-developed term for such advice or any theory of behavior to explain it, but the East does. And it specifies that the surest way to fail to reach one's goal is to try rather than to follow the *Tao.*

With such a perspective it is no wonder that the Eastern perspective places more emphasis than the Western on the meaning of silence and on saying nothing or as little as is necessary. The West has developed the study of nonverbal communication in recent years, but the approach thus far is hampered by the desire to fit it conceptually into a language system.

Gestures are described and labeled as if they function as verbal symbols in a language. Again the emphasis is on the cognitive representation of non-verbal behavior as "symbolic."

In the discussion of *ishin-denshin* in Japan or its counterparts in Korea and China, there is no attempt to reconceptualize the phenomenon as a special form of nonverbal transmission of messages, even though nonverbal gestures are involved. This is because the experience goes beyond mere symbol processing to a form of instantaneous, shared experience between two or more people. An appropriate understanding of this phenomenon must go back to the basic theory of perception in Buddhism.

A similar conclusion may be drawn regarding the effect of *kuuki,* or "mood," on human communication. It goes beyond words, or symbolic processing of any kind, to the mutual sharing of feelings about something as opposed to thoughts about it. The notions of "group think" or even "group pressure" popular in social theory in the West should not be considered as counterparts to *kuuki,* even if the outcomes are similar. Both group think and group pressure depend on verbal communication to function. What people think based on what they say and in what proportion is what "causes" the collective behavior to occur. When *kuuki* influences a group it does so without so much as one word of comment. Everybody present is aware of it at the same time; it is felt as much as it is thought. It is this difference between feelings and thinking which differentiate the Western and Eastern perspectives in this regard.

EMOTION AND RATIONALITY

The *kuuki* phenomenon found in Japan raises questions about emotion in general as opposed to the rational aspects of communication. Emotional response is central to the communication theory of the *Sadharanikaran* of India, as mentioned above, in a way that is consistent with the theory of cultural communication from the Western perspective. The main difference is that the theory of cultural communication focuses more on the forms of communication—ritual, myth, and social drama—than it does on the emotional responses that they evoke. According to the *Sadharanikaran* certain emotional responses perform a necessary and very positive function in the communication process.

Emotion plays a central role in the communication theory and practices that have emerged from the influences of Confucianism in Korea but in a quite different manner than in India. Overt emotional responses other than the neutral behavior of smiling is strongly discouraged in public settings. The emphasis is on maintaining human dignity and proper relationships. The seven emotions not only disrupt these relationships, they cause one to lose one's own sense of human dignity.

The same disregard for emotional, irrational responses is evident in the neo-Confucianist distinction between mass opinion and public opinion. One gets the impression that mass opinion is what would be tapped by today's opinion polls. Mass opinions are volatile, not necessarily well thought out, and subject to momentary influences. Nevertheless, there is something of value in the opinions of the people and somehow that msut be communicated to the king for proper conduct of government. The method preferred is to have it filtered through the wise deliberations of the most highly educated members of society who serve as advisers to the king.

The neo-Confucian perspective toward emotion in human affairs and government policy sheds little light on the positive functions that human emotion might play in both human communication as well as the political process. The convergence theory treats emotional response as simply another type of information which may influence the process of convergence. The theory of autopoiesis considers two types of input, from the ecosphere and the noosphere, and omits any discussion of the role that emotional response might play in the autopoietic process.

HUMAN RELATIONSHIPS

One of the recent directions which rules theory has taken is the exploration of the difference between the rules which govern different kinds of human relationships, such as the friendship and the marriage relationship, and the role of the self-concept in such relationships. The focus remains, however, on the instrumental nature of such relationships. The convergence theory moves the level of analysis from the individual up to the level of relationships, from dyadic to that of the members of intact cultures or organizations. The interest in relationships is limited, however, to the extent to which two or more individuals share information with one another and the extent to which they move toward mutual understanding and agreement. Other aspects of human relationships are not considered.

In the study of *uye-ri*, the main focus is the relationship itself, the conditions which support it, the consequences for Korean society, and the mutual obligations of those involved. Also specified are the levels of the parties involved, whether they are on the same level or superior/ subordinate within a social hierarchy. It is not surprising that these factors are given more attention in the Korean perspective because of the high value placed on human relationships and hierarchy in general within that culture. A culture such as the United States which places such a high value on equality, individualism, and freedom has a built-in bias which directs its attentions to other aspects of communication.

It is thus surprising to the Western reader to discover not only a preference for authority and asymmetrical communication in the traditional Indian model but also a belief that communication from a higher social level to a lower one would be more effective. Each person has a specific place within the scheme of the world, and it is a world which is by definition hierarchical. Those in higher positions always have more power, and this is taken for granted as the natural scheme of things. An opposite extreme is found in the warning by the citizens of Catalan, beween France and Spain, to their king in their constitution written in the Middle Ages: "Each of us is equal to you, and together all of us are greater than you."

Power, hierarchy, and especially coercive forms of communication are largely missing from modern theories of communication in the East and the West but especially in the West. Power is certainly present in many human relationships, but it remains relatively invisible in the theories of communication currently being developed. This aspect of human relationships along with many others are not considered central to our existing theories of communication. The comparison of Eastern and Western perspectives has highlighted this omission and has presented some useful lines for future inquiry.

CONCLUSION

The comparisons that we have made in this volume have underscored the extent to which history and traditional culture have influenced the content and nature of communication theories that have been developed. Many of the key issues in human communication have been explored, and the wide range of the papers has brought many overlooked aspects to light for future research. Finally, the unique contributions of each perspective have laid the foundation for theories and practical guidelines for intercultural communication which go beyond the surface behavior that occurs when people from the East and the West meet one another for the first time.

References

Abegglen, J. C. (1958). *The Japanese factory.* Glencoe, IL: Free Press.

Akutagawa, R. (1970). *Rashomon, and other stories* (2nd ed.) (T. Kojima, Trans.). Tokyo: Tuttle. (Original work published 1954)

Anand, U. (1969). *The romance of theatre.* New Delhi: National Council of Educational Research and Training.

Applegate, J. L. (1980a). Adaptive communication in educational contexts: A study of teachers' communication strategies. *Communication Education, 29,* 158–170.

Applegate, J. L. (1980b). Person and position centered communication in a day care center. In N. K. Denzin (Ed.), *Studies in symbolic interaction* (Vol. 3). Greenwich, CT: JAI Press.

Applegate, J. L. (1982a, February). *Contruct system development and identity-management skills in persuasive contexts.* Paper presented at the convention of the Western Speech Communication Association.

Applegate, J. L. (1982b). The impact of construct system development on communication and impression formation in persuasive contexts. *Communication Monographs, 49,* 277–289.

Applegate, J. L., Burke, J. A., Burleson, B. R., Delia, J. G., & Kline, S. L. (1985). Reflection-enhancing parental communication. In I. E. Sigel (Ed.), *Parental belief systems: The psychological consequences for children* (pp. 107–142). Hillsdale, NJ: Earlbaum.

Applegate, J. L., & Delia, J. G. (1980). Person-centered speech, psychological development, and the contexts of language usage. In R. St. Clair & H. Giles (Eds.), *The social and psychological contexts of language.* Hillsdale, NJ: Erlbaum.

Aristotle. (1976). *Metaphysics* (J. Warrington, Trans.). Cambridge, MA: Harvard University Press.

Ashby, W. R. (1956). *An introduction to cybernetics.* London: Chapman & Hall.

Asian Development Bank Report. (1980). *Rural Asia: Challenge and opportunity* (pp. 254–255).

Attreya, B. L. (1953). Indian culture, its spiritual, moral and social aspect. In *Interrelations of cultures* (pp. 139–140). Paris: UNESCO.

Austin, J. L. (1962). *How to do things with words* (1st ed.). Cambridge, MA: Harvard University Press.

Austin, J. L. (1975). *How to do things with words* (2nd ed.). Cambridge, MA: Harvard University Press.

Avens, R. (1980). Recovering imagination—discovering the East. *Thought, 55,* 152–168.

Baek, S. M. (1962). The origins of Korean thought. *Koreana Quarterly, 4,* 151–159.

Ballon, R. J. (1969). *The Japanese employee.* Rutland, VT: Tuttle.

Barker, R. (1960). Ecology and motivation. In M. Jones (Ed.), *Nebraska Symposium on Motivation.* Lincoln: University of Nebraska Press.

Barker, R. (1968). *Ecological psychology.* Stanford, CA: Stanford University Press.

Barnett, G. A., & Kincaid, D. L. (1983). A mathematical theory of cultural convergence. In W. B. Gudykunst (Ed.), *Intercultural communication theory: Current perspectives* (pp. 171–179). Beverly Hills, CA: Sage.

Baskerville, B. (1980). *The people's voice.* Lexington: University of Kentucky Press, 1980.

Beal, G., Rogers, E. M., & Bohlen, J. M. (1957). Validity of the concept of stages in the adoption process. *Rural Sociology, 22,* 166–168.

Beltran, L. R. (1976). Alien premises, objects, and methods in Latin American communication research. In E. M. Rogers (Ed.), *Communication and development: Critical perspectives* (pp. 15–42). Beverly Hills, CA: Sage.

Benedict, R. (1946). *The chrysanthemum and the sword.* Cambridge, MA: Houghton Mifflin.

Bennett, G. A., & Montaperto, R. (1971). *Red guard: The political biography of Dai Itsiaoai.* Garden City, NY: Doubleday.

Berger, P., Berger, B., & Kellner, H. (1974). *The homeless mind: Modernization and consciousness.* New York: Vintage Press.

Bernam, M. (1982). *All that is solid melts into air.* New York: Simon and Schuster.

Berry, W. (1978). *The unsettling of America: Culture and agriculture.* New York: Avon.

Bhartrhari. (1971). *The vakyapadiya: Critical text of cantas I and II* (K. R. Pillai, Trans.). Delhi, India: Motilal Banarsidass.

Blumer, H. (1969). *Symbolic interactionism: Perspectives and method.* Englewood Cliffs, NJ: Prentice-Hall.

Bohm, D. (1980). *Wholeness and the implicate order.* London: Routledge & Paul Kegan.

Borden, A. W. (1981, November). *Interpersonal values, Machiavellianism, and social cognition as indicators of communicative competence in persuasive contexts.* Paper presented at the meeting of the Speech Communication Association, Anahiem, CA.

Boulding, K. E. (1978). *Ecodynamics: A new theory of societal evolution.* Beverly Hills, CA: Sage.

Brown, P., & Levinson, S. (1978). Universals in language usage: Politeness phenomena. In E. N. Goody (Ed.), *Questions and politeness.* London & New York: Cambridge University Press.

Buber, M. (1958). *I and thou* (2nd ed.). New York: Scribner's.

Buber, M. (1964). *Daniel: Dialogues on realization.* New York: Holt.

Buber, M. (1965). *The knowledge of man.* London: Allen & Unwin.

Bunge, M. (1972). Metatheory. In *Scientific thought.* Paris: UNESCO.

Burke, J. A. (1979, April). *The relationship of interpersonal cognitive development to the adaptation of persuasive strategies in adults.* Paper presented at the meeting of the Central States Speech Association, St. Louis, MO.

Burleson, B. R. (1982a). *Developmental and individual differences in comfort-intended message strategies: Four empirical studies.* Doctoral dissertation, University of Illinois, Urbana.

Burleson, B. R. (1982b). The development of comforting communication skills in childhood and adolescence. *Child Development, 53,* 1578–1588.

Burleson, B. R. (1983). Social cognition, empathic motivation, and adults' comforting strategies. *Human Communication Research, 10,* 295–304.

Burleson, B. R. (1984a). Age, social-cognitive development, and the use of comforting strategies. *Communication Monographs, 51,* 140–153.

Burleson, B. R. (1984b). Comforting communication. In H. E. Sypher & J. L. Applegate (Eds.), *Communication by children and adults: Social cognitive and strategic processes* (pp. 63–104). Beverly Hills, CA: Sage.

Burns, R. B. (1979). *The self-concept.* New York: Longmans, Green.

Byrne, E., & Maziarz, E. (1969). *Human being and being human.* New York: Appleton.

Cappella, J. N. (1972). Style and the functional prerequisites of intentional communicative systems. *Philosophy and Rhetoric, 5,* 231–297.

Capra, F. (1975). *The Tao of physics.* Berkeley, CA: Shamhala.

Cardillo, J. P. (1971). *The effects of teaching communication roles on interpersonal perception and self-concept in disturbed marriages.* Doctoral dissertation, George Peabody College.

Carr, J. E. (1969). Differentiation as a function of source characteristics and judge's conceptual structure. *Journal of Personality, 37,* 378–386.

Carr, J. E. (1970). Differentiation similarity of patient and therapist and the outcomes of psychotherapy. *Journal of Abnormal Psychology, 76,* 361–369.

Carr, J. E., & Whittenbaugh, J. A. (1968). Volunteer and non-volunteer characteristics in out-patient population. *Journal of Abnormal Psychology, 73,* 16–21.

Cell, C. (1979). Communication in China's mass mobilization campaigns. In G. Chu & F. Hsu (Eds.), *Moving a mountain.* Honolulu, Hawaii: East-West Center.

Chang, R. (1977). *Physical chemistry with applications to biological systems.* New York: Macmillan.

Chang, W. H. (1972). *Communication and acculturation: A case study of Korean ethnic groups in Los Angeles.* Doctoral dissertation, University of Iowa, Iowa City.

Chen, J. (1957). *The new earth, how the peasants in one Chinese county solved the problem of poverty.* Peking: New World.

Choe, C. G. (1972). Concept of loyalty and filial piety vs. democracy. *Korea Journal, 12,* 13–20.

Choe, C. H. (1980). Korea's communication culture: An inquiry into spoken and written words. *Korea Journal, 20,* 41–52.

Choe, J. S. (1965). *Hankukin ye sahwejuk sung kyuk* (Social personality of Koreans). Seoul, Korea: Minjosa.

Choe, S. H. (1974). *On onkwan in the early days of the Yi Dynasty.* Seoul, Korea: Sumundang Co.

Chu, G. C. (1979). The current structure and function of China's mass media. In G. Chu & F. Hsu (Eds.), *Moving a mountain.* Honolulu, Hawaii: East-West Center.

Clark, R. A., & Delia, J. G. (1976). The development of functional persuasive skills in childhood and early adolescence. *Child Development, 47,* 1008–1014.

Cohen, B. D. (1978). Referent communication disturbances in schizophrenia. In S. Schwartz (Ed.), *Language and cognition in schizophrenia.* Hillsdale, NJ: Earlbaum.

Condon, J. C., & Saito, M. (Eds.). (1974). *Intercultural encounters with Japan.* Tokyo: Simul Press.

Confucius. (1938). *The analects of Confucius* (A. Waley, Trans.). London: Allen & Unwin.

Couch, C. A. (1955). *A study of the relationship between self views and role-taking accuracy.* Doctoral dissertation, University of Iowa, Iowa City.

Cronen, V. E., Johnson, K., & Lannaman, J. W. (1982). Paradoxes, double binds, and reflexive loops: An alternative theoretical perspective. *Family Process, 20,* 91–112.

Crook, I., & Crook, D. (1966). *The first years of yangy: Commune.* London: Routledge & Paul Kegan.

Cushman, D. P., & Craig, R. T. (1976). Communication systems: Interpersonal implications. In G. R. Miller (Ed.), *Explorations in interpersonal communication* (pp. 37–58). Beverly Hills, CA: Sage.

Cushman, D. P., & Hauser, G. A. (1973). Weaver's rhetorical theory: Axiology and the adjustment of belief, invention and judgment. *Quartlery Journal of Speech, 59,* 319–329.

Cushman, D. P., & Pearce, W. B. (1977). Generality and necessity in three types of human communication theory—special attention to rules theory. In D. Reuben (Ed.), *Communication Yearbook I* (pp. 173–183). New Brunswick, NJ: Transaction Books.

Cushman, D. P., & Tompkins, P. K. (1980). A theory of rhetoric for contemporary society. *Philosophy and Rhetoric, 13,* 43–77.

Cushman, D. P., & Whiting, G. (1972). An approach to communication theory: Towards consensus on rules. *Journal of Communication, 22,* 217–228.

Czbekhan, H. (1971). Planning and human action. In P. A. Weiss (Ed.), *Hierarchically organized systems in theory and practice* (pp. 123–230). New York: Hafner.

Dandekar, V. M. (1972). *Effectiveness in Agricultural Planning* Agricultural Development Council Teaching Forum, No. 19, Singapore.

Danes, J., & Woelfel, J. (1975, April). *An alternative to the "traditional" scaling paradigm in mass communication research: Multi-dimensional reduction of ratio judgements of separation.* Paper presented at the annual meeting of the International Communication Association, Chicago, IL.

Daniel, J., & Smitherman, G. (1976). How I got over: Communication dynamics in the black community. *Quarterly Journal of Speech, 62,* 26–39.

Delia, J. G. (1976). A constructivist analysis of the concept of credibility. *Quarterly Journal of Speech, 62,* 361–375.

Delia, J. G., Burleson, B. R., & Kline, S. L. (1979, April). *Person-centered parental communication and the development of social-cognitive and communicative abilities.* Paper presented at the annual meeting of the Central States Speech Association, St. Louis, MO.

Delia, J. G., & Clark, R. A. (1977). Cognitive complexity, social perception and the development of listener adaptational communication in six, eight, ten and twelve year old boys. *Communication Monographs, 44,* 326–345.

Delia, J. G., Kline, S., & Burleson, B. R. (1979). The development of persuasive communication strategies in kindergartners through twelfth graders. *Communication Monographs, 46,* 241–256.

Delia, J. G., & O'Keefe, B. J. (1979). Constructivism: The development of communication. In E. Wartella (Ed.), *Children communication* (pp. 157–185). Beverly Hills, CA: Sage.

Delia, J. G., O'Keefe, B. J., & O'Keefe, D. J. (1982). The constructivist approach to communication. In F. E. X. Dance (Ed.), *Human communication theory* (pp. 147–191). New York: Harper & Row.

Denbigh, K. W. (1975). *An inventive universe.* New York: Braziller.

Descartes, R. (1952). *Rules for the direction of the mind* (L. J. Lefleur, Trans.). R. M. Hutchins (Ed.), *Great books of the western world.* Encyclopedia Brittanica.

Deuchler, M. (1980). Neo-Confucianism: The impulse for social action in early Yi-Korea. *Journal of Korean Studies, 2,* 71–112.

Deutsch, E. (1969). *Advaita vedanta: A philosophical reconstruction.* Honolulu: University of Hawaii Press.

Deutsch, K. W. (1968). Toward a cybernetic model of man and society. In W. Buckley (Ed.), *Modern systems research for the behavioral scientist* (pp. 387–400). Chicago, IL: Aldine.

Diaz-Bordenave, J. (1976). Communication of agricultural innovations in Latin America. In E. M. Rogers (ED.), *Communication and development: Critical perspectives* (pp. 43–62). Beverly Hills, CA: Sage.

Dissanayake, W. (1981). *Personality, impersonality and transpersonality.* A paper presented at the International Conference on Culture and Communication, Temple University, Philadelphia, PA.

Dobson, J. K. (1970). *Predictions of individual student teacher behavior in classrooms for emotionally disturbed children.* Doctoral dissertation, University of Michigan, Ann Arbor.

Doi, T. (1973). *The anatomy of dependence* (J. Bester, Trans.). Tokyo & New York: Kodansha, 1973.

Drucker, P. F. (1971, March-April). What can we learn from Japanese management. *Harvard Business Review,* pp. 110–122.

Dudman, R. (1977). Headlines and deadlines: Chinese style. *Nieman Reports,* Spring-Summer, pp. 19–25.

Durkheim, E. (1966). *The rules of sociological method.* New York: Free Press.

Einstein, A. (1956). *Meaning of relativity.* Princeton, NJ: Princeton University Press.

Fay, B., & Moon, D. (1977). What would an adequate philosophy of social science look like? *Philosophy of Social Sciences, 7,* 209–224.

Fisher, B. A. (1978). *Perspectives on human communication.* New York: Macmillan.

Fisher, R. A. (1935). *The design of experiments.* (1st ed.). London: Oliver & Boyd.

Flavell, J. H. (1968). *The development of role taking and communication skills in children.* New York: Wiley.

Foerster, H. von. (1979). Cybernetics of cybernetics. In K. Krippendorff (Ed.), *Communication and control in society* (pp. 5–8). New York: Gordon & Breach.

Fraser, J. T. (1975). *Of time, passion and knowledge.* New York: G. Braziller.

Frey, J. C., (1972). *Some obstacles to soil erosion control in western Iowa* (Research Bulletin 391). Iowa Agricultural Experimental Station.

Friedman, M. (1955). *Martin Buber: The Life of dialogue.* New York: Harper Torchbook.

Fujioka, S. (1895). *Nihon fuzoku shi* (A history of Japanese manners and customs). Tokyo: Toyodo.

Galileo, G. (1914). *Dialogue concerning two new sciences* (H. Crew & A. De Salvio, Trans.). New York: Macmillan.

Gargi, B. (1966). *Folk theatre of India.* Seattle: University of Washington Press.

Gatlin, L. L. (1972). *Information theory and the living system.* New York: Columbia University Press.

Geertz, G. (1973). *The interpretation of cultures.* New York: Basic Books.

Goffman, E. (1959). *The presentation of self in everyday life.* Garden City, NY: Doubleday.

Goffman, E. (1968). *Strategies interaction.* Philadelphia, PA: University of Pennsylvania Press.

Grice, H. P. (1975). The logic of conversation. In P. Cole & J. L. Morgan (Eds.), *Syntax and semantics: Vol. 3. Speech acts.* New York: Academic Press.

Gross, E., & Stone, G. P. (1964). Embarrassment and the analysis of role requirements. *American Journal of Sociology, 70,* 1–15.

Gurevich, A. J. (1976). Time as a problem in cultural history. In L. Cadet *et al.* (Eds.), *Culture and time.* Paris: UNESCO.

Guthrie, W. K. C. (1975). *A history of Greek philosophy.* London & New York: Cambridge University Press.

Hall, E. T. (1977). *Beyond culture.* Garden City, NY: Doubleday.

Hamblin, R. (1974). Social attitudes: Magnitude measurement and theory. In H. Blalock, Jr. (Ed.), *Measurement in the social sciences.* Chicago, IL: Aldine.

Hannerz, U. (1969). *Soulside: Inquiries into ghetto culture and community.* New York: Columbia University Press.

Hanson, N. R. (1958). *Patterns of discovery.* London & New York: Cambridge University press.

Harre, R., & Madden, E. (1975). *Causal powers.* Totowa, NJ: Rowland & Littlefield.

Harris, G. A. (1968). *Interpersonal sensitivity in the counselor-client relationship.* Doctoral dissertation, University of Southern Mississippi, Hattiesburg.

Harris, L. M. (1979). *Communication competence: An empirical test of a systems model.* Doctoral dissertation, University of Massachusetts, Amherst.

Harris, M. (1974). Why a perfect knowledge of all the rules one must know to act like a native cannot lead to a knowledge of how natives act. *Journal of Anthropological Research, 30,* 242–251.

Heady, E. O. (1965). *Priorities in adoption of technology* (Tech. Rep.). Ames, Iowa: Iowa State University, Center of Agricultural and Economic Development.

Herrigel, E. (1971). *Zen in the art of archery* (R. F. C. Hull, Trans.). New York: Vintage Press. (Original work published 1953)

Hirokawa, R. Y. (1981). Improving intra-organizational communication: A lesson from Japanese management. *Communication Quarterly, 30,* 35–40.

Hocking, W. F. (1968). A brief note on individuality in East and West. In C. A. Moore (Ed.), *The status of individual in East and West.* Honolulu: University of Hawaii Press.

Hoffman, E. (1976). *Huna: A beginner's guide.* Rockport, MA: Para Research.

Hsu, F. L. K. (1963). *Clan, caste, and club.* Princeton, NJ: Van Nostrand-Reinhold.

Huai, Y. L. (1977, March). Television broadcasting in communist China. *Studies on Chinese Communism,* pp. 713–778.

Hull, J. H., & Levy, A. S. (1979). The organizational function of the self: An alternate to the Duval and Nicland model of self-awareness. *Journal of Personality and Social Psychology, 37,* 201–219.

Husband, R. L. (1981). *Leadership: A case study, phenomenology, and social-cognitive correlates.* Unpublished doctoral dissertation, University of Illinois at Urbana-Champaign.

Hymes, D. (1974). *Foundations in sociolinguistics.* Philadelphia: University of Pennsylvania Press.

Imai, M. (1975). *Never take yes for an answer.* Tokyo: Simul Press.

Imai, M. (1981). *Sixteen ways to avoid saying no.* Tokyo: Nihon Keizai Shimbun.

Johnson, R. T., & Ouchi, W. G. (1974). Made in America (under Japanese management). *Harvard Business Review,* pp. 61–69.

Johnson, S. E. (1965). *Combining knowledge, incentives, and means to accelerate agricultural development* (Tech. Rep.). Ames, Iowa: Iowa State University, Center of Agricultural and Economic Development.

Jones, J. L., Delia, J. G., & Clark, R. A. (1981a, May). *Person-centered parental communication and the development of communication in children.* Paper presented at the annual meeting of the International Communication Association, Minneapolis, MN.

Jones, J. L., Delia, J. G., & Clark, R. A. (1981b, May). *Socio-economic status and the developmental level of second- and seventh-grade children's persuasive strategies.*

Paper presented at the annual meeting of the International Communication Association, Minneapolis, MN.

Kang, K. (1984). *Transculturation: The relationship between breach management and family paradigm in experiencing a novel culture.* Doctoral dissertation, University of Massachusetts, Amherst.

Kang, K., & Pearce, W. (1984). The place of crosscultural concepts in communication research, with a case study of reticence. *Communication, 9,* 79–96.

Kapp, K. W, & Kapp, L. L. (1963a). *Hindu culture and economic development.* Bombay: Asia Publishing House.

Kapp, K. W. & Kapp, L. L. (1963b). *Retardation of economic development in Hindu culture and economic development and planning,* Bombay: Asia Publishing House.

Kasch, C. R. (1984, April). *Interpersonal competence, compliance, and person-centered speech: A study of nurses' and para-professionals' communicative strategies.* Paper presented at the meeting of the Central States Speech Association, Chicago, IL.

Kawabata, Y. (1970). *The sound of the mountain* (E. M. Seidensticker, Trans.). New York: Knopf.

Kawashima, T. (1951). *On no ishiki no jittaim* (The actual state of on consciousness). *Chuo Koron, 66,* 119–129.

Kearl, B. (1975). *Communication for agricultural development.* A paper presented at the East-West Conference on Communication and Change in the Developing Countries, Honolulu, Hawaii.

Kelly, G. A. (1955). *The psychology of personal constructs.* New York: Norton.

Kelman, H. C. (1961). Processes of opinion change. *Public Opinion Quarterly, 25,* 57–78.

Kim, C. M. (1969–1970). Korean thought patterns: How Koreans think and solve problems. *Korena Quarterly, 11,* 67–82.

Kim, H. I. (1981). A short survey of Buddhist logic. *Korea Observer, 12,* 78–100.

Kim, J. K. (1980). Explaining acculturation in a communication framework: An empirical test. *Communication Monographs, 47,* 155–179.

Kim, J. T. (1974). *Li-Jo Yu-hak-ye it-su-su byukidan-ye inyum gwa juntong* (Byukidan ideology and tradition in Li Dynasty Confucianism). *Journal of Kukje University, 2,* 339–359.

Kim, J. W. (1975). The thought of filial piety. *Research Review of Kyungbook National University, 20,* 239–256.

Kim, Y. Y. (1977). Communication patterns of foreign immigrants in the process of acculturation. *Human Communication Research, 4,* 66–77.

Kincaid, D. L. (1979). *The convergence model of communication* (Paper No. 18). Honolulu, Hawaii: East West Center, Communication Institute.

Kincaid, D. L. (1983). Communication technology and cultural diversity. *Informatologia Yugoslavica, 15,* 71–82.

Kincaid, D. L., Yum, J. O., Woelfel, J., & Barnett, G. A. (1983). The cultural convergence of Korean immigrants in Hawaii: An empirical test of a mathematical theory. *Quality and Quantity, 18,* 59–78.

Kitano, H. H. L. (1969). *Japanese Americans: The evolution of a subculture.* Englewood Cliffs, NJ: Prentice-Hall.

Kline, S. L. (1981a, November). *Construct system development, empathic motivation, and the accomplishment of face support in persuasive messages.* paper presented at the annual meeting of the Speech Communication Association, Anaheim, CA.

Kline, S. L. (1981b, May). *Construct system development and face support in persuasive messages: Two empirical investigations.* Paper presented at the annual meeting of the International Communication Association, Minneapolis, MN.

Kline, S. L. (1982). *The effect of instructional set on the provision of face support by persons differing in construct system development.* Paper presented at the annual meeting of the Speech Communication Association, Louisville, KY.

Kline, S. L. (1983). *Social cognition, metal cognition, and the provision of face support in persuasive communication.* Paper presented at the annual meeting of the Southern State Speech Association, Orlando, FL.

Kline, S. L. (1984, May). *Construct differentiation and strategy repertoire.* Paper presented at the annual meeting of the International Communication Association, San Francisco, CA.

Kline, S. L., & Ceropski, J. M. (1984). Person-centered communication in medical practice. In J. T. Wood & G. M. Phillips (Eds.), *Human decision-making.* Carbondale: Southern Illinois University Press.

Kodaka, K. (1943). *Nihon no yugi* (Games in Japan). Tokyo: Haneda-Shoten.

Kojien (Japanese Language Dictionary). (1955). Tokyo: Iwanami Shoten.

Krippendorff, K. (1971). Communication and the genesis of structure. *General Systems, 16,* 171–185.

Krippendorff, K., & Steier, F. (1979, August). Cybernetic properties of helping: The organizational level. In *Proceedings of the Silver Anniversary Meeting of the Society for General Systems Research* (pp. 88–97). London.

Kuhn, M., & McPartland, T. S. (1954). An empirical investigation of self-attitudes. *American Sociological Review, 19,* 68–76.

Lebra, T. S. (1976). *Japanese patterns of behavior.* Honolulu: University of Hawaii Press.

Lebra, T. S., & Lebra, W. P. (Eds.). (1974). *Japanese culture and behavior: Selected readings.* Honolulu: University of Hawaii Press.

Lee, D. J. (n.d.). *Yuhakye uye-ri sasang gwa hyunsil uyesike daihan kochal* (A study of the Confucian uye-ri thought and reality consciousness). Seoul, Korea.

Lee, J. H. (1978). *Jun-tong mun-hwa wa wae-rai mun-hwa* (Traditional culture and foreign culture). *Journal of the Humanities of Sung Kyun Kwan University, 3,* 81–96.

Lee, K. Y. (1967). *Bul-gyo wa, gundai-jok ingan-hyung* (Buddhism and modern man). In *Han-kook gundai-hwa ye i-nyum gwa bang hyang (Ideology and direction of Korean modernization).* Seoul, Korea: Dong Kuk University Press.

Lee, P. D. (1974). *The life and philosophy of Yi Yulgok.* Seoul, Korea: Sumundang.

Lee, P. D. (1977). Commentary. *Yulgokjib* (Collected work of Yulgok) (Vol. 1). Seoul, Korea: Min-jok mun-wha jin-heung whe.

Lee, S. E. (1967). On the ciriticism of Confucianism in Korea. *Korea Journal, 7,* 4–18.

Lee, U. Y. (1966). *Huksoke, jubram soke: E-gut-ee han-kook ida* (In the earth, in the wind: It is Korea). Seoul, Korea: Hyunamsa.

Legge, J. (Trans.). (1963). *The I Ching.* New York: Dover. (Original work published 1899).

Lerner, D. (1958). *The passing of traditional society: Modernizing the Middle East.* New York: Free Press.

Lerner, D., & Schramm, W. (Eds.). (1976). *Communication and change in developing countries.* Honolulu: East West Center and University of Hawaii Press.

Lew, S. K. (1970). Confucianism and Korean social structure. *Chulhak Yon-goo (Philosophical Studies), 5,* 13–38.

Lew, S. K. (1975). The peculiar and universal character of Eastern and Western thought. *Korea Journal, 5,* 22–28.

Long, B. H., Henderson, E. H., & Ziller, R. C. (1967). Developmental change in the self-concept during middle childhood. *Merrill Palmer Quarterly, 13,* 201–219.

Lyell, W. A., Jr. (1976). *Lu Hsun's vision of reality.* Berkeley: University of California Press.

Mach, E. (1915). *The science of mechanics* (P. E. B. Jourdain, Trans.). Chicago & London: Open Court.

Mandelbaum, D. G. (1959). Concepts and methods in the study of caste. *Economic Weekly, 10*, 147–162.

Mao, T. T. (1954a). On practice. *Selected works of Mao Tse-tung* (Vol. 1, pp. 259–308). New York: International University Press.

Mao, T. T. (1954b). On contradiction. *Selected works of Mao Tse-tung* (Vol. 1, pp. 311–347). New York: International University Press.

Maturana, H. (1975). The organization of the living: A theory of the living organization. *International Journal of Man-Machine Studies, 7*, 313–332.

Maturana, H. (1981). Autopoiesis. In M. Zeleny (Ed.), *Autopoiesis: A theory of living organization* (pp. 21–33). New York: Elsevier-North Holland.

McCann, C. D., & Higgins, E. T. (1984). Individual differences in communication: Social cognitive determinants and consequences. In H. E. Sypher & J. L. Appelgate (Eds.), *Communication by children and adults* (pp. 172–210). Beverly Hills, CA: Sage.

McFarland, G. (1970). *Effects of sensitivity training utilized as in-service education*. Doctoral dissertation, George Peabody College, Nashville, TN.

McKeon, R. (1941). *The basic works of Aristotle*. New York: Random House.

McKeon, R. (1957). Communication, truth and society. *Ethics, 67*, 89–99.

McLellan, D. (1980). *Marxism after Marx*. Boston, MA: Houghton Mifflin.

Mead, G. H. (1934). *Mind, self and society*. Chicago, IL: University of Chicago Press.

Mead, G. H. (1938). *The philosophy of the act*. Chicago, IL: University of Chicago Press.

Ming, C. (1976). Broadcasting network in rural China since the cultural revolution. *Ming Pao Monthly*, No. 121, pp. 93–100.

Mohanty, J. N. (1980). Subject and person: Eastern and western modes of thinking about man. *International Philosophical Journal, 20*, 265–274.

Morse, P. M. (1969). *Thermal physics* (2nd ed.). Reading, MA: Benjamin/Cummings.

Muni, Bharat. (1967). *Natyashastra* (Manmehan Gosh, Trans.) Calcutta, India: Chin Mohan Sehanavis, Mamisha Granthalya Pvt.

Nagata, K. (1969). *A statistical approach to the study of acculturation of an ethnic group based on communication-oriented variables: The case of Japanese-Americans in Chicago*. Doctoral dissertation, University of Illinois, Urbana.

Nakane, C. (1972). *Japanese society*. Berkeley: University of California Press.

Nakayama, N. (1973). *Mujunteki Sosoku no Ronri* (The logic of Soku). Kyoto: Hyakka En.

Nathan, A. (1979). *Mass mobilization and political participation in China: Do people believe the media?* A paper presented at the conference on Communication and Societal Integration in China, East-West Center, Honolulu, Hawaii.

Needham, J. (1956). *Science and civilization in China* (Vol. 2). London & New York: Cambridge University Press.

Nehru, J. (1961). His statement before the Inter-University Youth Festival. *The Hindustan Times*.

Newcomb, T. M. (1953). An approach to the study of communicative acts. *Psychological Review, 60*, 393–404.

Newcomb, T. M. (1956). The prediction of interpersonal attraction. *American Psychologist, 2*, 575–586.

Newton, I. (1962). *Sir Isaac Newton's mathematical principles of natural philosophy and his system of the world (Principia)* (A. Motte, Trans.). Berkeley: University of California Press.

Nordenstreng, K., & Schiller, H. I. (Eds.). (1979). *national sovereignty and international communication*. Honolulu, Hawaii: East West Center.

O'Connor, W. (1964). *Forms of modern fiction*. Bloomington: Indiana University Press.

Oh, T. K. (1976, January). Japanese management: A critical review. *The Academy of Management Review*, pp. 14–25.

O'Keefe, B. J., & Delia, J. G. (1982). Impression formation and message production. In M. E. Roloff & C. R. Berger (Eds.), *Social cognition and communication* (pp. 33–72). Beverly Hills, CA: Sage.

O'Keefe, B. J., & Delia, J. G. (1986). Psychological and interactional dimensions of communicative development. In H. Giles & R. St. Clair (Eds.), *Advances in language, communication, and social psychology*. London: Erlbaum.

O'Keefe, B. J., and Shepherd, G. J. (in press). The pursuit of multiple objectives in face-to-face persuasive interactions: Effects of construct differentiation. *Communication Monographs*.

O'Keefe, B. J., Delia, J. G. & O'Keefe, D. J. (1980). Interaction analysis and the analysis of interactional organization. In N. K. Denzin (Ed.), *Studies in symbolic interaction* (Vol. 3, pp. 122–155). Greenwich, CT: JAO Press.

Oliver, R. T. (1962). *Culture and communication*. Springfield, IL: Thomas.

O'Neil, W. M. (1969). *Fact and theory*. Sidney, Australia: Sidney University Press.

Osgood, C. E., Suci, G. T., & Tannenbaum, P. H. (1957). *The measurement of meaning*. Urbana: University of Illinois.

Pagnol, M. (1947). *Notes sur le Rire*. Paris: Nagel.

Parmar, S. (1975). *Traditional folk media in India*. New Delhi, India: Geka Books.

Pascale, R. T. (1978, March-April). Zen and the art of management. *Harvard Business Review*, pp. 153–163.

Pearce, W. B., & Cronen, V. (1980). *Communication action and meaning: The creation of social realities*. New York: Praeger.

Pearce, W. B., Kang, K. W., & Gielis, M. (in press). *Communication and the human condition*. Carbondale: Southern Illinois University Press.

Pearce, W. B., & Lannamann, J. W. (1982). Modernity makes immigrants of us all. *Journal of Asian, Pacific and World Perspectives*.

Pitts, W. H. (1965). *Self-concept scale manual*. Nashville: Tennessee Department of Mental Health.

Planning Commission. (1985). *Working document for the Seventh Five Year Plan 1985–1990*. Yojana Bhavan, New Delhi.

Porter, W. N. (1979). *A hundred verses from Old Japan*. Tokyo: C. E. Tuttle.

Potter, K. H. (1963). *Presuppositions of India's philosophies*. Westport, CT: Greenwood.

Prigogine, I. (1973). The statistical interpretation of nonequilibrium entropy. In F. G. D. Cohen & W. Thirring (Eds.), *The Boltzmann equation: Theory and application* (pp. 401–450). Berlin & New York: Springer-Verlag.

Prigogine, I. (1976). Order through fluctuation: Self-organization and social systems. In E. Jantsch & C. H. Waddington (Eds.), *Evolution and consciousness* (pp. 93–133). Reading, MA: Addison-Wesley.

Prigogine, I. (1978). Time, structure, and fluctuations. *Science, 201,* 777–785.

Prigogine, I. (1980). *From being to becoming: Time and complexity in the physical sciences*. San Francisco, CA: Freeman.

Prigogine, I., & Stengers, I. (1977). The new alliance. *Scientia, 112,* 319–332.

Prusek, J. (1964). The realistic and lyric elements in the Chinese medieval story. *Archiv Orientalni, 32,* 4–15.

Radhakrishnan, S. (1923). *Indian philosophy* (Vol. 1). London: Allen & Unwin.

Radhakrishnan, S. (1927). *Indian philosophy* (Vol. 2). London: Allen & Unwin.

Radhakrishnan, S. (1948). *Bhagavadgita*. London: Allen & Unwin.

Ramanan, K. V. (1966). *Nagarjuna's philosophy: As presented in the Maha-Prajna-paramita-satra.* Rutland, VT: Tuttle.

Rapoport, A. (1974). Various meanings of theory. In A. C. Michaloa (Ed.), *Philosophical problems of science and technology* (pp. 259–279). Boston: Allyn & Bacon.

Reserve Bank of India Report. (1985). *Report of Trend and Progress of Banking in India 1983–84* (p. 82).

Richards, M. C. (1976). *Centering: In pottery, poetry, and the person* (9th ed.). Middletown, CT: Wesleyan University Press.

Reincourt, A. de. (1960). *The soul of India.* New York: Harper.

Riesman, D., Potter, R., & Watson, J. (1960). Sociability, persmissiveness, and equality. *Psychiatry, 23,* 323–340.

Rogers, E. M. (1979). Freedom and control in the Peoples' Republic of China: Information, Persuasion, and Coercion. In G. Chu & F. Hsu (Eds.), *Moving a mountain* (pp. 2–26). Honolulu: University of Hawaii Press.

Rogers, E. M. (1983). *Diffusion of innovations.* New York: Free Press.

Rogers, E. M., & Kincaid, D. L. (1981). *Communication networks: A new paradigm for research.* New York: Free Press.

Rogers, E. M., & Shoemaker, F. F. (1971). *Communication of innovations: A cross-cultural approach* (2nd ed.). New York: Free Press.

Ryan, B., & Gross, N. C. (1943). The diffusion of hybrid seed corn in two Iowa communities. *Rural Sociology, 8,* 15–24.

Samter, W., & Burleson, B. R. (1984). Cognitive and motivational influence on spontaneous comforting behavior. *Human Communication Resarch, 11,* 231–260.

Scheiner, I. (Ed.). (1974). *Modern Japan: An interpretive anthology.* New York: Macmillan.

Schiller, H. I. (1976). *Communication and cultural domination.* White Plains, NY: International Arts and Science Press.

Schneidau, H. N. (1976). *Sacred discontent: The Bible and Western tradition.* Berkeley: University of California Press.

Scholes, R. E., & Kellogg, R. (1966). *The nature of narrative.* London & New York: Oxford University Press.

Schorer, M. (1967). Technique as discovery. In P. Stevick (Ed.), *The theory of the novel* (pp. 65–84). New York: Free Press.

Schramm, W., & Roberts, F. D. (Eds.). (1971). *The process and effects of mass communication.* Urbana: University of Illinois Press.

Scott, M. B., & Lyman, S. M. (1968). Accounts. *American Sociological Review, 33,* 46–62.

Searle, J. R. (1969). *Speech Acts.* London & New York: Cambridge University Press.

Sennett, R. (1976). *The fall of public man: On the social psychology of capitalism.* New York: Vintage Press.

Shatz, M. (1978). The relationship between cognitive processes and the development of communication skills. In B. Keasey (Ed.), *Nebraska Sympsoium on Motivation.* Lincoln: University of Nebraska Press.

Shui, H. C. (1963). *Water margin,* by Shih Nai-an (J. H. Jackson, Trans.). Hong Kong: Commercial Press.

Singh, K. J. (1980). Communication and tradition in revolution: Gandhi and Mao as mass communication. *Communicator, 15,* 37–41.

Sitaram, K. S., & Cogdell, R. T. (1976). *Foundations of intercultural communication.* Columbus, OH: Bell & Howell.

Steiner, G., & Fagles, R. (Eds.). (1962). *Homer: A collection of critical essays.* Englewood Cliffs, NJ: Prentice-Hall.

Stevens, S. S. (1975). *Psychophysics.* New York: Wiley.

Strauss, A. L. (1969). *Mirrors and masks: The search for identity.* San Francisco, CA: Sociology Press.

Sumner, W. G. (1979). In E. Sagarin (Ed.). *Folkways and mores.* New York: Schocken.

Szilard, L. (1964). On the decrease of entropy in a thermodynamic system by the intervention of intelligent beings (A. Rapoport, Trans.). *Behavioral Science, 9,* 301–310. (*Zeitschrift fuer Physik,* 1929, *53,* 840–856).

Taylor, C. (1970). *Behavioral sciences.* London & New York: Cambridge University Press.

Tewari, I. P. (1980). Sadharanikaran: Indian communication theory. *Indian and Foreign Review,* pp. 13–14.

Thomas, D. (1979). *Naturalism and social science.* London & New York: Cambridge University Press, 1979.

Thompson, W. (1972, June). *Correlates of the self-concept* (Monograph No. 6). Dade Wallace Center Monographs.

Triandis, H. C. (1960). Cognitive similarity and communication in a dyad. *Human Relations, 13* (2), 175–183.

Tsujimura, A. (1968). *Japanese culture and communication.* Tokyo: NHK Books.

Turner, V. (1980). Social dramas and stories about them. *Critical Inquiry, 6,* 141–168.

Tyler, L., & others. (1980). *Intercultural ready reference: A guide for "successful" interactions.* Provo, UT: Brigham Young University Press.

Tzu, C. (1968). *Complete works of Chuang Tzu* (B. Watson, Trans.), (pp. 36–49). New York: Columbia University Press.

Varela, F. J. (1975). A calculus for self-reference. *International Journal of General Systems, 2,* 5–24.

Varela, F. J. (1979). *Principles of biological autonomy.* New York: Elsevier/North-Holland.

Varela, F. J. (1981). Describing the logic of the living. In M. Zeleney (Ed.), *Autopoiesis: A theory of living organization.* (pp. 36–48). New York: Elsevier/North-Holland.

Varela, F. J., Maturana, H., & Uribe, R. (1974). Autopoiesis: The organization of living systems, its characterization and a model. *Biosystems, 5,* 187–196.

Vatsyayan, K. (1968). *Classical Indian dance in literature and the arts.* New Delhi: Sangeet Natak Akademi.

Verma, D. (Ed.). (1958). *Hindi sahitya kosh* (Hindi). Varanasi: Gyan Mandal Ltd.

Vogel, E. F. (1963). *Japan's new middle class.* Berkeley: University of California Press.

Vogel, E. F. (1979). *Japan as number one.* Cambridge, MA: Harvard University Press.

von Wright, G. H. (1971). *Explanation and unverstanding.* Ithaca, NY: Cornell University Press.

Weaver, R. (1964). *Visions of order: The cultural crisis of our time.* Baton Rouge: Louisiana State University Press.

Weinstein, E. A. (1969). The development of interpersonal competence. In D. A. Goslin (Ed.), *Handbook of socialization theory and research.* Chicago, IL: Rand McNally.

Whitehill, A. M., & Takezawa, S. (1978). Workplace harmony: Another Japanese "miricle." *Columbia Journal of World Business, 12,* 25–39.

Wiley, E. O., & Brooks, D. R. (1982). Victims of history: A nonequilibrium approach to evolution. *Systematic Zoology, 31,* 1–24.

Wilkening, E. A. (1949). *The acceptance of certain improved agricultural programs and practices in a Piedmont community of North Carolina* (Program Report No. 8). Raleigh: North Carolina Agricultural Experiment Station, Department of Rural Sociology.

Woelfel, J., & Danes, J. (1980). Multidimensional scaling models for communication research. In P. Monge and J. Cappella (Eds.), *Multivariate techniques in human communication research.* New York: Academic Press.

Woelfel, J., & Fink, E. (1980). *The measurement of communication processes: Galileo theory and method.* New York: Academic Press.

Yadava, J. S. (1979). Communication in an indian village. In W. C. McCormack & S. A. Warm (Eds.), *Language and society.* (pp. 627–636). New York: Mouton.

Yadava, J. Y. (1971). *Communication and parliamentary elections* (Mimeographed paper). New Delhi: India Institute of Mass Communication.

Yamamoto, S. (1977). *Study of Kuuki.* Tokyo: Bungei Shunju Sha.

Yang, H., & Yang, G. (1972). *Selected stories of Lu Hsun* (pp. 65–112). Peking: Foreign Language Press.

Yankelovich, D. (1981, April). A world turned upside down. *Psychology Today,* pp. 35–91.

Yi, H. D. (1973). Formation of confucian ethics in Korea. *Korea Journal, 13,* 10–16.

Yi, Yulgok. (1977). *Yulgokjib* (Collected works of Yulgok). Seoul, Korea: Min-jok mun-hwa jin-heung whe.

Yoo, M. J. (1975). *Han-kook Chul-hak-sa* (Korean Philosophy). Seoul, Korea: Il-Shin Sa.

Yoshino, M. Y. (1968). *Japan's managerial system: Tradition and innovation.* Cambridge, MA: MIT Press.

Yum, J. O. (1984). Social networks of five ethnic groups in Hawaii. *Communication Yearbook. 7,* 574–591.

Zajonc, R. B. (1960). The process of cognitive of tuning. *Journal of Abnormal and Social Psychology, 61,* 159–167.

Index

A

Absolute relativization, 35–36
Accomodation, 86
Acculturation, 185, 235–244
Action, 24, 29–31, 40–42, 46, 81, 152, 179–
  180, 185, 202, 215, 223–225, 229–230,
  241, 256, 266, 308
  collective, 182, 192, 210, 218
  disinterested, 179
  group, 181
  trivial, 118, 126
Action theory, 337
Adaptation, 196
Aesthetic pleasure, 166
Agreement, 184, 287
  mutual, 210
Agricultural extension, 176–179
Ah Q, 12, 45–56
Alazon, 47–50, 51
Alignment, 247–248
Allopoiesis, 184
Ambiguity, 14, 18–19, 84, 133, 138, 141 149
Ananda, 165–167
Antyodaya, 21–22, 180–182
Arguing, 266–267
Aristotelian model, 302–308
Aristotle, 2, 26, 167, 184, 190, 223, 243,
  277, 291, 299, 301–310, 315–317, 331,
  336

Art, 165
Asymmetrical obligation, 334
Asymmetrical relationships, 20, 167–169,
  191
Atama, 124
Atmosphere, 116, 124–126
Attachment, 81, 325–326
Attitudes, 219, 284–285, 288, 291–293, 316
Authority, 7, 9, 340
Autocatalysis, 204
Autonomy, 15, 36, 90, 93, 184, 197–198,
  203–207, 248
Autopoiesis, 183–184, 189, 196–208, 333–
  334, 339
Avoidance, 266–267

B

Behavior, 210–212, 216–217, 231
Behavioral self, 229–230
Behavioral settings, 126
Belief, 24, 152, 184, 197, 210–212, 215–
  217, 219, 249, 282–283, 285, 288, 290–
  293, 316
Bhagavad-Gita, 22, 164, 172, 179
Bhartrhari, 175
Bliss, 165, 167
Body, 27, 72, 81, 185
Bohr, Niels, 313
Boltzmann, Ludwig, 211

355